SINGLE
&
PSYCHO

SINGLE & PSYCHO

How Pop Culture Created the Unstable Single Woman

CAROLINE YOUNG

UNIVERSITY PRESS OF KENTUCKY

A note to the reader: This volume contains discussions of domestic violence, sexual abuse, and other sensitive topics as well as quotations that readers may find offensive. Discretion is advised.

Copyright © 2025 by The University Press of Kentucky

Scholarly publisher for the Commonwealth, serving Bellarmine University, Berea College, Centre College of Kentucky, Eastern Kentucky University, The Filson Historical Society, Georgetown College, Kentucky Historical Society, Kentucky State University, Morehead State University, Murray State University, Northern Kentucky University, Spalding University, Transylvania University, University of Kentucky, University of Louisville, University of Pikeville, and Western Kentucky University.
All rights reserved.

Editorial and Sales Offices: The University Press of Kentucky
663 South Limestone Street, Lexington, Kentucky 40508-4008
www.kentuckypress.com

Library of Congress Cataloging-in-Publication Data

Names: Young, Caroline, 1979– author.
Title: Single & psycho : how pop culture created the unstable single woman / Caroline Young.
Other titles: Single and psycho
Description: Lexington, Kentucky : The University Press of Kentucky, [2025] | Includes bibliographical references and index.
Identifiers: LCCN 2025004407 | ISBN 9781985902510 (hardcover) | ISBN 9781985902527 (pdf) | ISBN 9781985902534 (epub)
Subjects: LCSH: Women in popular culture. | Women in mass media. | Feminism.
Classification: LCC HQ1155 .Y38 2025 | DDC 306.81/53—dc23/eng/20250213
LC record available at https://lccn.loc.gov/2025004407

Member of the Association
of University Presses

Contents

Introduction   1

1. "I'm Not Going to Be Ignored": The Creation of the Bunny Boiler   13

2. The Madwoman in the Attic   26

3. Bachelor Girls   43

4. The Good Wife and the Bad Girl   51

5. 5 a.m. Breakfasts on Fifth Avenue and a Countercultural Shake-Up   69

6. The 1970s: Feminism, New Hollywood, and Blaxploitation   77

7. Is It Really Free Love?   85

8. From Feminism to Fighting for the Nuclear Family   94

9. Burnout, Biological Clocks, and Boiling Rabbits: The Career Woman's Despair   108

10. Baby Booms and Working Girls   125

11. Bitches from Hell   140

12. Sex and Fear: The Sharp Edge of the Erotic Thriller   156

13. The Threat Is inside the House   166

14. The Rise of the Singleton   183

15. Playboy Bunnies, Slut-Shaming, and the Aughts' Double Standards   201

16. Alcoholic, Divorced, and Highly Anxious   222

vi   Contents

17. *Fleabag,* Fourth-Wave Feminism, and the Destructive Single Woman   238

18. "I'll Show You Crazy"   256

19. Tradwives and Childless Cat Ladies   271

Conclusion   279

Acknowledgments   287

Notes   289

Index   301

Introduction

An hour into the movie *Fatal Attraction*, there's a moment that sums up all the stereotypes of the single woman as depicted in popular culture. Alex Forrest, played by a wild-haired Glenn Close, is sitting on her bed, surrounded by a box of Oreo cookies, a half-eaten tub of Häagen-Dazs, and a tumbler of white wine as she barks into her telephone, frantically trying to find out why her ex-lover's phone number has been disconnected. It's a familiar scene that, if played differently, could be from a romantic comedy or an episode of *Sex and the City*. Alex is a New York book editor who has a passionate, but very brief, fling with a married work colleague, Dan Gallagher, played by Michael Douglas. Her rejection by Dan unleashes a dark, twisted obsession as she takes her stalking to the extreme, kidnapping his daughter, boiling the family's pet rabbit, and breaking into the house with a kitchen knife to threaten his wife in the bathroom. From the moment she is destroyed in the bathtub, a demonic witch who needs to be put down, Alex would be the template for the desperate, and deadly, single thirtysomething woman. Her unhinged actions also coined a phrase, *bunny boiler*, that, for the next forty years, would hang like a threat over women who dared to ask for more.

Despite her dangerous, and cringy, deeds, Alex is a woman I have a degree of empathy with, stemming from my own experiences of thankless dating, bad relationships, and a struggle with infertility that sent me spiraling into empty-wombed despair.

These fears of perpetual singledom were first implanted in my early twenties. While everyone else around me seemed blissfully

2   *Single & Psycho*

loved up as they settled down with university boyfriends, and then bought homes together, held gorgeous weddings, and had children, I felt like the one left on the shelf, all the while wondering if there was something wrong with me. And then, as I approached forty, the message driven by Alex Forrest—that a single, childless woman of a similar age may as well count herself out—was one that had burrowed deep into my psyche. Alex's desperation is partly driven by her discovery that she's pregnant, and while Dan pleads with her to get an abortion, she is adamant she wants to keep it: "I'm thirty-six years old! It may be my last chance to have a child!" I was terrified of leaving an abusive relationship in my late thirties because, surely, this was my last chance too.

While this book will be an exploration of pop culture, as I dive into the movies that demonize, laugh at, and occasionally celebrate the complicated, unstable, and at times psychopathic single woman, I'll also share my personal stories and fraught encounters.

I'll examine the depiction of single women from the madwoman in the attic of gothic Victorian fiction to the femme fatale of 1940s film noir; Marilyn Monroe's real-life persona as the tragic, aging divorcée who is without a date on a Saturday night; the domestic thrillers like *Single White Female* and *The Hand That Rocks the Cradle* that were a staple of the early 1990s; the romantic comedies of the aughts; and Taylor Swift's domination as a serial-dating, love-obsessed pop star to chart how depictions of the single woman have changed with the fluctuations of the feminist movement. Many of these movies and cultural moments were the backdrop to my life, influencing and shaping my decisions as I found my own experiences reflecting and reflected within them.

Given the narrow lens of Western popular culture, there has long been a staunch resistance to exploring diverse, inclusive stories, and women of color were typically neglected in these depictions. As a teenager, my love of film was nurtured through Hollywood's output in the 1990s, where straight relationships and white characters were the focus of storytelling, and these very much echoed my own experiences too.

When I watched *Fatal Attraction* fully for the first time in my late twenties, I was both repulsed by and drawn to Alex, and as embarrassing as it is to admit, I could see myself in her. I think the reason the movie has made such a huge cultural impact in its almost forty years in popular culture is that, apart from the stalking and the animal cruelty, it has universal, relatable themes. Even though it's supposed to, and did, illicit sympathy for the poor, unwitting victim of an unhinged woman, it also strikes a chord with those who have felt the pain of rejection and who burn with anger at the double standards of a society in which a woman is punished for her singleness, her promiscuity, and her quest for love.

By the time I was in my thirties, I had a habit of either plunging into unrequited love, and feeling the pain and anxiety on a deep level, or pushing away the good guys in favor of the bad, almost as a twisted way of protecting myself from being scrutinized. I feared that someone who appeared too perfect, too stable, and too normal would inevitably discover my flaws, so maybe it was better to choose the sketchy ones who were walking red flags. That way, at least there would be that barrier to intimacy.

Sometimes the heartbreak at the end of a short-lived relationship was all-consuming, leaving me unable to concentrate on my studies or my job. During my college years, I was the girl whose friends would bring around sympathy bars of Dairy Milk, whose roommate made me an omelet and delivered it to me alongside a glass of wine while I lay in bed, thinking I might die from the numb agony of it. I was the reliable entertainment with my disastrous first-date stories, the one who would pretend to pocket dial her ex-boyfriend in the hope that it would trigger him into calling back, and the naive nineteen-year-old who, not having fully tuned into social cues, turned up uninvited to the object of my obsession's flat, leading to a very awkward thirty minutes.

I wasn't single or unlucky in love because I was concentrating too much on my career, as has been the stereotype over the last forty years; rather, I was failing because of my own insecurities and the deep-rooted sense within myself that I wasn't worthy of love. As much as I craved intimacy, I was also afraid of it, because it would expose all the things I didn't like about myself. I was also all too aware of the ticking time bomb warning me of the accepted timescale of life goals that I should be sticking to, and this led me to some dark, traumatic places.

4   *Single & Psycho*

There's a thread that runs between Alex Forrest and her more comedic incarnation, Bridget Jones, another character I feel a reluctant affinity with. Both their names are shorthand for a particular type of desperate singleton—and Bridget is the calorie-counting, wine-swilling, granny-pant-wearing younger sister of Alex, who can similarly never catch a break. As Helen Fielding wrote in the spin-off manual *Bridget Jones's Guide to Life*, released to capitalize on the movie adaptation in 2001, the word *singleton* is a "replacement for poison outdated word 'Spinster.'"[1]

Bridget herself believes that her position as a single woman could be a slippery slope into perpetual loneliness, and she blames her lack of a relationship on being too fat when it's quite clear she's not. But that doesn't matter when you are ruled by deep-set insecurities. In Bridget's mind, she'll only be happy when she reaches her target weight, which, again, is a feeling I can attest to.

I've been nicknamed "Bridget Jones" by friends for my disastrous love life, and I took it in the affectionate way I *hope* it was meant, with the relief that at least I wasn't being called Alex Forrest. I was, like Bridget, always thinking about the number on the scales and punishing myself for eating too much chocolate, drinking too much booze, and smoking too many cigarettes when huddled around the outdoor heaters of city-center bars.

As a teenager, marriage was a distant goal. I remember, in my first year of university, sagely announcing to friends that I wouldn't get married until I was at least twenty-seven. It was the sensible solution to what seemed like life's inevitability—that someday I would be married and have children, despite the absolute horror I felt around the gruesomeness of childbirth. From my room in student halls, with my zeitgeisty *True Romance* poster on the wall, I had zero awareness that once I was in my thirties and early forties, having children would feel like an impossible and gut-wrenching struggle, and when it came to relationships, it would also be a path lined with anxiety and heartbreak.

It didn't help that in high school I was incredibly shy and awkward and suffered bouts of terrible acne. I would avert my eyes from mirrors as I couldn't stand to look at myself, and I would shuffle around with my head down to avoid people seeing me. There were lunches spent in a toilet cubicle, eating my sandwich in blissful solitude, away from the noisy hellhole of the school dining room—an early glimpse at my avoidant nature. I reached my full height early, and then I stopped growing at five-foot-two, and what's more, my body, small-chested but with a curvaceous posterior, didn't follow the rules that were set in the 1990s that thin was in. This was long before Kim Kardashian would help make big butts a desirable trait. I so, so wished I could be beautiful like the popular girls with their willowy limbs and glowing skin who were on the hockey and basketball teams at high school or the page 3 girls in the British tabloid newspapers, with their naked, cheerful perkiness.

Women often lament that the best they ever looked was when they were twenty. Not me. I can attest that things absolutely do get better when you hit your thirties. I lost a bit of weight, which sharpened up my cheekbones and my frame and gave me confidence in how I perceived myself, and with the problem skin now gone, I was comfortable in myself for the first time. I felt a great deal of power in now being desirable, and I knew I was also excellent company on a first date because I saw it more like meeting a friend rather than an interview process.

There were many, many times when I enjoyed, and relished, the fun of dating, of experiencing an ego trip in going for drinks with perfectly nice men who always wanted to see me again. I got a kick out of the buildup to meeting a stranger for the first time, the butterflies in my stomach and the nervous sweat that gave my skin a youthful glow, then greeting each other over a candlelit table with uncertain smiles. With each new round of drinks, cheeks flushing and a growing intimacy with every silly joke and funny story. Walking home after a fun evening, there would inevitably be a text lighting up my phone, just because they wanted to tell me that they had a great time. But as Amy Dunne, from Gillian Flynn's *Gone Girl*, writes in her (fake) diary, "I'm tired of not knowing who I'll be with, or if I'll be with anyone."

I was all too aware, by the time I turned thirty-four, that I still hadn't cohabited, and being the last of my friend group to do so, I had the niggling worry that this made me a bit of a freak. I'd backpacked around the world solo when I was twenty-two, taking advantage of that time between studies and work, and in Australia, I'd met a Kiwi while staying in a hostel in Sydney. We traveled through the outback in a station wagon, Tom Petty blasting as we drove along endless

6   *Single & Psycho*

desert highways and surviving on the money made from fruit-picking work. We were together for almost a year, and I stayed with his family in New Zealand for a few months. He was already desperate to settle down and have children, but I felt like I had so much more I wanted to do, and so I returned to Scotland, he stayed in New Zealand, and that was that. Ten years later and I was still single after a couple of failed, not-quite-sure-what-they-were relationships, and the anxiety led me to make a rash decision in letting someone into my life who would turn out to be abusive and from whom it would be very difficult to free myself.

I never thought I would have much in common with Paris Hilton, the party girl of the aughts who was slut-shamed on a mass scale after an ex-boyfriend violated her by releasing a sex tape. I found it painful to watch a scene in her 2020 documentary, *This Is Paris*, where her boyfriend pushes for an argument just before she is due to deliver the most prestigious DJ set of her career at the Tomorrowland festival in Belgium. His relentless badgering of her, demanding that she give him more attention when she's psyching herself up for her performance, is a means of sabotaging her success. She pleads with him to stop, telling him he's stressing her out, that he's going to make her cry, and finally she rips off his all-access wristband and kicks him out of her life. She drew her line, even though she was disenchanted at another failed relationship.

This scene brought back memories of my painful relationship with a man—I'll call him Gavin—who was always jealous that my burgeoning writing career (which he referred to as a hobby even though I was getting commissioned by publishers) was taking my attention away from him. I worked full time in communications and PR, yet I squeezed in writing by getting up at 6 a.m. before heading to the office, and I tried to devote as much time to it as possible over the weekends. I probably was too preoccupied and focused, but it was my dream, my absolute love, and meeting the deadlines was very important to me. It was October 2016, and I'd managed to secure a book launch at Waterstones in Edinburgh, my first serious event, and the bookstore was packed with friends, family, and work colleagues who were incredibly supportive and pleased for me. As an introvert, I had been sick with nerves about standing in front of an audience, but I pushed myself into the zone and spoke proudly about my book to the compere. When it was time for questions, Gavin, who was sitting in the front row, was the first to raise his hand, with a satisfied smile creeping across his face.

"Now that you've finished this book, does this mean you are going to do more housework?"

I was mortified and embarrassed that he tried to take away this huge moment from me, but I smiled and laughed it off and moved on to the next question. Later that night, we had a huge argument about some comment I made that he found demeaning, and the adrenaline rush from my book launch quickly turned to anguish. I wondered why I didn't deserve a supportive partner who would champion and encourage me instead of tearing me down. As Paris says in the documentary, "I didn't really understand what love or relationships were. I thought that them getting so crazy meant that they were in love with me. Looking back, I can't believe I let people treat me like that."

This uncertainty, the perpetual disappointments, can be a real mind bender, especially with all those expectations of what your life is supposed to look like, so that you end up making a hurried bid for the wrong person. This is exactly what Alex Forrest and Bridget Jones tapped into; they struck a nerve among single women who were made to feel like failures, and by settling, they ended up in damaging situations. Through popular culture and the media, this fearful message has been a poisonous worm burrowing into the minds of women for decades. They are questioned for their choices, labeled as psycho if they demand more, or derided as "childless cat ladies" by politicians because their life doesn't follow the supposed proscribed plan.

On its release in 1987, *Fatal Attraction* not only reflected AIDS-era angst, when sex was now a dangerous pursuit, but tapped into the question of whether the feminist movement had given women unrealistic expectations that they could have it all. Single professionals were depicted as being deeply unhappy with their lot, having sacrificed the chance for a family of their own because they'd been too devoted to their career. This anxiety, at seemingly now being too far gone (at the ripe old age of thirty-six!) to find a husband and have children, triggers Alex's dangerous side, and she becomes a threat to married men, and good wives, everywhere.

In her influential 1991 book *Backlash*, Susan Faludi describes a much-repeated pattern of fearmongering as a response to women

8   *Single & Psycho*

asking for more rights. After the second wave of feminism of the seventies, it was inevitable that in the following decade politicians and the media would try to push women back into their rightful place at home.

Faludi quoted a number of studies in the 1980s that appeared to show that with every year that passed, a woman had ever-decreasing chances of getting married due to a "man shortage" and that she would struggle under the "infertility epidemic" because she left it too late to have children. These studies, including a 1982 report in the *New England Journal of Medicine* that claimed a woman's chances of conceiving dramatically dropped after the age of thirty, provoked a media storm in the mideighties with alarmist headlines that only served to cause more anxiety.

In June 1986, *Newsweek* infamously splashed the headline "Too Late for Prince Charming?"—and it set off alarm bells among single women in their thirties and forties, who were made to feel that midnight had already struck on their happily-ever-after. The article highlighted a study by Yale and Harvard Universities that suggested thirty-year-old, white, college-educated single women had only a 20 percent chance of finding husbands. At age forty, the probability fell to 2.6 percent, and the magazine would make the unfounded claim that this meant they were more likely to be killed by a terrorist than find a husband.

A thirty-eight-year-old *New York Times* columnist, Anne Taylor Fleming, who was going through the grueling process of fertility treatment, blamed feminism for a new middle-class "sisterhood of the infertile." She wished to cry out to all those outspoken figures of women's liberation, Gloria Steinem and Germaine Greer, "How does it feel to have ended up without babies, children, flesh of your flesh? Did you mean to thumb your noses at motherhood, or is that what we heard or intuited for our own needs?"[2]

As Faludi wrote in *Backlash*, "From 'the man shortage' to 'the infertility epidemic' to 'female burn-out' to 'toxic day care,' these so-called female crises have had their origins not in the actual conditions of women's lives but in a closed system that starts and ends in the media, popular culture and advertising—an endless feedback loop that perpetuates and exaggerates its own false images of womanhood."[3]

Introduction   9

It is these very concepts that are continuing to be drip-fed to women in contemporary popular culture and politics. Following the fourth wave of feminism of the 2010s, which used social media to rally voices against sexual harassment and body-shaming and called out powerful men for their transgressions, another backlash was inevitable.

In recent years, we've witnessed the dangerous rescinding of female bodily autonomy in the United States, with the US Supreme Court's overturning of *Roe v. Wade* in June 2022, meaning that abortion rights are no longer protected by the Constitution. With many states now seeking to ban abortion or making the cut-off point at six weeks (where the men who make these decisions clearly don't understand, or care, how weeks of pregnancy are calculated), these measures will have the most impact on younger women who are without support from a partner.[4]

Thousands of women marched in protest at their fundamental rights being taken away as these measures not only endanger poorer women's lives but also place the burden and consequences of unprotected sex on women rather than men. One right-wing politician even insinuated it was only desperate single women who were protesting against the "pro-life" movement by ranting in a speech, "Why is that the women with the least likelihood of getting pregnant are the ones most worried about having abortions?"[5]

The message in some quarters is the same as it was in the 1960s, '70s, and '80s—that women who step outside of societal conventions are deviant and, worse, ugly and destined for spinsterhood.

In my 2022 book *Crazy Old Ladies: The Story of Hag Horror*, I explored the phenomenon of the "hagsploitation" genre of movies of the 1960s and 1970s, which was sparked by the enormous success of *What Ever Happened to Baby Jane?*, starring Bette Davis and Joan Crawford. These camp gothic horrors cast famous older actresses as crazed spinsters who are living in regret at their lost beauty and missed chances, and I argue that the characters were designed as a response to the rising feminist movement. They were a warning: look what happens to women if they don't settle down and have families; they'll turn into an ax-wielding hag who is driven to mental despair by the increasingly frightful image staring back at her in the mirror. Alex Forrest is born from these characters, and her legacy lies in a

10   *Single & Psycho*

number of guises, from the dangerous man-killing bisexual of *Basic Instinct* to divorcée Rachel Watson in *The Girl on the Train*, driven to alcoholism because her unexplained infertility caused cracks in her marriage. The spirit of *Baby Jane* can also be found in 2024's horror movie *The Substance*, where Demi Moore's fading actress is desperate to try a cure against aging.

In 1951's *A Place in the Sun*, a pregnant and unmarried Shelley Winters nags and cajoles after being rejected by Montgomery Clift so he can be with his rich "cool" girl, Elizabeth Taylor. There are traces of the desperate single woman in Marion Crane, the female victim in Alfred Hitchcock's 1960 horror, *Psycho*, as played by Janet Leigh. Marion is the softer, more acceptable version of this wretched creature, but like Alex Forrest, she has her comeuppance for daring to step outside of proscribed female behavior. Marion is pushing thirty and worried about her future, particularly as her lover, Sam Loomis, says he can't afford for them to be together while his ex is still on the scene. Marion is so desperate for the relationship to succeed that she makes the fateful decision to steal money from a wealthy client at the bank where she works. As she flees to start a new life, she winds up at the Bates Motel, where she is murdered in the shower by Norman Bates, who has taken on the persona of his domineering, and now deceased, mother. With that scene, and Bernard Herrmann's unnerving score, the screech of a violin would be a shorthand signal that ex-partners and one-night stands were certifiably cuckoo. In these earlier examples of the Alex Forrest trope, women's lives are framed as morality tales in which the tainted, unwed woman is punished.

I'll also explore what became known as the children of *Fatal Attraction*. In the early 1990s, another film made it clear that there was nothing more terrifying than a single female and helped to coin an insult that became a part of the cultural lexicon in much the same way as *bunny boiler*.

In 1992's *Single White Female*, Jennifer Jason Leigh is the "flat-mate from hell," a mousy weirdo who tries to steal the life of successful career woman Bridget Fonda. Here we can see the echoes of Alex, and not just in the way she comforts herself with Häagen-Dazs and harms a beloved pet. The movie has an integral place in the "from hell" subgenre of movies that were so prevalent for a few years, including the barren "nanny from hell" in *The Hand That Rocks the Cradle*.

In the 2010s, there were hit novel adaptations like *Gone Girl* and *The Girl on the Train*, with complex and destructive women who are afflicted with mental illness due to the weight of expectations placed on them. Single women were not only grappling with the modern phenomena of dating apps and the pressure of having to curate the perfect life on social media but were also riddled with anxiety due to political and economic instability. This chaos morphed into the messy, single heroine of television and film, as seen with Lena Dunham's *Girls*, Phoebe Waller-Bridge's *Fleabag*, and Issa Rae's *Insecure*. She drinks too much, has one-night stands, throws up on the street, and loses her house keys, and she continually makes a fool of herself in her quest for love.

These antiheroic characters are, it's important to note, predominantly straight. When lesbians were depicted on screen, they were typically shown to be deviant and dangerous. From Mrs. Danvers in *Rebecca* (1940) to Shelley Winters in the little-seen "hag horror" *What's the Matter with Helen?* (1971), Sharon Stone in *Basic Instinct* (1992), and Megan Fox in *Jennifer's Body* (2009), bisexual and lesbian women displayed obsessive, homicidal tendencies, from burning down mansions to wielding icepicks and transforming into man-eating cannibals. And as for women of color being cast as viable love interests and femme fatales, they were largely passed over and ignored.

In their 2004 essay "Femme Noire: Dangerous Women of Color in Popular Film and Television," Jane Caputi and Lauri Sagle argue that while women of color are often depicted as dangerous and fearful under the dragon lady or queen bitch trope, the femme fatale character is so often white. Yet she often possesses the noir qualities that are "especially endemic in [depictions of] women of color: primitive emotions and lusts, violence, sexual aggression, masculinity, lesbian tendencies, promiscuity, duplicity, treachery." They assert that the Alien queen in *Aliens* (1986) is rooted in a stereotype of Black women as monstrous queen bitch, in the same way as *welfare queens* and *condom queens* were terms used to scapegoat Black women in the 1980s: "Moreover, her antagonist is now a white woman who achieves hero status by annihilating the queen."[6]

12 *Single & Psycho*

Increasingly, over the last decade, we've seen greater diversity in shows that explore the pressures and angst of single women of color, and these productions have often been created by women of color who take on the lead roles. Michaela Coel's 2020 BBC drama *I May Destroy You* was groundbreaking in its discussions of rape and sexual assault, periods, and stealthing, where a man removes the condom during sex without consent, while also grounding it within the Black British experience of being single. Similarly, the 2022 BBC drama *Mood*, created by and starring English-Jamaican Nicôle Lecky, tells the story of a London singer who has reached rock bottom after setting fire to her ex-boyfriend's garden and who is swept into a world of influencers and Only Fans. Developing and acting in their own stories has given these women the chance to voice their own experiences that have traditionally been given so little airtime.

In my own life, the pressure I felt to reach certain milestones, and to accept bad relationships for fear of being labeled *crazy* or *demanding*, was reflected in the media I consumed. With the sheer number of anxiety-inducing horror stories about catfishing scams and predatory behavior due to the ubiquity of dating apps, Alex Forrest's story seems more relevant than ever. Given the 2024 presidential election campaign was punctuated with sneers at "childless cat ladies," with blame placed on "selfish" women for declining birth rates, and with a growing "tradwife" movement that delivers the message that true happiness can only be found in being a domestic goddess, now seems to be the perfect time to explore the cultural history of being "single and psycho."

CHAPTER 1

"I'm Not Going to Be Ignored"

The Creation of the Bunny Boiler

During Donald Trump's first presidency, *Saturday Night Live*'s Kate McKinnon made headlines for her on-point impersonations of the key figures of his administration. One of these was Kellyanne Conway, the White House adviser and campaign manager who could effortlessly reel off breathless arguments to defend President Trump's policies on live television. This skill often led to ridicule, particularly for her comment during a January 2017 television interview about "alternative facts," when she defended the White House press secretary's claim that the numbers in attendance at Donald Trump's inauguration were "the largest ever . . . period."

In a sketch that aired on February 12, 2017, McKinnon depicted Kellyanne as Glenn Close in *Fatal Attraction*, complete with Medusa-blond hair, having broken into news anchor Jake Tapper's apartment as if she were a spurned lover. The pinnacle is when she delivers the line "I'm not going to be ignored" in Close's famously unhinged shrill. The only thing missing from that scene was the rabbit boiling in a pot.

Almost thirty years before, there was another *Saturday Night Live* skit on the February 25, 1989, show where Glenn Close was the special guest reprising the character of Alex. In between her terrorizing of the Gallagher family, she is taking part in a support group to help her get her relationship problems off her chest. Dressed in her signature black leather jacket, with maroon nails and her hair teased with mousse, she recounts her stalking of Dan and kidnapping of his child. "You know that guy I've been obsessed with? Well . . . I finally got up enough courage to throw acid on his car," she says before adding, "I

14   *Single & Psycho*

boiled the rabbit." Her confession earns claps from the audience and horrified reactions from those in the support group. *Saturday Night Live* regular Jon Lovitz says, "Didn't you tell us last week that Dan pretty much said he never wanted to see you again? And why did you boil the bunny?"

Alex may be positioned as the confident businesswoman with the dream job—who wouldn't wish to be an editor for a publishing firm in 1980s Manhattan, with all the swanky book parties and boozy lunches?—but when it comes down to it, it's just a facade. This single woman is a danger to the sanctity of the family, because she'll prey on the weak married man, picking him off when he's vulnerable, like a lioness catching a wildebeest. In the words of one reviewer in 1987, Alex's wild hair and her décolleté "resemble those of a drag queen."[1] The implication is that she's not a real woman; she's an impersonator because she isn't sufficiently soft and submissive.

The *Los Angeles Times* reviewer described Alex as an "over-30 publishing executive," as if thirty was the kiss of death for women, and Dan as a "basically decent guy."[2] He's just a simple man who takes the opportunity when it's handed to him on a platter. OK, so maybe he tries to hit on her after she slashed her wrists and then ghosts her after she tells him she's pregnant, but what's he supposed to do? It's Alex, as the unmarried seductress, who is the threat rather than the cheating husband because good women, as one reviewer wrote, "stay at home and mind the kids. Bad women don't have homes and need other women's men to sire kids."[3]

Fatal Attraction was the most talked-about movie of the year when it was released in September 1987. The following month, the *Los Angeles Times* wrote, "It's been called an anti-feminist film, a 'yuppie slasher' movie, an advertisement for safe sex and fidelity as well as a diatribe against being single. . . . The feelings it has elicited make it one of the most thought-provoking and—to some—disturbing movies of the decade."[4]

It made $155 million at the box office by the time the home video came out in June 1988, with more than 485,000 video cassettes shipped in advance. The film also received six Oscar nominations, including Best Actress for Glenn Close, Best Director, and Best Picture, although much like Alex Forrest and her doomed relationships, it went home with none.

"I'm Not Going to Be Ignored"   15

Alex was dubbed in one tabloid as "The Most Hated Woman in America" and was praised for inadvertently starting a monogamy trend, as married men were now said to be terrified of cheating. In the years that followed, there were warnings of "Real Life Fatal Attractions," like that of Amy Fisher, the "teenage temptress" who, in 1992, shot her lover's wife. It was served up as a gleeful cautionary tale that casual affairs could only end in revenge and shattered lives.

The movie's poster added to the intrigue: a black-and-white photo of Douglas and Close in an embrace, with a slash of red cutting through them like a bloody wound or a vagina. It hinted at the deadliness of women, particularly seductive, single women who dress powerfully in glistening leather trench coats and can manipulate a man into leaving the arms of his loving wife.

Once she won the role, Close carried out her own extensive research into whether Alex's conduct was realistic. She talked it over with her doctor father and spoke with a psychiatrist to map out a case history for the character, "something that would explain to me as an actress her behavior, because she's so very much out of control and tragically unaware of it."[5]

Alex's deep trauma was only hinted at. There's mention of a past relationship where she had a "bad miscarriage" and thought she couldn't have children, which is a detail I wish we could know more about. There was mention of her father, who died from a heart attack, but we're not sure where the truth lies. Then there's the moment when she's hiding in the Gallaghers' garden under the cover of darkness, watching a happy family scene unfold through the window as Dan presents his daughter with a cute and cuddly rabbit. This image is so sickening to Alex that she literally throws up. Close was intrigued as to the reason. What had happened to Alex in her past that made her vomit, or was it a reference to her early pregnancy nausea?

"I think she was victimized as a child—her behavior indicates that—with the result that she's emotionally crippled," said Close in October 1987. "Because she's very intelligent she's been able to cope up to now, but all the elements for a crack-up are there. I don't think any human being is black or white. We're all very complicated creatures, and Alex is a person in great pain."[6]

This visceral reaction leads to arguably the most famous scene in the movie: when Dan's wife, Beth, finds the beloved pet in a pot of boiling water with blood smeared across its fur. From this cinema shocker, the term *bunny boiler* was born. Alongside the slashing knife and violin-screeching action from *Psycho*, it quickly became an easy shorthand to describe a mentally disturbed single woman.

When the film's screenwriter, James Dearden, was given the chance to bring *Fatal Attraction* to the stage in 2014, he tried to do right by Alex by bringing her closer to his initial depiction of a lonely, tragic figure. But one thing he couldn't change was the shocking slaughter of the rabbit, because this was the moment that fans of the film would be waiting for. In his original short film *Diversion* (1979), on which the feature film was based, there was no boiled bunny; this water-cooler moment was conceived during the script development of the Hollywood adaptation. Paramount Pictures insisted on rewrite after rewrite to make Dan more likable, Beth more angelic, and Alex more psychotic. By the time the script was completed, the original, emotionally vulnerable Alex had faded away, and in her place was this archvillainess who takes her anger out on fluffy, floppy-eared pets; if she is the witch (with her surname, Forrest, further implying a connection to a witches' Sabbath secretly held under a blanket of trees at night), then the pot is her cauldron. This crucial plot device is hinted at early in the film, when Alex persuades Dan to come to her apartment for lunch and to bring his pet dog because "I love animals. I'm a great cook."

It was, as Dearden put it, now the story of "the Dark Woman and the Light Woman," and director Adrian Lyne further pushed Close into the performance of "a raging beast underneath" by coming up with the idea of her wearing black leather and living in a barren loft in the Meatpacking District. "Initially, I had her grilling the bunny," Dearden later said. "But I thought that was too grotesque. So we boiled the bunny instead."[7]

Despite Close's research, Alex's trauma went unheard, and instead, she became the stereotype of the desperate single woman in an era when women's mental health was not discussed in the way it is today. The way James Dearden described Alex in 2014 is much more nuanced than the character of 1987. "Was she not just driven to it by a series of disappointments in love? Love, at least initially, is a form of madness," he said.[8] This chimes with Edgar Allan Poe's much-quoted line that "I was never really insane except upon occasions when my heart was touched."

Dorothy Parker's short story "A Telephone Call," from 1928, is hooked around a woman's inner monologue as she waits anxiously for a man to call her. "Please, God, let him telephone me now," she prays. She tries to stop herself from compulsively looking at the clock, and as her fingers itch toward the telephone receiver, convincing herself that maybe *she* should be the one who calls, she begs God to stop her from doing it.

"I mustn't. I mustn't do this," she pleads to herself. "They don't like you to tell them they've made you cry. They don't like you to tell them you're unhappy because of them. If you do, they think you're possessive and exacting. And then they hate you."

It's amazing that these words from the 1920s could be the dialogue of a twenty-first-century woman. In the feminist backlash of the 1980s, these pleadings from an unhappily single woman, consumed by anxiety from the powerlessness of waiting for a phone call, were now laced with violence.

The film, and Alex's extremism, caused very passionate feelings among audiences. *The Los Angeles Times* spoke to moviegoers whose emotions were running so high after watching the movie that they said they were likely to go back to see it for a second or third time. While several who were interviewed found it refreshing to have Close play a psychotic-type role typically reserved for males, many single women were offended, adopting Alex as a symbol of all the pain they had suffered at the hands of men.

"I felt that it depicted the successful, single, intelligent career woman as being psychologically unhinged," said San Francisco actress Carolyn Gregory, who was thirty-four at the time. "On the other hand, the faithful devoted wife and mother symbolized emotional stability." West Los Angeles freelance accountant Carolyn Hench, described as a thirty-two-year-old single woman, said, "The whole movie took the side of the man. The audience definitely empathized with him."[9]

The film proved to be the perfect excuse to undermine women and their emotions as they navigated an often ruthless dating scene. *Bunny boiler* soon infiltrated the cultural lexicon, where it remains today, even among those who haven't seen the film and don't have an inkling as to its origins but are clear as to what it implies.

Taylor Swift, arguably the most talented songwriter of her generation, has continually been dismissed as a "bunny boiler" due to

18   *Single & Psycho*

her well-documented past relationships. While countless men have made a living from singing about real women (the Rolling Stones' controversial "Brown Sugar" and Bob Dylan's "Just like a Woman" are two examples), Taylor was mocked for using real-life situations and lovers as inspiration for her songwriting. "I'm Not a Clingy and Insane Girlfriend! Taylor Swift Opens Up about Her Bunny-Boiler Reputation," screamed one headline in *Her* magazine in 2013. The following year, she parodied this image in the music video for "Blank Space." She was shown luring men into her luxurious mansion and then turning into a possessive, mascara-smeared mess—very reminiscent of Alex Forrest with her inky tears and dead-eyed stare as she compulsively turns the side lamp on and off.

Bunny boiler is an expression similar to *gaslighting*, which has also shifted far beyond its source, the 1944 film *Gaslight*, starring Ingrid Bergman and Charles Boyer. It's now used freely to describe a form of manipulative behavior that makes someone question their own sanity. In the movie, Boyer is an abusive husband and thief who tells his wife, Paula (Bergman), that she is only imagining seeing the gaslights flicker in the evenings when he is out of the house. It is in fact he who is causing them to dim as he spends his evenings rifling through the attic for the jewels he wishes to steal, and as part of an elaborate plot, he attempts to drive his wife to madness by making her question her own mind. Both these phrases, with their cinematic origins, are perhaps the biggest cultural reference points to a woman's mental health in modern times.

I had firsthand experience of this abusive questioning of reality when I let Gavin move into my flat, even though I knew from the start that it was a mistake. I felt pressured by societal expectation that, given I was in my thirties, I should be cohabiting, and my excitement at having purchased my first apartment was quickly tempered by his presence.

With his boxes of junk crammed into every space, the smoke from his cigarettes permeating the air, his contributions to the bills becoming less frequent, and the living room now his lair for playing videogames and watching porn all night, the power I held over my own space quickly dissolved. As I pleaded with him to pay his share and stop smoking all the time, I was dismissed as a "nag" and a mental case and told that he would only listen to me once I became a "better girlfriend." It was an incredibly difficult situation, particularly as I became voiceless due to him being the one who could always shout louder, and there were many times I sought refuge in the bathroom as he screamed and ranted through the locked door, "Either you are a liar, or you are crazy. Which one is it?" Those are the words I remember, although now, as I look back on it, I can't recollect what I was supposed to have lied about.

Sometimes he woke me up at 3 a.m. for an endless diatribe about what was wrong with me and all the injustices leveled at him. When you know you have to go to work the next day and someone is keeping you awake in the middle of the night with their resentments, it's like a form of torture and instills a deep anxiety. I drank too much, tried over-the-counter sleep remedies, and pushed away the pain through denying that this was an abusive relationship.

At least he didn't hit me, I reasoned with myself. Instead, he pushed me against the wall and held the back of my head, pointing and yelling at me just inches from my face as if he were threatening to do it. But after these huge one-sided rows, when I would flee outside, wandering the dark, rain-soaked streets because it seemed safer than my flat, he was contrite. He cried big wet tears, his body shook in pain, and I felt powerful for that brief moment because I was the one who now held all the cards. And I forgave him. Sometimes, when things were good between us, I felt great relief because now I didn't have to worry about trying to get him to leave. Besides, where would he go? I knew he would dig in and make my life hell, and I couldn't subject my parents to the knowledge about what was happening. I also felt sorry for him because he was a broken human, and so maybe it wasn't really his fault.

By the time I turned forty, that dreaded age that sounds like a death rattle, I knew I had to get away. I'd had a chronic twitch in my eye for over a year, and I could feel the stress seeping from every pore in my body, consuming me, hollowing me out so that all that was left was the shell of who I used to be. The tipping point was when he berated me in the center of Edinburgh after we'd spent what was supposed to be a joyous evening watching a Christmas light show at the castle. The gothic streets of the Old Town may have been given a festive glow, but I'd shot him a hostile look, he said, and he kept asking me why.

20   *Single & Psycho*

"It's just my face." I shrugged defensively. "I've no idea what look I gave you."

"No, you gave me a look like you hated me." I tried to walk away from him just to make him stop, but he followed after me as angry, unhinged words tumbled out of his mouth. I tried not to make a scene; I just wanted to get away from him, to hide from all the vitriol. He grabbed my arm and gripped on tightly to pull me back to him, and as I struggled to release myself, I could see out of the corner of my eye that there were people watching us with concern. And I could tell that one was about to intervene. I refused to be that person, the pitiful woman being yelled at on the street, the figure that people needed to rescue. What I needed was to be away from him. So I did it, although in an avoidant, roundabout way. I'd been wanting to get a new heating system installed for years, and with all the furniture piled up in the bedroom so that workmen could pull up the floorboards to access the pipes, I told him it was best if I moved back to my parents' house. I didn't cut ties immediately; I acted as if it were temporary, but as soon as I was back in my childhood bedroom, I felt safe, and I didn't want to leave.

I was forty years old, I was living with my parents, I was miserable at work, and he still didn't believe we had broken up until one day I finally told him, as unambiguously as possible, that I couldn't do it anymore. It was a hard conversation; he cried and begged, but I had to be strong. In the spirit of change, I also quit my job as the stress had just become too much for me, and I plotted an overseas trip, like the ones I'd done in my early twenties. It was a crazy itinerary—Japan, Korea, Hawaii, California, New York—and I was due to leave on March 18, 2020. Then, as news of a global pandemic spread and international borders were closing one by one, I was forced to cancel.

When stay-at-home orders were put in place, there was no choice but to remain in the same childhood bedroom I'd grown up in, and so I would hunker down for the next three months with my parents. I told him he could stay in my flat for lockdown, and then I hoped he would make alternative arrangements. This would prove to be wishful thinking as I ended up being kept out of my own home for almost a year. I couldn't tell my parents the full story—I was too ashamed and they would be upset—but at least now I felt like I could finally breathe. The lockdown order saved me.

Obviously, I should have broken up with him years before, but the critical voice inside told me that at my age, I was running out of options. Sometimes I felt like the little girl who was scared of everything—and I was also incredibly soft. My mother once told me that when I was little, I had cried at the nursery rhyme "Humpty Dumpty" because he had fallen off a wall and couldn't be put back together again. As a child, that had been a devastating tragedy. And as an adult, I still couldn't stand the idea of seeing someone like Gavin broken—I wanted to fix him, to the detriment of myself.

Gavin had continually told me I was a nightmare to live with and no one else would want me. We're all aware of toxic relationships, gaslighting, and coercive control—concepts that weren't up for discussion at the time *Fatal Attraction* was made—and when you are in the center of it, it sometimes takes a while to see.

In her 2022 memoir, *Why Did You Stay?*, actress Rebecca Humphries describes the pain of being made to feel like a psycho when she was convinced her comedian boyfriend was having an affair. He was one of the celebrities learning ballroom dance on BBC's *Strictly Come Dancing*, and he dismissed her fears that he was getting too close to his dance partner. When their kiss was splashed across a tabloid newspaper, Rebecca was thrown into a media storm, and she also realized she had been correct all along.

As she writes, "Perhaps you're not insane. Perhaps it's not your period, or your gender. Perhaps you don't 'always do this,' and you did remember it right. Perhaps your actions didn't cause their reaction, and you're not too sensitive, and you can take a joke, and you can't be more like someone else's girlfriend and nor should you need to be. Perhaps they're a bit of a dick."[10]

Ending that five-and-a-half-year relationship was the hardest, but the best, decision I made. Soon after, I went on a date to see the 2020 reboot of *The Invisible Man*. The reimagined monster is now an obsessive boyfriend whose tech genius allows him to create invisible technology in which to gaslight his ex-girlfriend Cecilia (Elisabeth Moss). As she escapes from his controlling grip, I held my breath and gripped the seat because I felt like I had just gone through the same thing and survived.

I was angry that I wasted a good five years—the crucial five years of my mid- to late thirties. But I was so afraid of confrontation, of

22   *Single & Psycho*

change, of being alone, and I felt like my perception of reality was skewed. It's this notion that I really wanted to examine in this book. We are so scared to be called out for being crazy, for being "bunny boilers" and psychos—and with those supposed life deadlines hanging over us—that we allow and make excuses for bad treatment.

As part of my research, I was interested in tracing exactly when the term *bunny boiler* was coined and searched through newspaper archives to find the earliest example. The first mention I came across was in an article in a syndicated dating column by Laura Kavesh and Cheryl Lavin in May 1989, with a headline that declared "One Tantrum Doesn't Make You a Bunny Boiler."

The article read, "Does one temper tantrum a Fatal Attraction make? Just because a woman makes a scene at one little party, does that mean Glenn Close is her role model?" It recounted the predicament of a woman called Amanda, whose college boyfriend, Donald, was showing no signs of proposing and instead was complaining that he needed space. After he told her he wanted to break up, she found excuses to call him—her cat was sick, her car was making funny noises—and she accidentally-on-purpose bumped into him. Despite his wish for a clean break, he still considered her a friend with benefits, and one night at a party at Donald's apartment, Amanda erupted in jealousy when she saw him flirting with another woman. Donald retaliated by telling her she was "weak and dependent and just like that character in Fatal Attraction." Amanda knew "he wasn't talking about Michael Douglas." When she told her friends what he'd said, many of them shared similar experiences, that as soon as they showed emotion, their boyfriends accused them of "pulling a Fatal Attraction." As Amanda insightfully said, "It's like whenever men can't understand a woman's emotional outburst, they attribute it to psychotic behaviour."[11]

In the aftermath of the film's release, a woman's clinginess was being compared to "that character from *Fatal Attraction*," but by early 1989, she had a name—Bunny Boiler. Glenn Close had lampooned Alex and her penchant for bunny-boiling in her February 1989 guest appearance on *Saturday Night Live*, and, further, in a March 9, 1989, interview in the *Liverpool Echo*, as part of the promotion for her latest movie, *Dangerous Liaisons*, her character in *Fatal Attraction* was referred to as "Alex the Bunny Boiler."[12]

"I'm Not Going to Be Ignored" 23

In an interview Close gave to *Ladies' Home Journal* in December 1990, she was now using that expression herself: "There's nothing like portraying a psychopathic bunny-boiler to boost one's self-esteem. I couldn't wait to show everyone that I could be sexual. On a personal level I had never really liked myself, but after that movie good things started clicking in my mind."[13]

Alex Forrest was a character who chimed with women who were struggling in their own relationships. Rather than being listened to, the woman asking for clarity in her relationship became a bunny boiler.

If *Fatal Attraction* coined a new name for an unhinged single woman for the 1990s, then Helen Fielding's neurotic character Bridget Jones, created first for a newspaper column and then in the 1996 novel *Bridget Jones's Diary*, was all too aware of the stereotypes.

Helen Fielding was inspired to create her as a response to the retrograde way single women in their thirties were being portrayed in books and films. "The air of Miss Havisham and the tragic barren spinster left on the shelf was still hanging around us," she said. "The film *Fatal Attraction* presented the single 36-year-old as a desperate bunny boiler. Friends of one's parents would whisper: 'Why aren't you married?' in tones of appalled dismay. We weren't Miss Havisham or bunny boilers. We were products of a new generation, with our own flats, cars, incomes and expectations . . . we just didn't need to settle for someone who wasn't right, simply to keep life afloat."[14]

Bridget, in the 2001 companion book, *Bridget Jones's Guide to Life*, describes a bunny boiler as a "hateful concept suggesting that if a woman is 36 and unmarried, she is going to start murdering other people's husbands and boiling their children's rabbits."[15]

She also has her own floppy-eared moment when she squeezes into a homemade Playboy bunny costume in the mistaken belief she's going to a "tarts and vicars" party. She ends up feeling humiliated because, as Elle Woods in 2001's *Legally Blonde* can attest, being a desperate bunny is only one step removed from being a bunny boiler.

What's more, as the mascot of the Playboy brand, the bunny is the pervading symbol of antifeminism. Alex Forrest was all that was wrong with the movement with her demanding shrillness and masculine traits, and when she boiled that bunny, she was comparable to a radical witch, destroying what Playboy celebrated—the soft,

24   *Single & Psycho*

pliable version of womanhood through the lens of heterosexual men. Bridget's concept of feminism was trying to keep up with the expectations of being sexy in the way that lad mags like *Loaded* and *FHM* stipulated, but she typically failed miserably.

These magazines were the reading choice of young men when I was studying at Glasgow University in the late 1990s. The Lynx-scented bathrooms of my male friends were always stocked with piles of them, and they blue-tacked to their walls images of large-breasted models like Kelly Brook, who typically had a soundbite about how much she enjoyed sex. The content of these magazines, and the impression they made on young men, put an awful lot of expectations on women that they should also be "up for it." Her body, like the page 3 girls of British tabloids, was both thin and voluptuous, making it even more unattainable than the "size 0" models on the catwalks.

By the early 2000s, thanks to *Sex and the City*, women were now talking frankly about sex, but there was so much pressure for young women to be sexual and skilled in the arts of strippers and porn stars while never being too demanding. Being the "cool girl" like Cameron Diaz was the primary aim, and it was imperative to avoid doing anything that would lead to accusations of being a bunny boiler or to have the *Psycho* violins hummed behind your back.

In the Australian reality comedy *Balls of Steel*, which first aired in 2011, different comedians must act out certain behaviors to provoke members of the public. In one popular segment, the actress Ally Pinnock plays the part of the bunny boiler, a blond bombshell who takes on different tasks such as playing a surf instructor who flirts with other women's boyfriends.

The phrase was so well known that it became a confessional expression for women to reflect on their own conduct. *Cosmopolitan* in January 2019 ran a first-person piece by a woman who described herself as a "bunny boiler" girlfriend. Choosing to be anonymous because of her shame, she compared herself to Alex in *Fatal Attraction*. She was independent, had a good job, was outgoing in social and professional situations, and initially felt in control of her dating life. But then, the minute she started to like a man, she said she became addicted to her infatuations, and "I almost suffocate the poor guy."[16]

"I never realized, 30 years later, people would still be talking about bunny boilers," said Adrian Lyne.[17] But this concept, of creating an easy soundbite to undermine a woman's mental health or to malign single women as "bad," has been a long-standing feature of popular culture. *Bunny boiler* may have its origins in Alex Forrest's obsessive behavior, but its concept as a suspicion placed on the behavior of single women is centuries old. The unmarried woman's mental stability has frequently been questioned, particularly during periods of history when they've asked for more rights or when a man wishes to cover up his own sins of illicit sex, just like Dan Gallagher. And with the spinster, the old maid, the witch, and the hysteric, there have been plenty of expressions over the centuries that have been used to ensure women are kept in their place.

CHAPTER 2

The Madwoman in the Attic

On Boxing Day, 1851, Charles Dickens sacrificed an evening at the pantomime in favor of paying a visit to London's St. Luke's Hospital for the Insane to observe their festive dance around the Christmas tree.

It was pitch black outside when he arrived, and he found the hospital wards eerily quiet. He was cautious about what he could expect to see, given the history of these places with their restraints and torture devices dressed up as cures. Instead, he was struck by the festive jollity and how the ball was not just "proceeding with great spirit, but with great decorum." Writing up his visit in the magazine *Household Words*, partly as a means of encouraging others to care for those who were poor and suffering but also to give readers a flourish of his style, he painted an image of some of the characters there, including a "brisk, vain, pippin-faced little old lady" and "a quiet young woman, almost well, and soon going out." He also observed that "insanity is more prevalent among women than among men. . . . Female servants are, as is well known, more frequently afflicted with lunacy than any other class of persons."[1]

According to the British census of 1871, for every thousand male inmates at asylums, there were 1,182 women, with former servants making up the largest group. The number of women working as domestic servants rose by a third between 1851 and 1884, and alongside the sheer drudgery of the work, there was an expectation that they should grant their employer sexual favors. Given the power imbalance, it would have been impossible to say no, and with the scarcity of contraception, they ran the risk of falling pregnant and catching sexually transmitted infections. If they became a problem for their employer, the easy solution was to place them in an asylum, where they would be out of sight and out of mind. There's a similarity to how Monica Lewinsky was treated over one hundred years later—seduced by a powerful man who sought to hide his own sins by dismissing her as mad and ensuring she was shunned by society.

The domestic servant category also included governesses, the profession of the middle-class spinster, as depicted in Charlotte Brontë's 1847 novel *Jane Eyre*. Not only were they financially vulnerable, but as single women, governesses didn't have the support of a husband who could speak for them.

Charlotte Brontë and her author sisters, Emily and Anne, lived a humble life in their father's Yorkshire parsonage, and knowing that their poverty would make it difficult for his daughters to marry, he equipped them with the skills to teach. When Charlotte received a marriage proposal from the Reverend Henry Nussey, she considered it carefully. She asked herself, "Do I love him as much as a woman ought to love the man she marries?" and knowing the answer, she turned him down. In her rejection letter, she wrote to him, "I will never for the sake of attaining the distinction of matrimony and escaping the stigma of an old maid take a worthy man whom I am conscious I cannot render happy."[2]

Charlotte was devastated when her sisters died of tuberculosis within a year of each other, and racked with grief as the surviving child, she made the decision to accept a second proposal, from Arthur Bell Nicholls, an Irish clergyman. She had believed "it is a solemn, and strange, and perilous thing for a woman to become a wife," and the decision to marry would be fatal.[3] She died during a difficult pregnancy, at the age of thirty-eight.

The gothic novels of the nineteenth century often used the theme of mental health to explore how a patriarchal society repressed women and allowed them to be easily committed for insanity. Jane Eyre struggles valiantly through life without a father or husband as protection, taking up a position as governess for a little girl, Adele, who lives with her father, Edward Rochester, in Thornfield Hall. Jane discovers that her employer and future husband, Rochester, has a wife, Bertha, whom he has imprisoned in the attic of their home due

28   *Single & Psycho*

to her madness. Bertha also has an "otherness" because she's not white enough. Not only is she from a wealthy family who lived in Spanish Town, Jamaica, where the tropical climate was, in the Victorian era, said to unleash wild, unstable passions, but her dark skin and dark hair are due to her mother being a Creole woman. There's a suggestion, a common trope at the time, that her violent madness is inherited through this mixed-race lineage.

She is the motif of the repressed woman in Victorian society, the hidden interior of women like Jane, who must keep their true spirits locked away. As Jane believes, "Women are supposed to be very calm generally: but women feel just as men feel." Charlotte had experienced her own inflamed passions when she fell for her married teacher while studying in Brussels. Her infatuation was revealed in love letters that she wrote from the Yorkshire parsonage in 1844, which were kept by the Belgian professor's wife. Bertha's anger is dismissed as madness, her laughter "hysterical," and her only means of expressing her rage is by setting fire to a bed and ripping Jane's wedding veil, a warning against marriage if ever there was one.

In the Victorian era, there were plenty of reasons given for why a woman's mental health might be so delicate that she was committed, from epilepsy to masturbation, nymphomania, and grief, and for being too educated, too well read, and too lovelorn. The *Illustrated London News* on March 14, 1860, noted that governesses were particularly susceptible to madness due to their education and "the lunacy of the servant to religious hysteria and unrequited love."[4]

In Henry James's 1898 novella *The Turn of the Screw*, a young governess arrives at Bly Manor to take care of two children. She becomes increasingly anxious and irrational as she believes she sees the ghosts of two people who once worked there, and her isolation further enhances her paranoia. The lone working woman, without a husband and children to occupy her mind, is vulnerable to dark imaginings and slow-building insanity.

Charles Dickens was continually fascinated with the insane, often paying visits to asylums for his own altruistic purpose, as well as to mine them for material for his writings. As much as he argued against the cruel treatments that were dished out to the inmates, he wasn't above trying to place his wife, Catherine, in one. It's been revealed in a recently discovered letter that he had once sought to declare

The Madwoman in the Attic 29

her mad. Despite, or because, she'd given birth to his ten children, Dickens was anxious to replace Catherine with a younger actress he was in love with. Luckily, the doctor he had asked to certify her as mad refused to do so, and she was saved from a terrible fate in an asylum.[5]

A decade later, Dickens created one of the most sinister characters in gothic fiction—the eternal spinster, Miss Havisham, in *Great Expectations*, which was first published in serial form in 1860.

Having been abandoned on her wedding day, the ultra-wealthy Miss Havisham has been fated to live in perpetual bitterness and regret, still wearing the wedding dress and veil she was jilted in. Her house, and her heart, has become a prison, falling into a state of disrepair and coated with layers of dust. Now half-mad, she is described by Dickens as the "the witch of the place" and with "bridal flowers in her hair, but her hair was white." This juxtaposition of the virginal bride with the old crone reveals that white in Victorian fiction did not only signal innocence—it was also linked with death.

As he describes, "The bride within the bridal dress had withered like the dress," and while her gown had originally been fitted to her once ripe body, as an unloved middle-aged woman, she had now shrunk to "skin and bone."

In the many adaptations of the novel, Miss Havisham is portrayed as an elderly hag. But in Dickens's notes, he wrote that she was "scarcely forty"—perhaps her resentment and isolation as an old maid had prematurely aged her. She was the Victorian incarnation of Bette Davis's Baby Jane Hudson in *What Ever Happened to Baby Jane?* (1962), who is grotesque in her caked-on horror-show makeup and the frilled little-girl dresses copied from the ones she wore when she was a child star. Jane is similarly a prisoner of her past, taking out her vengeance on her disabled sister, Blanche (Joan Crawford), just as Miss Havisham raises her young and beautiful ward, Estella, to be a cruel heartbreaker.

A single woman in the mid-nineteenth century, particularly when over the age of twenty-five, the acceptable cutoff for still being unmarried, was a suspicious and pitiful figure. In popular imaginings, they would either be driven mad by loneliness from enforced celibacy, or, in the case of governesses, their bookishness could jeopardize their fertility. There's a famous unattributed quote, "A

30 *Single & Psycho*

well-read woman is a dangerous creature," and this thought, that education and books were a root cause for eternal spinsterhood, has had a resurgence during times when there has been a pushback against feminism.

In 1873, as a response to a rising movement of women seeking the right to study, a physician and Harvard University medical professor, Edward H. Clarke, warned that too much education would make a woman infertile. He wrote his study "Sex in Education" as an argument against allowing women admission to Harvard because, with their inferior intelligence, the extra work demanded of their brains would divert blood away from their reproductive regions, and would ultimately lead to "hysteria."[6]

This was a term first coined by the ancient Greek physician Hippocrates, in the fifth century BCE, to describe how mental disturbances in women were supposedly caused by a wandering uterus. By the nineteenth century, French physicians like Paul Briquet and Jean-Martin Charcot studied hysteria to define its symptoms and root causes.

Women were said to be more emotional, more susceptible to weakness in their bodies, and given that their ownership was passed from their father to their husband, they had very little power or independence. If they exhibited stress, anxiety, or depression, or even if their husband wanted to get rid of them, as Dickens plotted, they could be diagnosed with insanity or hysteria and placed in an asylum. Here, they were expected to be silent and have little communication with other patients, presumably so they couldn't compare notes about why they were there. Given it was believed that a woman's sexual organs were responsible for her mental issues, the proscribed treatment sometimes included a hysterectomy or an ovariotomy and even a clitoridectomy.

One of Charcot's students, Sigmund Freud, further developed his theories around hysteria, which formed the basis of psychoanalysis. While he believed men also suffered from it, he concluded that for women, it was a response to the metaphorical absence of a penis and that they would be in equilibrium after regaining one through sex (and marriage) with a man. Thanks to Freud, hysteria was a convenient explanation for perplexing female conduct. If she was moody or depressed, if she liked sex too little or too much, then that was the

The Madwoman in the Attic   31

simple diagnosis. It's hard to believe it wasn't until 1980 that hysteria was removed from the *Diagnostic and Statistical Manual of Mental Disorders.*

There are certain words that have traditionally been attached to a single woman of a certain age, and the majority aren't flattering. According to Amy M. Froide, who has carried out research into unwed females in early modern England (before the seventeenth century), the positive terms *maid* and *virgin* highlighted a young woman's purity in the years before her inevitable marriage. But for single, unmarried women, the terms became more unpleasant the older they got.

A *thornback* was a seventeenth-century New England expression for those over thirty—named after a type of fish with thorny spines that keeps predators from touching them.[7] Then there are the classics that have been used as pointed insults: *spinster, old maid,* and *witch.*

When we hear the word *spinster,* it makes us think of an older woman, perhaps a maiden aunt with gray hair in a bun or the old crone in the fairy tale *Sleeping Beauty,* who lures the young princess to prick her finger on the needle of her spinning wheel. Its origins date to the thirteenth century, at a time when Western European men were traveling to the Middle East to fight in the Crusades, with many dying on the battlefields or on the exhaustive journey. They left behind widows or unmarried women who were now without much prospect of finding a husband. These surplus single women were tasked with spinning cotton and flax, a vital function in producing textiles for clothing and furnishings. Prior to the invention of the spinning wheel in the 1300s, most women would carry a portable spindle where they could spin and twist threads as they did other tasks, such as trading in the market or collecting water. But now, with the stationary wheel, they were housebound and worked in isolation, and so the unmarried spinster became invisible.[8]

By the seventeenth century, *spinster* was part of legal terminology, commonly appearing on marriage banns in England and Scotland. In her research, Amy Froide calculated that 30 percent of the adult female population in England was single; the Civil War had decimated the men, and the women who were left were often too poor to make an attractive marriage prospect at a time when it was very much a business transaction.

32 *Single & Psycho*

With a surfeit of unfortunates who had grown old without the opportunity to marry, and with concerns around decreasing marriage rates, the terms *spinster* and *old maid* were now applied negatively as the opposite of the youthful, virginal maid who looks forward to her wedding day. She was untouched and unwanted, left on the shelf after the age of twenty-five. A 1713 pamphlet entitled "A Satyr upon Old Maids" described these tragic cases as "odious" and "impure"— and in illustrations, the old maid was often depicted as wrinkled and shriveled, even if she was supposed to be in her late twenties.[9]

In 1526, Anne Boleyn, a lady-in-waiting to Henry VIII's wife, Catherine of Aragon, was catching the eye of admirers at court for her fashion flair and her wit and charm. One devotee was the most powerful man in the country; the king was so transfixed by Anne that he lavished her with gifts of silk, furs, and jewels in the hope that she would agree to be his mistress. There is some dispute about the year she was born—either 1501 or 1507—but if it was the former, she was skating close to the limits of marriageability, and by sleeping with the king, she knew she would lose any powers of negotiation. So she refused to lay with him unless he agreed to marry her. According to Alison Weir in her biography *The Six Wives of Henry VIII*, Anne "accused the King of having kept her waiting; she might, in the meantime, have contracted some advantageous marriage, she said, and had children—a pointed barb, this."[10]

The king grew increasingly frustrated that she wouldn't let him into her bed, and over the summer of 1527, he proposed. There were two slight problems—his existing queen and that the Catholic church forbade divorce. His eventual solution was to dissolve his links with Rome and establish the Church of England so he could divorce Catherine and marry Anne in 1533. If Anne was the original *Fatal Attraction*, using her witchy femininity to seduce the married king, then her destiny was death. Henry tired of her when she failed to carry a male child to full term, and after he put her on trial for adultery and incest, she was doomed to lose her head. While Catholicism considered celibacy as a means of getting closer to God, under the dominant Protestant regime of Elizabethan England, it was now a sin not to marry as a woman's duty was to procreate. The religious houses where single women had sought refuge were closed down, and rather than the chastity of nuns being celebrated, women were a temptation, divided into the marriageable or the sinful. The Protestant reformer Martin Luther even declared that virgins were "not women."[11]

This belief inspired a curious Elizabethan proverb: "They that die maids, lead apes to hell." One of its mentions was in Shakespeare's 1590–1592 play *The Taming of the Shrew*, about a free-spirited and independent woman, Katherina, who is resentful of her sister marrying first. She tells her father, "I must dance barefoot on her wedding day, and for your love to her lead apes in hell." The ape was a symbol of man's base desires, of sex and sin and foolishness, so to be destined to lead a lecherous fool to hell was a grotesque prospect.

There were other variations of the term, including "maydens above twenty lead apes in hell" and "coy mayds lead apes in hell," which was a warning against prudishness as a woman's extended virginity was a violation of God's will. As Gwendolyn B. Needham wrote in a 1962 essay on the proverb, its implication for celibates was that as a "symbol of their uncleanness . . . persons who do not mate normally on earth must couple with apes in hell."[12]

From the sin of being a virginal "old maid," this would tie into the fear of the devil-worshipping witch. As Alison Weir writes, centuries of Christian teachings drilled into society the notion that "woman was an instrument of the devil, the author of original sin who would lure man away from the path to salvation—in short, the only imperfection in God's creation."[13]

Puritanism (an extreme form of Protestantism) swept through Europe and the United States in the sixteenth and seventeenth centuries, and unmarried, childless women of a certain age, typically shunned as outsiders in their communities, fell under the suspicion of witchcraft. It was a grim fate if they were accused—they would be tortured to confess and, if found guilty, hanged at the gallows and, in some cases, burned at the stake.

Think of how art and literature have so often depicted these witches—old and wrinkled, with a crooked nose and sagging skin, and boiling all sorts of weird ingredients in their cauldrons to cast spells on men. In *Macbeth*, Shakespeare describes the three "weird sisters" chanting as they make their witches' brew from dissected frogs, snakes, and bats. All that's missing in the list of ingredients is a rabbit.

Yet rather than wearing a pointy hat, the real-life witches were ordinary women, more likely to be holding a broom due to the burden

34   *Single & Psycho*

of housework than using it to fly to the Sabbath. In communities that were under religious and political control, she was not just a scapegoat but a measure of normality—*if she's this weird, then I can't be so bad.* These women were often mentally ill, uneducated, poor, or unable to defend themselves, and without a husband, there was no man willing to speak for them.

In 1590, King James I (and VI of Scotland) was crossing the North Sea from Scandinavia with his new bride, Anne of Denmark, when his ship was hit by severe storms. He believed that his near-death experience was caused by the dark arts, and he blamed a coven of witches in the coastal village of North Berwick, who were tried and condemned. The king questioned them himself, and as they confessed, it convinced him that witchcraft was a real threat.

In 1604, he sponsored the compilation of a new bible that would adhere to the Church of England, and on its publication in 1611, the King James Bible would have a huge cultural impact on Europe and the New World. It would also offer a command in Exodus 22:18—"Thou shalt not suffer a witch to live." His reign sparked a witch panic, which continued into the English Civil War with the Witchfinder General Matthew Hopkins, a terrorizing figure whose Puritan fervor sought out and executed deviant women.

There had been witch hunts prior to this. The first witchcraft act in England was passed in 1542, with the moral panic reaching a peak in England in the 1580s. In the village of St. Osyth, Essex, in 1582, fourteen women were suspected of witchcraft, including the most famous to be hanged, Ursula Kemp. She was a poor midwife who was accused of causing the death of a baby using one of her spirit creatures, or familiars, which inhabited the body of animals, including a rather sweet-sounding gray cat called Tyffin—although sucking the blood from her witch's teat was not quite so endearing.

Almost a decade later, in 1662 in Bury St. Edmunds, two elderly widows, Rose Cullender and Amy Duny, were accused of bewitching a group of girls. According to Katherine Howe in *The Penguin Book of Witches*, these examples were the template for the panic that spread to New England. There was a common supernatural thread on both sides of the Atlantic, where witches were said to cast spells with the aid of their talking imps and cats and were skillful in making potions from herbs that could cause physical and mental harm to those who drank them. They also tended to be midwives, placed under suspicion because of their uncanny knowledge of female bodies and their contact with young women.

As the Puritans fled England after the Civil War for the New World, they established highly religious communities, in which those who were outsiders could be scapegoated. Sometimes they were blamed for the failure of vital functions, such as butter not churning and crops not growing. "Witchcraft was perceived as harming families and household goods, the two primary engines under women's control for their economic security," Howe writes.[14]

The first English settler recorded as being accused of witchcraft was a Virginian midwife, Joan Wright, who was blamed for the death of a baby she helped to deliver. This was supported by the facts that she was left-handed, claimed to be a healer, and was accused of forcing a servant girl to dance naked, but despite her confession, she was acquitted.

There were other witch hunt outbreaks in the colonies, but by far the most famous was the 1692 Salem witch trials, which resulted in the death of nineteen people. It was triggered when a group of girls all fell ill at the same time. Their convulsions and blackouts seemed to come out of nowhere, as if they were under a curse. Desperate for an explanation, a local beggar woman, Sarah Good, was targeted for blame because she hadn't attended church due to her shame over the rags she wore. She was put on trial with two other outcasts—Sarah Osborne, a woman who had shown deviancy by living with a younger man and who had also been notably absent from church, and Tituba, an enslaved woman from Barbados, whose confession laid the blame on others. These women were said to have been in partnership with the devil, ridden a stick to Sabbath, and used their coterie of devilish spirit creatures to bring harm to children.

Other women were put on trial, including Martha Corey, a respectable member of the church; Rebecca Nurse, who was ill and bedridden; and Rachel Clinton, who was forced to beg after being abandoned by her husband. On breaking into a neighbor's house to steal milk and meat, she reacted in anger when she was forced to leave. As Katherine Howe writes, it showed "how dangerous it was to be an angry woman in the early modern period, especially at the fringes of society. Rachel Clinton's frustrations at being without food led to her being accused of witchcraft."[15]

36 *Single & Psycho*

The widespread moral panic eventually died down and the laws against witchcraft in Britain were repealed in 1736. But the concept of the witch would live on in folklore. Not all witches were spinsters and widows, yet they were still condemned for their outsider status, and throughout the nineteenth century, single women would continue to be judged. As Philippa Levine described in her 1989 essay, "So Few Prizes and So Many Blanks: Marriage and Feminism in Later Nineteenth Century England," for the woman who didn't marry, by choice or chance, "spinsterhood marked her as one of society's unfortunates, cast aside from the common lot of the sex."[16]

We can see these witchy stereotypes in the depictions of single women in the horrors and domestic thrillers that I will discuss in later chapters. She is a cat lady, with her creatures as bidders of her work in *The Cat People* (1942); she preys on and corrupts younger women, like the elderly coven in *Rosemary's Baby* (1968); and she sacrifices animals in her cauldron, like Alex Forrest, who then must be executed. It takes a strangling, a drowning, and a bullet through the heart to finish her off. And in *The Hand That Rocks the Cradle*, Rebecca De Mornay's psycho babysitter tries to kill the virtuous mother, munching on an apple like the wicked queen in Snow White as she plots her trap. Except for the Castevets of *Rosemary's Baby*, these characters have failed to find a loving sexual or marital relationship.

By the nineteenth century, due to the losses from the Napoleonic Wars, a surplus of single women caused serious concern. The 1851 British census revealed that out of a population of 20 million, there were around 500,000 more women than men. Given their narrow contribution to society as dependents, it was even proposed that those who had failed to partner up should be sent overseas to one of the colonies.

Frances Power Cobbe, in the 1862 essay "What Shall We Do with Our Old Maids?," argued that with one in four women "certain not to marry," they should receive education and employment to help them be self-sufficient. By being given these tools, many single Victorian women were, like Florence Nightingale and Mary Seacole, pioneers in nursing, and they excelled as scientists, social reformers, authors, and journalists. Their accomplishments were no doubt even greater due to their single status because marriage, while elevating her position in society, meant a loss of agency and a life filled

The Madwoman in the Attic 37

with domestic drudgery and dangerous pregnancies. Middle- and upper-class women living on the other side of the Atlantic during the American Revolutionary period, between 1780 and 1840, according to historian Lee Virginia Chambers-Schiller, "manifested a dramatic new form of female independence" by rejecting marriage to become a member of an unofficial category known as "the cult of Single Blessedness." Many of the reformers, educators, and writers of the time, such as writers Louisa May Alcott and Emily Dickinson, suffragist and abolitionist Susan B. Anthony, and Clara Barton, founder of the Red Cross, believed they would lose their creative and intellectual selves if they married.[17]

In 1848, the suffrage movement was launched by Elizabeth Cady Stanton and Susan B. Anthony at a women's rights convention in Seneca Falls, New York, and along with the right to vote, they called for equality in education, jobs, and marriage. As a response, they were lambasted in the press. Up for particular ridicule was their penchant for a more comfortable style of dress of Turkish-inspired trousers, as championed by dress reformer Amelia Bloomer, because it made them look too "manly."

As the early feminists discovered, an easy way to dismiss their cause was to paint them as bitter man-hating spinsters whose jealousy of other women's happiness was driving their desire to break the bonds of marriage. Betty Friedan, author of the groundbreaking 1963 book *The Feminine Mystique*, was adamant that the early feminists "all loved, were loved, and married."[18]

But there was a truth to the notion that many wouldn't suffer the indignity of marriage. Susan B. Anthony turned down at least two offers from men. Rebecca Traister, in her book *All the Single Ladies*, found this fabulous quote of Anthony's: "I've been in love a thousand times! . . . But I never loved any one so much that I thought it would last. . . . I never felt I could give up my life of freedom to become a man's housekeeper."[19]

She preferred to spend the money she earned as a teacher on a beautiful wardrobe, feeling she was the envy of her married peers for her vivid clothes, such as a purple wool dress, which paints a picture of her as the Carrie Bradshaw of social reformers. Female authors in the nineteenth century were similarly torn between societal expectations and the burning desire to express their inner life through

38   *Single & Psycho*

writing. They were all too aware of the battle they faced to be taken seriously, with many opting to publish anonymously or by adopting an ambiguous pen name, like the Brontë sisters. They also knew that a husband and children would reduce the amount of time they could devote to their inner life.

As I experienced with Gavin, certain insecure men can be jealous of the time a woman spends nurturing this creative side. I found sweet escapism in writing; it was a means of tapping into different lives, different worlds, to express myself in ways that I couldn't in real life. I was avoidant of conflict and struggled to even ask in past relationships, "Where do you think this is going?"

In 2018, I discovered the perfect writing retreat in Greece. Situated on a quiet volcanic peninsula, reachable by a two-hour journey by sea, the residencies were held in a long white-painted house with terracotta tiles, with an arch-covered porch that offered sheltered seating areas with sweeping sea views, and with steps leading down to its own private beach. The grounds of the house were dotted with different alcoves and raised areas, which all had a table and chair. Here, a writer could find their perfect spot with views of the turquoise waves lapping against the rocky shore and with the gentle hum of cicadas in the surrounding olive and pine trees as an inspiring soundtrack. Most of the guests were women who had come here as a solitary escape, momentarily switching off from the demands of their busy lives to breathe in the pine and sea air.

My theory is that men typically take over the domestic space, and women politely fit themselves around what's left, whether that's to find a place to set up their yoga mat or to even decide what's being watched on television. They are also burdened with most of the housework and childcare, and therefore, to explore their creativity, they must take time for themselves away from the home. The first two times I visited, I was struggling with thoughts of my future. Not only was my flat not my own anymore—instead, it was a smoky, crammed, and sordid hole filled with anxiety—but now that I was in my late thirties, I also believed that time was running out.

I'd given up thinking about marriage years ago. I'd found, through extensive dating and unsatisfactory relationships, that men who were still single in their thirties were often commitment-phobes. As much as I had fantasized when younger about the perfect wedding dress, the idea of being the focus of everyone's gaze for an entire day had always made me feel uneasy. Besides, it was a huge expense, and surely there were better things to spend the money on. My ambivalence toward weddings also stemmed from the fact that I definitely did not want to marry Gavin. Besides, he would occasionally make comments dressed up as jokes that he should really be named in my will so that if I died, he would inherit my property. There were times toward the end of the relationship that I did wonder whether he might really kill me.

What I did want was a baby, and the thought of it gnawed inside me as if my ovaries were burning. As my periods became more painful the older I got, it was as if my body was telling me I should be pregnant. And then there were the dreams. I can remember a particularly vivid one where I was holding and nursing a baby in my childhood bedroom, my safe sanctuary. The dreams didn't ever involve a man; rather, it was just me with this new baby, which sometimes took the form of a talking cat. Was this my witchy, childless cat lady voice coming out?

When I first met Gavin, he told me he wanted kids someday, and we discussed it over the years. We tried, or I tried, with visits to the doctor to ask for advice, and we even secured an appointment with fertility specialists. In Scotland, three rounds of IVF are fully funded by the NHS with certain criteria attached—that the woman is under forty, that a couple has been trying unsuccessfully for two years, and that they don't smoke. There's also a year's waiting list. Gavin had admitted to the fertility doctor that he was a heavy smoker, and so there would be no funding until he could prove he had quit for at least six months. I knew that this was never going to happen, and so I was tormented with the realizations that I would likely never have the family I wanted and that time was most definitely something that could be taken for granted.

At this point, I couldn't admit to myself how damaged Gavin was. He hadn't descended into the abuse that would mark the last year of our relationship, and so I defended him to my friends, who were already starting to worry about me.

"What are you doing, pal? You want kids, and you're going to get to the age of forty and realize you've wasted this time," my friend Conrad lectured me as we sat in the pub one evening. He didn't like

Gavin; he felt he was sketchy, but I wasn't at a place where I could take people's advice.

At the retreat, I spoke to other women who were my age, some of whom were single, some who had gone through fertility issues and early menopause or had accepted that children wouldn't be in their life. Back home, I felt like one of the few, but here, I was in a community of shared experiences. We all enjoyed our seclusion, relished squeezing as much time for writing into our day as possible, and some of us escaped here to reflect on and accept the different life path we were on.

In the nineteenth century, a woman who married, unless she had a particularly sympathetic husband, would be destined for a life of domestic drudgery. Multiple pregnancies would inevitably follow, with childbirth often a harrowing ordeal to survive. Charlotte Brontë had died during her pregnancy, a fate made even more tragic by her previous uncertainty about marriage and children.

Jane Austen's novels may have been reflective of the Georgian woman's occupation with securing a marriage, but in reality, the author would never make her own perfect match. Her outlet was in writing, and she couldn't sacrifice the creative spirit that drove her. When her father died, Jane, her mother, and her sister were left in a difficult financial situation, and this further drove her to find success as a writer. After a doomed romance with Tom Lefroy due to both of them lacking money, she turned down a marriage proposal in 1802 from Harris Bigg-Wither because she knew she wouldn't be happy. As she wrote to her niece, "Anything is to be preferred or endured rather than marrying without Affection."

Little Women author Louisa May Alcott had known from a young age that she didn't want to marry and instead opted to retain her independence as a teacher and writer. She considered old maids happy rather than the miserable image that was painted of them, saying, "I put in my list all the busy, useful, independent spinsters I know, for liberty is a better husband than love to many of us."[20] She created Jo March as an alter ego—a strong-willed woman who turns down the marriage proposal of Laurie, her best friend, because her desire to find success as a writer is unflinching.

Rather than the idea of the Victorian middle-class spinster being left on the shelf, many women embraced the freedom of not having

The Madwoman in the Attic 41

to answer to a husband. London's bohemian circles in the mid- to late nineteenth century often lived together in freer ways, yet their art typically captured women as romantic but tortured figures. In John Everett Millais's *Ophelia*, first exhibited in 1852, he chose to depict Shakespeare's heroine in a tragic light rather than as a temptress. She falls into a state of madness after her love is rejected by Hamlet and drowns herself in a flower-strewn river. The model for this work, Elizabeth (Lizzie) Siddal, would have an equally tragic life, forever known as a long-suffering and doomed muse.

Flame-haired Lizzie was the live-in lover of pre-Raphaelite artist Dante Gabriel Rossetti for many years before he eventually married her when she was struggling with ill health. A talented artist and poet in her own right, she was drawn to the romantic medieval ballads and poems of nineteenth-century writers Alfred Tennyson and Sir Walter Scott in her illustrations and poetry. Her painting *St Agnes Eve*, based on the Tennyson poem, was inspired by the medieval legend of the eve of the Feast of St. Agnes on January 21, when unmarried girls and women would fast before bed in the hope they would dream of the man they were destined to marry. She also took inspiration from Tennyson's "The Lady of Shalott," in which the heroine, trapped in a tower, destined to a life of weaving, is placed under a curse where she must never look out her window toward Camelot. Instead, she watches the world through her mirror, weaving what she sees. When she sees a reflection of Lancelot riding past, she is compelled to turn her head to watch him, and a curse of unrequited love falls on her. Rather than being trapped under this curse, she chooses death. She leaves her tower and floats downriver to Camelot, where her body is discovered by Lancelot, who remarks on her lovely face. Only in death is the sweetness of this single woman appreciated.

Lizzie was from a lower economic class than Rossetti, having been plucked from obscurity as a milliner in a hat shop to become a model for the pre-Raphaelite brotherhood of artists. She knew that marriage would offer her the security she so desired, but Rossetti refused and instead embarked on affairs with other artists' models.

As her depression led to a devastating laudanum addiction, her health deteriorated. It was only when Rossetti thought she might die that he agreed to finally make it official. Sadly, her happiness would be short-lived. Their daughter was stillborn, having died in the womb three weeks before, and the trauma sent her into a spiral of depression until, one evening, she took a fatal overdose of laudanum. Her disillusionment and bitterness around love were evident in her poetry, including in "Dead Love," where she cried, "Oh never weep for love that's dead / Since love is seldom true," and in "The Passing of Love": "Will tears of anguish never wash / The passion from my blood?"

For Lizzie Siddal, the medieval tales of tragic love seared into her soul, and this notion of a woman dying for love, and of a single woman being more appreciated in her death, would be a much-explored theme in movies a century later.

CHAPTER 3

Bachelor Girls

Sometimes all it takes is good branding to completely rethink the way women are seen. An article in the *Philadelphia Inquirer* in August 1903 celebrated the rise of the "bachelor girl," who, it enthused, was a new kind of "old maid." The bachelor girl was attractive, independent, and earned her own salary; she sometimes lived alone in an apartment, with just the company of a "canary or a household pet," and she had a very active social life. She enjoyed casual restaurant lunches, and her evenings were a mix of receiving gentlemen friends to her home, hosting dinner parties, and visiting the theater, either by herself or with a companion. It painted a picture of a thrilling lifestyle, not so far removed from the one *Sex and the City* would promote a century later.[1]

The bachelor girl sprung from the "new woman" of the late nineteenth century, a feminist concept for educated, independent women who were living their best lives. She also tied in with the Gibson girl, an immensely popular series of illustrations by Charles Dana Gibson, who redrew modern femininity as narrow-waisted, curvaceous, and athletic. They weren't abnormal spinsters; rather, they were free and thriving, they traveled alone on bicycles, and they went to work. The movement was captured in Ella Hepworth Dixon's 1894 novel *The Story of a Modern Woman*, in which her heroine, loosely based on herself, makes an independent living as a journalist.

In her 1899 article in *Humanitarian*, "Why Women Are Ceasing to Marry," Hepworth Dixon celebrated the liberty of the new woman, who, in lieu of wifedom and motherhood, could now "go to college, to live alone, to travel, to have a profession, to belong to a club, to give parties . . . and to go to theatres without masculine escort."[2]

44 *Single & Psycho*

The traditionalists, however, believed that this freedom would come with a price—they would be tormented by feelings of incompleteness when they realized it was too late to have a family. In an article in *Woman* on June 9, 1897, entitled "Does the Old Maid Improve?," the author argued that while these bachelor girls were proof "of the advance of womankind," the single life wasn't worth the sacrifice: "Occasionally she glories in her freedom; and then perhaps we, who are weak enough to prefer the chains of little arms about our necks, may chance to smile, knowing that the price of absolute freedom is a high one."[3]

The new woman had modern tools to enhance her free-flying lifestyle. The bicycle was the first form of transport to give women the option to travel on their own, and to make it easier to peddle, they donned the divided skirt, which provoked much pearl-clutching for hinting at the shape of the legs. These free-living bachelor girls provoked anxiety in the parts of society that considered it to be a double crime to be unmarried and childless. There were whispers that she must be a lesbian, a feminist, or both, and this stigma continued with female-led campaigns for suffrage and equal rights in the years before World War I. It was true that some Victorian women had found female friendships more fulfilling or chose to live with a man without commitment.

Elizabeth Wolstenholme-Elmy, who fought for fifty years for women's suffrage and whose campaigning achievement was the 1882 Infants' Act, which gave widowed mothers custody of their children, strongly believed that women should have control over their own bodies. When she fell pregnant to her live-in partner, women's rights supporter Ben Elmy, she was pushed into tying the knot by other suffragists who feared a baby out of wedlock would cause harm to the cause. She was one of the promoters of the "free love" movement, which condemned marriage as a harmful contract to women, and believed women could be empowered by embracing their sexuality for their own pleasure rather than solely for breeding.

During this time, female campaigners believed that to protect women from sexual abuse, rape, coercion, and infectious disease, the sexual behavior of men needed to change. Members of the Social Purity Movement took exception to the sexual double standards where women were divided into the "pure" and the "fallen" while excusing the male sex drive as a part of nature. Sex workers may have been forced to undergo demeaning testing for STDs, but the men who used them were "only sowing his wild oats."[4] They believed that men should be reeducated through male chastity leagues that would help promote self-control and with the Purity Society circulating literature to appeal to men.[5]

In the two decades leading up to World War I, factions of the women's movement fell on different sides of the argument around sexuality. One side believed that the key to equality was to target the accepted notion that a man's sex drive was at the mercy of nature. Christabel Pankhurst, cofounder of the militant suffrage organization Women's Social and Political Union, announced that her spinsterhood was a protest against marriage as a form of sexual enslavement. By 1913, 60 percent of this organization was made up of spinsters, and alongside their slogan "Votes for Women," they also believed in "Chastity for Men." As Sheila Jeffreys wrote in *The Spinster and Her Enemies*, "Spinsters provided the backbone of the feminist movement in the late nineteenth and early twentieth century."[6]

On the other side of the argument, a new group of "sexologists" believed that the biological sexual urges of men were vital for female well-being. As they promoted male dominance and female submission, they painted the celibate spinster as sterile, in comparison to the married woman, who thrived with vitality due to her willingness to please her husband sexually.[7]

In her book *The Truth about Woman* (1913), Catherine Gasquoine Hartley used the analogy of the beehive to equate the infertile female worker bees to spinsters who can't or won't marry. Their poisoned sting was created out of their egg-laying tube, and so spinsters, by being unable or unwilling to have children, would be "left the possessor of the stinging weapon of death." Here, she made clear that a spinster had the potential to be a danger—to other women, to men, and to society as a whole. She's the Alien queen, Annie Wilkes in *Misery*, and Alex Forrest all wrapped up in one.

Women's lives had shifted dramatically in the first decade of the twentieth century, and they would be further upended with the outbreak of World War I. They operated machinery, drove ambulances, and rode motorcycles for the war effort, and this taste of freedom was incredibly tantalizing. With every progress for women's rights, there was often a step back. In the United Kingdom, women over

46   *Single & Psycho*

the age of thirty who met a property qualification won the right to vote in 1918, and in the United States, the Nineteenth Amendment gave women the right to vote in 1920, although this change to the Constitution excluded the majority of Black women. Now that it was felt the job was done, the image of feminism would be very different from that of the militant suffrage movement before the war.

With millions of men dying in the trenches and on the battlefields of the Western Front, women grieved for this lost generation of boyfriends and husbands and for those young men who returned from the front maimed, depressed, and shell-shocked. *Testament of Youth*, Vera Brittain's account of losing her fiancé, her brother, and all the young men she knew, was the heartbreaking reality of many women who lived through the Great War. In the years following armistice, the United Kingdom was populated with 9 percent more women than men, which meant that many missed out on their chance at a married future. It also led to concern about what to do with another generation of "surplus" women. In the nineteenth century, there had been discussions about shipping them off to the colonies, but now, with the popularity of Freudian theory, single women were diagnosed with a variety of problems, including frigidity and depression.

A new form of feminism adopted by sexologists in the 1920s pushed women to reject prudishness for fear of turning into bitter man-haters. The message, that they should embrace their sexuality, was an about-turn for the feminism of the suffragettes who promoted celibacy, but it was still expected to take place within the confines of marriage.[8]

Single women coming of age after the war were collectively known as "flappers," and their short dresses and outrageously boyish bobbed hair, their cocktails and cigarettes and Charleston dances, created a stir. Their free and easy way of life was heavily criticized as disrespectful to marriage, even down to their haircut: "Shingles Leave Girls Single," said one headline. They developed their own vocabulary, which was impenetrable to the "old fogies," and their distaste for convention was evident in the use of *alarm clock* for *chaperone*, *handcuff* as an *engagement ring*, and *eye-opener* for *marriage*.[9]

They could be as fun and frivolous as they wished when they were young, but if they were lucky enough to land a man, they were expected to embrace marriage in sober seriousness. In Hollywood,

Bachelor Girls   47

flappers like Clara Bow and Colleen Moore fizzed and popped as good-time girls who were only promiscuous on the surface; they were still looking to secure the ring on their finger. The vamp, played by Theda Bara and Greta Garbo in her silent period, slinked onto the screen, and with the intensity of her heavily kohl-rimmed eyes, she lured men to their death with her seduction technique. Vamps were also grounded in an "exoticism" to make them appear dangerously foreign. The virgins, on the other hand, were played by all-American women like Mary Pickford and Lillian Gish, who were sweet and chaste and would eventually find a husband. This would mirror the messages in later movies, particularly *Fatal Attraction*—that the femme fatale, or deadly single woman, was an "other," infiltrating the domestic sphere, which was home to the "good wife."

For wealthy women in the twenties, it was chic to be daring and sexually adventurous, and painter Tamara de Lempicka, actress Tallulah Bankhead, and writer Mercedes de Acosta were unapologetic in their relationships with women. They were protected by the bohemian communities in London and Paris, but ordinary women didn't have that privilege. Lesbianism was almost made illegal in the United Kingdom in 1921, when members of Parliament voted to criminalize it. The House of Lords, however, vetoed the bill as they argued it would only serve to advertise same-sex relations to impressionable women who might think it a glamorous lifestyle choice.

The "normal" woman embraced heterosexual love, while the "abnormal" spinster and lesbian were to be feared and pitied. Marriage champions believed that women would suffer from "repression," which would turn them into bitter, fanatical killjoys if they remained celibate. Some even spoke against masturbation because if women embraced self-love, then they might find it more fulfilling than going through the paces with a man.

In movies, the repressed lesbian spinster could be terrifying, as seen with Mrs. Danvers in Hitchcock's *Rebecca* (1940). The middle-aged and unmarried housekeeper, played hauntingly by Judith Anderson, glides into rooms unannounced as she terrorizes the young bride who has married the widowed Maxim de Winter. She exhibits a cold cruelty to the new wife (Joan Fontaine), all the while memorializing de Winter's beautiful first wife, Rebecca. As she strokes the luxurious items in Rebecca's wardrobe, caressing the underwear that was

48   *Single & Psycho*

woven especially for her by nuns, it's clear that her affections to this deceased woman run deep. By the end of the movie, she becomes the madwoman in the attic, willing to go down in flames over her obsessive love for Rebecca.

There was also coded lesbianism in *The Cat People* (1942). Irena (Simone Simon), a mysterious beauty from Serbia, home of a tribe of "cat people," is so repelled by the thought of sex with her husband that she turns into a panther whenever he approaches her. While celebrating their marriage in a restaurant, she meets another woman who hints that she is also a cat person and who recognizes Irena as a sister of this secret club.

Although marriage rates had dipped in the years after the war, by the 1930s, they had bounced back as a conservative response to the global depression following the Wall Street crash in October 1929. Given how tough it was to make ends meet in those times, more women than ever entered the workplace, although the majority would give up work once they married. While millions of American men had lost their blue-collar jobs, what was considered women's work in department stores, schools, and offices was insulated. In Hollywood, the working woman thrived on screen. Powerful, independent women like Katharine Hepburn, Joan Crawford, and Barbara Stanwyck were depicted making their own fortunes through their sheer will. However, in their final moments, they typically sacrifice their professions, and sometimes, in the case of Greta Garbo, their lives, for the sake of love.

As Molly Haskell writes in *From Reverence to Rape: The Treatment of Women in the Movies*, "In no more than one out of a thousand movies was a woman allowed to sacrifice love for career rather than the other way around. Yet, in real life, the stars did it all the time, either by choice or by default—the result of devoting so much time and energy to a career and of achieving such fame that marriage suffered and the home fell apart."[10]

In 1937, Marjorie Hillis published *How to Live Alone and Like It*, an etiquette guide for the single girl, and in 1940, Ginger Rogers starred in *Kitty Foyle* as the beloved heroine of Christopher Morley's hit novel. Kitty's relationship struggles while holding down a job as a shop girl and secretary connected with millions of single women who were dealing with the same issues. The movie adaptation sanitized the major heartbreak of her story—her pregnancy out of wedlock and the death of her baby.

The opening scene is set in the 1900s, when a bachelor girl boards a tram, and the gentlemen on board immediately offer her a seat. She marries, and we see her in domestic harmony, pregnant and with a husband who comes home to her with his salary. "But this was not enough," the next title card says, as suffragettes protest in the streets. Women may have won equal rights, but those crammed into the trolley cars to go to work were now forced to stand. "They wanted equality, and they got it!" is the message.

The next scene takes place in the elevator of a department store in the present day, which is crammed with salesgirls.

"Got a date tonight, Jane?" asks one.

"Same date I have every night—with the *Saturday Evening Post.*"

One woman chastises them for talking about men all day. "I can think of a thousand better ways of being happy . . . isn't independence worth anything to you? After all, what's the difference between men bachelors and girl bachelors?"

We then see Ginger Rogers pile out of the elevator too. "Men bachelors are that way on purpose," she wryly comments, suggesting that these women aren't necessarily enjoying being single; rather, they're biding their time until that coveted marriage proposal.

Kitty Foyle was part of a series of melodramas known as "women's pictures," in which the protagonist undergoes a journey of self-discovery. This genre includes *Now, Voyager* (1942), one of the biggest successes of Bette Davis's career. The scene when Paul Henreid lights two cigarettes at once and then passes one to Bette was copied by would-be Romeos everywhere on the film's release.

Bette Davis plays the archetypal spinster, Charlotte Vale, whose family is forced to call a doctor due to her nervous breakdown. Born to a mother in her forties whose husband died shortly after, she was treated as the "ugly duckling" of the family, with her older, overly protective mother causing her untold damage. Dressed dowdily, with glasses and a bun and eyebrows that need a good plucking, Charlotte anxiously wrings her hands as her family dismisses her as nothing but a spinster aunt. The limited pleasures she has, she embraces: "Cigarettes and medicated sherry and books my mother won't allow me to read!"

50   *Single & Psycho*

After a spell in a sanatorium, she loses weight, gains a new wardrobe, and goes on a cruise to South America to further aid her recovery. There she meets architect Jerry (Paul Henreid), her soul mate, but she still carries the scars of a domineering (because she's older) mother who ruined Charlotte's chance at a relationship when she was younger because she wanted to keep her in a repressed state.

As she tells Dr. Jaquith (Claude Rains), "I'm fat. My mother doesn't approve of dieting. Look at my shoes. My mother approves of sensible shoes. . . . I am my mother's well-loved daughter. I am her companion. I am my mother's servant. . . . My mother says . . . my mother, my mother, my mother!"

Charlotte feels great shame at having been kept from having normal relationships, and when she meets Jerry, he isn't turned off by her own description of being the spinster aunt. On a road trip to the mountains, their car breaks down, and they spend the night together—hinting that they have sex, further allowing Charlotte to enter adulthood. Jerry, like Mr. Rochester in *Jane Eyre*, is tied to a wife whom he can't divorce but doesn't want to be with, and so Charlotte must accept the decision they will never marry, and she will take on the role of mother to his unhappy younger daughter, with whom she feels a great affinity.

"Don't let's ask for the moon; we have the stars," she says, and as a wartime weepy, the self-sacrifice message touched a nerve, alongside her stoicism and strength. During the war, being a spinster was more acceptable due to the inevitable absence of men, but this attitude shifted dramatically after the war.

In Frank Capra's *It's a Wonderful Life* (1946), George Bailey (James Stewart) contemplates killing himself due to financial worries. He is saved by his guardian angel, who shows him what his world would be like if he didn't exist. One of the consequences is that his wife, Mary (Donna Reed), is now a fearful "old maid" in glasses and a tweed suit, who is destined to spend her years working in a library. This was painted as a tragic fate, but at the same time, the *Sliding Doors* glimpse into Mary's future, where she is happy in her work and surrounded by books, doesn't appear completely undesirable.

CHAPTER 4

The Good Wife and the Bad Girl

A crowded dance floor is filled with young couples swaying cheek to cheek, and they slowly part to reveal a tiny but curvaceous figure on the stage, shimmering under the spotlight as she croons into the microphone. This bombshell with the blond peek-a-boo hairstyle is arguably the most beautiful woman in the room, and the actress playing her has just made one of the most impactful movie debuts of all time.

1941's aviator film *I Wanted Wings* would have been a forgettable wartime drama if not for Veronica Lake; as nightclub singer Sally Vaughn, she packs a punch as the original psycho ex-girlfriend. Made in conjunction with the Army Air Corps as a propaganda piece to prepare the United States for possible entry into World War II, the story follows a group of aviators at training camp. To break up the flying sequences, the film features a love quadrangle, with Veronica Lake's Sally competing for the attention of Jeff Young, played by Ray Milland. He's in love with a dark-haired photographer, Carolyn Bartlett (Constance Moore). At the same time, William Holden's Al Ludlow has previously been in a relationship with Sally and warns Jeff against going out with her because, he suggests, she's a brazen harlot and a gold digger.

There wasn't really an expression in the forties that described a clingy, obsessive girlfriend—there was no *bunny boiler* or *single white female*, and even the term *psycho* wasn't used the way it is now. What was implied was that she was "easy"—that she would spend boozy nights in bars, picking up men and falling into bed with them. One of the terms used was *B girl*, for *bargirl*, which described a woman

52 *Single & Psycho*

who earned money as paid entertainment both on stage and off. She would become a staple of film noir, the doomed type so often played by Gloria Grahame, with her glossy, pouting lips and hoop earrings rattling as she sways to jazz music. She is an exotic entity, an other, and she is the antithesis of the good girl, the one the hero will inevitably marry.

Jeff uses Sally as a comfort blanket to help him recover from the trauma when one of his crewmates is injured in a crash. But after sleeping together, he swiftly dumps her in favor of the brunette good girl, Carolyn. Over the phone, Sally begs to see him, but he is so casually cruel in the way he fobs her off.

"What does that mean?" she erupts. "Goodbye, good luck, we've had our fun, you go your way and I go mine? Don't try and sell me that routine, Jeff."

He then finds Sally skulking behind the cars in the garage on his base, and she begs and then threatens him into taking her back. When that doesn't work, Sally does the classic pretend-to-be-pregnant move. Proving how loyal he is as a friend to Jeff, William Holden's Al agrees to marry Sally so as not to jeopardize Jeff's engagement to Carolyn. Poor Sally is the consolation prize, and when she reveals to Al that she had in fact lied about being pregnant, he's understandably angry and abandons her too.

The next we see of Sally, she is on the run from the police after having killed a new boyfriend, and she returns to the air base to seek help. "You were born to hurt somebody," Al tells her, even though it's clear Sally was defending herself against an abusive partner. But rather than eliciting sympathy, she finds herself trapped in an aircraft as it takes to the air, and when it crashes, she dies in the wreckage. A bomber is no place for a woman, except for when her luscious silhouette is painted on the side as wartime nose art, and so the blond bombshell is destroyed for invading the sanctity of the male space. As William Holden's Al embraces her beautiful, dying body, with just the right amount of cleavage on show, he decides that, after all, he really did love her. It's as Susan Faludi would write forty years later, "The best single woman is a dead one." Sally is punished for her sexual desires and for daring to ask for more.

It may have been her first major acting gig, but Veronica Lake easily ran away with the movie, and she was hailed as the next screen siren for her villainous role. As the film critic at the *Bangor Daily News* wrote, "Never have we seen a portrait of more sheer feminine perversity. Most army cantonments have their Sally Vaughns, but seldom are they disposed of by fate in quite so dramatic a way." This was in contrast with Constance Moore's Carolyn, whom the critic noted was "the right kind of girl."[1]

Veronica Lake was a new type of seductress who would lurk in the shadowy nightclubs and foggy alleyways of 1940s and 1950s film noir. By the end of the war, as society had been shaped by violence and mass casualties, a sexual woman was considered a destructive force. She was referred to as a *bombshell* or a *firecracker*, and the two-piece swimsuit was given a similarly weaponized name—the bikini—after Bikini Atoll in the South Pacific, where the US government tested nuclear weapons.

Following the outbreak of war in Europe in 1939 and then America's entry into a now global war in December 1941 after the Japanese attack on Pearl Harbor, women were needed in the workplace more than ever. With a mass mobilization into factories, farms, and offices to fill the space of men who were fighting overseas, their icons were the muscle-bound factory worker Rosie the Riveter and Wonder Woman, first introduced in DC Comics in 1941. Yet women were also fed the message through wartime propaganda that it was only a temporary measure and that they must, at all times, continue to be pleasing to men; even in factory overalls, a slash of red lipstick and a winning smile was a must.

After peace was declared in 1945, men returned home from fighting overseas to find women had coped well without them, and frankly, they wanted life back to how it was before. While polls revealed that 61–85 percent of women wished to keep their jobs after the war ended, millions were fired, and by 1946, women's employment fell from a wartime high of 19 million to under 17 million.[2] For Black women in particular, with 6,500 having volunteered for the Women's Army Corps, the loss of wartime work often meant a return to domestic employment, which offered little security, although some were able to take advantage of funding under the GI Bill to study nursing and other skills.

There was a desire among both sexes to return to normality, for a quiet, homebound life to make up for the lost years in limbo. With

54   *Single & Psycho*

the introduction of the GI Bill, it also meant there was a degree of security for men that there hadn't been during the Great Depression; those who had fought in the war now had access to education, well-paid jobs, and affordable housing to help them raise that longed-for family. They were sold the message that they were fighting for the promise in the Norman Rockwell advert and that freedom was to be found in a happy, well-nourished family.

From 1946, film noir dominated Hollywood's output as it exposed the insecurities of postwar life, of returning soldiers dealing with the guilt and trauma of the violence they had taken part in and witnessed, and of the paranoia around what their sweethearts had been up to at home. With movies casting a mirror to society, the femme fatale trope was a reflection of the fears that their girls had been unfaithful during the war. Like Sally Vaughn, she was tempting but duplicitous, and her words couldn't be trusted as she would pretend to love a man but then betray him.

Ava Gardner's Kitty Collins in *The Killers* (1946) was the embodiment of the calculating woman whose black-satin-clad body drives men to cheat and kill. When Burt Lancaster's the Swede first casts his eyes on her at a party as she leans against a piano, singing like a siren on a rock, Lilly, the girlfriend he's arrived with, knows that her time is up. Because Lilly is the good girl (even the name evokes purity), we soon discover that she was snapped up for marriage not long after being dumped by the Swede, but as for Kitty, she's too devious to find her happy-ever-after. For all the single women in movies who didn't behave in the appropriate way, they would be destined to live a miserable life, rotting in a prison cell or a grave.

In *Out of the Past* (1947), Jeff (Robert Mitchum) escaped from a dangerous woman to begin a new life as a small-town petrol station owner, with a plan to settle down and marry. But the past catches up with him in the shape of Kathie (Jane Greer), who has manipulated Jeff into killing and stealing for her and who is one minute professing her love, and the next doing the bidding of Kirk Douglas's gangster.

It wasn't just the single women whom men in film noir had to watch out for—the married women could also be devious. There was Barbara Stanwyck in *Double Indemnity* (1944), a woman whose sleaziness is revealed through her ankle bracelet as she seduces Fred MacMurray's insurance worker and dupes him into bumping off her

The Good Wife and the Bad Girl   55

rich husband. Similarly, John Garfield's drifter is hooked on Lana Turner in *The Postman Always Rings Twice* (1946) as soon as he sees her lipstick rolling across the floor and then the shapely legs clad in tight white shorts. Men were the suckers, and the sexually aggressive, immoral woman was the counterpoint to the devoted, and lauded, housewife, as personified by Myrna Loy in *The Best Years of Our Lives* (1946).

By the end of the forties, women were being blamed for the ills of society, and this would be reflected in Hollywood's fondness for female characters who were mentally disturbed. Psychoanalysis and psychiatry were increasingly popular at this point and would be used to diagnose women who had been cast aside as outsiders, whether they were unwed mothers, hopeless spinsters, or dipsomaniacs who sought solace in a glass of white wine.

As Marjorie Rosen in her 1973 book *Popcorn Venus* noted, "The list of forties female victims reads like a Who's Who hospital roster" as unmarried working women are shown undergoing psychiatric treatment. Ginger Rogers may have played the career girl icon *Kitty Foyle* in 1940, but by 1944, her magazine editor in *Lady in the Dark* was suffering a crisis of confidence as she seeks psychiatric treatment when she can't decide whom to marry.

With the desire to make up for lost time, marriage rates skyrocketed, with a record 2.2 million couples wed in 1946, and 20 percent more babies were born in 1946 than in 1945. People were also getting married at a younger age than the generation before, and to keep up with the pace, women were warned that they shouldn't leave it too late for fear of becoming an old maid. They could be bitter and twisted, as seen with Jessica Tandy's poisonous spinster Janet in *A Woman's Vengeance* (1948). Janet is in love with the married Henry (Charles Boyer), and she plots to be with him by drugging his invalid wife, Emily. Instead of choosing Janet as his rebound, as she had expected, he marries a much younger woman (Ann Blyth), and as revenge, Janet allows him to be charged and condemned to death for the murder of his wife.

In *Possessed* (1947), Joan Crawford is admitted to a psychiatric ward after she becomes dangerously obsessed with an ex-lover. Olivia de Havilland's career diverted from swashbucklers into experimentation in the late 1940s as she took on a series of complicated,

56   *Single & Psycho*

tortured women in darker dramas. Her character in *The Snake Pit* (1948), Virginia Cunningham, is an inpatient at a mental hospital who, in a series of flashbacks, reveals what drove her to insanity.

De Havilland won a Best Actress Academy Award for her powerful performance in *The Heiress* (1949), where she plays Catherine, a supposedly plain woman in 1840s New York (evident by the heavy eyebrows and ill-fitting gowns) whose father believes that her social awkwardness and lack of beauty will leave her on the shelf.

After being courted by Montgomery Clift's Morris Townsend at a dance, where she had initially been treated as a wallflower, she can't believe that someone as handsome as he would love her. Catherine and Morris plan to elope, but her father, who is convinced Morris is using her for her inheritance, threatens to cut her off from his fortune, and on discovering that this would result in a dramatic drop in her income, Morris abandons her. Catherine is absolutely devastated by this betrayal, and it destroys her innocence and naivety. This is further compounded by her father making clear he struggled to love her due to his disappointment that she wasn't as beautiful and accomplished as her late mother.

After her father dies, she inherits his wealth, and Morris, who has lost his fortune out West, calls on her again. But her time alone has left her angry, and she takes revenge on this man who abused her trust. She pretends to have forgiven him, but then when he arrives at her door, she refuses to answer, leaving him hammering desperately outside as she coolly completes her embroidery, the last task of a hopeful maid. She may have felt the satisfaction of revenge, but in the process, she's become a bitter spinster. In the final shot, she climbs to the top of the stairs, the first time we see the house from this angle, and it offers a future insight into her life as the woman living alone, retreating to the upper floors of her home. In horror movies and gothic literature, this is often the dwelling place of the mad, single, and childless hag.

A few years before, de Havilland had won her first Oscar for Best Actress for *To Each His Own* (1946) as a young woman during World War I who falls pregnant after one night with a fighter pilot who is then killed in action. Despite the depictions of Sally Vaughn types faking their pregnancies, the conditions of war had led to a surge in the number of babies born out of wedlock. In the United States

The Good Wife and the Bad Girl   57

between 1940 and 1964, the rates of so-called "illegitimate" pregnancy skyrocketed from 89,500 to 275,700, respectively. Girls coming of age in the 1940s had been fed the wartime propaganda that it was their patriotic duty to provide comfort for men before they were sent to fight. The stigma of being unmarried and pregnant was very real, and girls often kept their pregnancies secret as they were likely to be expelled from school or college or fired from their jobs. Up to 25,000 women were admitted to maternity homes each year, and many were encouraged to give up their babies for adoption.

There were cautionary tales splashed in the pages of the *Ladies' Home Journal*, which placed the onus on girls and women to "put the brakes on" when petting with the boys (a good girl never lets him go too far), and an article in 1958 argued that the reason for accidental pregnancies was not that the girl was bad but that she craved affection. This was a common belief—that rather than being the result of unprotected sex, the pregnancy was a misplaced means for a woman to grasp for love.

An article in *Look* magazine in July 1949 titled "The Problem of Unwed Mothers" claimed that "there are some startling facts connected with this problem: A very high percentage of illegitimate babies were born to 'good' girls; the 'bad' ones know how to take care of themselves."[3]

Cautionary tales in the movies depicted the inevitably tragic consequences for these pregnant single women. Susan Hayward in the late 1940s and 1950s was critically acclaimed for her roles as tortured, unstable women, including as an alcoholic in *Smash-Up, the Story of a Woman*, which earned her a Best Actress nomination at the Oscars in 1948. In *My Foolish Heart* (1949), she plays a woman who must deal with the consequences of sleeping with her boyfriend just before he is sent off to war. Being pregnant and unmarried was a doomed status, leading not only to heartbreak but also to mental problems numbed by drink.

There were psychologists who offered theories, such as character disorders, narcissism, and psychosis, on why women "allowed" themselves to fall pregnant. Leontine Young, in 1954's *Out of Wedlock*, argued that illegitimate pregnancies were the result of a young woman's unhappiness and unconscious needs, and because she was likely suffering a mental illness, she would be an unfit mother.[4]

58   *Single & Psycho*

These diagnoses ensured that the blame for out-of-wedlock pregnancies lay solely on the young woman who had somehow allowed herself to become pregnant, and it removed any responsibility from the man, even with the possibility that he may have pressured her into sex. At least in Hollywood's depictions in the 1950s, he would pay the price for his negligence.

In *No Man of Her Own* (1950), Barbara Stanwyck is Helen, a woman who is eight months pregnant and unmarried, and despite her pleas to her boyfriend to help her, all he gives her is a one-way train ticket to San Francisco to get her out of his life. On the journey, she is befriended by a lovely couple, Hugh and Patrice Harkness, but when the train crashes and the couple is killed, Helen is mistaken for Patrice, who was also eight months pregnant. She keeps up the ruse and, like a cuckoo, moves into the Harkness home, where Hugh's brother Bill falls in love with her. When Helen's ex-boyfriend gets wind of her plan, he tries to blackmail her, but having been so deceptive, does Helen deserve to be happy ever after?

The consequences of an out-of-wedlock pregnancy would also lead to catastrophe in *A Place in the Sun* (1951), based on Theodore Dreiser's novel *An American Tragedy*. Driving the narrative is a love triangle among Montgomery Clift's George Eastman; Elizabeth Taylor's sophisticated, cool, and marriageable brunette, Angela Vickers; and Shelley Winters's down-at-the-heels blond, Alice Tripp.

George Eastman arrives in a small California town hoping his rich uncle, the owner of a swimsuit factory, will be able to fix him up with work. He's given a job on the factory floor, but due to his status as the poor relation, his uncle and cousins keep him at a distance. In his lonely room at night, he sees the sign "Vickers" flashing on and off, which reminds him of the beautiful and rich Angela, whom he only caught a fleeting glimpse of at his uncle's house but whom he is now infatuated with. If George is Jay Gatsby, a poor outsider who strives to belong in rarefied, privileged circles, then she's Daisy, the symbol of success.

She's the type of good rich girl who can afford to flirt with men as she is secure in the knowledge she will always be destined for marriage. Accepting that Angela is out of his league, George strikes up a relationship with downtrodden Alice. Coming from a poor farming family, she has no choice but to work in a monotonous job in the factory, and she is thrilled when George appears to be so intensely into her, kissing her passionately and sweet-talking her into believing she's the only girl for him.

One rainy night, after one of their dates, Alice gives in to George's passionate embraces, and as the storm is unlikely to break, she invites him into her boardinghouse. With the soft sounds of bossa nova jazz on the radio and the pattering of rain outside, there's a sense of illicitness in the air, and when he sneaks out of the house in the morning, it's clear they slept together.

George's uncle finally elevates his nephew to a better position in the company, moving him off the factory floor into an office, and he is also invited to one of the celebrated Eastman parties. Feeling out of place among the chattering society people, George hides in the billiards room, and it's here that Angela first notices him. Like many a woman, she's instantly impressed by the rebel with a pool cue, and she falls for his nervous charms, particularly when he makes an awkward phone call to his religious mother. Alice struggles with her sense of worth, and as a reaction to her insecurities, she nags him about the pretty girls in pretty dresses. "Honey, why do you have to keep needling me all the time?" George says, masking his guilt over Angela by gaslighting her.

Alice reveals she's pregnant, or, in censorship code parlance, she's "in trouble." Just as he imagines a beautiful future with Angela, the pregnant and pitifully dowdy Alice is now demanding that he marry her. She has become a major problem, and it drives him to think it would be better if she's dead. George is invited to Lake Tahoe to spend time with Angela and her family, and when a very pregnant Alice gets wind of it, she arrives in town, threatening to tell Angela everything unless he marries her. The soft, loving Angela is the opposite of Alice, who screams and nags at him, jeopardizing the future he envisions without her. This moment is rehashed fifty years later in Woody Allen's *Match Point* (2005) with Scarlett Johansson as the less dowdy but just as naggy pregnant shackle.

As Alice continually harasses him, we feel for George's predicament. We want him to be with Elizabeth Taylor—and Alice is just too desperate, too much of a gripe, too much of a stalker. But at the same time, Alice's helplessness would have been even more impactful on contemporary audiences who were aware of the difficult choices women faced. Abortion was illegal, and for women without money,

60   *Single & Psycho*

it could only be accessed through dangerous, unregulated clinics. Single mothers would also face a difficult life as their employment and housing prospects would be limited due to the social stigma.

Ultimately, for George to achieve the life he feels entitled to, Alice must die. He hires a boat and rows them into the middle of a deathly quiet lake, but rather than kill her as he planned, it becomes an accidental sacrifice as she falls into the water during a heated argument. George swims to shore, leaving her body floating in the water. But his path to marrying Angela is doomed, and it's only a matter of time until fate catches up with him.

By the fifties, young women were sold the idea that marriage was their destiny. There was an expectation that they should at least secure an engagement by the time they were in college to safeguard against being an eternal spinster. The message that was delivered through the movies, in print media, and in advertising was that education and jobs were detrimental to a woman finding happiness and long-term security, and if they weren't sufficiently feminine (code for asking too many questions about their place in the world), then they were likely to end up an old maid. A woman's true happiness, they were told, was to be found in domesticity. They were tempted with the new consumerist culture—the latest kitchen gadgets, the makeup to attract the perfect mate, and the corsets that cinched in their waists for that desirable hourglass figure.

The Christmas 1956 issue of *Life* was devoted to the "fascinating, puzzling" American woman, and it explored how expanded "women's rights" had "produced a backwash of unforeseen emotional and psychological problems for the emancipated woman." It detailed how the number of women in work had risen from 16.5 million in 1950 to 22 million in 1956, which was one-third of all American jobs, and in an accompanying article by Robert Coughlan titled "Modern Marriage," he noted, "Studying causes of our disturbing divorce rate, psychiatrists note wives who are not feminine enough and husbands not truly male." Coughlan diagnosed the problem as being hers; the "emerging American woman" was too demanding and assertive, and if husband and wife were both "wearing trousers" and "coming home equally tired," it was going against nature.[5]

This message, which harked back to the Victorian era, was constantly drip-fed in women's magazines. In a 1960 article in *Good*

Housekeeping magazine called "How to Know When You're Really Feminine," women were told their real character was naturally "womb-centered," and, reflecting the fears of the 1920s, there would be an "emotional penalty" for not following their destiny as wife and mother—the fate of lesbianism or spinsterhood.[6] The only way to catch a man was to be the epitome of gentle, soft femininity, and they also had to be very mindful of the ticking clock.

Thirty-five was, according to psychologist Dr. Clifford R. Adams and writer Vance Packard in their 1946 book, *How to Pick a Mate: The Guide to a Happy Marriage*, the age "when an unmarried woman can no longer consider herself a 'young maid.'" They also claimed that psychiatrists were in agreement that "except in unusual cases women who live alone will become neurotic and frustrated."[7] It was quite different from Marjorie Hillis's message less than a decade before, in her popular manual *Live Alone and Like It*.

Being a spinster, or an old maid, was not just emotionally dangerous. It was also physiologically dangerous. In Family Circle's *Complete Book of Beauty and Charm*, childless women were "more likely to have nervous and emotional troubles, poorer bodily function, and generally more precarious health than the mother."[8]

In her groundbreaking book *The Feminine Mystique*, Betty Friedan spoke of her memories of growing up in the 1930s, that she feared being one of the sad single women who worked in her town: "None of these women lived in the warm center of life as I had known it at home. Many had not married or had children. I dreaded being like them, even the ones who taught me truly to respect my own mind and use it, to feel that I had a part in the world."[9]

Friedan noted that by the end of the decade, the average age for a woman in America to be married was twenty; 60 percent of female college students dropped out to get married, and the number of children born to teenagers rose 165 percent between 1940 and 1957. Many were even choosing to get married in high school if the right opportunity presented himself.[10] For those who didn't wed in college, and instead went into the workplace, there was a gnawing anxiety around securing a domestic future. The Barbizon Hotel was where "almost every unmarried woman who came to New York in the 1930s resided" according to historian Paulina Bren, and in the fifties, its guests included Grace Kelly, Joan Didion, and Sylvia Plath. Although

62 Single & Psycho

many of the women who stayed there thrived as single women in the city while working as writers and models, it was also a waiting area until marriage. Most tragic of all were the spinsters and wallflowers who didn't have the charms of Grace Kelly and were given the moniker "Lone Women" by *New York Post* writer Gael Greene. She went undercover in the hotel and wrote a ten-part series on the Barbizon for the Post in 1957. Tragically, given the pressure to look and act a certain way, of waiting for the calls that never came, there were several suicides during this time, and they most often happened on Saturday nights, date night.[11]

Rona Jaffe was an associate editor for a publishing company in New York City when she had a fateful meeting in 1956 with Columbia Pictures producer Jerry Wald, who was looking for "a modern-day Kitty Foyle. A book about working girls in New York."[12] What she wrote was *The Best of Everything*, a novel designed to tie in with an adaptation by Wald for the screen and that struck a chord with young women living in the big city. Jaffe had in fact interviewed women working in Manhattan, who shared stories of their travails in love and in their careers.

"Back then, people didn't talk about not being a virgin," she wrote in her foreword to the 2005 reissue of her novel. "They didn't talk about going out with married men. They didn't talk about abortion. They didn't talk about sexual harassment, which had no name in those days. But after interviewing these women, I realized that all these issues were part of their lives too."

She was told by many women that the book changed their lives, not only empowering them and giving a voice to their thoughts and feelings about love but also, decades before Carrie Bradshaw did the same for Manolos and cosmopolitans, inspiring them to move to New York and seek a job in publishing. Her original intention was for it to be a cautionary tale against falling too quickly into dangerous love, but on reflection, she wrote, "an exciting life, even if very difficult, is better than a dull one, even if it changes you forever."

The opening chapter of the novel, taking place on January 2, 1952, describes the hundreds of women descending on Manhattan each morning at a quarter to nine, filing out of Grand Central Station, crossing Lexington and Park and Madison and Fifth Avenues: "some

The Good Wife and the Bad Girl   63

of them look eager and some look resentful, and some of them look as if they haven't left their beds yet."

One of these young women, Caroline Bender, recently jilted by her fiancé, has now found a job at a publishing house, Fabian, as a secretary for demanding editor Amanda Farrow (played by Joan Crawford in the movie), whose bitterness at the younger women in the company could be down to the fact that she's in her late thirties and still unmarried.

While Caroline has ambitions to move up the ladder in publishing, which she achieves, the question the girls at Fabian ask one another is whether they want to get married or work as an editor—it's not a choice to do both. They may be thrilled to have glamorous jobs in the city, but their adventures are just a stopgap until they secure that ring on their finger. Mary Agnes, smug in her own engaged status, believes that the girls in their late twenties who aren't married may have "something psychologically wrong with them."

Another secretary, April Morrison, is sexually harassed by her boss, Mr. Shalimar, and is then strung along by a rich preppy, Dexter, who insists she get an abortion and then does the slow-fade afterward. She keeps calling him in his office, and then at his home, until she convinces herself to crash his family Christmas party: "Maybe it was a crazy thing to do but she didn't care. Knowing she was going to do it made her feel happy for the first time since Dexter had left her."

Caroline's roommate, Gregg, desires to be an actress, but alone in her apartment, with only her loyal cat for company, Gregg is tortured by the shadows of singledom that are waiting to swallow her up. There's an empty glamour to a career girl's apartment, with the stockings drying over the shower rod, the canned orange juice and bottles of wine in the icebox, and the collection of matchbooks from the trendiest eateries around the city. For these lovelorn women, the excitement soon wears thin.

Forty years before Bridget Jones worries about being eaten by an Alsatian, Gregg frets about dying on her own in New York, "behind the locked door of your apartment and no one would ever know until some neighbor complained of the smell."

When she meets the playwright David Wilder Savage at a party, she quickly becomes obsessed. She wants to take care of him, emptying his ashtrays and making curtains for him, and while he's happy

64   *Single & Psycho*

to sleep with her, he never gives her the full attention she desires. She spends her evenings searching for him in the bars of the theater district, hiding in booths in the hope he asks her to join him, rummaging through his bureau drawers, and trailing him as he walks through a park. As long as she is near him, she feels everything will be OK "because he meant warmth and life and cheerfulness."

Gregg, who, like Alex Forrest, could have done with a copy of *He's Just Not That into You*, does everything she *shouldn't* so she can just be close to him. Eventually he tires of her clinging, choking behavior, and when he finally dumps her, she fantasizes about suicide to punish him. She calls him incessantly just to hear his voice and searches through his bins, hoarding pieces of garbage as if they are tiny clues about the other women he's sleeping with. One evening, as Gregg sits in her usual hiding place outside David's apartment, she is startled by a drunk man approaching her, and in her fright, she falls down the stairs to her death. She's a tragic warning about obsessive love and the dangers of falling for the type of man who is never going to commit.

If a woman doesn't find the security of marriage, there was the worry she might suffer the fate of Hollywood actresses whose complicated love lives were dissected in the celebrity fan magazines. They reported on how beautiful women like Ava Gardner and Rita Hayworth often went from man to man, marriage to marriage, trying to find the elusive happiness.

In an article in *Parade* magazine in November 1960, celebrity gossip columnist Lloyd Shearer divulged his thoughts on the number of actresses who had killed themselves over love. He had been inspired by the recent reports of Brigitte Bardot having taken an overdose of Nembutal on her twenty-sixth birthday. "Fame, fortune, beauty and power do not protect the emotionally unstable actress who falls victim to love frustration," he wrote. "Take sex-kitten Bardot. Ever since she was 16, this well-bred daughter of a French industrialist has been falling in and out of love with men."

Shearer ruminated on other tragic stories, including that of Lupe Vélez and Carole Landis. Mexican-born actress Vélez, typecast as a fiery Latina, was a tabloid favorite in the thirties for her reputation in Hollywood as a party animal with a tempestuous love life. Her on-and-off-again romances with Gary Cooper and Johnny Weissmuller hit the

The Good Wife and the Bad Girl   65

headlines, and as she was nicknamed "the Mexican spitfire," she was considered hot-tempered, wild, and irrational. In December 1944, she was found dead in her bed, having washed down seventy-five Seconal pills with brandy. In a suicide note, she accused French actor Harald Ramond of refusing to marry her when she was pregnant with his child: "How could you, Harold, fake such a great love for me and our baby when all the time, you didn't want us?"

Her tragic death sparked a media sensation, and rather than sympathizing with Lupe's plight, Shearer blamed Lupe for vindictively ruining her former lover's career with her devastating suicide note.

Carole Landis, a World War II pinup and star of movies *One Million BC* (1940) and *Moon over Miami* (1941), was found dead in her Pacific Palisades home by her lover, Rex Harrison, having taken an overdose of pills. Shearer similarly laid the blame on Landis's overly emotional attitude to love. With four marriages and divorces by the time she was twenty-nine, she was "perennially in love with one man or another, and in the last few days leading up to her suicide in 1948, the man was Rex Harrison." He wrote:

I remember lunching with Carole at Mike Romanoff's restaurant one afternoon. For an actress who had "been around," she struck me as surprisingly gullible. Carole kept spinning what seemed to be impossible daydreams, in which she described her future life with Harrison as a perfect idyll.

She realized that her motion picture career wasn't going any too well—she was never very successful as an actress—but marriage to Harrison, she felt, would compensate for all her past defeats and unhappiness. Exactly when she realized that Harrison had no intention of marrying her—which many in Hollywood had previously surmised—I do not know. But when the cold truth dawned, her loss of self-esteem was so complete that she apparently abandoned any hope of regaining it. Evidently she could not accept defeat both in her career and in love.[13]

In the late 1950s and early 1960s, there was one actress in particular who evoked the perpetually single woman—Marilyn Monroe. After her divorce from playwright Arthur Miller, she was painted as an unstable marriage-wrecker who was desperate for love. And

66   *Single & Psycho*

these weren't your regular married men—they were John F. Kennedy and Robert Kennedy, two of the most powerful men in the country. Marilyn was often depicted in the media as a tragic, lovelorn mess who was in the grips of hysteria due to her failed marriages, her inability to carry a child, and her aging body.

As her biographer Charles Casillo wrote, "There was something almost Shakespearean about Marilyn's saga in her final year. She was the beautiful, mad, aging queen, referring to her mirror and then turning to the mighty king and his ambitious brother to make sure she was still desirable, her position safe."[14]

Marilyn purchased her first home, an L-shaped hacienda-style bungalow in Brentwood, just six months before her death, and as she signed the ownership papers, she was saddened that she was buying it as a single woman. "I couldn't imagine buying a house alone," she ruminated. "But I've always been alone so I don't know why I couldn't imagine it."[15]

Marilyn is most closely associated with the character of the gold digger, who relies on her beauty to lure rich men. She was the ditsy, wide-eyed naïf of *The Seven Year Itch*, but she also played surprisingly vulnerable women who, despite their beauty, were tottering on the edge of stability.

Her first standout lead role was in *Don't Bother to Knock* (1952), as a mentally unstable babysitter who has been pushed to madness by the death of her fiancé during the war. Nell, who is suffering from delusions, is tasked with watching over a child at a New York hotel while the parents attend a banquet downstairs. After trying on the mother's expensive negligee and jewels, she catches the eye of a pilot, played by Richard Widmark, who is also staying at the hotel. She invites him to the room, ensuring the little girl is hidden away, but as they flirt, he becomes increasingly alarmed at her erratic behavior. The trauma of losing her fiancé has left her in an unnatural state— perhaps with symptoms of nymphomania and psychosis, as well as a desire to harm a child who gets in the way of a potential relationship.

With her roles in *Gentlemen Prefer Blondes* and *How to Marry a Millionaire* (both 1953), Monroe established her "dizzy blond" persona. In one of her most famous musical numbers, "Diamonds Are a Girl's Best Friend" from *Gentlemen Prefer Blondes*, she sings that "men grow cold as girls grow old, and we all lose our charms in the end."

The Good Wife and the Bad Girl   67

As she got older, her characters were increasingly jaded at the prospects of finding love. In *Some Like It Hot* (1959), singer Sugar Kane, touring with an all-female band, encounters Jack Lemmon and Tony Curtis's musicians, who must disguise themselves as women to hide from the mob. She laments to Curtis's Josephine that she's "tired of getting the fuzzy end of the lollipop." Her weakness is for saxophone players, and having had her heart broken so many times by them, she made a promise to herself to stay away from male bands.

Donald Zec, showbusiness columnist for the *Daily Mirror*, and someone who had grown close to Marilyn, speculated on the reasons for her admission to a hospital in New York in 1961 for mental exhaustion. He wrote that "the best-known and one of the most mixed-up beauties was facing up to a harrowing problem—the problem of being Marilyn Monroe. She is restless, nervous, anxious and ill at ease. She has been taking tranquilizer pills by day and sleeping pills by night." His guess was that "after some years of studying and talking with this tragic beauty . . . she is waking up to the fact that she is thirty-four years old" and "there comes a time when a 'sex symbol' had had its day, when the flashes from a 'heavenly body' grow dimmer, when what was child-like is . . . a little less so."[16]

After she turned thirty-six, she felt she was on the downward slope to forty, and it terrified her. She had been married three times before: the first when she was sixteen, to Jim Dougherty; the second to baseball legend Joe DiMaggio; and the third to Arthur Miller, during which they were frequently referred to as "beauty and the brains." Their marriage disintegrated because of Miller's disenchantment in his wife not being the angel he thought, rather a flawed, insecure woman, and Marilyn's realization about his disappointment. She'd had several miscarriages during their marriage, which were devastating given how much she wanted to create a family. It must have been even more heartbreaking to discover that Miller's new wife had fallen pregnant soon after they married. She would give birth in September 1962, just a month after Marilyn died.

By all accounts, the last year of Marilyn's life was tumultuous as she fought depression and angst around her career and love life. She had a fleeting affair with President Kennedy, but he was warned to stay away because her vulnerability made her unpredictable. She may have appeared as the confident sex kitten on the surface, but there

68　*Single & Psycho*

were concerns she could make his life difficult if she chose to. In her fictional biography of Marilyn, *Blonde*, Joyce Carol Oates imagines that during her first time with the president, she hopes "my empty womb this man might fill." In another moment in the book, Marilyn waits days on end for the phone to ring as her happiness and joyfulness depend on him calling her.

Marilyn died on a Saturday night, Clare Boothe Luce wrote in *Life*'s August 7, 1964, edition: "The girl whose translucent beauty had made her the 'love object' of millions of unknown lonely or unsatisfied males had no date that evening."[17] It was a tragic thing for the most beautiful woman in the world to be at a loss on the most romantic night of the week, and much was made about her age, even though she was only thirty-six—the same age as Alex Forrest. Marilyn may have been married three times, but she was now considered a spinster, an empty womb, fated to die alone. As Sarah Churchwell notes in *The Many Lives of Marilyn Monroe*, Marilyn has no reason to exist apart from the men who desire her, and if they reject her, she shrivels up and dies: "The spinster is the dead, negative flipside of the Virgin, and she is associated with a failure of home, a failure of fertility, with emptiness and with death. Unmarried, childless, a professional success, she will still be branded a personal failure. The prospect of the most desirable woman in the world becoming a spinster is finally what will kill her. She will die when the men have left the tale. She will die because she was a woman alone on a Saturday night—a fate worse than death."[18]

The three explanations for Marilyn's death, homicide, suicide, or accidental overdose, all link back to her rejection by men—the only possible explanation for a single woman's suffering.

CHAPTER 5

5 a.m. Breakfasts on Fifth Avenue and a Countercultural Shake-Up

Marilyn's death marked the end of the 1950s American dream, and the conventions that guided women down the "right" path to marriage would soon be shaken up. The following, more permissive, decade was one led by youth culture, where a new sexual revolution was sparked by the approval of the birth control pill in 1960. Fashion designer Mary Quant described it as "the atomic bomb of human relationships, and possible saviour of the planet."[1]

It was revolutionary in allowing women to have agency over their bodies as they could now avoid the fate of Alice in *A Place in the Sun* or Barbara Stanwyck in *No Man of Her Own*. Just as the feminists of the early twentieth century had been concerned that birth control would result in increased sexual coercion, in the sixties, some were worried about the damage free love would do to a woman's reputation. This period of being on the cusp of feminism was a confusing time for young women, caught between fifties traditionalism and the youthful experimentalism in the air.

Natalie Wood, with her deep brown eyes that yearned for more, perfected the angsty teenager who was the opposite to the perky blonds like Sandra Dee or Debbie Reynolds. In *Rebel without a Cause* (1955), her character, Judy, is tormented by her father calling her "a little tramp" for the lipstick and too-tight sweaters she wears, and as Deanie in 1961's *Splendor in the Grass*, she is a cautionary tale for falling too fast, and too obsessively, in love. The latter also reveals the patriarchal and societal pressure placed on young people and how these life values can crush them.

70   *Single & Psycho*

Deanie is in love with her devastatingly handsome high school boyfriend, Bud (the film debut of Warren Beatty), but is raised to believe that good girls are chaste, while the loose, unmarriageable girls solely exist for male pleasure. Her mother tells her, "I just gave in because a wife has to. A woman doesn't enjoy those things the way a man does. She just lets her husband come near her in order to have children."

A similar lesson has also been hammered into Bud by his father: "Dad says there's two types of girls—one type of girl to get the steam out the system, and the other for marriage." Because of this messaging, Deanie won't go further than a goodnight kiss, while Bud is tortured by his sexual frustrations. Deanie keeps a shrine to Bud in her bedroom, kissing his photo before she goes to sleep every night. She is completely infatuated, gazing up at him as they walk along the corridor at high school together and looping their names together in her notebook, like the lovesick teenager she is. "I am nuts about you, I can't get along without you, and I would do anything for you," she swoons.

Bud is advised by his father to break it off with Deanie and to find gratification with one of the easier girls, and ultimately their relationship is destroyed because their desire for one another has no outlet. The breakup proves too much for Deanie, and she suffers a mental breakdown.

"I can't eat, I can't study, I can't even face my friends anymore. I want to die," she cries to her mother, who is shaken at the sight of her daughter stripping off her clothes and screaming. But it's the only way she can express her mental torture.

After a suicide attempt at a local waterfall spot where young people go to make out, she is committed to an asylum, losing out on the milestones that she should have experienced as a young woman coming of age. Finally able to overcome her teenage infatuation, she realizes that she can still find joy in life, even if the optimism of youth, the splendor in the grass, has gone.

If the fifties was about disaffected rebels like James Dean and Marlon Brando, in the sixties, they were young women like Deanie who were skirting close to insanity. In *Lilith* (1964), Jean Seberg plays a schizophrenic young woman who beguiles an ex-soldier, Vincent (Warren Beatty again), when he works as an assistant at the mental asylum where she is a patient. On his arrival, he is shown the women's ward and told, "It's not as disturbing on this floor is it. Somehow insanity seems a lot more sinister to watch in a man than in a woman."

The female patients are a mix of "eccentric spinsters" and "witless girls," but Lilith shines with intelligence and artistry. We first meet her properly when the patients are taken for a picnic near a river. As she stands on the bridge, she spits into the water, causing all the other patients to burst into laughter. When she breaks out into hysterical laughter, too, there are looming clouds above and dramatic music to indicate her madness. As part of her mental illness, she's a nymphomaniac who tries to seduce and kiss young boys and is in an intimate relationship with another woman. After she and Vincent sleep together, he feels deep jealousy, accusing her of being a "dirty bitch" for her promiscuity.

Lilith tells Vincent that she wants to "leave the mark of her desire on every living creature in the world . . . she's Lilith, she has to do it with her body." Lilith destroys men by being a tease—first her brother, with an implication that she chased an incestuous relationship; then Vincent, whose misogyny leads to him calling a woman in a bar "bitch"; and Stephen, an inmate who is in love with her. His suicide destroys Lilith, severing her last connection with reality as she is fully inhabited by her madness. On the cusp of the sexual revolution, Lilith was a warning about the dangers of permissiveness in women, who were emotionally unequipped to deal with new freedoms.

While Deanie cares too deeply for love and Lilith is a psychotic nymphomaniac, *Breakfast at Tiffany's* Holly Golightly, with her desire to run free, without commitment, was a new screen heroine for a new decade. She is a single woman living in an apartment on her own, which in those days was rare and bohemian, and despite her questionable methods of earning money, she appears to live a glamorously untethered life. The poster for *Breakfast at Tiffany's* may have adorned countless student walls, but what many fans didn't realize is that Audrey Hepburn's independent and carefree singleton, Holly, is in fact a sex worker, a detail that was clear in the Truman Capote novella it was based on but that was glossed over in the Hollywood adaptation.

Audrey was the good girl of cinema, beloved for her doe-eyed beauty and for her roles in fairy-tale movies like *Roman Holiday* and

72   *Single & Psycho*

Sabrina. With Audrey having just been Oscar-nominated for *The Nun's Story* (1959), the character of Holly Golightly was a surprising shift. Holly is the wild child who window-shops on Fifth Avenue just as the sun is coming up, and before she's been to bed, and who takes fifty dollars from men every time she goes to the powder room. Her life is chaotically alluring—waking up in a man's tuxedo shirt, keeping the phone in the suitcase, having nothing to eat in the fridge, and then looking like a million dollars as soon as she throws on a black Givenchy dress. She demonstrates pure individuality with every whim. No time to get changed for a party? She'll just wrap a bedsheet around herself, like a toga. Her ginger cat is a symbol of her own liberty and nonconformity—she refuses to give him a name so that he remains without ownership. Holly Golightly helped single women to feel excited about their status. Rather than being tied to the mop handle or spending hours washing and folding laundry, they could throw out the old rule books.

Helen Gurley Brown's 1962 how-to guide, *Sex and the Single Girl*, was similarly revolutionary in changing the way women thought about sex. The flamboyant editor of *Cosmopolitan* magazine instructed women to enjoy being single as it would be the greatest freedom they would ever experience—a time that was sandwiched between the protective blanket of their parents and the restrictions of marriage.

Sex and the Single Girl was on the bestseller list for almost seven months, transforming the spinster from dowdy to pleasure-seeking and glamorous and offering an alternative to fretting at still being unmarried at twenty-five. The pill was becoming more widely available, and Gurley Brown actively encouraged women to enjoy no-strings sex. As she wrote, "Theoretically, a 'nice' single girl has no sex life. What nonsense! She has a better sex life than most of her married friends. She need never be bored with one man per lifetime. Her choice of partners is endless and they seek her."[2]

Gurley Brown spoke from experience. She married for the first time at the age of thirty-seven, and while she told her readers she didn't consider herself particularly striking or brilliant, she said she still managed to land an in-demand motion picture producer at an age that many dismissed as akin to an old maid. But, she said, she worked hard to "become the kind of woman who might interest him." She was worldly, financially secure, and "adorned with enough glitter" to make up for what she claimed was her lack of natural beauty.

While Gurley Brown still believed a woman's goal was to marry, she thought women should have fun and be as independent as possible in their "best years." She was also radical in reassuring women they could still have children beyond their forties and that the most important truth is that "the single woman, far from being a creature to be pitied and patronized, is emerging as the newest glamour girl of the times."

To readers in the 2020s, be warned the book is spoiled by homophobia and fat-shaming ("Your figure can't harbor an ounce of baby fat"), and she also expressed the unsisterly belief that married men were not off limits. But as a modern guide to life in the sixties, it was groundbreaking in its message to women that they had options and that they should love all of themselves, right down to their menstruation and reproductive organs. She paved the way for Candace Bushnell's *Sex and the City* to inspire women to take pleasure and enjoyment in being single, and thirty years before Samantha Jones romped through Manhattan, she insisted "career girls are sexy."

While Gurley Brown's declaration was empowering to her readers, in August 1963, a double murder would cause a moral panic around the dangers to young single women in the city. When Janice Wylie, a twenty-one-year-old researcher at *Newsweek*, and her roommate, Emily Hoffert, twenty-three, were found brutally murdered in their New York Upper East Side apartment, newspapers dubbed it the Career Girl Murders. Their bodies had been discovered by their surviving roommate, who worked in publishing for Time Inc., much like the young women in *The Best of Everything*.

Janice's father, the novelist Max Wylie, traumatized by the brutal murder of his daughter, wrote a book entitled *Career Girl, Watch Your Step!* It was designed to warn about the dangers women faced when living alone and questioned their desire for independence and freedom without male protection. There were other similar cases that hit the headlines, such as that of bartender Kitty Genovese, stabbed to death outside her Queens apartment in March 1964, which became notorious for the "bystander effect" when it was reported incorrectly that there were thirty-eight witnesses who didn't come to her aid. Despite these horrific incidents giving pause to progress, there would

74   *Single & Psycho*

be a further shake-up in how women considered their place in society, thanks to Betty Friedan.

Friedan had, through a survey of students at Smith College, Massachusetts, in the late fifties, found that young women were using college as a means for meeting men rather than to educate themselves. They weren't having fun being single; instead, they felt pressured by expectations to invest their time in finding a husband. She was informed by one blond senior that girls only went to college because their parents expected it, and those who took their studies too seriously were labeled "peculiar, unfeminine." The ultimate goal was to leave college with "a diamond ring on her finger" rather than an education as grounding for a career.

The feminine mystique was the term Friedan coined to describe the damaging belief that a woman's sole purpose, her feminine calling, was to be a housewife. As many struggled to find fulfillment in spending their endless days cleaning their home and looking after their children, without the mental stimulation to give them a purpose, it became "the problem with no name."[3]

She also wrote her text as a cautionary tale about how easily new freedoms could be taken away. She includes within her pages the history of the first-wave feminists who worked tirelessly to win the right to vote and helped give women a sense of pride in education and work outside of marriage, only to retreat to Victorian values by the end of the 1940s.[4] As Gaby Hinsliff writes in her introduction to the 2021 edition, "The ghosts of the attitudes she described hover over us still. They are present every time a single woman is portrayed as suffering for lack of a man, and every time female ambition is portrayed as selfish or a threat to her children's happiness in ways that male ambition is not."[5]

Friedan found that married women were stunted in their development because they had gone straight from being under the care of their father to under the care of their husband. As they struggled with the sense that their individuality was being erased, falling into a depression at the lack of creativity and the dull sameness of their days, they entered into a cycle of pills and drink, sought help from psychiatrists, and some even ended their lives.

She described the typical housewife as having "a childlike kind of dependence," very different from the self-sufficient women of the forties. "They have no vision of the future, except to have a baby," and their attitude was focused on the belief that "in order to be a woman, I have to be able to have children."

The Feminine Mystique made a huge impact on its publication in February 1963, as Friedan finally put a name to the frustrations felt by millions of women. The book sparked a movement, and with her founding of the National Organization for Women (NOW), the second wave of feminism was born. In part due to the sway of Friedan's book, the Equal Pay Act was passed in 1963, which made it illegal to pay a woman less than a man for doing the same job. Friedan didn't want NOW to be exclusively for white women, and with Black lawyer Pauli Murray as one of the founders, they approached Black women to set up chapters of the organization across the country. The Civil Rights Act, passed in 1964, banned discrimination on the basis of race, sex, and religion, which included firing a woman for being pregnant.[6] One of their major achievements was to ban airlines from forcing air stewardesses to resign either at the age of thirty or on marriage. But there was so much more to do in the quest to be equal.

The feminine woman was supposed to be graceful and childlike, she spoke gently and deferred to men, but the new feminist rejected the trappings of the patriarchy—the bras, the makeup, everything designed to keep a woman in her place. In September 1968, the Miss America pageant in Atlantic City, New Jersey, became a protest site for the women's liberation movement, and they symbolically threw into a trash can the repressive tools of femininity. This included high-heeled shoes, curlers, false eyelashes, the bra, and copies of *Playboy*, *Cosmopolitan*, and *Ladies' Home Journal*. They didn't get the chance to burn the contents, but the concept of the bra-burning, man-hating, perpetually single feminist stuck.

To mark the fiftieth anniversary of women winning the right to vote on August 26, 1970, thousands of protesters gathered en masse on New York's Fifth Avenue to demonstrate that feminism was more than just a fad. It was a global movement, a revolution, and as Friedan said, "It suddenly became both political and glamorous to be a feminist."[7]

Throughout the sixties, pop culture took a mirror to the growing feminist movement. Female characters on television were given magical abilities, such as the good witch Samantha in the TV series

76 *Single & Psycho*

Bewitched and the sexy genie in *I Dream of Jeannie*. These were acceptable witches, still in possession of their youth and beauty. But given that the feminist movement was an existential threat to male dominance, this fear would be reflected in the depictions of the single and deranged older woman in horror movies such as *What Ever Happened to Baby Jane?* (1962), *Hush . . . Hush, Sweet Charlotte* (1964), and *Fanatic* (1965), where the aging female antagonist has been driven mad by the lost opportunities of her youth and by the grotesque reflection she now sees in the mirror. I fully explored this subgenre of horror, known as "hag horror," "hagsploitation," "grand dame Guignol," or "psycho-biddy," in my book *Crazy Old Ladies: The Story of Hag Horror*, so I won't go over the same ground. But one of the messages that ran as a thread through these films was the poisonous regrets of a middle-aged woman who hasn't achieved stability in her family life and who takes out her bitterness on the younger generation.

I include 1968's *Rosemary's Baby* in the hag horror subgenre because it depicts a coven of elderly people who abuse the fertility of young women to breed the devil's seed. It was a film that represented New Hollywood, a movement of young filmmakers who explored the new social and political mores. Cinema attendance in the United States had reached 78.2 million a week in 1946, but by 1971, it had plunged to 15.8 million a week, and with a dramatic slump in profits, it was up to this new generation to revitalize the industry with their experimentation in depicting violence and sex on screen. But the question was, how would these new directors, free from the constraints of the old censorship codes that had been abandoned in favor of a ratings system, choose to depict the single woman under the conditions of the feminist movement?

CHAPTER 6

The 1970s

Feminism, New Hollywood, and Blaxploitation

It's 1971. In January, Charles Manson and his female followers are found guilty of murder after a shocking circus of a trial held in Los Angeles. In March, the United Kingdom's first women's liberation movement protest takes place in London, and in July in Washington, DC, at the founding meeting for the National Women's Political Caucus, Gloria Steinem delivers her "Address to the Women of America" as she calls for a society free of racism and sexism. In the midst of this sea change, on March 31, *The Beguiled* is released in American cinemas, to a lukewarm response.

Considered the very opposite of the peace and love generation, Clint Eastwood's appeal as an actor in the seventies was based on his old-fashioned charisma and strong good looks, the machismo and swagger in his actions, and his reputation as a ladies' man in real life. So his starring role in *The Beguiled*, playing a man at the mercy of feminine wiles during the Civil War, was the antithesis of what people expected of an Eastwood film. In retrospect, it has been criticized as misogynistic, but what it does offer is a fascinating insight into the time it was made. The film's dreamy aesthetics, of makeup-free women with flowing hair and long cotton dresses, are straight out of a hippie commune, and with its all-female society, it's a vision of "the future is female" before the T-shirt was conceived.

Clint Eastwood plays John McBurney, a Union soldier in the American Civil War, who is discovered wounded in the moss-hung forests of Louisiana that surround an all-girl seminary. The headmistress, Martha Farnsworth (Geraldine Page), agrees to hide him from Confederate soldiers until his injuries are healed, and his presence

78 *Single & Psycho*

among the teachers and pupils twists their sexual repression into jealousy and lust. Because these women have been starved of men for so long, they exhibit the unhinged behavior of desperate spinsters. Miss Martha simmers with buttoned-up lust; the repressed teacher, Edwina, holds on to hope that he's her ticket to marriage and happiness; the enslaved Black woman, Hallie, bonds with him; and Carol, the precocious schoolgirl, seduces him.

Veteran director Don Siegel, a long-standing collaborator of Eastwood's, uses hazy fantasies and flashbacks to reveal the untapped desire of these spinsters, including an alcohol-fueled dream in which Martha imagines being entwined with Edwina and McBurney, taking on the positions of the religious pietà, a print of which hangs above her bed.

The film was based on the 1966 novel by Thomas P. Cullinan, and the scriptwriters, Albert Maltz and Irene Kamp, were so disgusted by Siegel's deviations, where he aimed for something more akin to the twisted horror of *Rosemary's Baby*, that they asked to be credited under pseudonyms—John B. Sherry and Grimes Grice.[1] After its limp box office returns, Eastwood blamed the marketing. The misleading poster featured the actor brandishing a gun as if he's Dirty Harry, with a smaller picture of him being surrounded by Union soldiers, even though the character was a failure in war and among housebound women. The artwork completely erased the women of the film, as if the studio felt that a film about female desire wouldn't sell unless they pretended it was really about men.

That was the thing with cinema in the seventies—its output was so male-centered that there was little space for women to be anything other than the girlfriend or the creepy spinster. She was kept in her lane by the male-bonding movies that inevitably starred the uber-masculine Burt Lancaster, Burt Reynolds, Lee Marvin, or Eastwood. The ongoing Vietnam War, coupled with the call for women's rights, had shaped a preoccupation with male anxieties, and movies now focused on depicting their relationships with one another. *The Beguiled* offered the rare chance for actresses to play complex women who get the better of the man, even if the finale is more *Village of the Damned* than empowerment.

Leading the female cast was Geraldine Page, a character actress who had developed a reputation at the time for playing deviant widows

The 1970s   79

and spinsters. Kevin Thomas of the *Los Angeles Times* praised her as "always best in demented Grand Guignol parts." Previous roles had included 1969's hag horror *What Ever Happened to Aunt Alice?*, playing a conniving widow who murders her maids for their money. In an interview, Page described Martha as "a terribly complicated, complex lady," which was somewhat of an understatement. She isn't just a prim school mistress and genteel Southerner with unfulfilled urges; the briefest of flashbacks reveals an incestuous relationship with her late brother. Elizabeth Hartman plays Edwina, a teacher who has no experience with men, and with a sense of what she might be missing out on, she tries to hide her disappointment at the prospect of spending the rest of her days bonded to the chaste environs of the school.

Tragically, both actresses would die within days of each other. Hartman suffered long-term depression, and after a period of intense success, she struggled to work. In 1987, at the age of forty-three, she killed herself by jumping from the window of her Pittsburgh apartment. Just a day after the news of her close friend's death was reported, Page suffered a fatal heart attack. Poignantly, Hartman had said in a 1971 interview, "I can't wait till I'm 45 and get all those great parts."[2]

The flirtatious school pupil Carol, played by Jo Ann Harris, also lusts for McBurney, and after she lures him into her bed, Edwina is horrified when she catches them in the act. McBurney's promise that he loves her rings in Edwina's ear, and she reacts in fury at being betrayed, hitting him with her candlestick until he falls down the stairs, breaking his leg.

"You lying son of a bitch, you bastard, you filthy lecher. I hope you're dead!" she screams at him, now a woman possessed by rage.

With McBurney so gravely injured, Martha decides that the only option to prevent gangrene is for his leg to be amputated, but he believes it is her revenge for being rejected. "You dirty bitch," he hisses in shock. "Just because I didn't come to your bed. Just because I went to someone else's bed."

He erupts in violence, threatening the women with rape and holding a gun to them. What happens to McBurney next is either a valid punishment for his brutality or women's sly revenge, using one of the most powerful weapons witchy women have—the knowledge of poison.

In 2017, Sofia Coppola released her remake of *The Beguiled*, with Colin Farrell as McBurney, Nicole Kidman as Martha, Kirsten Dunst as

80   *Single & Psycho*

Edwina, and Elle Fanning as Carol. Her version was criticized for one glaring omission, that of the only Black character in the story, Hallie.

In the Eastwood film, she is the only woman in the house who seems to understand and see through John McBurney, and her presence also speaks for race relations as she possesses a self-assurance and power that the white women don't have. In a 2017 podcast by the *New York Times* writers Wesley Morris and Jenna Wortham, they question why Sofia Coppola omitted the character of Hallie, played by Mae Mercer in the original. The director had said she didn't want to make an error in telling this part of history, but they question whether it was an act of "artistic cowardice."[3]

Hallie's characterization follows the Hollywood cliché of the Black woman as the protective force of the household. She was Mammy in *Gone with the Wind* (1939), who stands up against Union soldiers, and Delilah in 1934's *Imitation of Life*, who not only gives Claudette Colbert her waffle recipe, forming the foundation of her business, but also supports her through every crisis. But to lose a complex Black woman from the story is a disservice.

In the blaxploitation movies of that decade, Black writers and directors, in response to the civil rights movement, created powerful heroines like Cleopatra Jones and Coffy—women who are in control of their own sexuality as they fight against institutional racism and sexism, although their pain was also exploited as titillation for the audience. Pam Grier played Coffy in the 1973 film of the same name, and it made her a huge exploitation star. Coffy uses her desirability to enter the seedy world of LA drug dealers, brothels, and prostitutes while seeking revenge on the men who got her little sister hooked on heroin. After discovering that her pseudo-boyfriend, a politician, is not only in league with the bad guys but, much worse, has been cheating on her, she takes her revenge by shooting him between the legs. Again, the message was clear—be careful of the vengeful, hot single woman and her jealousies.

Grier followed it with *Foxy Brown* (1974), again using her body and her charisma to seek revenge on those who killed her boyfriend. Along the way, she is drugged and raped, which are a further driving force for vengeance.

What *The Beguiled* taps into is the dangers of an all-female environment, particularly as the women compete for the attention of one man. And this concept had very much been in the news at the time with the horrors of Charles Manson and his band of hippie followers, mostly young women who had run away from home. Over two nights in August 1969, the Manson family terrorized Los Angeles, butchering pregnant actress Sharon Tate and four others at the Bel-Air home she shared with *Rosemary's Baby* director Roman Polanski, and the next night, murdering Rosemary and Leno LaBianca in their own home.

The horrors of these murders, and the apparent randomness of the brutality, effectively tarnished the hippie dream, and what made it even more haunting was that it was a group of disturbed young women who were mostly responsible for the killings, in which they scrawled messages on the walls in their victims' blood. Susan Atkins, Leslie Van Houten, and Patricia Krenwinkel were tried for murder alongside Manson, and the news footage of them arriving at court together was incredibly creepy. Dressed in little-girl dresses and with their long hair swishing, holding hands and singing, they appear the picture of innocence. But what's terrifying is that they are so utterly brainwashed by Manson that they are glassy-eyed and seemingly incapable of reason—like the haunting Grady sisters in *The Shining*.

Young women weren't supposed to have these murderous impulses, and it was unthinkable for them to have stabbed to death Tate, an eight-month pregnant woman whose unborn child died with her. It indicated something rotten in society that they could have been so corrupted by the counterculture movement, and it spoke of the dangers of free love, of the sexual permissiveness that would be so damaging to women in the long term.

While Eastwood's McBurney has the charisma and charm to play with each member of the group, knowing which buttons to push to get them on his side and to seduce them, ultimately, he's no Manson-style cult leader as his power falls apart quickly. This is a man at the mercy of women and their jealousies and vengeances. Pam Grier may have shot her cheating, duplicitous ex in the balls, but the deadliness of women is often subtle—they use their knowledge of poison mushrooms rather than physical violence (see 2017's *Phantom Thread*) to control a man.

There is one particularly uncomfortable moment in the first minutes of *The Beguiled* that sums up the sexual inappropriateness of the 1970s. Amy, one of the young pupils, discovers McBurney injured in the woods and tries to help him. He asks her how old she is, she replies twelve, and on uttering "old enough to be kissed," he plants

82   *Single & Psycho*

his lips on hers to stop her from crying out when soldiers approach. While Vincent Canby in the *New York Times* conceded in his review that "discriminating moviegoers" would consider the film "a sensational, misogynistic nightmare," at the same time, he didn't have too much of a problem with "the lovely opening sequence" where he "gives her a long, not really friendly kiss on the mouth. She's confused, but immensely happy."[4]

What's disturbing about the seventies is that it was an era when men appeared particularly infatuated by the concept of the Lolita. Because adult women were demanding too much liberation, some men turned their attention to the younger, more naive, and less ardent version. There was Brooke Shields in *Pretty Baby* (1978) and *The Blue Lagoon* (1980), Mariel Hemingway in Woody Allen's *Manhattan* (1979), and just Woody Allen's output in general. When I rewatched *Annie Hall* (1977) a few years ago, I was shocked by a glib line in it—a joke about having a threesome with two sixteen-year-old twins.

Entering into the seventies, it was clear that feminism was a fully formed threat, not just to the sanctity of marriage but also to men's dominance in Western society. In 1971, Betty Friedan helped to establish the National Women's Political Caucus alongside leading feminists including Shirley Chisholm (who in 1968 had become the first Black woman to be elected to the US Congress), Bella Abzug, Fannie Lou Hamer, LaDonna Harris, Jill Ruckelshaus, and Gloria Steinem, who delivered the rallying address at the founding meeting in Washington, DC, in July 1971. "This is no simple reform," she declared. "It really is a revolution."

As well as aiming to drive more women into elected positions, the caucus pushed for the ratification of the Equal Rights Amendment while being fought against by conservatives like Phyllis Schlafly, who hadn't left the fifties with her belief that women's happiness was centered on being a housewife. In the 2020 television miniseries *Mrs. America*, she is played by Cate Blanchett in all her hypocritical glory. There was an irony in her campaigning for the preservation of housewives while she spent her days away from her home, attending conventions and writing newsletters and creating flyers in her office. Fighting against the progress of her own sex was a full-time job.

Gloria Steinem, like many second-wave feminists, had begun her activism as a campaigner for civil rights and then transitioned toward women's rights after having to undergo an abortion. What separated Gloria from other feminists was her style—the streaked hair; large, tinted glasses; and the miniskirts. It was her conventional beauty that had allowed her to report undercover as a Playboy bunny at the New York club in 1963. She and Letty Cottin Pogrebin launched *Ms.* magazine in 1971, choosing its title to make a pointed comment on the way a woman is judged by her marital status. She was often questioned about her own plans to marry, but she thoroughly embraced and enjoyed being a single woman as she considered those who married "half people" and quipped, "I can't mate in captivity."[5]

In *The Feminine Mystique*, Betty Friedan had revealed how trapped and unfulfilled women felt as housewives, but she was a supporter of marriage as a concept. While she said of Steinem's pronouncement, "I guess it gave some comfort to the singles," she believed Steinem was hypocritical as she "always *had* a man. And I used to catch her hiding behind a *Vogue* magazine at Kenneth's having her hair streaked."[6] Friedan also sidelined lesbian feminism, describing them as a "lavender menace" as she was deeply concerned they would brand the movement as "man-hating" and thus drive away support from moderates like her.

Throughout the next decade, the feminist movement made incredible gains in improving the lives of women, including helping them be autonomous single people. In 1972, the Supreme Court extended the right to birth control to unmarried people with its ruling in *Eisenstadt v. Baird*, and the Equal Rights Amendment passed in both houses of Congress.[7]

As feminists like Gloria Steinem championed the benefits of being single, and Andrea Dworkin described marriage as evolving from rape, they shook the foundations of matrimony. With these voices, it became more acceptable for women to embrace their singlehood and avoid rushing into marriage. *The Mary Tyler Moore Show* debuted in 1970 on America's CBS and was hailed as the first program to show a successful independent woman, with the encouraging theme song "You're Going to Make It on Your Own." Mary Tyler Moore played Mary Richards, a television journalist in her thirties who moves to Minneapolis to work on a local station after breaking up with her boyfriend. It offered an alternative life plan for women to choose fulfillment in their careers over marriage and to enjoy their singleness, even if they were in their thirties.

84 *Single & Psycho*

New Hollywood, like Old Hollywood, was dominated by white men, and this masculine posturing would be more pronounced and ramped up over the next decade. Movies reflected the fears of feminism and the disaffection at the sacrifice of American youth to an overseas war—both themes being central to *The Beguiled*. Hanging out with young directors Brian De Palma, Steven Spielberg, and Walter Hill and actors Richard Dreyfuss and Bruce Dern were two young actresses, Jennifer Salt and Margot Kidder, who were hedonistic spirits of the free love generation and whose Malibu home was a creative space for this new generation under a haze of pot smoke.

Peter Biskind described wild child Kidder as "cute and scrappy, funny, a tomboy, and enormously bright," but she was also "sexually aggressive" and "slept with nearly every man who crossed the threshold." Yet she and Salt played up to their traditional roles as nurturing women as they served the men who came to their Malibu home. Kidder told him, "The reality was that we always got the drugs and we always got the food and we basically served our guys, the whole time putting down the notion that we as women would do that. There was a real contradiction in what we perceived ourselves to be doing and what in fact we were doing."[8]

Brian De Palma cast the two struggling actresses in his new film, *Sisters* (1972), which told the story of conjoined twins (both played by Kidder) who undergo a separation procedure, during which only one survives. The remaining twin, Danielle, a beautiful model, takes on the darker, murderous personality of her deceased sister, Dominique. When she brings a man home to her apartment after a date and they have sex, it appears that her twin has arrived unexpectedly at the apartment and slashes at him with a knife until he's dead. The slaying is witnessed by a reporter, played by Salt, who believes that the police aren't taking her seriously because the murdered man is Black. In her investigations, which take her to a mental hospital, she discovers that whenever Danielle has sex, the guilt and trauma bring out the murderous Dominique personality. This places her as one of the psychotic single women of seventies' feminism, who is a deadly and deceitful threat to men. As film critic Robin Wood would suggest, "Simply, one can define the monster of *Sisters* as women's liberation."

CHAPTER 7

Is It Really Free Love?

If being single was now a valid choice for women, then they were also supposedly free to sleep with whomever they wished. The sexual revolution was meant to have diminished this idea of women being damaged goods if they indulged in hookups. Yet some radical feminists saw free love as just another way of controlling women. Psychologist Paula J. Caplan believed this new permissiveness led to "a strange combination of liberation and disturbing pressures with regard to sex." She argued it placed a greater burden on women because, without the fear of unwanted pregnancy, there was no reason to say no.[1] This meant a corruption of the archetypal good girl, where even being nurtured by a rigid family unit couldn't protect a young maid from descending into hell.

In *Looking for Mr. Goodbar* (1977), this promiscuity would be deadly for Diane Keaton's Theresa Dunn, a Chicago schoolteacher for the deaf who spends her nights picking up men in bars. She appears to be the most unlikely patron in the dive bars she frequents, yet she buys cocaine from street dealers, sleeps with hustlers, and turns up for work the next day to teach her young wards. Richard Brooks's film was based on Judith Rossner's novel of the same name, which in turn was inspired by the real-life 1973 murder of Roseann Quinn in New York City. Theresa has been raised in a strict Irish Catholic family, and while she appears to be prim and buttoned up, she uses casual sex to cure her broken heart over a damaging affair with her married professor.

After moving into her own apartment, she relishes the freedom away from the watchful eye of her parents and spends her evenings

86   *Single & Psycho*

in bars, where she sits at the counter with a book as a safety blanket while hoping she can drop the reading and strike up conversations with men. Those she meets turn out to be aggressive and controlling, including Richard Gere's street hustler Tony and the parent-approved but obsessive James, who scares her with his love and commitment. It's almost as if the dangerous men are appealing because they allow her to avoid facing up to her own insecurities. Having been treated as an ugly duckling, she is also traumatized by the childhood scoliosis that left her with mental and physical scars and a fear of passing the affliction to any future children.

She develops a cocaine habit, neglects to wash her dishes so that her flat becomes a cockroach-infested hovel, and invites a series of men to her apartment for sex. She doesn't appear to particularly enjoy the act; it's more a means of filling her loneliness. With her day job having suffered from her late nights, she vows to give up the drugs and barhopping, but on New Year's Eve, she fatefully meets the violent murderer who will end her life.

In *Closing Time: The True Story of the "Goodbar" Murder*, the 1977 true crime account of the murder of Roseann Quinn, Lacey Fosburgh, who renames the victim Katherine Cleary, writes evocatively of this double life: "The person who worked at St. Joseph's and loved the children was not the same woman who took books to bars, and the woman who couldn't fall asleep at night was not the same person who chattered at parties." Katherine, like Deanie in *Splendor in the Grass*, had been warned by her mother that "sex can be a woman's downfall" and "men are after only one thing. They'll take all you've got, but they only want to marry someone good like their mother."[2]

With Theresa's tragedy connecting deeply with audiences, *Looking for Mr. Goodbar* would leave a lasting legacy. Madonna's 1992 music video for "Bad Girl" took inspiration from the depiction of a woman whose drinking habits and promiscuity are a recipe for disaster. The themes feed into a long-held belief that a woman sitting at a bar on her own is asking for trouble and to enjoy a drink is to damage her reputation.

I always found this idea confounding, because why doesn't a woman on her own belong in this public space, and why can't she enjoy a drink? I've been perfectly content sitting on my own in a bar with a glass of wine, although, like Theresa, I always brought a book to read; having this prop made me feel I had a purpose in being there. I didn't want to appear as some barfly lush waiting to be picked up; I was feeding my soul with the words on the page and the contents of the glass in front of me.

I've been torn by a quest for a solitary life and my desire to have company when I want it. It's the classic introvert conundrum of how to thrive socially while fighting the tendency to want to hide in a corner. At fancy work events where the fizz flowed and the room filled with chatter, I often struggled with the sensation that I was on the outside looking in, and this displacement sent a rush of anxiety through me as I worried about whom I should be talking to and what on earth I should say as small talk. Sometimes, if it got too much, I would retreat to the bathroom, my safe space when at high school, and, locking myself securely in a toilet cubicle, I would catch up on the BBC news headlines and prepare myself to face the crowd again.

A line from Lacey Fosburgh's book particularly struck a chord with me when she writes of Katherine's sense of being alone, even in a crowded room, where she would "feel a vast chasm separating her from life and hope and a future, and wonder why she of all the people she knew had been marked with the ugliness, doubt, and memories. Why was she chosen for this?"

My socializing was so often encouraged by alcohol as I realized from a young age that having a drink in my hand instantly gave me confidence. Growing up in Scotland, it's just what we did. I was a late starter; I didn't have my first one until I was fifteen, and it was stolen gin from my parents' cupboard, topped up with orange juice. There were the bottles of cheap cider, the sickly sweet alcopops so prevalent in the late 1990s, then frothy pints of lager in student dive bars. Despite my crippling shyness as a teenager, there was a sociable extrovert inside me waiting to burst out, and I had learned that I needed to flood my brain with endorphins to fully relax and allow this side of me to thrive. And I suppose it did become a lifelong crutch. I loved drinking. I relished that first tangy sip on the tongue, and as it slid down the throat, it was an instant relaxer. Chilled white wine became the drink for me, the solace of unhappy thirtysomethings everywhere.

A few years before *Looking for Mr. Goodbar* was released, Clint Eastwood made his directorial debut with a thriller that also

88   Single & Psycho

questioned whether women could really handle the concept of free love. But rather than being the victim, this single woman would be as dangerous and deranged as Alex Forrest. *Play Misty for Me* (1971) is a prototype of *Fatal Attraction*, not just in its narrative around a one-night stand gone wrong but also with its reference to the doomed heroine of *Madame Butterfly*, a hollow suicide attempt, and the *Psycho*-esque slash of a knife wielded by a crazy-eyed spinster.

Eastwood plays Dave Garver, a handsome local radio DJ who is something of a celebrity in the coastal town of Carmel-by-the-Sea, where Eastwood lived in real life. He soon finds himself at the mercy of one of his fans, an attractive woman who always phones in to request "Misty" by Erroll Garner and who grows increasingly unhinged after their two-night stand. *The Beguiled* and *Play Misty for Me* offer different responses to the counterculture era and the sexual revolution, with both asking in different ways whether free love is really free love after all. Women may have felt they could have unattached relationships, but was it that simple?

When Eastwood read the original story by Jo Heims ("a gal I knew in the old days when she was just a secretary and I was an actor"), he liked it so much that he optioned it with a plan for it to be his directorial debut. It was based on a story of a Mendocino County DJ who was stalked by a fan, and it struck a chord. Eastwood had a similar experience in his own life when he was pursued by an older woman when he was a nineteen-year-old burgeoning actor. "There was a little misinterpretation about how serious the whole thing was," he said.[3]

It also referenced, probably unconsciously, his own womanizing behavior. A profile in *Life* magazine in July 1971 described Eastwood as a man's man who liked a beer and liked admiring women. "The character Eastwood plays is invariably a man in total control, able to handle anything," the article declared. "He is his own law, and his own morality—independent, unfettered, invulnerable, unfathomable and unbelievable. He is a nondimensional symbol of man as pure superiority. He is a heavy dude. He is a superstud."[4]

Eastwood conceded in an interview in 1971 that he was concerned about women pretending that they were fine with casual relationships, but in reality they wanted more: "A girl may say: Sure, I feel the same way; I don't want any part of marriage. But then next week, slowly, there's that kind of throwing a blanket over a person . . . that

Is It Really Free Love? 89

makes it personal to the audience as opposed to just a horror movie. If you've had any kind of experience in your life where somebody has just tried to move in too fast, or has just held on too hard; I think everybody has had something like that. It's something that could happen."

In real life, Eastwood didn't have the best reputation with women, and he treated his long-term girlfriend in much the way that women are often casually dismissed in his movies. Nominated for a Best Supporting Actress Oscar for her acting debut in the 1968 drama *The Heart Is a Lonely Hunter*, Sondra Locke first met Eastwood when she was cast opposite him in the 1976 Western *The Outlaw Josey Wales*, and their love affair would last for the next thirteen years. In her autobiography, she described her attraction to him as immediate and powerful and that he would tell her she convinced him to be monogamous. The two starred in five movies together, where she was positioned as his muse. But she claimed in her 1997 memoir, *The Good, the Bad, and the Very Ugly*, that he wasn't happy that she chose to direct her own films, which included *Ratboy* (1986) and *Impulse* (1990), rather than to continue acting in his.

But it wasn't just her career—Eastwood was also in another, secret relationship with Jacelyn Reeves, who he went on to have two children with. What made it even worse for Locke was that he had persuaded her to have two abortions and then an irreversible tubal ligation because he claimed not to want more children.

While she was making *Impulse*, she returned to her beloved home to find that Eastwood had changed the locks and moved all her things out of the house. When she sued him, he dismissed her as his "occasional roommate," and her marriage to her gay childhood friend Gordon Anderson, which had been an act of kindness and friendship, was used against her.

They settled out of court, and as compensation, she was given a 3-year, $1.5 million deal with Warner Brothers. But it was in name only, and despite all the ideas she submitted to the studio, she was never allowed to direct a film. She considered it sabotage and took him to court again. It was settled in 1996 for an undisclosed sum.[5] Her claims that he was abusive were ignored by the media, and ultimately it was she who suffered and was labeled a bitter ex and a gold digger.

90   *Single & Psycho*

She directed two more films, both obscure, and she died in 2018 after a lengthy struggle with bone and breast cancer. Even following her death, her obituary in the *Hollywood Reporter* had the headline "Actress Sondra Locke, Embittered Ex of Clint Eastwood, Dies at 74."

The female stalker storyline of *Play Misty for Me* felt fresh, even though it had popped up in early films and novels (a softer version in *I Wanted Wings*, for example, or Gregg's destructive behavior in *The Best of Everything*). But Eastwood came up against studio executives who weren't convinced of having a female villain. "The studio people said, 'Why do you want to do a movie where the woman has the best part?'" Eastwood said. "My reaction was: 'Why not?' I figured, 'Why should men have all the fun playing disturbed characters?'"

When he finally got a deal with Universal to direct, he was supported by *The Beguiled* director Don Siegel (who even makes a cameo as the bartender at his local bar and eatery), and he used a cast of unknown actors to keep the costs down. The film captures the breezy bohemian glamour of Monterey, where he'll meet the one-night stand from hell who transforms into a clinging, parasitical nightmare.

Dave Garver regularly goes for drinks at a place called the Sardine Factory, and it's here that his number one fan, Evelyn (Jessica Walter), waits for him one day so that she can strike up a conversation. She confesses that she went there on purpose to meet him, and like Alex Forrest, she's direct and confident in expressing what she wants.

"You don't want to complicate your life. Well, neither do I," she convinces him. "But that's no reason we shouldn't sleep together tonight if we feel like it." In this era of consequence-free sex, a woman could pretend that she was cool with casual, but what she fails to reveal is that she is after more than a "zipless fuck," an expression later coined by Erica Jong in her groundbreaking 1973 novel *Fear of Flying*.

Again, like Alex Forrest, Evelyn gives off a "cool girl" vibe at first, claiming she's happy for it just to be a fling. But then she shows her insecurities and neediness, which manifest into toxic rage. Evelyn is desperate for Dave to commit to her, and her initial actions are like the "what not to do" list from 2003's *How to Lose a Guy in 10 Days*. She turns up uninvited at his home, passing judgment on the minimal contents of his fridge, and is giddy at the thought of playing the domestic goddess. Dave is a little concerned at this overfamiliarity, but the alarm bells aren't ringing just yet. "I'm trying to tell you there's a telephone and I pick it up and I dial it, and you answer, and I say, hey what are you doing?" he says as he tries to set his boundaries.

But still, he lets her cook a steak for him, and they sleep together again. "There are no strings, but I never said anything about not coming back for seconds," she says. We don't know much about Evelyn, what she does, where she's from, what she likes, apart from her favorite song being Erroll Garner's "Misty" and that she has a penchant for poetry and a tendency to explode at the slightest things.

Dave sees the first glimmer of Evelyn's psycho behavior when a neighbor tells them to be quiet while they are saying goodbye after their evening together. She aggressively honks the horn of her car and yells back at him, "How'd you like to go screw yourself!" Next, she has a key to Dave's apartment cut and then erupts in uncontrollable, irrational jealousy when she sees him with an older woman, a potential new employer whom he's been trying to impress. Safe to say that Evelyn calling her an "old hag" doesn't serve Dave well in his job prospects.

Even after she turns up at his house with a big fluffy toy, he's naively blind to what a danger she is. When he finally expresses his feelings of suffocation and tries to break it off with her, she bursts into angry tears: "You're nothing. You're not even good in bed. I just felt sorry for you. You poor pathetic bastard." After pleading and crying, she resorts to cutting her wrists so that he'll be guilted into staying the night with her.

What Dave fails to tell Evelyn is that there's another woman in his life—sweet, pretty artist Tobie (Donna Mills), whom he is trying to win back. Tobie is tired of his womanizing, but he convinces her he's given up his philandering ways, which is a lie, considering he's only just recently slept with Evelyn. Tobie is the definition of a "cool girl" as she knows the boundaries of propriety, telling Dave, "The thing I hate most in the whole world is a jealous female and that's what I was getting to be." She is the grounded "good woman," the one he can imagine marrying, and their love scenes, tenderly soundtracked to Roberta Flack's "The First Time Ever I Saw Your Face," are juxtaposed with Evelyn's time in a psychiatric hospital.

Evelyn's sweet, girlish smile can unnervingly transform into wide-eyed desperation and then spitting, violent anger. As she descends

92 Single & Psycho

into madness, she becomes a Norman Bates figure, slashing at her victims, including Dave's thankless Black maid, with a knife. In the film's climax, taking place between long scenes of musicians and the crowds of visitors to the Monterey Jazz Festival, Evelyn holds Tobie prisoner at her cliffside house, and it becomes, like *Fatal Attraction*, a fight to the death.

Dave possesses the quiet masculinity that was a signature of Eastwood's characters, where his stoical reactions, the stillness of his actions, downplay the horror that Evelyn clearly displays. And this made it a frustrating watch for some reviewers. "A lot of good movies are weak on sense—though they don't often require a leading man to be quite so dense for quite so long in interpreting the behavior of a psychotic leading woman," wrote the *New York Times*.[6]

Adam Knee, in his essay "The Dialectic of Female Power and Male Hysteria in *Play Misty for Me*," describes how Dave Garver was an acknowledgment by Eastwood that machismo was outdated as feminism swept into mainstream thought, and instead he possesses "signifiers of 'sensitivity' and 'hipness' . . . to make him a man in tune with the 1970s." Evelyn, he writes, is "an overt manifestation of the threat posed by the flourishing of the women's liberation movement. David's trepidation over the new deference to women required of him as a man of the 1970s—his fear of women with newly-won social power—surfaces in the form of an ultimately violent, sexually desirous female aggressor."[7]

Dave may be a pathological philanderer, while Evelyn can't handle sex without commitment, but their gender roles shift. She takes on the typically masculine characteristics that Dave, as the everyman facing the tyranny of women's liberation, has given up. She is the one who is sexually aggressive and violent, while Dave is the repressed figure who can only react to her irrationality. This characterization of a man who is victim to female obsession also played out in François Truffaut's *The Story of Adele H* (1975). It combined the Civil War setting of *The Beguiled* and the stalker theme of *Play Misty for Me* to tell the story of a young woman, Adele (Isabelle Adjani), who becomes increasingly obsessed with a British lieutenant.

The script was based on the diaries of Adele, the real-life daughter of the author Victor Hugo, who was later placed in an asylum. In the movie, she arrives in Halifax, Nova Scotia, where she hopes to track down a former acquaintance, Lieutenant Albert Pinson. Each time she pursues him, he rebuffs her, making clear he's not interested in a relationship, but still she continues to follow him. In Adele's mind, the two will be married, and her behavior becomes increasingly unhinged—hiring a prostitute for him, trying to use hypnotism to make him love her, and then following him to Barbados, where she aimlessly wanders the streets while claiming the two are married. Suffering from extreme obsession, with her fantasies having taken over her reality, she experiences a full mental breakdown.

The ideals of the sexual revolution, where women could find fulfilling sexual relationships without the worries of falling pregnant, did not offer the freedom that was promised. Misogyny became even more apparent as the patriarchy took advantage of the permissiveness, much to the detriment of women. With more extreme forms of pornography further reinforcing notions of women as sex objects, feminism was split into two by those who saw pornography and *Playboy* as damaging and those who believed it was empowering for women to have this choice.

By the eighties, the work of feminism was considered complete—women had careers, independence, freedom to pursue relationships and to display their bodies as they wished. So it was inevitable there would be a conservative backlash that targeted single, working women for going against nature and damaging the very foundations of Western society. It was a fight for family values.

CHAPTER 8

From Feminism to Fighting for the Nuclear Family

In late December 2006, I was flying back to Scotland from a year studying in Australia, and waiting in line for check-in, I struck up a conversation with a woman from Melbourne who was my age and was going to be spending some time in Edinburgh. We agreed to sit together on the plane, and through the duration of the long flight, we bonded over the excitement of selecting movies on the in-flight entertainment system. We both decided on *An Officer and a Gentleman* as neither of us had seen it before. I didn't know very much about it, apart from seeing a clip of Richard Gere lifting Debra Winger into his arms to an eighties power ballad.

What I learned was that he plays Zack, a navy aviation cadet who falls in love with a local "townie," Paula (Debra Winger), but he is terrified of commitment because of a terrible childhood. The recruits are warned that these local girls hang out at the base to catch an officer for a husband, and they will use an "accidental" pregnancy to trap him into marriage. That old trope was at play again, and Paula's friend Lynette is conniving in her quest to earn a wedding ring from Zack's best friend Sid. When Lynette lies to Sid that she's pregnant, it leads to him dropping out of training, but a life spent in North Carolina rather than traveling the world as an officer's wife is a grim prospect, and she cruelly reveals she faked her pregnancy and turns down his proposal. This lie has devastating consequences, and Paula must prove to Zack that she's not like Lynette or the other girls and that as much as she wants to be with him, she'll never resort to tricks.

As I watched it on the tiny little airplane screen, I wasn't struck by the emotions of the love story so much; rather, it was the female

From Feminism to Fighting for the Nuclear Family   95

naval cadet, Casey, who struggles to pull herself over the wall of the training camp obstacle course, that I found the most powerful. At the end of the movie, my new travel buddy and I both professed how it was that moment when Richard Gere sacrifices completing the course in record-breaking time to cheer and encourage Casey into pulling herself over that wall that brought us to tears. It was a woman overcoming barriers, with a man supporting her, and it was incredibly spiriting.

As this scene proves, filmmakers could tell powerful stories of women who weren't necessarily on a mission for love but were fighting for other goals, such as Casey's valid ambition to be a naval pilot (despite the overarching theme of predatory women on the base). Other groundbreaking female characters from this time included Ripley in *Alien* (1979) and Sarah Connor in *The Terminator* (1984), two action heroines who outrun and outlast the men in the face of a terrifying, and seemingly unstoppable, threat.

As a film-obsessed teenager, compiling lists of my top ten movies and pasting them onto my school folder, I found it was James Cameron's ramped up sequel *Aliens* (1986), *The Terminator*, and *Thelma & Louise* that took the top spots, with *Pretty Woman* up there, too, for some rom-com balance. I'd borrowed the VHS tape of *Aliens* (special edition, of course) from a schoolmate, and I was gripped from the very beginning. The action was nonstop edge-of-your-seat, there were two amazingly tough women (Ripley and Vasquez) who fought alongside the men and took control of the situation, and I wished I had the same ability as Vasquez to do pull-ups and deliver a one-liner with cool efficiency. I was also stirred by watching the growing love between Ripley and Michael Biehn's Corporal Hicks, where his love token is a tracker to wear on her wrist like a digital watch so he can always find her. One of James Cameron's skills as a storyteller is not only to create strong kick-ass women and thrilling action scenes but also to bring that tenderness and sensitivity. As with *Titanic*, at the heart of *The Terminator* and *Aliens* is a love story.

What I didn't realize when I was watching it as a young teen was that *Aliens* was entwined with symbolism around family. In Ridley Scott's *Alien*, Ripley, a single working mother who makes a living

96   *Single & Psycho*

through delivering cargo intergalactically, is the sole survivor of the grizzled crew of the Nostromo hauler. She escapes in a shuttle after setting the Nostromo to destruct, but as we discover in James Cameron's 1986 sequel, *Aliens*, it takes fifty-seven years for her to be rescued, and in this time, her daughter, left behind on Earth, has grown old and died, while she, like Sleeping Beauty, has remained the same age, thanks to the hypersleep chamber. Having survived an alien attack, Ripley is sent with a group of marines to a colonized planet to discover why all communications have been lost. The aliens have wiped out all the settlers on this planet, and in a fight for survival, she creates a new family with Newt, a little girl who has lost her parents to an alien attack, and Hicks, who is one of the more level-headed of the band of marines.

There's another mother here, a monstrous alien queen whose jaw drips with ghastly secretions as she opens it to reveal her vagina dentata. As Ripley tries to escape from the planet with Newt, she discovers the queen's lair where her huge ovaries have laid steaming fresh eggs. With the little girl in her arms, Ripley uses a flame-thrower to destroy the lair, and seeing all her labor destroyed, the alien is hellbent on revenge. With the alien queen having managed to scramble onto their aircraft carrier, Ripley is forced to defend Newt by stepping into a power loader, like an armored extension of her body, as she cries out, "Stay away from her, you bitch!"[1]

Again, what I hadn't been consciously aware of in my early viewings of *Aliens* was that the underlying drive of Ripley and the alien queen, and of Sarah in *The Terminator*, is their overwhelming maternal instinct to defend, and fight to the death, for their children. It's as if a woman's sole agency comes from that primary urge. By protecting herself from being assassinated by the time-traveling terminator, Sarah is saving the life of her unborn son, who will become a war hero against the machines in the future. For Ripley, as the adopted mother of Newt, who now calls her "Mommy," she'll use her sheer strength and will to defend the new family she has created for herself.

The nuclear family was sacrosanct in the conservative eighties. The decade was marked by President Reagan's aggressive anti-Soviet response, his Star Wars missile-defense proposal, and the new space race, all of which was reflected in a surge of science-fiction action movies like *Aliens* and *Predator* (1987). The United States may have

From Feminism to Fighting for the Nuclear Family 97

faced the humiliation of losing the war in Vietnam, but high-octane action movies depicted victory in other spheres. Further, these outside forces represent the communist threat that was playing out with Russia's tech domination during the tail end of the Cold War, whereas the strength of America was to be found in the family and the pioneer spirit of survival.

For queer Chicana feminist Gloria Anzaldúa, she found the alien to be a tragic, identifiable figure because she saw her as a representation of all the fears of white America rolled into one. She said the movie "seemed like they were taking all the things they fear and hate about themselves and projecting them onto the monster. Just like we did with blacks and like people do with queers—all the evils projected. My sympathies were not with the people at all; they were with the alien."[2]

In November 1980, former actor Ronald Reagan swept to victory in the forty-ninth US presidential election, defeating Democratic president Jimmy Carter in a campaign that railed against gender politics. His election was a promise to return to the 1950s era of prosperity and family values, which was reinforced with the *Morning in America* advertising campaign for his 1984 reelection. The clip featured men and women in their business suits as they briskly walked to their city offices and happy couples buying a beautiful new suburban home or getting married in a church in front of their proud families (6,500 young men and women each day, according to the ad).

But single women didn't quite fit with this vision. He used the racist-tinged expression "welfare queens" as he fought to reverse the decline in people getting married, which had been blamed on the wave of feminism experienced in the last decade. With the fervent support of antifeminists like Phyllis Schlafly, he struck off the Equal Rights Amendment from the Republican Party's platform; he planned to reverse *Roe v. Wade*, which protected a woman's right to abortion; and he supported a media blitz against unmarried women.

On the other side of the Atlantic, the Conservative Party's Margaret Thatcher had been elected as British prime minister in May 1979 with a social-economic policy that promised to quash trade unions and calm inflation. She may have been the first female British prime minister, an extraordinary achievement that led to the next

98   *Single & Psycho*

generation of young people never questioning whether a woman could run a country, yet she refused to appease her sex and sneered at the concept of feminism. She even pulled up the ladder of equality after her by declining to promote women to her cabinet because, she insisted, they weren't good enough (although she seemed to be OK with mediocre men). She promoted family values and decried women who relied on nannies while at the same time removing policies that helped support struggling parents, such as free milk for primary school pupils.

When Jenni Murray, a BBC *Woman's Hour* journalist, interviewed Thatcher in the 1980s, she found her to be artful at dodging any questions around her feminist credentials. Thatcher confided that she'd been saddened, on a trip to Russia, to see children being dropped at nurseries by their struggling working mothers, and she didn't want Britain to be a crèche society. Mothers, she thought, should only consider a little part-time work "to keep the brain engaged." Never mind that she herself had always worked despite having two children and that her husband, Denis, was very much in the shadows; for other women, she couldn't acknowledge their ambitions. She was against giving women any sort of special attention and failed to recognize that others weren't in her own fortunate position.

As Jenni Murray wrote, "She was the Mummy, the Nanny, the Governess, the Wife, the Matron, the Flirt or Boudicca, depending on which role was required for any given moment, but woe betide the hapless hack who asked what it was like to be a woman PM. 'I have no idea, dear,' she would sneer, 'as I have never experienced the alternative.' 'I didn't get here by being a strident female,' she once intoned. 'I don't like strident females.' Self awareness was never her strong point."[3]

In both Britain and the United States, these two new fiscally and ideologically conservative powerhouses would oversee an aggressive, booming 1980s, not only undoing public support systems but also relegating feminism to a relic of the previous decade. The message would be the sacrosanct of the family, even in popcorn flicks like *Die Hard* (1988). Bruce Willis's straight-talking all-American hero John McClane faces off against a foreign threat while also demonstrating his devotion to his wife. This is particularly apparent in the 1990 sequel, set in an airport, as he bats away interest from attractive

From Feminism to Fighting for the Nuclear Family   99

single women while flashing his wedding ring. He's a devilishly handsome chick magnet, but he respects his marriage vows.

It may have been a new conservative era, but there was an increasing desire among audiences in the early eighties for films that pushed boundaries in sex and violence. In 1968, the censorship system was replaced by a new ratings system, and the X certificate, for adults only, was designed to allow filmmakers to have more expressive freedom. Films like *Midnight Cowboy* (1969) and *A Clockwork Orange* (1971) achieved commercial success despite the rating, but the X was soon co-opted by pornography, which meant that newspapers were wary of advertising an X-rated movie, and movie theaters were reluctant to show them. As audiences were looking for titillation without having to go to grim and grubby adult-only theaters, mainstream Hollywood directors experimented with more sex and nudity while skirting close to the boundaries of an R rating, using glossy production values to elevate their erotica above the usual sleazy porno flick.

Neo-noirs *Body Heat* (1981) and *The Postman Always Rings Twice* (1981) not only harked back to the film noir of the 1940s, with their devious femme fatales manipulating men, but helped to popularize the erotic thriller. Brian De Palma's sex- and violence-filled movies were blatant odes to Alfred Hitchcock. *Dressed to Kill* (1980) and *Body Double* (1984) were revolutionary in their softcore sex scenes that explored and exposed female desire, with tongue kept firmly in cheek, although *Dressed to Kill* is unsettling in its transphobia. These films would lay the groundwork for the success of *Fatal Attraction*, using a domestic setting and a narrative that touched on topical social concerns to strike fear into the heart of yuppies.

There was also the added nostalgia factor. Each generation tends to eulogize the pop culture of thirty years before, and in the eighties, the classic postwar film noir was looked back on with fondness. In the fast-paced corporate world of sexual equality and new technologies, such as the videotape, old movies reflected a simpler, more glamorous time when men were hardboiled and women were beautiful but devious.

As Bettijane Levine wrote in the *Los Angeles Times* in June 1982, "Bad girls are back. They're the whole new generation now seeing Lauren Bacall vamp Humphrey Bogart for the first time—on late-night TV. They're also discovering Rita Hayworth, Veronica Lake

100   *Single & Psycho*

and the other bombshell beauties whose non-explicit wickedness left everything to the imagination without putting anything X-rated on the screen. It was an era when a wink, a hair style, the cut of a neckline or the shape of a shoe served as a kind of code—a symbol of how the heroine really behaved when nobody else was around."[4]

If it was felt that by the late seventies, feminism had run its course, a group of activists, which included Susan Brownmiller, Gloria Steinem, Shere Hite, and Robin Morgan, banded together to fight on the new battlefield—that of the dangers of pornography. Andrea Dworkin wrote *Pornography: Men Possessing Women* (1981), and Shere Hite had penned the bestselling *The Hite Report: A Nationwide Study of Female Sexuality*, in which she collated her findings from a mass questionnaire of American women about their sex lives—and the conclusion was that the majority of women were unsatisfied. It was a shock to the male ego, but porn was further placing women as compliant objects rather than fallible humans. The pornification of culture on the back of the sexual revolution sent a confusing image to single women as to how sexual they should be.

With the slogan "Pornography is the theory, rape is the practice," antiporn feminists believed they were saving women from degradation and male domination, but on the other side of the argument were the sex-positive feminists who believed that women should be free to perform or watch it as they wished. This freedom was represented by Melanie Griffith as a porn star in Brian De Palma's *Body Double* and who, in press for the film, spoke of her character as being feminist in her right to choose what she does with her body.

Despite the family-friendly fare of Steven Spielberg and George Lucas and the cheeringly strong female characters of James Cameron's action movies, Hollywood in the 1980s was rampant with misogyny. Big-shot producers like Don Simpson racked up lines of cocaine while dishing out casual sexism during lunch meetings at glitzy Beverly Hills restaurants. I'd read Peter Biskind's *Easy Riders, Raging Bulls* in 2021, when researching *Crazy Old Ladies*, and what struck me was how damn misogynistic Hollywood in the seventies was. As much as I admire the directors and actors, there were eye-wateringly awful moments in the book when women were treated as bimbos and arm candy. The author recounted an anecdote from Warren Beatty's assistant in the late 1960s, Susanna Moore, who had been nineteen years old when she applied for the job. At the end of the flirtatious interview with Beatty, he asked her to lift her skirt so he could see her legs and then said, "Okay, you got the job."

Was this the end result of the sexual revolution, where women had been encouraged to sleep around, yet their wants and needs were never considered? The *Basic Instinct* screenwriter Joe Eszterhas's boisterous and arrogant, yet surprisingly moving, 2004 memoir *Hollywood Animal* gives further insight into that mindset, even from the viewpoint of a man who professed to being a socially conscious liberal.

The Hungarian-born screenwriter emigrated with his family to the United States at the age of six, having survived as displaced persons in Europe's postwar refugee camps. Working for the *Plain Dealer* newspaper in Cleveland, he was one of the first reporters to cover the Kent State student shootings. His first screenplay, *F.I.S.T.* (1978), was inspired by his investigations into Midwest labor unions, and the movie, directed by Norman Jewison, became a star vehicle for Sylvester Stallone.

According to Eszterhas's memoirs, he and Stallone met at the Universal commissary to discuss the script. Stallone was working on the gritty sports drama *Paradise Alley* (1978), a movie he'd written, and was having an affair with his costar Joyce Ingalls during filming, despite being married. Suggesting that he was struggling with her clinginess and unhinged behavior, he recounted to Eszterhas how Joyce was "driving me crazy. Certifiable, you know what I mean?"

In another passage in the book, Eszterhas is afternoon-drinking with producer Don Simpson and a female writer from the *Village Voice*. Both men were fighting over who would go home with the attractive reporter, and when she left with Joe, despite Simpson's bragging that "I know more about pussy than anybody in Hollywood with the possible exception of Robert Evans," the producer was enraged. He ranted over the phone the next day to Joe, screaming that she was a "fucking bitch." This was the type of language used to describe women that was going around Hollywood at the time—"certifiable," "crazy," "bitch" (or its opposite, "fuckable")—so no wonder it filtered into scripts and onto the screen.[5]

As the head of production at Paramount, Simpson was interested in producing *Flashdance*, a screenplay by journalist Thomas Hedley

102   *Single & Psycho*

that told the story of students at the Fashion Institute of Technology who earned extra money by stripping on the side. Simpson commissioned Eszterhas for rewrites, and he shifted its location to blue-collar Pittsburgh and focused the story on a beautiful working-class woman with ambitions to be a ballet dancer, who is, famously, a welder by day and a stripper at night.[6]

Alex was described by Eszterhas as "pretty" but "not all that special" and "skinny but still fuckable," and they were looking to cast an actress who also had to be a great dancer. Following auditions, there were three shortlisted to play Alex—Demi Moore, Leslie Wing, and Jennifer Beals. To decide which one should be chosen, the three actresses took part in a screen test, which was shown to two hundred men working on the Paramount lot. They were then asked which of the three "you'd most want to fuck." They overwhelmingly went for Jennifer Beals.[7]

Following the phenomenal success of *Flashdance* on its release in 1983, Eszterhas was asked by producer Martin Ransohoff to write a courtroom drama involving sex and "a shocking, bloody crime," in which Jane Fonda was set to star as a talented but unmarried lawyer who is convinced of her client's innocence. The script became *Jagged Edge*, and after Fonda dropped out, Glenn Close was cast in her place. It tells the story of a San Francisco publisher, Jack Forrester (Jeff Bridges), who is charged with the gruesome murder of his wife and her maid. His defense attorney is Teddy Barnes (Close), who at first is convinced of his innocence, partly because she's attracted to him and he charms her into believing it. They have an affair, and now, as a woman in love, it clouds her judgment.

Marty Ransohoff was against the casting of both Jeff Bridges, whom he considered too farm boy to play a suave editor, and Glenn Close, who, despite her brilliance as an actress, he dismissed as completely unsexy. Eszterhas recalled him saying, "She's a matron in training. There's a love scene in this movie. Would you want to fuck her? I wouldn't want to fuck her!"[8]

Beginning her career on the stage, Glenn Close transitioned to film in the early 1980s, earning an Oscar nomination for her first movie role in *The World According to Garp* (1982). As Dr. Sarah Cooper in *The Big Chill* (1983), she plays one of the more level-headed of a group of college friends who come together to mourn the suicide of one of their own. They grieve the loss of their sixties idealism and their transition into confused, unhappy yuppies. Mary Kay Place plays a single attorney, Meg, who is unfulfilled in her career and approaches her male friends to ask if they would donate their sperm so that she can have a child. As the ultimate gift to her friend, Sarah nobly asks her husband, Harold (Kevin Kline), to have sex with Meg with the aim of impregnating her. This acceptance of a woman choosing to have a baby on her own was groundbreaking, and as the eighties progressed, this theme, of whether it's possible for single women or a working woman to cope with motherhood and a career, would be explored in a more critical eye.

"When I did Sarah Cooper, there were a lot of articles coming out about Superwoman—you know, career, wife, mother—and I was very much aware of her being tugged in a lot of different directions," said Close. "But she was basically doing it—coping very well. Now, three or four years later, when I was preparing for Jagged Edge, it was a coincidence that a lot of articles were coming out . . . that said it was almost impossible to do that."[9]

Before agreeing to sign on to *Jagged Edge*, Close expressed her concerns that the ending, with Teddy Barnes wielding a gun, made it more akin to a vigilante piece. She was also uncomfortable about the nudity and sex, and so she asked that these scenes be filmed with a closed set to limit the number of people in the room. Ransohoff felt that he, the producer, should be allowed to watch her perform these intimate scenes, and he was incensed to be told no. Eszterhas reported him ranting, "I don't want to fuck her for Christ's sake. Who'd want to fuck her? I'm not gonna get any jollies looking at her. I want to make sure there's heat in the scene."

As revenge for being refused, he belittled Close and constantly insulted her looks to everyone at the studio. One day, during the filming of a courtroom scene, Ransohoff was on the set with his daughter when Close complained that they were both in her line of vision, and so they were cleared from the set. Later, Marty exploded, calling her a "cunt" for embarrassing him in front of his daughter and promising to get his final revenge by insisting she do the sex scene again, this time fully nude, with him watching: "I'm gonna be standing there watching her fat white ass and I'm gonna be fucking it with my eyes. She's gonna know it, too. She's gonna know I'm standing there, fucking her with my eyes!"[10]

104   *Single & Psycho*

It's shocking stuff to read, if Eszterhas's account is true, particularly from a man in such a position of power to abuse and humiliate his star in such a way. On its release, critics were mixed in their reviews of *Jagged Edge*, and its misogyny was a particular contention for female reviewers given that the murder victim was slashed on her breasts and in her vagina. Rita Kempley of the *Washington Post* found it to be another example of the graphic violence meted out to women. She derided it as "commercially packaged abuse" and wrote that "violent crime against women is not entertainment. . . . Not only is the character foolish enough to fall in love with and make love to her client—a man she knows might have just sliced up his wife—but she's not even professional about it."[11]

She described Glenn Close's character as the "lovelorn attorney for the defense, a career woman whose vulnerability (what we all want in a criminal lawyer) suckers her into a romance with her client and into harm's way."[12] Glenn Close's Teddy was representative of the predicament of the single career woman. She may be in control at work, but what she really wants is to be submissive in the bedroom. She's climbed to the top of her profession, but she isn't fully satisfied with this new equality.

In the erotic drama *9½ Weeks* (1986), directed by Adrian Lyne, Kim Basinger is a successful art gallery owner who is willing to be a love slave to a stockbroker, played by Mickey Rourke. He blindfolds her, orders her to strip, and insists she stay silent, and she is willing to sacrifice the control she has in her career to become subservient to a man.

In 1981, Joan Collins joined the second season of the soap opera *Dynasty* to play Alexis Colby, the ex-wife of an oil tycoon, who is an unashamedly sexual and powerful "bitch." Like a more glamorous Margaret Thatcher, teaming her power suits with pearls and red or hot pink lipstick, she is as ruthless in business as she is uncompromising in love.

"I didn't feel that Alexis was bitchy, I felt that Alexis was strong, and I think she was bitchy with other women," Joan Collins said in an interview with the Television Academy Foundation in 2010. "I liked the fact that she was strong enough to control the boardroom, that she was powerful enough to run oil companies and gold companies and all kinds of companies. She was the female Donald Trump."

From Feminism to Fighting for the Nuclear Family 105

Like the classic femme fatale, she acts as a counterpoint to the good girl, Krystle Carrington (Linda Evans), and throughout the different seasons, she has an endless series of lovers whom she uses and then dismisses. Even though she has left her children and her marriage, she wields her power and doesn't suffer regrets or consequences.

Alexis was considered the eighties version of Joan Crawford, Bette Davis, and Tallulah Bankhead—all shoulder pads and scathing put-downs—and the woman you love to hate. As Stephen Schiff wrote in *Vanity Fair* in December 1984, "Like the aging Crawford looming in her swivel chair at Pepsi-Cola board meetings, Collins's Alexis is oddly reassuring to women and to gay men. Your looks needn't flee with your youth, she promises. And there is power—practical, world-beating, money-making power—in femininity. And—the bitch's credo—a well-turned insult can defeat an arsenal." Although the reporter also described her as "flinty, unmarriageable, mannish" and said that her "broad-shouldered, over-tailored suits" made her look like a "female impersonator."[13]

So what happened in between the depictions of a woman choosing to have a baby on her own (and her friend offering up her husband's sperm) in *The Big Chill* and the larger-than-life, power-dressing Alexis? Why were brilliant, unattached women now filled with anxiety? Alexis came on the scene when there was an unprecedented rise in the number of women in the workforce. By 1980, women were 43 percent of the US labor force, up from 29 percent in 1950. This surge was linked to delays in getting married, an increase in divorce and separation, and lowered fertility, and so, as the decade became more aligned with conservative values and feminism was considered well and truly cooked, there was an about-turn in positive messaging.[14]

An *Associated Press* article in November 1980 reported on the worries of women who were entering their thirties and hearing "the insistent ticking of a baby clock." These women, who had spent their twenties devoted to college and career, were now soul-searching about what they really wanted in life: "In other times—before the pill, before feminism and the two-career family—having babies was almost automatic, the normal thing to do."[15]

The article was measured in its optimism—that it was possible for women in their forties to still have children thanks to medical advancements and general health improvements, even if the mental

106 *Single & Psycho*

biological clock set the deadline at thirty-five. It also listed the advantages in being older first-time parents, such as being more financially secure and emotionally equipped and with "a greater capacity for giving."

However, in February 1982, the *New England Journal of Medicine* published a study that revealed that between the ages of thirty and thirty-five, women's fertility dramatically dropped. As the *New York Times* advised, "The study shows the decline coming earlier and more precipitously than had generally been thought."[16]

By the mideighties, women were overwhelmed by the fearful warnings that having a career in lieu of a stable home life was damaging to their health. There were articles that laid out concerns that high-powered career women were suffering from "stress-induced disorders" including alopecia, frayed nerves, alcoholism, and heart attacks.[17] Feminism was now being blamed for undermining the family, and laws that were designed to help women advance were being reversed.

Ginny Dougary wrote in March 1992 in the *Times*, "The Equal Rights Amendment was defeated in 1982; the federal government stalled funding for battered women's programmes, defeated bills to fund shelters and shut down its Office of Domestic Violence, only two years after opening it. And then the media joined in. Suddenly women were told they should live like Stepford Wives or face a dreadful fate of childless, careerist spinsterhood."[18]

The press only inflated single women's fears by reporting on these stories with exaggerated relish. Faludi reported that between 1980 and 1982, American magazines ran only five feature articles about single women; between 1983 and 1986, they ran fifty-three, which were negative in slant.[19] The buzzword was the *biological clock*, designed to terrify women in their thirties that time was not on their side and that they had the statistics to back it up. In her 1987 book *The Biological Clock: Reconciling Careers and Motherhood in the 1980s*, Molly McKaughan referred to childless, working women as "clock watchers" and claimed feminism had created a plague of infertility among middle-class women.[20]

The blame was placed on feminists, who in their drive for equality had failed to warn women of the risks of pursuing a successful career. Just as Betty Friedan had referred to the feminist mystique as the "problem with no name," there was a new problem. As *Newsday* reported in a 1987 investigation into twenty years of feminism, critics claimed it "seduced and abandoned a generation of women who have exchanged marriage for a world of independence and self-sufficiency, only to find themselves in a discriminatory job market with inadequate financial support. And, they say, it has led a younger generation of women down a path of glamorous career expectations that could only be achieved by delaying their desire for a family until it was too late."[21]

As we'll see in a new raft of movies in the middle of the eighties, the career woman was now a workaholic, spending her evenings alone in her apartment, spooning peanut butter out of the jar in lieu of a proper meal, and poring over case files and briefs as she tries to ignore her regrets while the lonely tick of that biological clock punctuates the air.

CHAPTER 9

Burnout, Biological Clocks, and Boiling Rabbits

The Career Woman's Despair

In 1987, Roy Lichtenstein released a pop art lithograph featuring a woman with hot-red lips who despairingly holds her head in her hands, with the speech bubble floating beside her: "I can't believe it. I forgot to have children!" This print, soon emblazoned on posters and T-shirts, perfectly nailed the mood and anxieties of Western women at the time, that they may have fought for, and won, equal rights, but they now faced a new crisis.

There was a gnawing sadness in the pit of their stomach, a visceral ache in their womb and their ovaries, as they imagined a future without a family of their own because they'd left it too late. Fourteen years later, in season seven of *Friends*, Jennifer Aniston's Rachel Green would sum up how a woman's life is dictated by time. On her thirtieth birthday, surrounded by balloons and bunting, and with a gold crown on her head, she opens a card from Monica and Chandler and reads out the words "Happy Birthday, Grandma, it's better to be over the hill than buried under it." The words make her cry because "to be a grandmother you have to be married and have children, and I don't have any of these things."

Chandler's choice of card triggers her into plotting out a life plan where she envisions herself as married with three children. But as she does the calculations in her head, she realizes it doesn't add up: "I should probably have the first of the three kids when I'm thirty-five, which gives me five years. . . . But I do want to be married for a year before I get pregnant. So I don't have to get married until I'm

Burnout, Biological Clocks, and Boiling Rabbits   109

thirty-three . . . but wait a minute though. I'll need a year and a half to plan the wedding, and I'd like to know the guy for a year, year and a half before we get engaged, which means I need to meet the guy by the time I'm thirty."

There was a growing anxiety by the mideighties that women had been sold a false promise that they could have it all when really they were destined to be regretful spinsters. The March 31, 1986, edition of *People* magazine featured the headline "Are These Old Maids?" with images of recognizable women of the time—Diane Sawyer, Sharon Gless, Donna Mills, and Linda Ronstadt—and the provocative claim that "most single women over 35 can forget about marriage."

This article was based on a 1985 study from Harvard and Yale researchers titled "Marriage Patterns in the United States," and it sparked a blitz of coverage that distorted the stats. The reporting of this study was the backbone to Susan Faludi's *Backlash*, as she examined how this willful misrepresentation created a wave of anguish for single women. The pinnacle of this fearmongering was in the June 2, 1986, edition of *Newsweek*, with a cover story, "The Marriage Crunch," illustrated by a graph that showed, with its use of a plummeting line, the chances of marriage dropping with every year gone. White, never-married, college-educated women over forty, it declared, were more likely to be killed in a terrorist attack than get married, and this alarmist statement provoked widespread fear. The magazine later printed a retraction, and the Census Bureau asserted that rather than the 2.6 percent quoted, women over forty had a 17–23 percent chance of marriage for the first time.[1]

But the message that a violent death was more likely than finding a husband, so a woman over forty may as well give up, was ingrained. The impact was still being felt seven years later, when Nora Ephron referenced it in *Sleepless in Seattle*. Annie (Meg Ryan), a Baltimore journalist, and her best friend and editor, Becky (Rosie O'Donnell), dismiss the marriage versus terrorism statistic after two male colleagues bring it up as fact. They are discussing how Tom Hanks's widower Sam has become the focus of attention from single women, who are now clamoring to meet him, after he reveals on a radio show his devastation at the loss of his wife.

110   *Single & Psycho*

"There are a lot of desperate women out there looking for love," one of the male reporters says.

"That's not true, that statistic is not true," protests Annie.

"But it feels true," quips Becky.

"There's practically a whole book about how that statistic is not true."

Let's talk about Cher for a minute. We know her as a fearless feminist icon and fashion maverick, someone who has continually fought for her position as a pop queen and critically acclaimed actress and who has bounced back from career slumps to achieve career highs. By 1979, she had been married and divorced twice—to Sonny Bono and then Gregg Allman—resulting in a child from each marriage, and she built her career on her persona as an independent woman who doesn't need a man for her happiness. Sure, she could date younger actors like Tom Cruise and Val Kilmer, but she always gave the impression she was content being single, with newspaper articles at the time referring to her as "love-em-and-leave-em Cher."[2]

In one of her most famous interviews, a 1996 edition of NBC's *Dateline*, the interviewer, Jane Pauley, questions why she once said "a man is not a necessity, a man is a luxury." Cher coolly replies, "Like dessert, yeah. A man is absolutely not a necessity."

When Pauley then asks, "Did you mean that to sound mean and bitter?" Cher shoots back, "Not at all. I adore dessert. I love men. I think men are the coolest, but you don't really need them to live. My mom said to me, 'You know, sweetheart, you should settle down and marry a rich man.' I said, 'Mom, I am a rich man.' My experience with men is great because I pick them because I like them. I don't need them."

After experiencing a downturn in her pop career by the early eighties, she reinvented herself as a serious actress, earning an Academy Award nomination for *Silkwood* (1983) and winning Best Actress for *Moonstruck* (1987). Cher may have been killing it in all aspects of her life, but the character she played in the 1987 thriller *Suspect* was more aligned with the message that focusing too much on a career would lead to burnout.

She plays a Washington, DC, public defender, Kathleen Riley, who is exhausted because she works too hard, is too serious (signposted by the large glasses she wears), and therefore has no time for a personal life. We first meet her stuck in traffic on the way to court, when

Burnout, Biological Clocks, and Boiling Rabbits   111

she's assaulted and robbed in her own car by a couple of thugs. She makes a futile attempt to chase after them as they rip her mother's locket from around her neck but then returns to her car, defeated. She's alone and isolated, and no one has come to her assistance, even though she was attacked and robbed during morning rush hour. She's the unprotected single woman living and working in the terrifying city, who goes home to her lonely apartment, where her supper is spoons of peanut butter direct from the jar while she stays up into the wee hours with paperwork spread out in front of her.

What Kathleen really needs is a vacation, but instead she is given an impossible-to-win case. She is tasked with defending a deaf and mute homeless Vietnam vet (Liam Neeson), who is accused of the violent murder of a young woman. While drinking cans of beer together in her office late at night, Kathleen tells her male coworker just how much she is suffering from burnout: "I don't know what I'm doing anymore. I don't have a life. The last time I went to the movies was like a year ago. The only time I listen to music is in my car. I don't date. I'd like to have a child but I don't even have a boyfriend so how can I have a child? I spend all my time with murderers and rapists, and what's really crazy is I like them. I don't think I can do it anymore. I'm tired, I'm really tired."

Her anxieties are in direct contrast to Dennis Quaid's boisterous charmer, dairy industry lobbyist Eddie Sanger, who has been selected as a juror for the case she is trying. He's unfettered by his bachelorhood, easy in his jokes and his banter with the court staff, and he has a one-night stand with an older congresswoman to help pass one of his bills. He is also willing to jeopardize Kathleen's career as he actively investigates the case he is on the jury for and continues to contact her directly, despite the clear laws against jury tampering. The single man, this film demonstrates, is free from the shackles of anxiety that a woman in the same position would feel.

Suspect was released at the end of October 1987, the same month as another neo-noir thriller, *Someone to Watch Over Me*, directed by Ridley Scott. Here, a desirable and fabulously wealthy single woman, played by Mimi Rogers, is clearly set up as the threat to a happy marriage. Tom Berenger is recently appointed Manhattan detective Mike Keegan, who lives in Queens with his wife, Ellie (Lorraine Bracco), and their son and is assigned to protect a rich socialite, Claire

112 *Single & Psycho*

Gregory (Rogers), after she witnesses the murder of her friend at a swanky party. When Mike first sees Claire, we can tell he is attracted to her. She exudes glamour, with the fur coats, glossy painted lips, and, we can imagine, the intoxicating, expensive scent. Her enigmatic silences, coupled with her positioning as damsel in distress, further emphasize her seductive aura.

Her characterization is in sharp contrast to Tom's working-class wife, Ellie, who swears like a sailor, slugs beer, and knows how to fix her own car. Mike doesn't give much resistance to his immediate attraction to Claire, and the two have an affair, but it leaves us wondering what the point of it is. Their relationship is built on lust, and while they say they love one another, she isn't so infatuated that she can't say goodbye to him, and he doesn't appear to wrestle with any guilt. Roger Ebert described the film as a cliché in its one-note concept—"Detective from working-class background falls in love with society beauty"—yet it's Ellie, the betrayed wife, and the sparky performance by Bracco that breathe life into the movie. As Ebert conceded, "There is something fundamentally wrong with a script in which the hero sleeps with the wrong woman."

Ellie's first inkling of Mike's growing infatuation with Claire is when he pulls her up for swearing: "I've been talking like this for sixteen years, Michael, and all of a sudden, you find it vulgar." Believing that he's slipping away from her, Ellie begs him to stop working nights protecting Claire, and when she confronts him with her suspicions, he refuses to deny it and instead moves out of the family home. When the criminal who is after Claire kidnaps Ellie and their son, it's down to Ellie to save her family. Having been doing target practice at a shooting range, she is able to take out the villain with the gun that she hid under her kitchen table. She transitions from housewife to gun-toting heroine who will use force to protect her loved ones. Like Sarah Connor and Ellen Ripley, in eighties cinema, the mother will do whatever it takes to defend her family.

As Mike, Ellie, and their son embrace in a Reagan-era tableau, Claire is alone and only able to watch this family unit from the sidelines, and without saying goodbye, she retreats into the shadows. As the single woman, Claire must exile herself by leaving for Europe to mend a broken heart, Ellie must try to forgive and forget her husband's infidelity, and as for Mike, he receives no comeuppance for his

Burnout, Biological Clocks, and Boiling Rabbits   113

betrayal except for a mild discomfort at being temporarily kicked out of the house.

While *Someone to Watch Over Me* was playing in cinemas, there was another domestic thriller showing at the same time that was outperforming it by miles. It also dealt with a similar theme—the dangers of a seductive single woman to a family unit—but this time the threat levels would be ramped up to ten.

Fatal Attraction went straight to number one on its release on September 16, 1987, and it would remain there for eight weeks until mid-November, when it was knocked off the top spot by the Arnold Schwarzenegger movie *The Running Man*. If concerns had been raised about burnout for single career women, then Adrian Lyne's movie hit sexual politics and the concept of family values like a sledgehammer as it cast single women in an even more dangerous light. It was the watercooler moment of the year, with everyone having their own stories about a spurned lover refusing to take no for an answer. It also revealed the mental despair of a woman who was so desperate for love (and babies) that she was prepared to take what wasn't hers.

Both *Suspect* and *Someone to Watch Over Me* had offered different takes on the loneliness of the single woman, and in *Fatal Attraction*, Alex would combine the driven, undomesticated side of Kathleen and the morally questionable temptress of Claire. "We didn't set out to make a heavy message picture," said its producer, Stanley R. Jaffe, "but it has touched a chord." It was described as the film that represented the growing AIDS crisis with its depiction of illicit sex as a threat and, as an article in *People* asserted, a "put-down of women, perverse proof of women's liberation . . . a retrograde portrait of sex-loving women as loony sluts."[3]

Despite the accusation of misogyny leveled at it over the years, the cultural phenomenon of *Fatal Attraction* was down to the determination of one woman, a very powerful woman in Hollywood, Sherry Lansing. A former math teacher, actress, and script reader, she became the production president of Twentieth Century Fox in 1980 at the age of thirty-five, the first woman to ever hold this position at a major studio. After resigning in 1982, she formed a production company with Jaffe, and they aimed to create buzzy productions that would tap into cultural moments.

114   *Single & Psycho*

After watching a 1979 British short film, *Diversion*, Lansing immediately saw it had the potential to be remade as an American thriller. "Diversion would not leave my mind," she said. "I had my own experience when I was rejected [by a man], and I felt like he took my soul."[4]

She understood from a female point of view the enormous pain caused by ghosting and breadcrumbing, concepts that very much existed before they were given an official name. In trying to explain why it struck such a nerve and pushed "all sorts of buttons," she tapped into her own pain and confusion around rejection: "We've all felt unrequited love at some time. We've all dialed a phone number in the middle of the night when we shouldn't have."

Diversion tells the story of a man who has a one-night stand when his wife is staying at her mother's and then finds that the woman he cheated with is becoming increasingly deranged. As *Fatal Attraction* is very 1980s New York, *Diversion* is very 1970s British, and its tension builds up slowly. It opens with the sound of a ringing telephone on a black screen, often the sign of hope for a single woman who is waiting for a call. But by the end of the film, this ringing telephone strikes fear in a man who doesn't know what level of psycho he'll be getting on the other end.

Lansing hired *Diversion*'s writer and director, James Dearden, to pen a feature-length script. But when she took it around the studios, it was continually rejected as the male production heads couldn't believe in a story about a man who cheats on his wife for no reason. Eventually it was picked up by Adrian Lyne, who had created his own cultural moment with *Flashdance* in 1983 and saw the potential in *Fatal Attraction* as a film that would make people talk.

One of the aspects of *Fatal Attraction* that makes it so interesting is the way it acts as a time capsule of a mythical New York in the eighties. Outsiders often view a place through an entirely different lens, capturing elements that are taken for granted and enriching them to higher realms. This is true of *Fatal Attraction*'s British director, Adrian Lyne, in the same way that Ridley Scott uses the dusty highways of the American Southwest to elevate the heroism of *Thelma & Louise*. Lyne also applies the similar MTV aesthetics of *Flashdance* and *9½ Weeks*, with its water-soaked love scenes and backlit smoke, to contrast the sleazy, fast-paced city life with that of the rural ideal of the Gallaghers.

Burnout, Biological Clocks, and Boiling Rabbits   115

Lyne's New York is a place where danger is always underneath the surface of its glitzy book launches and publishing meetings. Rain beats down on the bustling midtown streets, as its office workers hold up umbrellas while trying to flag down taxis, and gather in the leather booths of its restaurants, sipping wine and chain-smoking as they hash out business deals or negotiate illicit affairs.

Actor Michael Douglas had been on board from the beginning, but they struggled to find the right actress to play Alex. Lyne, according to casting agent Billy Hopkins, asked that he find him the "new Kim Basinger," but numerous actresses, including Debra Winger, Jessica Lange, and Ellen Barkin, turned down the part.[5] Miranda Richardson later confirmed that she rejected the role because it was "demonizing of ladykind that I didn't really love."[6] She added that it was too similar to her role as Ruth Ellis, the last woman to be hanged in Britain, in 1985's *Dance with a Stranger*, because after that part, "the last thing you want to do is be someone brandishing a knife."[7]

When Glenn Close read the script, she was absolutely certain she could do justice to this complex character, and she campaigned hard for the part, meeting with Jaffe in New York to beg for an audition. Lyne and Douglas both thought she was wrong for it, that she couldn't do sexy, and, she remembered, they "didn't even want me to read because they were embarrassed." Eventually they agreed she could do a reading with Douglas, and when she arrived in a tight black dress, her hair worn loose and wild because she didn't know what to do with it, Douglas and Lansing were blown away by her intensity during the flirtatious restaurant scene when Alex offers a challenge to Dan: "Are you discreet?"[7]

As Lyne told *People* magazine in October 1987, "She's a person you'd least expect to have this passion and irrational obsession. When she and Michael tested, an extraordinary erotic transformation took place. She was this tragic, bewildering mix of sexuality and rage—I watched Alex come to life."[8]

Glenn Close, and Alex, continually faced criticism that she wasn't attractive enough to cheat with when Anne Archer, the more conventionally beautiful woman, is the one waiting at home. It's Anne Archer who, like Mimi Rogers in *Someone to Watch Over Me*, is lit by a warm glow as Dan watches her apply makeup and stroke her skin with moisturizer as if it's a seductive ritual, although when they

116   *Single & Psycho*

try to have sex one evening, they are interrupted by their daughter. There is a telling moment, after Dan has just slept with Alex, when he breathes "thank God," as if the frustration has been building up due to a lack of sex in his marriage.

Fatal Attraction's overtly stylized sex scenes became a part of the myth of the film long after its initial release. In the kitchen sink scene, for example, Alex is seemingly turned on by the splashes of water on her piles of dirty dishes as if, like Theresa in *Looking for Mr. Goodbar*, she was literally saying "fuck it" to being a domestic goddess who washes her plates after every meal. Later, they get it on in the creaking wrought-iron elevator, with their movements like a coordinated dance of power. Alex, the dangerous single woman whose apartment is in an industrial wasteland, is the predatorial instigator, pressing the red button on the elevator so that she can go down on her catch.

After their night of sweaty dancing in a salsa club, Dan's arm is wrapped around Alex as they wander through an early morning meat market on their way back to her apartment in the Meatpacking district. Alex is drunk on the promise that she's being guided by this man out of her own meat market and into her idealized version of a relationship. With that lion-mane hair, Alex is also positioned as the butcher, leading her prey past strung-up carcasses and burning oil drums and into her industrial loft conversion, which is completely devoid of any homey touches. Compared to the Gallagher home, with its books and picture frames, Alex's is all brick and white paint, like the hipster hangout of a bachelor circa 2010—a perfect symbol of her unused womb. It was, as the *Los Angeles Times* described it in its review in 1987, "nearly barren, surrounded by sinister wet streets—as if she were a bohemian who hadn't shaken the '60s."[9]

She may have been labeled the psycho bitch from hell, but there's something poignant about Alex in her early interactions with Michael Douglas, which could be from a very different film. By the end of their affair, Alex appears to have lost her independence, existing only for Dan. But when he first meets her, she's very much the poised, confident woman, and he is attracted to her because of that self-assurance. After their night of passion, of sex on the kitchen sink, in an elevator, and sweaty dancing in a nightclub, he reluctantly agrees to spend the day together. It unfolds like a perfect date, with the type of falling-in-love montage in Central Park that could be straight out of a romantic comedy. But then Dan pretends to keel over from a heart attack while they play ball with his dog. Alex rushes over in panic, and realizing he's just kidding, she berates him because it triggered the memories of the death of her father in a similar way when she was a child. She then laughs it off as another "gotcha," and he wonders who he's dealing with.

One common query about the plot of *Fatal Attraction* is whether Alex was faking her pregnancy. It's the sort of desperate, tricky move that women have long been accused of and was a major plot point in *I Wanted Wings* and *An Officer and a Gentleman*. Elizabeth Hurley, for example, was publicly shamed when the father of her child, Steve Bing, insisted she take a pregnancy test. Despite this common trope of the treacherous woman who lies about her pregnancy, the evidence points to it being true for Alex. The rising hormones could also be an explanation for her increasingly irrational actions. But that part of the plot is brushed away, and Alex is disbelieved, so that the fetus in her belly is conveniently forgotten when she is strangled, drowned, and then blasted against the bathroom tiles, like the execution of a witch.

In October 1987, Nancy Webber, an art and film appreciation teacher, and Lowell Alexander, an art therapist and psychiatric nurse, penned an article in the *Los Angeles Times* in defense of Alex. "A woman and her unborn child are sacrificed," they wrote. "Alex's compulsion does not negate the legitimacy of her claims or rights. For the sake of its unity, this happy little family justifies the murder of this woman who at first sought only respect and fair dealing."[10]

The letters page in the *Los Angeles Times* was filled with readers who were provoked by Alex. One described her as "a picture of an obsessed, manipulative, explosive, violent and psychotic woman filled with anger and disgust." But another, Linda Warren from Hollywood, said, "After seeing the film, I was very disturbed because of my strong identification with the character. There are many women who have suffered greatly and been driven to extreme psychiatric disorders because of cruel rejection by a man they loved. Someone who has never known the pain of being used as a convenience by someone they truly cared for, then discarded, ignored and neglected, can never realize the feelings of worthlessness, severe anxiety, panic and desperation a woman feels when this happens."[11]

118   *Single & Psycho*

Rather than Alex receiving sympathy as a pregnant woman grappling with rejection, she was now placed firmly as the insidious threat to family life.

I have a confession to make. When I rewatched *Fatal Attraction* for the first time in many years, I had forgotten about the pregnancy subplot. It happened to be on television one night, and so I watched it with my rebound from Gavin, Paul, who had been a source of entertainment and comfort throughout the first year of COVID-19. We'd met on Bumble in February 2020, just before the pandemic struck, when I'd escaped Gavin and had sought sanctuary at my parent's house.

It was a funny, in-between sort of relationship, stilted by a global shutdown, where we hadn't discussed where it was going. What was our status? I wasn't sure, but by February 2021, it had been over a year since our first date; we chatted over WhatsApp every day when we weren't allowed to meet in person for many months, and then when the social distancing rules relaxed, we would go for drinks, to the cinema, and to exhibitions. After a year with my parents, I had finally managed to claim my home back from Gavin. Friends and family had been skeptical that he would relinquish it, trying to persuade me to call the police to have him forcibly removed. Being the overly emphatic avoidant, I didn't want to resort to force, and to everyone's surprise, after a year, he packed up all his cardboard boxes and left with minimal fuss. So my flat was my own, and it was bliss as I rearranged the furniture, invested in fresh Egyptian cotton bedsheets, and even bought a new oven for the baking I found so mentally soothing. A new lockdown before Christmas 2020 was tough, only communicating with the outside world over Zoom calls, but Paul would come over for dinner and spend the night.

Then my period was late, and I noticed my breasts were bigger than usual. I'd typically always had irregular periods, but that morning there was something about the cramps in my stomach that made me wonder, so I walked to the supermarket to buy a pregnancy test. There was a very faint line there, so faint I thought it didn't count. But then I googled it. There were forum discussions that even the faintest line was a positive, and when I tried again, there it was. I was bewildered. I was over forty, and with those fertility issues with Gavin, I didn't think I had much chance of pregnancy. I'd also been monitoring my cycle on an app, but of course, we should have been more careful.

My being pregnant was a shock to both of us, even though we weren't exactly in the first flushes of youth. It was a surreal feeling, but it was also joyous. In the same way that Alex Forrest expresses it as being her last chance at having a child, I felt the same as I'd had reason to believe I was infertile. Paul refused to speak about it, apart from telling me he was walking the streets late at night for hours, as if the pressure was too much for him. Not once did he ask how I was feeling or how I was coping, and I struggled with the conflict of being happy for myself and anxious and guilty because I was pretty sure that he didn't really want this.

"I wouldn't ever tell a woman what to do with her body," he told me nobly when I asked what he wanted to do. He liked to position himself as the good guy who believed in a woman's right to choose. As fiercely pro-choice as I am, an abortion was definitely not the route I was going to take. I grappled with the idea that I would likely be a single mother, but at the same time he was still here— semi-supporting me while refusing to talk about the future. We just did our usual—I'd cook dinner, and he'd come over, and we'd then watch a movie together, which, one evening, was *Fatal Attraction*, because it was showing on the BBC. And then that scene came on. Alex tells Dan she's pregnant, and in his shock, he asks, first, if it's his, and then he begs her to get an abortion. My cheeks flushed, and I sat frozen, like a teenager having to watch a sex scene with their parents. I wondered if he was thinking all those things that Dan was saying. Did he think I'd done this to trap him? The guilt and burden of an accidental pregnancy falls on the shoulders of women, when it is two people who are very much responsible for it. I had no intention of trapping him; he could decide how much he wanted to be involved, but when he refused to speak about it, almost pretending it wasn't happening, it was difficult, distressing even. I had many days when the hormones caused me to be overwhelmed by anger or to spend afternoons in tears as he sent me funny gifs and TikTok videos—everything but what we should be speaking about. I so wanted this baby; I smiled to myself as I went for walks in the spring sunshine and enjoyed the changes in my body and the growing curve in my stomach.

120 *Single & Psycho*

My parents were also pleased when I'd told them, because I think they'd assumed grandkids were off the cards, although my dad immediately went into protective mode as I hadn't mentioned I'd been seeing anyone since Gavin. "Who is he?" he said, as if he wanted to get a shotgun and march out there to confront him.

"Someone I've been with for over a year," I justified. "But because of lockdown, we couldn't see each other much. He's nice, though."

I had read that miscarriage was a very real possibility, particularly for those over forty, but as the weeks went on, the statistics appeared to decrease. I wasn't booked in for a scan until week thirteen, but as I approached week eleven, when the fetus growing inside me was now supposedly the size of a fig, I felt optimistic. I was imagining the future, giddy at the thought of the baby who would eventually be in my arms. I thought of those images that people post on Instagram, with their child next to a card that reads "I'm three weeks," "three months," "six months," with every milestone bringing a different joy.

I didn't know what sex it was yet as I hadn't had a scan, but I was sure it was a girl. And I could raise her on my own if I needed to, I knew it.

Then, one sunny, late-April morning, the pains started. I tried to ignore them because, after all, Google had said it was normal to have growing aches and cramps. I spent the whole day with the sense that something was wrong. When I poked my breasts, they weren't as tender as they had been, and I was in a jittery, weird mood, not feeling quite right. When I went to the bathroom, there was a spot of blood. It must be normal; it must be. By eight o'clock in the evening, I could feel waves of pain in my back, like contractions, and I lay on my bed, trying to fight back the fear, pretending it wasn't happening.

I texted two of my close friends to tell them I thought I was miscarrying. Call NHS 24 they said, so I dialed the number and was put on hold. Then I suddenly needed to go to the bathroom. Blood poured out of me, and I felt something push out and plop into the water. I scrambled onto the floor and looked into the toilet bowl. I could see an object there, pale and coated in mucus, and I plunged my hand into the water to try to grab it, but it slipped out of my grasp. I'd heard about a mucus plug. Maybe that was it. Because what had just come out of me wasn't a fig; it was more like the size of a strawberry. So I flushed the toilet and tried to wipe the blood away, but there was so much streaming out.

When my call finally went through to an adviser, a kind nurse told me to put two sanitary towels in my pants and come to the emergency room to be checked over. "Is anyone with you?" she asked. "No, I'm on my own," I said, my voice wobbling and cracking through the tears.

I messaged Paul, and to his credit, he was over in twenty minutes. He drove to the hospital, and I stared out the window at the glare of streetlights, the other cars streaming past. Life was moving outside, but my world was in slow motion. I couldn't believe this was happening. I wanted to go back to the day before, when everything was fine; it felt like a sliding doors moment, that this was the awful version, whereas there should be the better, more positive reality where I was still pregnant. At the hospital, I was checked over, but there was nothing they could do at that time of night, so they sent me home to come back the next day for a scan. Every time I went to the toilet, tissue kept coming out of me, thick, bloody, livery, and I knocked back painkillers to deal with the intense stomach pains. Paul stayed over and made up a hot water bottle for me, and the next day, after a restless night trying to sleep despite the uncontrollable tears, we went back to the hospital for a scan. They confirmed my womb was empty, and that was that.

Paul and I drove back into town. We went for some Italian food, where I noticed him eyeing up the waitress, and then browsed in a bookshop, where I bought a very expensive hardback about the fashions of the Tudors. He dropped me back at my flat and said he needed to have a shower and change into clean underwear, but he'd check on me the next day. I really didn't want to be on my own, but I didn't tell him that. Instead, I texted my friend Conrad. He was always reliable for a drink. We met in the pub, and I struggled to fight back the tears as I told him what had happened. He was sympathetic, kind, but he didn't know what to say either. We went to the local store, and I bought a bottle of wine to drink back at his place, and he got a few beers. It was the end of April, and there were still glimmers of daylight as I walked back home at 9 p.m., numb, drunk from that whole bottle of wine.

It was so quiet, so empty in my flat, like my body, and I sank down onto the kitchen floor and screamed and cried. I just wanted this

122 Single & Psycho

baby back inside me, and I felt so alone. I took some co-codamol to help knock me out, and then the next day Paul messaged to see how I was doing. I was hungover, devastated, and I couldn't sleep. Paul didn't come to see me that day, as he said he would, but he drove me to the hospital for each follow-up appointment. They needed to check my blood every few days to make sure the hCG was decreasing and that the fetus and tissue had fully expelled.

He made sure I ate, but what I really wanted was a hug—for him to wrap his arms around me and soothe me and tell me it was OK and for us to talk about what had happened. But he didn't. Instead, he slowly ghosted me over the next few months, and so I posted on Instagram and Twitter about my loss because I needed people to pay attention to me, I needed to shout about what happened, I needed to receive sympathy from friends and strangers. People would tell me miscarriages were very common, but that wasn't a comfort. It wasn't common to me; it was the most devastating thing, and I didn't want to be just a statistic.

I met people for drinks, acquaintances who had reached out to me with their own experiences, and I quelled the anxiety and filled that emptiness with alcohol so I could just numb myself for a while. I also put my profile back on Bumble and Tinder and Hinge and hooked up with an ex from ten years before, because Paul was practically gone from my life. The last time I'd seen him, we had gone to the cinema to see *Cruella*, but he was snappy and cold, keeping his arm crossed against his chest throughout the film, and he didn't take up my offer to stay over. I felt like I was becoming irrational and unstable as I was grasping to find what my next move could be and how I could fill that ache and longing inside me. So when Alex Forrest mentions a bad miscarriage that made her believe she was infertile, and when she goes off the rails after being rejected by the man who impregnated her, I could really understand her. Her pain and anger connected with me.

Despite being game for poking fun at her famous character, as seen with the *Saturday Night Live* sketch, Glenn Close was unhappy with the way that Alex was ultimately depicted because, clearly, she is suffering a mental illness, triggered by the deep pain of rejection and, I would argue, the confusion of being pregnant and abandoned. As she said during publicity interviews for *Fatal Attraction* in 1987, "I

Burnout, Biological Clocks, and Boiling Rabbits   123

think it's a wonderful part—so outwardly sexual and yet so disturbed. She is a tragedy. That's what appealed to me—I thought I could bring a lot to the role and make it more believable."[12]

Close's performance was so powerful that Paramount knew they had a hit on their hands, but when test audiences watched it, it was clear they had a visceral loathing for Alex and wanted her to be punished. The ending that had originally been shot, and was shown to the test audiences, just wasn't satisfying enough in her take-down.

During the rosy moments of getting to know one another, Alex and Dan listen to the soundtrack to *Madame Butterfly*, and Dan reveals to her that the first experience of seeing the opera was with his father. It was one of the only times his father was ever kind to him, comforting him as he cried during the suicide scene.

In the movie's original ending, Alex would use this memory against him. Sitting cross-legged on the floor and with the opera soundtrack blasting in the background, she takes a large carving knife and slowly and methodically slits her throat. For unforgiving test audiences, killing herself was too easy a way out, and instead a new scene was written where Alex breaks into the Gallagher home armed with the same kitchen knife and is shot by a gun-wielding Beth. In the final moment, the camera lingers on a picture frame with a photo of the smiling Gallaghers, providing the reassurance that now that the witch is dead, the family unit has been restored.

Glenn Close fought the new ending for two weeks as she was horrified about turning "a character I loved into a murdering psychopath." Financially, it proved to be a savvy choice as it generated another $100 million profit and helped to make it one of the most influential thrillers of all time, but it destroys the film's pathos. "The grotesque, botched climax, conversely, has a definite aroma of 'market research,'" wrote Michael Wilmington in the *Los Angeles Times*. "The ending is bad precisely because it subverts everything the story and the actors have built up previously."[13]

When this final version was released, cinemagoers in the United States became so caught up in their hatred of Alex that they erupted with boos and cries of "kill that bitch!" and "take her down!" "It's quite extraordinary," Adrian Lyne said at the time. "I wasn't prepared for how much of an audience-participation movie it was going to be. In the last act, the reaction is so vocal."[14]

124   *Single & Psycho*

People magazine placed Close and Douglas on the front cover of its October 26, 1987, edition, with a tantalizing headline that promised real-life fatal attractions would be revealed inside. "It's not just a movie," the cover declared. "All too often, 'casual' affairs end in rage, revenge and shattered lives."

"It is like a Rorschach test come to life, this psycho parable of a rejected woman wreaking havoc and bloody revenge on a one-weekend lover and his comfy family," the article continued. "Men leave the theater shaken, silently or openly reaffirming their marriage vows; women leave resolving to make their husbands see it."[15]

In January 1988, film critics concluded that while *Fatal Attraction* was the most talked-about film of the previous year, it was also the most overrated because, as Peter Larson said, "when it comes down to it, it's really nothing more than Friday 13th by and for yuppies with a cliché copout final."[16]

He concluded that 1987 was not only the year that "adults came back to the movies"; it was also the year of "bringing up baby in the 80s." A raft of films about raising babies further reinforced the clash between the domestic sphere and the workplace and posed the question as to whether it was possible for women to excel in both.

CHAPTER 10

Baby Booms and Working Girls

A high-flying Manhattan businesswoman is recovering from breaking her leg in a skiing accident while on vacation, and she trusts her secretary to look after her luxury apartment for her while she's in the hospital. When she's finally able to come home, still on crutches, she discovers that this secretary has not only been staying there but has also been borrowing her clothes, copying her hairstyle, impersonating her in business meetings, and even sleeping with her boyfriend. It sounds like a nightmarish plot of an early nineties' domestic thriller, but it is in fact the 1988 comedy *Working Girl*, starring Melanie Griffith and Sigourney Weaver as two women competing at work and in love, one who is blond and the other who is brunette.

The smash success of *Fatal Attraction* would trigger a wave of copycat thrillers where the home is under threat from a pernicious single woman, but as these took time to develop, the questions raised around the ambitions of women were, in the meantime, addressed in a series of comedies. Rather than the film being about a threatening secretary who is trying to steal this woman's life, Sigourney Weaver plays Katharine Parker, the boss from hell, and Melanie Griffith is Tess McGill, her put-upon working-class assistant. Burning with ambition, Tess decides to take control of her career path after discovering her conniving boss has stolen her idea.

These two career women are both single and childless, and Weaver's character, who is older, has a ticking biological clock and a desperate focus on receiving a marriage proposal from her boyfriend, Jack Trainer (Harrison Ford). What appealed to Ford, he said at the time, was that he was in the position of love interest. "I played the

126   *Single & Psycho*

girl's part, basically, and that to me was intriguing," he said. "If you take away the names, I was playing the love interest which in most films is the girl's part."[1]

Long before the Me Too movement, *Working Girl* explored what it took to succeed in business as a woman while facing off against misogyny. There may have been attempts to keep the workplace doors bolted for women, but an educated female workforce was now competing with men and demanding to be taken seriously. Yet women still grappled with sexism, workplace harassment, and a belief that once married, they would eventually give up their career. As Donald Trump would say in the nineties, "Putting a wife to work is a very dangerous thing." The hot topic of sexual harassment was also explored in the British film *Business as Usual* in 1987. Glenda Jackson plays the manager of a clothing store who is sacked when she complains that her shop assistants have been victims of harassment by the regional manager, which leads to a strike action. But this was a very new topic, and a very new buzzword, with victims so often disbelieved.

In the opening scenes of *Working Girl*, Griffith's Tess McGill, with her big mullet haircut and gauche makeup, is just one of a stream of ambitious young women making their morning commute on the Staten Island ferry. This vision is much like the opening of Rona Jaffe's *The Best of Everything*, with the girls piling out of the subways and into their offices each morning. Here, the women wear their sports shoes for comfort before changing into their heels once arriving at the office.

Jaffe's single working girls were more focused on their marriage prospects, but in the mideighties, for women like Tess, ambition was an equal priority. The career woman came into her own in this decade as she earned her place in pop culture, from Dolly Parton's *9 to 5* (1980) to the sitcom *Murphy Brown*, which premiered in November 1988. Candice Bergen played the titular character, a celebrated journalist who is over forty, single and childless, recovering from alcoholism, and has no intention of stepping away from her career.

Clearly, Tess has the brains and the acumen, having earned a degree in business by taking night classes, and in the early scenes, she's driven out of her stockbroker job by her disgusting colleagues who treat her like a bimbo and set her up to be sexually assaulted.

Kevin Spacey's coked-up executive forces her to view pornography in the back of a limo and expects her to perform for a promotion. As costar Oliver Platt would later say, they "were the pigs, sort of the inciting #MeToo'ers. Here's the sad thing: Those pigs were a dime a dozen on Wall Street. I thought I was playing a rare pig, but what we've discovered is that there was nothing unusual about that guy at all."[2]

Offered a new position under a female boss, mergers and acquisitions associate Katharine Parker (Weaver), Tess believes it will be a cinch. Katharine seems fair; she masks her ruthlessness with niceties and even takes the opportunity to listen to Tess's profitable idea for a new merger. After Katharine breaks her leg while skiing, she asks Tess to look after her apartment while she's out of action, and it's here, while using her exercise bike and trying on her clothes, that she discovers Katharine has passed off Tess's idea as her own. It sets in motion a plan to impersonate Katharine so Tess can set up the deal herself, beginning with borrowing a sophisticated black dress to wear to a party in the hopes of meeting and impressing Jack Trainer, one of the most talented associates in mergers and acquisitions.

Tess is the type of ambitious go-getter who is always in a hurry, who vacuums topless and in heels, who proclaims she has a brain for business and a "bod for sin," and who completely charms Harrison Ford's Jack, even when she passes out from a heady combination of sleeping pills and booze, played as if it's a screwball comedy rather than something more sinister.

Melanie Griffith found that *Working Girl*'s themes of sexual harassment and gender and class barriers were way ahead of their time and that the film resonated strongly with women in the same situation. "There are millions of women who had that experience, and that's why so many women love that movie and to this day tell me how we changed their lives," she told *Hollywood Reporter* in 2018, to mark the thirtieth anniversary of the film.[3]

Just as Tess struggles to be taken seriously, Melanie Griffith saw a similarity in the dismissive way she was treated in the industry, and she had to fight to win the role of Tess. She had been frequently dismissed as just an airhead with a helium voice. As the daughter of Tippi Hedren, she was famous before she knew what that meant, and living in proximity to Hollywood, she grew up quickly. By the age of

128   *Single & Psycho*

fourteen, she was sleeping with future husband Don Johnson, her mother's costar in *The Harrad Experiment* (1973). She won her first major role at the age of seventeen in Arthur Penn's *Night Moves* in 1975, in which she controversially appeared nude, and while it led to more films, it affirmed an uncomfortable reputation as a Lolita figure, particularly after another teenage temptress role opposite Paul Newman in *The Drowning Pool.*

Newsweek's profile in 1975 illustrates the lack of boundaries when speaking of teenage girls: "She has the body of a sensuous woman, the pouting, chipmunk face of a teenager and the voice of a child— and, suddenly, she's showing them all." It also said of her role as a beauty pageant contestant in *Smile* (1975) that "she fully lives up to the script's description of the character as 'hot, sweet and dumb.'"[4]

At eighteen, she married Don Johnson in Las Vegas, they divorced, she had an affair with the much older Ryan O'Neal, and she then married and had a child with actor Steven Bauer. By the early eighties, reports of her hard partying, along with a publicized accident where she was hit by a car while drunkenly crossing Sunset Boulevard, tainted her with the reputation of being another nepo baby with substance-abuse issues.

Eventually, in 1984, she was given the chance to bounce back when she was cast as porn star Holly Body in Brian De Palma's *Body Double.* She also had to fight for that role, with De Palma auditioning porn actresses before even considering Griffith. "Can you handle it? It's pretty strong stuff," he told her. She said yes, she was a powerhouse, and was willing to do what it took.

Griffith hailed Holly as a symbol of feminism, body-confident and disarming with the girlish voice and the no-nonsense approach in how she lays down her boundaries. "There are some things I like to get straight right up front so there are no misunderstandings later on," she says. "I do not do animal acts. I do not do S&M or any variation of that particular bent."

In an interview with Bobbie Wygant, Griffith defended Holly as a "businesswoman . . . she likes what she does, and she does it very well. But she's got a great amount of pride in the fact she is a woman. And as far as the women's movement goes and everything, she's very much a part of it, in saying that 'I'm going to do what I want to do.'" When Bobbie Wygant asked if her vocal intonation was one of the reasons she got the role, she looked flummoxed and then laughed it off: "Hopefully not, gosh, I hope it was my ability to act!"

In Jonathan Demme's *Something Wild* (1986), Griffith's character has two different identities—that of the crazy, living-life-on-the-edge free spirit and the homey, down-to-earth woman. This schizophrenic personality is something many single women contend with. There are societal expectations in choosing the right path in life, and these compete with the internal desire to be free and untethered. Griffith could easily identify with these two opposing personas, and not only did the film become a cult classic, with her Louise Brooks black bob the inspiration for Uma Thurman in *Pulp Fiction*, but it helped to convince *Working Girl*'s director, Mike Nichols, that she was just the right amount of funny, vulnerable, and sexy. As producer Douglas Wick said, "We needed an old-fashioned movie star. Someone who, when they had glasses on, you believed they had a little anonymity, and as soon as they took them off, you saw they were a beauty. You needed someone fiercely intelligent but in a slightly more unique way."[5]

Even on its release, Griffith was billed third, behind Weaver and Ford, when clearly hers is the starring role. Filming took place in New York, and it was an intense time for her. She was thirty years old, single and with a young child to care for, and struggling with some of the concepts of the film, such as "trying to understand *Pygmalion* and how that correlated to *Working Girl*. At the time, it was like, 'What the fuck do you mean?' It wasn't like I knew what *Pygmalion* was."[6]

She was also gripped by a cocaine addiction, heightened by the temptations of the Downtown party scene, and when she turned up high on set, production was shut down for twenty-four hours. Nichols agreed not to report her to the studio if she paid the costs of eighty thousand dollars out of her own pocket. It was the wakeup call she needed, and when she finished playing Tess, she checked into rehab with a determination to get sober and called up her ex-husband, Don Johnson, for his support.[7]

Working Girl was the film that made Griffith a bona fide star. Winning a Golden Globe for Best Actress and earning Oscar and BAFTA nominations, she was elevated to a position beside Michelle Pfeiffer and, later, Demi Moore as the actress on every producer's wish list.

130   *Single & Psycho*

During the press junket for *Working Girl*, Griffith was profiled as if she embodied the same ambitious characteristics of Tess. News had just broken that she and ex-husband Don Johnson had reunited, and she was described as making diva-like demands to those around her while also fixating on her love life. The *Los Angeles Times* reported in detail her behavior in her hotel suite, that she was berating the front desk for sending up unannounced visitors and not collecting her dirty breakfast dishes, and criticizing the waiter for forgetting her midday coffee order.[8]

In the *New York Times*, she was likened to "the quintessential career woman taking a quick break between corporate conferences" as she sat in her trailer nibbling on a rainbow salad, dressed in a Wall Street–style tan business suit, and with a "girlish voice reminiscent of Judy Holliday."[9]

These comparisons with Judy Holliday, who won an Oscar for playing a ditzy, uneducated woman in *Born Yesterday* in 1950, seemed apt as it was a time when women were often dismissed for their ambitions and flooded with messages about the importance of family values. The eighties were tinged with nostalgia, and there was a real sense of harking back to the Golden Age of Hollywood, the good old days of the studio system. Griffith possessed the kittenish-soft Marilyn Monroe appearance and voice, combined with the resilience of a plucky 1940 heroine. The *Seattle Gay Times* suggested "1980s Judy Holliday or Marilyn Monroe with her whispery/husky voice, her little-girl vulnerability, and an audience-pleasing ability to cut through the bull. It's more than a little sad to see Melanie's character Tess put in all that energy just to land a man and an office cubicle of her own."[10]

In this postfeminist world, strong, independent female characters were also supposed to be adorable and compliant, and an article in the *Los Angeles Times* compared the appearances of actresses in recently released movies—Kim Basinger in *My Stepmother Is an Alien*, Geena Davis in *The Accidental Tourist*, and Griffith in *Working Girl*. "What seems to have emerged is a woman who mixes the pure lovability of a '50s Marilyn Monroe with the contemporary accomplishment and intelligence. Does this trio succeed only because they are adorable, gorgeous or cuddly?" asked the *Los Angeles Times*.[11]

Griffith had in fact been in the running for *The Accidental Tourist*, but after being advised that *Working Girl* would make her a star, she chose the latter. It not only affirmed her fierce ambition but also landed her on tabloid front covers as her colorful love life made her perfect gossip fodder. Griffith couldn't just be a woman focused on her career; she had to have a redemption arc, which was softened by the prospects of marriage. In an article in *People* in February 1989, it described her "curled up like a kitten on the sofa of her suite in the Beverly Hills Hotel . . . luxuriating in the glow of her newly brilliant career. Two days before, she'd won a Golden Globe for *Working Girl*, and her future had never looked brighter. It had taken her 13 films over 13 years to get this close to real stardom. But right now, the one thing more dazzling to her than her professional prospects was a four-carat rock on the third finger of her left hand."[12]

The magazine reported that as part of her tumultuous on-off relationship with Johnson, the short-lived marriage, and their addictions and partying lifestyles, she was now pregnant (with future star Dakota Johnson) and was opting to choose family over career. "I kind of like being a housewife right now," she said.[13]

Just as Melanie Griffith was compared with Judy Holliday or Jean Arthur, Sigourney Weaver considered her character, Katharine Parker, on a par with Bette Davis or as Rosalind Russell in *The Women* and *His Girl Friday*. She saw her as a strong 1930s and '40s heroine, and she said, "When I burst into the board room, that was my Bette Davis scene."[14]

While Katharine shared that belief that she should be on top, Weaver understood from her research at brokerage houses on Wall Street that women tended to downplay their success, despite their capabilities. "I think there still was a lot of concern about how they were being perceived, both by men and by women within their firms," she said.[15]

Thanks to *Working Girl*, it appeared as if the depictions of working women had greatly improved since *The Best of Everything*. Yet Betty Friedan was cynical around the progress. She told the *Los Angeles Daily News* in 1989 that despite the breakthrough of the women's movement, there was a return to the "new traditionalism," where the message was "that feminism is dead, all women are interested in is a husband and a home. This is the new feminine mystique. The message is to forget about equality and childcare. It's serious, the attack on women's rights."[16]

132   *Single & Psycho*

According to Friedan, eight years of the Reagan presidency, with plans to dismantle the Equal Rights Amendment, abortion rights, and funding for child care facilities, had created a reactionary atmosphere against feminism, as shown in films like *Working Girl*, with two women pitted against one another as they play male power games, and in *Fatal Attraction*, with the single woman as a domestic terrorist. Friedan said,

> The career woman was painted as pure evil, and she's killed by the sweet housewife. The character was painted in very menacing, evil overtones, and there is a certain amount of bad polarization between working women and housewives, and the media is playing to this. If they do stay home, or if they go out and work, and have to juggle a career and home life, they've both got a political problem or not really good choices. . . . A lot of books and movies like *Fatal Attraction* are playing to this. . . . All reactionary groups are threatened by women's empowerment, their individuality. I don't lose sight of the fact that it's an unfinished revolution, and the danger of a new feminine mystique is there.[17]

Working Girl was released in December 1988, and at the Oscars the following March, its three actresses were nominated for awards—Griffith for Best Actress and Weaver and Joan Cusack for Best Supporting Actress. Geena Davis won the Best Supporting Actress award for *The Accidental Tourist*, and as Best Actress, Jodie Foster won for *The Accused*. Both of these movies are interesting studies of single women living their lives outside of the norm, and *The Accused* was particularly provocative in its subject matter.

Jodie Foster is Sarah Tobias, a young woman who is brutally gang-raped in the back room of a bar while a baying mob watches, but because she has a chaotic lifestyle of barhopping and smoking weed, she isn't taken seriously as a victim. District Attorney Kathryn Murphy (Kelly McGillis) sees how wrong this preconceived judgment is and puts on trial the men who were cheering on Sarah's rapists. *The Accused* raised the question of the deserving victim and how rape and sexual assault victims were often judged for their lifestyle choices and clothing.

An article in the *Daily Mirror* on February 10, 1989, headlined "Asking for It?," read, "She plays a brassy, rough-and-ready blonde . . . a

Baby Booms and Working Girls 133

bit of a tart. She is nobody's idea of a conventional victim. But the film's message is that it is any woman's right to dress and behave as provocatively as she likes and still say No."

There were similarities within the dynamics of *The Accused* and *Working Girl*—a blond, working-class woman who is at odds with the dark-haired, well-educated professional who wears pearls and throws sophisticated dinner parties and has had all the educational chances to help her push to the top. In one of the film's most dramatic scenes, Sarah challenges her lawyer. "You ain't gonna defend me cause I'm some low-class bimbo," she says, with all the anger of a woman who knows very well how powerless her social standing makes her.[18]

The film was based on a true story, that of the 1983 sexual assault of Cheryl Araujo, who was gang-raped in a bar in New Bedford, Massachusetts. The victim and the assailants were Portuguese-American, and the racist way in which the assault and the trial were reported caused a conflict within the different communities in the town. As the first rape trial to be televised, Cheryl's name and address and the details of her assault were broadcast on cable news. Public sentiment soon turned on Cheryl, who was met with threats and aggression in the town she had been born in. She had gone into the bar to buy cigarettes and then decided to have a drink on her own, but this, according to the moral judgment meted down on women, meant she was clearly procuring for sex. The message was the same as in *Looking for Mr. Goodbar*, that a woman in a bar on her own, whether she was reading a book or stopping off to buy cigarettes, was a slut.

The defense lawyer even asked, "If you're living with a man, what are you doing running around the streets getting raped?" The four men on trial for assault were convicted, and the two who were charged with being accessories were acquitted.

After sixteen thousand signed a petition asking for leniency for the accused, and with the Portuguese community protesting on the streets to condemn her as a liar, Cheryl was forced to move to Miami with her sister to escape the abuse. In 1986, she was tragically killed when she crashed her car while intoxicated, with her children in the back seat surviving.[19]

The trauma of the rape and of then being blamed for it proved too much for her, as not only was she forced to leave the only home

134 *Single & Psycho*

she knew but was also actively blamed and scapegoated for a violent, humiliating act that was inflicted on her. The 2020 Netflix series *Trial by Media* devotes an entire episode, "Big Dan's," to the case, and hearing other women condemn her for being in a bar on her own, and for supposedly asking for it, is just so incredibly unjust.

Jodie Foster saw the lead-up to the rape scene as revealing the strength of Sarah. She's punished for trying to be one of the guys and for expressing herself as a single, free woman by choosing to drink, dance, and flirt.

As she noted in an interview, Sarah's in the bar that night because she said

> "no" to her boyfriend . . . and left. She's wearing a great outfit. More and more, she's becoming herself. When she plays pinball, she's one of the boys. She tells them, "I'm a winner." She feels like she's on top of things. Then her favorite song comes on . . . I've been in this situation a million times. Your favorite song comes on. You feel great about yourself. You feel totally un-self-conscious. There's no reason in the world why you shouldn't be allowed to do exactly as you feel, to be expressive . . . and it's precisely that moment of will, of her feeling equal, being able to be a woman and one of the guys that is so incredibly anger making.[20]

If Sarah's hedonistic choices were condemned, there was one particularly pervasive narrative theme in late eighties pop culture that took a mirror to the single person's unfettered lifestyle. By introducing a baby to yuppies' fast-paced but selfish existence, it would demonstrate that child-rearing, as difficult as it was, would give their shallow lives meaning.

Nancy Meyers's *Baby Boom*, released on October 30, 1987, starred Diane Keaton as J. C. Wiatt, an ambitious Manhattan yuppie whose lack of maternal desire is echoed by her gender-neutral name. When her distant cousin dies, she is shocked to discover that her inheritance is not a pile of cash, as she had hoped, but is in fact their baby. Now completely out of her depth, she learns how difficult it is to manage her work and home life, particularly as a single career woman. The film opens in much the same way as *Working Girl*, with soaring shots of Manhattan's skyscrapers, of working women rushing to their offices in their sneakers, and with a voiceover proclaiming the groundbreaking changes women are currently experiencing.

Her monochrome suits show that she's all business, even in bed, where she wears a man's bathrobe, and her emasculated partner (Harold Ramis) is in a face mask. As she warms to the baby, pastel colors and softer skirts show a more feminine side, and this subliminal messaging predicts that she'll abandon the rat race and find true happiness as a devoted mother.

In Woody Allen's *Annie Hall*, Diane Keaton had set trends as the kooky single woman whose mix-and-match androgynous wardrobe spoke to the boomers who were still trying to find their feet in a newly feminist world. Now, in *Baby Boom*, she was representing the modern woman of the eighties who may have protested as a twentysomething but was now middle-aged and focused on work.

Diane Keaton was forty-one at the time of the film's release, single and child-free, and during the press tour, she was quizzed by reporters on her own maternal instincts. Charles Champlin of the *Los Angeles Times* noted that when he met her five years before, she had expressed a desire to have children but that she had said none of the men she knew were feeling particularly paternal. I'm sure she appreciated him pointing out to her that "it is a late hour on the biological clock," but she politely conceded, "Life is full of trade-offs, and you have to accept that you can't have everything."[21]

She was asked in another interview whether working with the twins who played the thirteen-month-old girl in the movie inspired her to want children of her own. "Sure. Yeah. Yeah," she said, obviously trying to brush off her frustration at being asked the same questions. "Of course I did, because you're around them all the time, and there they are. There you are. I think it'd be nice. Really great. It's a question of, you know, other things."[22]

So often, a woman had to choose between being a mother or following her career, and Keaton pursued this theme further in the serious drama *The Good Mother* (1988), directed by Leonard Nimoy. She is a devoted mother who is in a new relationship with an artist, played by Liam Neeson. He criticizes her for having given up on her previous career as a pianist, and she fights back: "That was the plan for me, but I wasn't good enough! So I made a different kind of life for myself, with Molly! And I really hate being told there's no honor

136 *Single & Psycho*

in it!" As well as sacrificing her talents, she is also punished for dating Neeson's character while being a single mother, and after a court battle with her ex-husband, where she is condemned for exposing her child to her sexual relationship, she loses custody.

The movie was met with mixed reviews, and the *New York Times* described it as "the most extreme among recent films that take quirky issues and atypical characters, then try to inflate melodrama to the status of social issues."[23]

Nimoy's previous film, released just a month after *Baby Boom*, in November 1987, was a much more comedic take on domesticity, and it proved to be one of the biggest hits of the year. In *Three Men and a Baby*, three male roommates learn how difficult it is to care for a baby while generating laughs with their bumbling ineptitude.

Steve Guttenberg, Tom Selleck, and Ted Danson are the three professional, middle-aged bachelors whose party lifestyle is interrupted when a baby is left on their doorstep. The girl, Mary, has been abandoned by a struggling British actress, Sylvia (Nancy Travis), and was the result of a short-lived affair with Jack, Ted Danson's irresponsible actor. Later, when she comes back to collect her baby, the first thing Jack asks her is, "How do I know it's mine?"

Sylvia tries to care for Mary by herself, but she realizes that as a working woman, she'd struggle to do this on her own. She wonders how it would be possible for any single woman to look after a child, but luckily she has the help of these three men, and so, with their blessing, she moves into the bachelor pad so they can raise Mary in an unconventional family unit.

In *Backlash*, Susan Faludi was cynical of its intention, where it appears on the surface to have "feminist tendencies" in its heartwarming depiction of men being the primary caregivers. "But," she writes, "the movie does not propose that men take real responsibility for raising children. It derives all its humor from the reversal of what it deems the natural order." She also wryly comments that such is the terror that a baby in a masculine space might lower the testosterone that "the guys are forever lifting weights, sweating it out on the playing fields and jogging to the newsagents for the latest issue of *Sports Illustrated* and *Popular Mechanics*."[24]

In the 1990 sequel, *Three Men and a Little Lady*, Mary is now five and has begun asking questions about her unique living situation,

Baby Booms and Working Girls   137

where she has one mother and three fathers. Sylvia is also fretting about her future as she wants to get married and have more children (and in the nineties, the former is still very much the prerequisite to the latter). Her three roommates decide that marriage is a concept that can be easily fulfilled if they find the right man for her, but she makes the decision the next day—choosing to marry her pompous British theater producer, with a wedding due to take place at his English country estate.

The anxiety around marriage that Sylvia portrays was a universal concern at the time. In *When Harry Met Sally*, Sally (Meg Ryan) worries about still being single at thirty because it's a slippery slope to forty—the death knell for having any hope, as the *Newsweek* article had scare-mongered. In well-worn movie tropes, a single woman over forty is either a horror character or a joke. In *Three Men and a Little Lady*, Peter (Tom Selleck) is pursued by a spinster headmistress (Fiona Shaw) who has chocolate frosting stuck to her lips when she is first introduced to him and whose loins are clearly burning with unfulfilled passion.

Forty had always been a looming, terrifying number for me, and I imagined it as a bookend, a sturdy antique tome that separated youth from middle age. The lead-up to this huge milestone felt like the approaching apocalypse, the end of time. This was the age when I wouldn't be able to get IVF on the NHS; this was the age that characters in movies like *When Harry Met Sally* had also been terrified of, and I'd read all the articles, heard the comments that criticized a woman's appearance over this age. "Can You Believe She's Forty?" was a typical headline in the *Daily Mail* when describing the bikini snap of a celebrity; there were the comments—"old hag," "desperate case"—or, worse, the invisibility. I had even hoped that the people at my work wouldn't decorate my desk with bunting or bring a cake, and to avoid that possibility, I took the day as annual leave and instead treated myself to lunch with a friend and a trip to a spa. It was a nice day, although Gavin was an hour late to meet me for a drink. We then went round to my parents', and I have little memory of it except that we were probably mildly drunk from having had another round in the pub.

To be single at forty was a daunting prospect, and despite the misery of being trapped in my flat with Gavin, I couldn't imagine a future

138   *Single & Psycho*

without him, as grim as this future with him was. I had a fantasy of what my life should be like. I imagined dating a creative man with a beard, someone who had a big family, and we would all sit around a cozy wooden table in a farmhouse somewhere, chatting over home-cooked shepherd's pie and bowls of salad. Right now, my life was with a chain-smoking drug addict who lied about having a job. And there had to be a better option for me out there.

I'd thought about going back on online dating sites, but I worried that the pool of men would be greatly reduced. I'd been hammered with the message that no one wants to date a forty-year-old; she's the spinster with chocolate frosting on her mouth, after all, and she has desperation written all over her face. As one of my male friends also kindly pointed out to me as I regaled him with my woes, she's unlikely to be able to have children. I also knew that even if I did break up with Gavin, he would refuse to leave my flat, and I would be stuck there, for months, while he raged at me and made my life hell. Finally, I made my escape just before the COVID-19 pandemic gripped the world, and so, for me, forty was being back at home with my parents. As hard as the lockdown was, the daily death counts, the worries that health-care workers didn't have the right protective equipment, the not knowing if we would ever get out of it, I used the time as best I could.

I threw myself into doing home workouts, GRIT sessions and yoga every day, and I got really fit and healthy. I cooked and baked, and wrote and read, and it was a beautiful spring with sunny days and light-filled evenings for sitting outside. And I'd also met Paul. Rather than being the anxious mess of the past few years, I was now feeling attractive and wanted. We messaged every day during those six months of enforced stay-at-home orders and social distancing. He sent me TikTok videos and Star Wars jokes, we discussed *Tiger King*, he ranted about Prime Minister Boris Johnson. I felt the flush of excitement of a new relationship; there was a hope and a stirring of my sexuality. Gavin had killed off the confident, assured part of me, but now it was reemerging. This was forty, and it was giving me the chance to start over.

As conservatives in the eighties railed against feminist progress, there was a push to return to the 1950s, which was idealized as a golden era of simple family values (read: women in the kitchen rather than at work). To fill this appetite for nostalgia, Hollywood began to remake movies from that decade, such as *Father of the Bride* (1991), which further reinforced the message of marriage as the goal for all young women. There were also reruns of *I Love Lucy* on television (with a clip featured in *Pretty Woman*), and fashion was returning to a "conservative chic" of white gloves, sheer hosiery, and an hourglass silhouette.

By 1990, the full impact of *Fatal Attraction* would be felt in a wave of thrillers that explored the existential threat of the feminist movement and its impact on women's choices. As the number of women in the workplace increased, and women were opting to get married and have children later in life, there was a huge amount of concern as to what this meant to society. And Hollywood was there to feed into this yuppie paranoia.

CHAPTER 11

Bitches from Hell

In May 1988, the Directors Guild of America distributed to its members a list of guidelines on how AIDS- and HIV-related issues should be portrayed in movies. Directors were advised to show the consequences of unprotected sex, to avoid depicting casual sex unless it was vital to the story, and to "recognize and respect abstinence." There were some directors who objected to the guidelines on principle as they saw it as a puritanical return to the censorship codes of the studio era. Even so, these moralistic parameters would, for a short time, impact the way sex was shown on screen.[1] It was perhaps why there had been a boom in baby-themed movies and why major studio sex thrillers like *Fatal Attraction* were a vessel to warn of the murky dangers of one-night stands.

"It was natural that Hollywood would become interested in Aids," wrote the *Sunday Times* in March 1990. "And while the industry was slow to warm to the subject, when it did so, it was with a vengeance, launching probably its greatest concentrated propaganda effort since the second world war."[2]

The article used the example of *Cocktail* (1988), where formerly promiscuous bartender Tom Cruise rejects casual sex for stability, and described *Fatal Attraction* as doing for adultery and one-night stands what "Reefer Madness was supposed to do for marijuana." The article was served with a dollop of sexism in its description of Alex as a "svelte but not especially attractive co-worker" but concluded, "A man who risks everything near and dear for a night of passion. It almost sounds like . . . Aids?"[3]

Given the lengthy process from script to screen, it wasn't until July 1990 that there would be a thriller that built on *Fatal Attraction*'s

Bitches from Hell 141

success and followed the similar narrative arc of a sexually active single woman who threatens the sanctity of the family.

Released in July 1990, *Presumed Innocent* featured Greta Scacchi as the beautiful but dangerously ambitious single woman whose workplace affairs provide a justification for her violent murder. Carolyn Polhemus, like Claire in *Someone to Watch Over Me*, is a sensual woman, with shimmering bronzed skin, come-hither eyes, and a knack for getting ahead in her career as a prosecutor in the district attorney's office by sleeping with her colleagues. This includes Harrison Ford's Rusty Sabich, whose wife, Barbara, played by Bonnie Bedelia, resembles Lorraine Bracco's Ellie in her earthiness. Barbara, like Ellie, is also mother to a son, and having devoted herself to being a housewife, Barbara now wants to start thinking about nurturing her career.

Carolyn is happily promiscuous, even undergoing a tube-tying process to ensure she doesn't accidentally fall pregnant. When this is discovered in her postmortem, the implication is that she's even more unnatural and manipulative for not wanting children. This reminds me of Nicole Kidman's character in *Malice* (1993), whose villainy is demonstrated through her willingness to undergo an operation that will render her sterile as part of a million-dollar scam.

Given that Carolyn's murder kickstarts the narrative, we only see her alive through Rusty's memories, which often link her lustful bedroom gaze to her death. What we do see in these flashbacks is that she is brilliant at her job. As she interacts with an abused child, it's clear that she really cares about the vulnerable victims of the crimes that come through the DA's office.

"I never did understand why you put a broad like that in charge of rape and all that sicko shit," says one of Rusty's colleagues. She is offered little dignity in death, with policemen making casual comments about her breasts and referring to her as a "bitch." When they look at the crime scene photos of her tied up with slipknots, it's presumed that her sexual kinks led to her murder.

Rusty is the antithesis of Ford's typical heroic on-screen persona as he's incredibly passive; his wife drives him to the ferry that takes him from the suburbs and into Chicago every morning, he's managed by his secretary, and even when fighting for his freedom after being accused of Carolyn's murder, his response is muted. Perhaps this is

142 *Single & Psycho*

one of the reasons he's given such a bad haircut; the audience needs to know that this is a very different Harrison Ford from Indiana Jones and Han Solo.

Carolyn ended her affair with Rusty because he didn't show enough ambition in trying to overthrow the district attorney, who, it turns out, also had a brief relationship with Carolyn. They've swapped roles—she possesses overtly masculine ambition, which will be her downfall, while he has stereotypically feminine traits. Rusty becomes obsessed with Carolyn, begging for her to continue their affair, following her at night, calling her apartment continually so that he can hear her voice. The note he receives from her when he arrives in the office on the morning of her murder, "Stop it I know it's you," is, we can assume, a reference to her awareness of his stalkerish behavior.

His actions are more aligned with that of the single and psycho woman, but as a married man, it's up to his wife to remove Carolyn as the threat. Barbara is initially placed in the position of the good wife—she appears homey in her casual shirts and slacks and is clearly devoted to her family. We also discover she knew about and forgave her husband's affair, even though it's clearly painful to her. The bitterness simmers under the surface.

"There are 150 lawyers down there. They couldn't find one who didn't fuck her to put in charge?" she seethes to Rusty. "She's dead, and you're still obsessing."

There are a few hints that all is not as it seems with Barbara. Rusty finds her lying on their bed dripping in sweat, as if she's just finished an exercise video. She makes a crack that she's been masturbating as it's the only solace of the lonely housewife. In early 1990s thrillers, those who indulge in self-pleasure are typically considered deviant.

Unlike *Fatal Attraction*'s Beth Gallagher, Barbara has career ambitions. She had been the best mathematician in her class but dropped out to have their son. Now that he's older, she wants to return to her studies. "I'm still working on my dissertation at my age. It's ridiculous," she says.

In a dramatic plot twist, it's revealed that Barbara is Carolyn's killer, having exacted her revenge on the other woman by bludgeoning her to death, tying her up with a complicated system of knots, and then inserting her husband's sperm into her vagina. "The destroyer is destroyed," she says calmly, too calmly, to Rusty, apparently without any regret around her decision to kill.

Rusty is horrified that his wife is a cold-blooded killer, but he will ensure the murder remains "unsolved" because he doesn't want to deprive his son of his mother. Pablo Picasso, the notorious womanizing artist, may have said that there were "only two kinds of women—goddesses and doormats," but here, the doormat refuses to be walked over in favor of the goddess. We know that after the film's conclusion, Rusty will forever be tortured by the horrific knowledge that his wife killed his mistress.

As John Lyttle reflected in the *Independent* in May 1993, "Bedelia murdered spouse Harrison Ford's slutty mistress and framed him for the killing by using his very own sperm. Beware when Good Wives go bad."[4]

Rather than the married couple being punished for their mistakes (adultery and murder), it's the single, promiscuous, sexually confident woman whose death is justifiable. Just as the hag horror subgenre in the sixties and seventies offered a grim alternative for those pushing for female emancipation, by 1990, the backlash against second-wave feminism was delivering the same message. There had to be something wrong with a woman in her mid- to late thirties who was still living on her own. These were the messages in the movies that I was brought up with in the 1990s. It was this belief that led me to rush into a live-in situation with Gavin when I hadn't been sure, and that correlated with my fear of being on my own again.

In Rob Reiner's adaptation of Stephen King's *Misery*, released in November 1990, an isolated spinster with a sledgehammer becomes dangerously obsessed with a bachelor writer. Kathy Bates was inspired by the hags of classic horrors like *What Ever Happened to Baby Jane?* to shape one of the most notorious villains of all time, Annie Wilkes. The former nurse rescues author Paul Sheldon (James Caan) when his car crashes in a snowstorm and hauls him back to her isolated Maine cabin to recover from his serious injuries. Annie is Paul's self-described number one fan, and she is absolutely obsessed with his series of novels about the beloved Victorian heroine Misery Chastain. She's horrified to discover that in the final novel in the series, he's killed off Misery in childbirth because he wants to reinvent himself as a serious writer.

144   *Single & Psycho*

Keeping him captive in her remote cabin, Annie demands he write a new manuscript that has an ending to her liking, and he complies for fear of her explosive, dangerous temper. Annie is a villain of "grand dame Guignol" proportions. At times she is tragic, almost pitiful in her isolation, and at others she is a grotesque who, it is revealed, has a scrapbook of her previous murders, including the babies she cared for as a nurse.

The film was not, however, an easy comparison to *Fatal Attraction* as the major difference is sex. Despite Annie's obsession for Paul, it doesn't cross into lust; rather, it is her deadly fixation with honesty in storytelling that is responsible for his imprisonment. The movie acts as a projection of the masculine fear of the unknowable internal world of women—that she may appear unthreatening on the surface, that she utters hokey expressions like "cockadoodie," but she is so unstable that one wrong move can send her into murderous rage.

At the same time as these messages were playing out on screen, female celebrities who happened to be single were depicted as being deeply unhappy, even hugely successful ones like Madonna, who was the biggest-selling female artist of the eighties and had orchestrated the hugely successful, and controversial, Blond Ambition World Tour in 1990.

In a *Vanity Fair* profile in April 1991, the mega-star recounted how she had been traumatized by a fortune teller whom she had invited to perform at her New Year's Eve party in her Manhattan apartment. After having her palm read, Madonna was told by this fortune teller that she was never going to have children: "And I was just like, Get the fuck out of here. I was devastated." So she did something she said she never usually did—she got drunk, passed out, and missed her own party.

"I long for children," she told the *Vanity Fair* interviewer. "I wish that I was married and in a situation where having a child would be possible."

Published the year before she would release her boundary-pushing *Sex* book, filled with erotic photos that celebrated a woman's right to indulge in her fantasies, this article depicted Madonna as the lonely career woman, undomesticated, living like a bachelor, and fretting about her future marital and maternal prospects. Her apartment was described as state-of-the-art, with high-tech gym equipment, steam showers, and a kitchen, although she admitted that she never cooked there herself. It was "very much a place for one person," with the inference it was more masculine than feminine.

Madonna confessed to the interviewer that she missed the domesticity of her life when married to the actor Sean Penn and particularly took pride in doing the laundry. "I liked folding Sean's underwear. I liked mating socks," she said wistfully. It was often reported that Penn couldn't handle her work ethic and dedication to her career, and it led to the end of their marriage.

In the 1993 music video for "Bad Girl," directed by David Fincher, Madonna was inspired by Diane Keaton in *Looking for Mr. Goodbar* to play a destructive single woman who is murdered after going to bed with the wrong guy. We first see her lying dead on her bed while the room fills with detectives. She plays Louise Oriole, a bleach-blond New York businesswoman who strides through her office in dark glasses like Miranda Priestly, smokes and drinks at bars as she flirts with men, and then invites them back to her apartment for sex. In a reference to her earlier collaboration with Fincher, the music video for "Express Yourself," where she pours a saucer of milk over herself, she is now the lonely cat lady, licking cat food from her fingers and then knocking back a white wine.

After work, she goes to bars, where she sits at the counter on her own and inevitably picks up a string of men and takes them home, but, as Madonna sings, she's not happy living like this. She is punished for this promiscuity and destructiveness when one of the men she picks up is a serial killer. She appears to submit to her murder, lying back on her bed as if it's a relief to end her relentless lifestyle, and in the afterlife, she is greeted by her guardian angel, Christopher Walken, who allows her to be free.

"It's something of a cliche," Madonna told the *Vanity Fair* reporter while sitting on a stool in the kitchen, "but you can have all the success in the world, and if you don't have someone to love, it's certainly not as rewarding. The fulfillment you get from another human being—a child, in particular—will always dwarf people recognizing you on the street."[5]

As a young film fan in the early nineties, I tried to read as many Hollywood interviews as I could, which, pre-internet, involved real skill in trying to source the magazines—not easy on limited pocket

146   *Single & Psycho*

money. The waiting area in the hairdressers was useful, as were the parents of my best friend, because they were regular magazine purchasers. When I was researching this book, I came across a profile of Geena Davis in *Vanity Fair* in September 1992, which I distinctly remember reading when it came out as I was a huge fan of hers. Thirty years later, it seems eye-wateringly sexist in its lascivious scrutiny of Geena's appearance, where she is described as "Rita Hayworth on steroids" and where her legs, and their "thirty-six-inch inseam," were referenced several times.

The thing that I had remembered from reading it as a teen was being impressed with the list of her inventions and the cinnamon toothpicks that she pulled out after eating. I didn't recall director Stephen Frears's comments on the reasons he cast her in his 1992 film *Hero*, which the interview was to publicize.

"She's sort of magnificent. She's so . . . well, American," he said. "That's what's so nice about her. She's got long legs and that big American face. I wanted a woman who could sit *on* a desk and not behind one." He's then jokingly told off by the interviewer, Kevin Sessums, because he might come across as a bit sexist in the way he's describing a "feminist icon."[6]

In her memoir, Geena Davis recounted that as a child, she and her best friend would pretend to be the male characters in a western TV show, *The Rifleman*, because there weren't any female characters they wanted to emulate. Years later, as a working actress, she understood the type of women she wanted to play, those who took charge of their destiny, yet the scripts with inspiring female parts were few and far between.

"I'd realized by now that I really didn't want to play the kind of typical female roles I was seeing," she wrote. "I wasn't conventionally pretty enough to be cast as eye candy, and I didn't want to just be the girlfriend of the guy who goes off to do something cool; I wanted to have cool challenges, too." She said that she was drawn to the characters who were "bold and self-possessed, probably because I felt myself to be so far removed from those qualities."[7]

After reading Callie Khouri's script for *Thelma & Louise*, she considered it the best she'd ever read. "It was smart, funny, and dark, and very moving—written by a woman, about women, with two— TWO!—strong female leads."[8]

Khouri had the bad luck of being mugged twice in a short space of time, and driving home one night when her car tire caught fire, it sparked an idea in her mind of two women embarking on a crime spree. Ridley Scott bought the script with plans to produce, but when he approached directors with the script, it was typically dismissed as just "two bitches in a car." Ridley replied, "Why are they bitches? Because they have a voice?" and he realized that it was a film he needed to direct himself.[9]

Geena's agent called Ridley Scott every week for a year to ask for a meeting with him, but it was only after other actresses (Michelle Pfeiffer, Holly Hunter, Goldie Hawn) turned it down that she was offered the part of Thelma. Cast opposite her was Susan Sarandon, who possesses the tough, no-nonsense approach of Louise. Geena found working with Susan life-changing as she taught her how to stand up for herself and not to be afraid of saying no. It was invaluable advice for a woman who was a self-confessed people-pleaser.[10]

Ridley Scott envisioned his movie to be an epic odyssey, against the same heroic landscape that had previously been used in westerns. However, on its release in the summer of 1991, *Thelma & Louise* kicked up a hornet's nest around the dangers of feminism, with indignant op-eds claiming it was encouraging women to hate men and to even resort to violence. It was considered a shocking depiction of feminist rage, as if all that hard-done-by resentment from women had bubbled to the surface and then exploded. In his column in the *New York Daily News*, Richard Johnson called for it to be banned as it was "degrading to men" and "justifies armed robbery, manslaughter and chronic drunken driving as exercises in consciousness raising."[11]

When I was around twelve years old, my best friend, Susie, brought the videotape of *Thelma & Louise* round to my house for a movie night, and it left me with the most incredible feeling. I didn't know what it was—a sort of adrenaline rush, an electric thrill that made me want to punch the air, but also a deep sadness that their journey had come to an end with that cliff dive. This was how boys felt when they saw their action heroes, but girls weren't often given the same chance to feel it too.

I can distinctly remember saying to Susie that it was the opposite of sexist—I guess I had some notion of misogyny at that time, without knowing the word, and this film felt exciting, and empowering,

148 *Single & Psycho*

and like nothing I'd experienced. This was before I'd watched *Aliens*, which was another film that had a visceral impact on my introverted mind, that this toughness was inside me somewhere, as I imagined an alter ego with the no-bullshit gutsiness of Ripley and Louise Sawyer. The appeal wasn't that they were dissociating from men because I also adored the growing attraction between Ripley and Hicks (one of the reasons I'm still angry at *Alien 3*), and I liked seeing romance on screen. *Pretty Woman* was on my top ten list, after all. I think there can be both—there's space for girls to learn about relationships, and love, and compromise, but it's also important to show that they don't need to depend on it for their happiness.

As Geena said, "It brought home for me in a very powerful way how rarely we give women the chance to feel that way coming out of a movie. Men can come out of almost every movie having identified with the lead character or one of the important male characters and feeling empowered."[12]

Davis and Sarandon were featured on the cover of *Time* magazine on June 24, 1991, not because the film had been so financially success-ful but because of the controversy. The headline read "Why *Thelma & Louise* Strikes a Nerve." Men professed outrage that women were mimicking the actions of men, and Richard Schickel, in the accom-panying article, wrote, "Does it offer suitable 'role models'? Is the 'violence' its heroines mete out to their tormentors really 'empow-ering' to women, or does it represent a feckless sacrifice of the high moral ground? Is its indiscriminate 'male bashing' grossly unfair to an entire sex?"

Is it male-bashing for a rapist to be punished, for a controlling husband to lose his wife, or for a pervy truck driver to have his vehi-cle blown up as punishment for harassing female drivers? It's hardly anti-male—Harvey Keitel's detective is kind and thoughtful, and he roots for the two women right up until the end. And in the words of Geena, there's also "a guy who steals their money—but gives Thelma a six-thousand dollar orgasm."[13]

It may have been advertised as a female buddy movie, with the unsavory elements scrubbed from the trailer, but it had a dark heart to its core—that when it came to rape, women wouldn't be believed. "We don't live in that kind of a world," says Louise. It celebrated the friendship of two women who weren't focused on trying to find a man;

rather, they were discovering themselves. They sought to escape the narrow parameters of their lives by finding freedom and an awakening. "Everything looks different. You know what I mean . . . Everything looks new. Do you feel like that? Like you've got something to look forward to?" says Thelma as they explore the awe-inspiring landscape at night.

It was also an interesting critique of marital sex. In all her years in a controlling marriage to car salesman Darryl (Christopher McDonald), Thelma had never had an orgasm, but now, as a free woman who picks up a hot hitchhiker and acts with complete sexual freedom, she finally understands "what all the fuss is about." She chooses him because he's Brad Pitt, and it's his body that the camera lingers on.

The final moments in the film also created a mixed reaction from audiences, with their suicide a punishment for two women daring to be different, and for being, in the words of the truck driver, "bitches from hell." But it was their choice to be free rather than spending the rest of their lives in prison. As the car plunges off the Grand Canyon, there's a freeze frame, keeping it suspended in midair and never showing us the consequences of that final drive. Instead, it cuts to a montage of images of the two women on their adventures as if we're looking through an album of holiday snaps. It's a surprisingly upbeat ending that forces the audience to remember the positives of their journey rather than this grim ending.

"When I saw how women reacted after seeing *Thelma & Louise*," Geena said, "it wasn't like they ordinarily do, in a mall, when they say, 'Oh, well, I really liked your work.' They'd say, 'That movie! I loved it! It changed my life! My friend and I now call each other Thelma and Louise!' I thought, My God! There are really not movies like that for women."[14]

Susan Faludi told *Vanity Fair* in 1992 that *Thelma & Louise* "was not just a movie about strong women; other films have had strong women in them—women who defend the family farm or protect their children. It was a film in which women were strong in their own autonomy, which is a new concept for Hollywood. Yet the reaction to the film is as important as the film itself, because it pointed up the willful, intentional misinterpretation of feminism that is now going on."[15]

150 *Single & Psycho*

Geena Davis was often asked whether *Thelma & Louise* could be considered a "feminist movie." Reporters delivered this question to her in a "conspiratorial tone," as if it was a cheeky, provoking question, and when she answered affirmatively that she was indeed a feminist, they looked shocked at this admission. With the early 1990s backlash, *feminism* had become a dirty word, much like how *communist* had been used in the 1950s and the equivalent of the "woke brigade" in the 2020s. As Faludi concluded in her book *Backlash*, at the time of *Thelma & Louise's* release, feminism was considered "so seventies," and it was now a "post-feminist" world, not because women had achieved equal justice but because people were too fatigued to care.[16]

Its advocates were considered a homogenous group of puritanical, humorless enforcers, just waiting to profess their outrage and ruin all the fun. They were ugly harpies or lesbians, an inference that remains the same thirty years later. People would add a caveat—"I'm not a feminist, but . . ."—and Geena Davis refused to play that game. The recession of the late eighties and early nineties brought with it a fear around the job market. Just as men returning from the European and South Pacific battlefields at the end of World War II drove women from the workspace and into the home, there was a visceral concern that women were dominating education and employment markets. It felt like the patriarchy was unraveling, and with a rail against sexual harassment, one wrong move and a man might be accused of date rape.

By the early 1990s, more women were feeling confident in speaking up against harassment, and they were bravely going to court to testify against sexual assault and rape. But at the same time, women attacked other women for leading men on, a similar mode of defense later adopted during the Me Too movement. In February 1993, for example, Carol Sarler, writing in the *Sunday Times*, railed against "prick-teasing," that it was unkind to "dangle the promise of sex in front of a man and then to snatch it away again."

The narrative of Martin Scorsese's *Cape Fear* (1991) was driven by an under-arching theme that women who reported rape and sexual assault were often disbelieved. The cigar-smoking, Hawaiian-shirt-wearing convicted rapist Max Cady (Robert De Niro) terrorizes his former lawyer, Sam Bowden (Nick Nolte); his wife, Leigh (a sultry Jessica Lange); and precocious daughter, Danielle (Juliette Lewis) as he blames Sam for his conviction. Bowden knew that Cady was dangerous, but the victim's "promiscuous" back story would lead to the insinuation that she "asked for it," and so Bowden hides the evidence.

Illeana Douglas plays Lori Davis, a colleague of Sam's, who indulges in workplace flirting with him. She is the archetypical single woman in her thirties, hoping this dalliance will turn into more, and like Theresa in *Looking for Mr. Goodbar*, she hangs out in bars trying to meet men due to frustrations around her future. Because of this illicit relationship, she is targeted by Max Cady as part of his revenge plan, and after purposefully picking her up in a bar one night, he brutally rapes her, knowing she'll be too scared to testify. As a courthouse clerk, Lori sees rape cases all the time, and like Louise Sawyer, she's all too aware how tough it is for victims who agree to testify.

Douglas based her performance on a real-life victim of an infamous murderer in the 1980s. Jenifer Levin was strangled to death in Central Park in 1986 by Robert Chambers, known as the Preppy Killer for his supposed affluent background, but he pleaded guilty to manslaughter by claiming it was a case of "rough sex" gone wrong. She chose to have her character break into drunken laughter when Cady handcuffs her to the bed rather than immediately freak out as the original script stipulated, and this not only adds further to her vulnerability but offers a dramatic contrast from joy to pain and fear when he violently assaults her.

Just months after the release of *Thelma & Louise*, the media was covering the testimony of Anita Hill, a law professor in her midthirties who had accused Supreme Court justice nominee Clarence Thomas of workplace sexual harassment. As part of his confirmation hearing, she was called before the Senate Judiciary Committee in October 1991 to give evidence on her claims. During the televised hearing, people could watch as Hill was questioned by the exclusively white male panel, and rather than highlighting her achievements, she was painted in the press as an unstable single woman who struggled with being rejected by men. There was a bizarre moment when Senator Orrin Hatch waved around a copy of *The Exorcist* novel, with a claim that she had been inspired by some of the language in it. Hill was considered unreliable exactly because she was single; there was no man to give her a stamp of approval, and without it, there was speculation that there must be something wrong with her. Newspaper

152   *Single & Psycho*

headlines queried why she had never married. Was she one of the feminists who was a man-hater, or was she just an unmarriageable spinster?

A year after her testimony, Anita Hill delivered a speech at Georgetown University Law Center where she reflected on how the senators, and society, judged her. "Not only did the Senate fail to understand or to recognize me because of my lack of attachment to certain institutions, like marriage and patronage, they failed to relate to my race, my gender, my race and gender combined, and in combination with my education, my career choice and my demeanor," she said.[17]

The way Anita Hill was treated sparked an important conversation around sexual harassment, but when women put forward their own stories and experiences, rather than being believed, there was often a question of doubt. The Demi Moore and Michael Douglas movie *Disclosure* (1994) was one of those buzzy films that tapped into a hot topic and offered a twist on sexual harassment. This time it was a woman doing the harassing, but by asking "What about the men?" it only served to feed the doubters who refused to take women's claims seriously. It was women, the argument went, who were becoming more dangerous as they sought career advancement, and they were using feminism as a cover to seek vengeance against men.

Douglas plays Tom Sanders, a manager of the CD-ROM division at a Seattle computer company who expects a big promotion to the top of the company. His excitement turns to dismay when he discovers that the founder, Bob Garvin (Donald Sutherland), has instead opted to promote a woman, Meredith Johnson (Demi Moore), to "break the glass ceiling." Tom lives in a beautiful suburban home with his wife, Susan (Caroline Goodall), and two children, and like Rusty in *Presumed Innocent*, there is a subtle nod to his emasculation as his wife drives him to the ferry to complete the rest of his commute into the city.

On the ferry, Tom makes work calls in anticipation of his promotion while an older man who has been laid off from his high-paying job complains to him about the state of the world. Tom offers him his business card and suggests he call Cindy, Tom's PA, to help with any potential job opportunities. This older man then takes the opportunity to express his bitterness at the advancement of women: "Used to have fun with the girls. Nowadays she probably wants your job."

The modern office headquarters is dominated by staircases in which workers advance upward, and Tom catches sight of a pair of tanned legs and black heels climbing up this symbolic corporate ladder. We soon discover that these legs belong to Demi Moore's Meredith and that she has now taken the job that Tom had assumed was his. Meredith is beautiful and steely, and she has a heart that, according to her boss, "is made out of that plastic they use for football helmets."

As Tom complains to his team privately about her, the men use aggressively sexual language, and Tom reveals that they once had a passionate affair. Meredith invites Tom to her office after hours to discuss business over a glass of fine wine. What she does instead is seduce him, first by taking off her jacket to reveal her toned arms, asking him to rub her shoulders, and then forcing a blow job on him. He tries to resist, but in a moment to show that Douglas is a red-blooded male and not a complete pushover, he takes over the sexual domination. It's only when he catches his reflection that the guilt gets the better of him, and he pushes her away. Meredith responds in anger, screaming after him that she'll have her revenge. The next day, she accuses him of sexual harassment, and Tom is forced to fight back, accusing her in return.

After his wife finds out about Meredith's accusations, he expresses to her the travails of men in the early 1990s, who are continually being told how toxic they are: "Why don't I just admit it? I'll be that evil white male you're all complaining about, then I can fuck everybody." He is angered that "they" can come between "me and my wife, move my family out, take my job and take the family and house that we've made."

One gets the impression with this speech that it was exactly the issues that Douglas was passionate about, that it was the men who were being overlooked, who were depressed, struggling on the job market, and frustrated at the quirks of modern society, a theme he explored fully in *Falling Down* (1993). While the film did touch on passive sexual harassment, with Cindy admitting that his touches and slaps on the butt make her feel uncomfortable, ultimately it's Tom who is the victim of a maleficent career woman.

There was an expectation that *Thelma & Louise* would be a turning point in gender representation and that it would open the floodgates

154 *Single & Psycho*

for female-led movies, yet as *Disclosure* demonstrated, these didn't materialize in the way that had been anticipated. Instead, men were now painted as the victims of feminism. It took another five years for a similarly punch-the-air female-led movie to hit screens—and this time with a Black cast.

Set It Off (1996), directed by F. Gary Gray, tapped into the *Thelma & Louise* phenomenon for a Black audience. The *New York Times* wondered if, in "formulaic terms," it would be described as "Thelma and Louise Ride Shotgun in the Hood while Waiting to Exhale" because there were so few Hollywood movies that offered an opportunity to tell Black stories.

Queen Latifah, Jada Pinkett Smith, Vivica A. Fox, and Kimberly Elise are four unmarried friends who grew up together in a Los Angeles project and now earn a pittance as cleaners. After a series of injustices, they decide to become bank robbers to not only get rich quick but also rail against a society where they can't win. They are a generation of young Black women who have observed how the world is weighted against them. That Anita Hill, a lawyer, wasn't believed demonstrates that they will never be treated fairly by society. Instead, they take control of their own destiny, no matter how doomed this decision may be. "Deal with this," said the poster, as if it was a rallying cry that young, single Black women would no longer be ignored. Frankie (Vivica A. Fox) is held up by robbers at the bank where she works, but because she is Black and from the same neighborhood as the perpetrators, the investigating police assume she's involved, and she is immediately dismissed from her job. Stony (Jada Pinkett Smith) has been supporting her younger brother in the hopes he will go to college, but she is devastated when he is gunned down by police in a case of mistaken identity. And TT (Kimberly Elise) has her son taken off her by Child Protective Services purely because she couldn't afford to care for him while she worked.

Screenwriter Takashi Bufford told Blackfilm.com in 2011 that New Line Cinema initially rejected it three times because "they thought black males would not support a film with gunslinging black females. That obviously proved not to be true."[18]

It was a box office success, confirming that there was a desire for stories about women, and Black women, taking a stand against the racism and sexism that held them back. One of the most explosive characters is Queen Latifah's butch lesbian Cleo, who is in a relationship with a feminine lesbian, whom Cleo wishes to spoil with the stolen loot. The *New York Times* praised Queen Latifah for making "this potentially unsympathetic character the most endearing of the four."[19]

This depiction of a queer relationship in a positive light, despite her lover being silent, was also groundbreaking for the time, and wild card Cleo, who doesn't have the motivation of revenge as the others do, is the protective force of the group. Hers is a lesbian character who is loyal and upfront, and it was a depiction far removed from the devious *Basic Instinct* stereotype that had caused so much controversy just a few years before.

CHAPTER 12

Sex and Fear

The Sharp Edge of the Erotic Thriller

In 1992, British Home Office figures revealed that violent crimes by women had increased by 350 percent over the last decade. As Margarette Driscoll wrote in the *Times*, while it was difficult to interpret the trend, those "who a couple of years back dismissed dramatic portrayals of female violence, such as the film *Fatal Attraction* and latterly Thelma and Louise as bearing no relation to real life, have begun to re-assess their initial assumptions. Some now believe that we are seeing the tip of a post-feminist iceberg in which women who have learned to assert themselves in everyday life have also begun to take the law into their own hands."[1]

Rather than random violence, women were believed more likely to be driven to extreme acts when their relationships were threatened. One example that was splashed across UK media at the time was that of Susan Christie, a Northern Irish woman in her early twenties who murdered the wife of the army officer she was having an affair with. When Christie told her lover, Captain Duncan McAllister, she was pregnant, he insisted she have an abortion, when at the same time, his wife, Penny, was also expecting a child. In March 1991, Susan lured Penny into a forest on the pretext of walking their dogs and slit her throat.

In another much-reported incident from 1992, Christine Dryland, the wife of an army major, was sent to a psychiatric unit in London after she was found guilty of the manslaughter of Marika Sparfeldt, her husband's German mistress, whom she knocked down with her car and then drove back and forth over her body.

In May 1992, on the other side of the Atlantic, seventeen-year-old Amy Fisher, nicknamed the Long Island Lolita, shot Mary Jo

Buttafuoco, the wife of her much older lover, Joey Buttafuoco, in the face. When she pled guilty to first-degree assault later that year, she was propelled to the front pages of tabloids and newspapers as a media sensation. Three American networks broadcast their own dramatization of the events, and the story was even in direct competition with the November 1992 presidential campaign and the inauguration in January 1993.

The Amy Fisher phenomenon was a means of undermining the "feminist cause" that date rape, sexual harassment, and child abuse were byproducts of the patriarchy. Instead, antifeminists jumped on the case as evidence that it was women who were the destroyers. As William Congreve said three centuries ago, "Heav'n has no rage like love to hatred turned, nor hell a fury, like a woman scorned."

"Amy Fisher is America's Diana, our tabloid princess," wrote Camille Paglia in an essay in the *Sunday Times* on Valentine's Day 1993. "The instant myth of Amy Fisher turned feminist dogma on its head: as in the hit films *Fatal Attraction*, *Basic Instinct* and *The Hand That Rocks the Cradle*, woman rules and destroys. The femme fatale is for real." She also added, "Surely somewhere in Amy's childhood there had to be 'abuse', the feminist stock response to anything ambiguous in human behaviour."[2]

In this saga, Mary Jo was the loyal wife who refused to leave her husband, Joey, even when suffering facial paralysis and chronic tinnitus due to the bullet still embedded in her head. She denounced Amy while defending her husband as a victim of the manipulative Lolita, and she in turn was placed as the victorious wife who successfully seized back her man from the younger rival.

Given a prison sentence for first-degree assault, Amy was told by the judge that she was "motivated by lust and passion" and had pursued Mary Jo "like a wild animal stalks its prey." It may have been men who were typically blamed for their aggression and violence, but here, a woman could be equally motivated by animalistic behavior. This would be further evidenced in the raft of new thrillers in which women exhibited manipulative, vengeful personas.

As depicted in *Fatal Attraction*, *Presumed Innocent*, and *The Hand That Rocks the Cradle*, explored in the next chapter, female violence was often directed at the other woman rather than the man. Some felt it was an indication of too much power, that women had

158 *Single & Psycho*

traditionally put up with bad marriages, but now, thanks to the feminist movement, they were fighting back and overcompensating with extreme rage.

If Thelma and Louise were dangerously untethered from the domestic sphere, then Sharon Stone in *Basic Instinct* was the pinnacle of the psychotic single woman who uses her sexual powers to dominate. Her character, Catherine Tramell, was a femme fatale for the nineties, but rather than being punished for it, like Phyllis Dietrichson in *Double Indemnity* (1944), or undergoing a redemption arc like Rita Hayworth in *Gilda* (1946), she is victorious in getting away with it.

"If you're going to be bad on-screen, then be bad," said Sharon Stone. "Don't go, Wink wink wink: I'm really good at home. Go, 'I'm bad and this is what's going to happen to you, fool.' . . . My theory is that the Devil, or whatever the Devil is, is usually dressed up in a pretty suit."[3]

After *Fatal Attraction*, *Basic Instinct* provided Michael Douglas with another opportunity to act out choreographed sexual trysts in a zeitgeisty movie. The actor had won an Oscar for producing *One Flew over the Cuckoo's Nest* and was now one of the leading actors in Hollywood. He considered *Basic Instinct* to be an explicit statement against the desire to sanitize sex. He said he was drawn to the script because "I instinctively felt the restrictions of the 1990s. Doing *Basic Instinct* was not a question of breaking new ground, but possibly getting back to the 1960s or the 1970s. In other words, I think we have regressed in certain areas and ways. Moral majorities have much more control. I figured we were going to take some heat but I thought it was important."[4]

When Shane Black received a record $1.75 million for his script *The Last Boy Scout*, Joe Eszterhas was determined to beat it. He wanted to write a modern film noir with a "brilliant, omnisexual, and evil" femme fatale that would be the erotic film for the nineties. Originally called *Love Hurts* (switching to *Basic Instinct* for the final draft), his script was sold to Carolco for an unprecedented $4 million, with $1 million to go to producer Irwin Winkler and with Paul Verhoeven signed on as director.[5]

Famously, a long list of actresses, including Geena Davis, Kim Basinger, and Michelle Pfeiffer, turned down the role because of the nudity that would be involved. Lena Olin didn't want to work with Verhoeven, and Kelly McGillis and Margaux Hemingway both were rejected after their screen tests. And then there was Sharon Stone. She had to fight hard to win the role of Catherine, having been dismissed as "unfuckable," a term rampant in misogynistic Hollywood. Stone had been slogging away in the industry for many years, and despite having made eighteen films, she hadn't successfully broken through. Now that she was in her thirties, she said, "I knew this was the last chance—I was aging out of the business I hadn't really gotten into yet."[6]

Even though she had been directed by Verhoeven in *Total Recall*, playing Arnold Schwarzenegger's manipulative wife, her manager still had to call the Dutch director every day for months to secure an audition. Finally, after twelve other actresses turned it down, she nailed the ice-cool evil of Catherine in her screen test, and it made her an overnight sensation.

She was often referred to as "the last movie star" for her old-fashioned beauty and a diva-like, no-bullshit personality that was reminiscent of Bette Davis and Joan Crawford. And like those two veterans, she was considered tough, difficult, and unstable.

"When I was in my twenties, my boyfriend's best friend told me his simple theory of relationships: men are stupid and women are crazy," she wrote in her 2021 memoir. "Many years have passed, and although I do not ascribe to the 'crazy' theory, I do easily accept that I could be seen as a quirky broad."[7]

Catherine is a single woman who is in complete control of her sexuality and her power. Like a more violent and less humorous Samantha Jones in *Sex and the City*, she doesn't need a man in her life as she's independent, filthy rich, and a talented and famous author. Rather, she uses people to fulfill her sexual needs and then dismisses them (or kills them). She is cold, calculated, and psychotic, the type of woman the patriarchy is afraid of; her pansexuality and her casual dismissal of men were born from feminism.

Douglas anticipated pressure from "feminist extremists" who he thought would likely take exception to the nudity and sex. What he didn't anticipate was that filming in San Francisco would be interrupted by protesters who objected to the film's negative image of lesbians and bisexuals. This was sparked by a column in the

160　*Single & Psycho*

Philadelphia Inquirer, where Liz Smith teased that the movie was a "sexual shocker" with "ice-pick-wielding lesbians as the villains."[8]

Organizations such as Queer Nation and the Gay and Lesbian Alliance against Defamation (GLAAD) printed out T-shirts and walked down San Francisco streets with loudspeakers, announcing "Don't See It—Catherine Did It!"

As a self-described ally to the gay community, Eszterhas persuaded the director to come with him to a meeting with community leaders in a San Francisco hotel, where they faced a barrage of questions around the perceived homophobia. They were asked why LBGTQ characters always had to be the villain and why there had never been any action heroes who just happened to be gay. While the writer understood their point and agreed to take out a homophobic slur, he didn't necessarily agree. "I don't get it," he said to the room. "If someone is bisexual, he or she is not just homosexual—he or she is also heterosexual." He also argued that *Basic Instinct* was the least offensive of the current raft of movies and that Martin Short's depiction of a wedding planner in *Father of the Bride* was much more objectionable.[9] Around the same time as *Basic Instinct* was released, Queer Nation protested against homophobia and queer hatred in *Silence of the Lambs* at the 1992 Academy Awards. The Best Picture winner featured a serial killer who dresses in women's clothing, further pushing a prevalent transphobia in screen depictions of transwomen and crossdressers.

On its release in March 1992, *Basic Instinct* shocked and provoked with its extensive erotic scenes that, in the era of AIDS, placed sex as something to be feared. But most controversially of all, it showed more of an actress than ever had been seen before outside of pornography. It was one that producer Robert Evans grotesquely referred to as "the hundred-million-dollar pussy-hair shot."[10] Sharon Stone would later reveal that it had been filmed without her consent.

The moment had been set up in the previous scene, when Douglas's character ogles Catherine in the mirror as she gets changed, and we see her put on her dress without underwear. But the genital flash was a moment that Sharon Stone had not been expecting would be part of her role. She was only given the chance to see the final version of the film, and the infamous moment in which she uncrosses her leg, with the director, producers, and a room full of suits who hadn't even been involved in the production.

Having been asked by Verhoeven to remove her underwear as the white reflected the light, and with the promise that nothing would be seen, she was horrified to see the close-up of her most intimate part enlarged on the screen. She slapped her director and then went straight to her agent to ask her what her rights were. She was advised that she could get an injunction against the film and that she was protected by the Screen Actors Guild, but after giving it some serious thought, and considering all the effort it had taken to win the role, she chose to allow it because, she said, "it was correct for the film and for the character."[11]

All this controversy amounted to free publicity, and when it opened, it went straight to number one at the American box office. *Basic Instinct* grossed more than $400 million and became the watercooler film of the year, with discussions about the graphicness of the sex scenes and whether Sharon Stone was really the icepick killer at the end.

As Paul Verhoeven said, "At the end I feel we made clear that she did it, but *still* you do not want her to be caught. You might even prefer for Michael to be killed than for her to be caught, which is a statement about our interest in evil."[12]

The film proved to be stratospheric for Stone's career, and with that moment of crossing and uncrossing her legs, she went straight to the top of the A-list. As she secretly toured movie theaters in New York on the day it was released, she was awed to see the audience in Harlem cheering at her character. Catherine was the rare villainous single woman who wasn't punished for her crimes, and maybe that was progress. For a short time.

While some feminists found *Basic Instinct* offensive in its portrayal of a bisexual woman as a dangerous bitch, Camille Paglia was fully supportive. She proclaimed it marked the return of the sexually dominant femme fatale and called Stone's performance one of the greatest by a woman in cinema history. In the interrogation scene, "all those men around her, and a fully sexual woman turns them to jelly! The men are enslaved by their own sexuality!"[13]

While Sharon Stone found that the role dehumanized her, she tried hard not to be pigeonholed. In a March 1992 interview on *The*

162 *Single & Psycho*

Dennis Miller Show, she opined that female characters tended to be the fantasy of the male writer, walking and talking and acting in the two-dimensional way they saw women to be.

"There are so many rules in life, and when you are a girl there are more rules, and when you are a girl in movies, there are more rules," she said. "Because you don't really play real women very much. You play some guy writer's idea about how the woman makes him feel. So you are not really playing real people. So suddenly you're playing this person who's very out-there, not like any typical woman you've ever seen, and then she does all these things that are acceptable guy behavior, but when she does them everybody shatters."

After *Basic Instinct*, it seemed inevitable, and expected, that she would follow its success with another erotic thriller. *Sliver*, also penned by Joe Eszterhas, was set in an imposing New York apartment block, known as the Sliver, where a killer is apparently attacking and murdering its residents.

Stone had been unsure about doing another erotic movie, but rather than playing the femme fatale, her character, Carly, is a timid reflection of a bruised single woman who is struggling to get over a failed relationship. She may be a glacial blond in her thirties, but you couldn't imagine Catherine Tramell weeping when she has sex, as Carly does with Billy Baldwin's character, Zeke. He's a morally ambiguous tech millionaire who has installed hidden cameras throughout his apartment building, which allows him to watch Carly masturbating in her bathtub. Given how creepy that scene is, it's jarring that Billy Baldwin is set up as the romantic hero of the film, as if the script wasn't quite sure what to do with him.

Carly, like Alex Forrest, is a book editor, and her best friend in the office fulfills all the stereotypes of that role—with her glasses and bangs, she looks more like a schoolteacher, and she hungrily vies for a man: "How am I going to meet any attractive men if I have to do it by myself?" She also coaches Carly that now that she's single, she's ready for "new horizons. New lovers. New orgasms."

"I'm thirty-five, I'm not twenty-five." Carly laughs. "I don't need a date, I need a relationship."

Throughout his memoir, *Hollywood Animal*, Joe Eszterhas captures the seedy, misogynistic side of Hollywood, particularly when taking the reader behind the scenes of the making of *Sliver*. When

Robert Evans was looking for a redemption project following a cocaine bust, he hoped that *Sliver* would return him to greatness. Evans—who lived in indulgent splendor surrounded by, in Eszterhas's words, "bimbos"—sent a model in just a mink coat to the screenwriter's hotel, where she proceeded to pull a note out of her vagina. In the note, Evans professed it was the best first draft he'd ever read. "This movie," he said, "is all about pussy."[14]

Stone was disgusted by the unsavory behavior of Evans, and she demanded the same as Glenn Close during the making of *Jagged Edge*—that the sleazy producer be banned from set. Evans, in retaliation, did the same as Marty Ransohoff to Glenn Close; he denigrated her looks and her age. "You can't even shoot her ass anymore," Eszterhas quotes him as saying. "She's over already. She's too old. Who'd want to fuck her anymore? Who's gonna buy their popcorn and come watch her?"[15]

At the same time as *Sliver* was set to be released, Sharon was embroiled in her own *Fatal Attraction* scandal as she was depicted as a conniving single woman who seduced a married man. The man was producer Bill MacDonald, and he had only recently married Naomi Baka when he fell head over heels for Sharon on the set of *Sliver*. The headlines around the world blazed with descriptions of her as a homewrecker, and her name proved to be a subeditor's dream, generating headlines such as "Heart of Stone" and "Stone-Cold." To make it worse, Baka told the press that she had been pregnant, miscarried due to the stress of being jilted, and, describing a manipulative move to rival that of Anne Boleyn, claimed Stone lured MacDonald by refusing to sleep with him until he left his bride. Appearing on Fox's *A Current Affair* in April 1993, she said, "We were very happy. We were househunting. We were planning our future together. . . . Sharon gets what Sharon wants. . . . It's like an execution. It was cold-blooded and heartless."[16]

Shortly afterward, Joe Eszterhas left his wife of twenty-five years to marry Baka, and it would be a lasting love, complete with four sons. With Sharon Stone being treated as the homewrecker of Alex Forrest proportions, from then on, her single status and her decision to adopt children out of marriage would continue to generate tabloid gossip headlines. "Those sad *People* magazine covers don't help us get work, unless they are about being single again. As we've learned, fuckable is hirable," she wrote.[17]

164   *Single & Psycho*

The early nineties was a boom time for erotic thrillers, where the single woman exhibited increasingly psychotic behaviors. In the Hitchcockian thriller *Final Analysis*, released in February 1992, Kim Basinger plays Heather, the elder sister of Uma Thurman's Diana, who is being treated by psychiatrist Isaac Barr (Richard Gere) for obsessive compulsive disorder. Heather explains her sister's behavior as being triggered by painful memories of their father, with childhood abuse typically a cynical plot point to explain away irrational behavior. Isaac, who hasn't been in a relationship for a while, throws away his code of ethics because Heather is so irresistible and appears to be a damsel in distress who is married to an abusive gangster, Jimmy (Eric Roberts). As soon as she touches a drop of alcohol, she becomes a gnarling, violent psychotic, and this comes in handy when she kills her husband and relies on Isaac to help her to be found not guilty due to "pathological intoxication."

However, Isaac discovers he has been manipulated by Heather, and she becomes increasingly deranged as she escapes from prison and then tries to kill him, actions for which she must be punished in a dramatic, storm-whipped lighthouse showdown. By the end of the film, Diana has taken on Heather's persona ("caterpillars become a butterfly"), and in the final scene, as she enjoys a dinner date with a wealthy man, we see her expression switch to reveal her devious nature.

In 1992's *Damage*, Juliette Binoche is another sexually enticing but damaged woman who wreaks havoc on a family when she has an affair with her fiancé's father, played by Jeremy Irons. As Carol Sarler in the *Sunday Times* wrote, in words that could describe Catherine in *Basic Instinct* and Heather in *Final Analysis*, she is "a woman who leaves a trail of destruction in her wake and then exits, immaculate, without remorse or censure."[18]

There was, however, a hit film from 1991 that was more closely aligned with the storytelling device of *Fatal Attraction*, but instead of a woman, the villain was a man. *Sleeping with the Enemy* was Julia Roberts's first starring role since *Pretty Woman*, the film that made her an overnight star, and audiences lapped up this domestic thriller that inverted the *Fatal Attraction* formula. It explored, in the words of *Entertainment Weekly*, "what happens when a beautiful young woman finds and marries her Prince Charming—and he turns out to be a psychotic monster?"[19]

With the architecture porn that's so typical of this genre, Martin (Patrick Bergin) and Laura (Roberts) live in a pristine but clinical beachfront house on Cape Cod, and at first, it seems like a perfect yuppie marriage until hints about his controlling nature give way to full-on domestic violence. She follows his request to wear the black dress to the party, she appears fearful that the tea towels aren't in a straight line, and his soundtrack of choice while having sex is Wagner. His domination becomes clear when he beats Laura savagely after seeing her chatting with one of their neighbors.

After executing the perfect fake death, thanks to a well-timed storm at sea, Laura starts a new life in a typical all-American town. She blends in with the locals by moving into a cozy wooden house with a porch, baking apple pies, watching a Fourth of July parade, and falling in love with the local drama teacher.

These scenes play out like a romantic comedy and even feature a dressing-up montage to "Brown Eyed Girl" that feels like a different movie but is clearly a homage to the beloved shopping scene in *Pretty Woman* that made Roberts a huge star. As Martin's dark presence threatens this perfect domestic sphere, it further shifts tone to that of a home invasion flick. The ending is almost a carbon copy of *Fatal Attraction*, with its overflowing bathtub, a gun that finds its way into the plot, and a jump scare as the villain seemingly rises from the dead.

The domestic thriller and home invasion formula of *Sleeping with the Enemy*, combined with the threat of an unhinged single woman, would give birth to a short-lived but prolific new subgenre sometimes known as the "blank from hell" movie. If *Fatal Attraction* was responsible for inventing the bunny boiler, then this new generation would give us the single white female, the psychotic frenemy who wants to steal your boyfriend and your life.

CHAPTER 13

The Threat Is inside the House

In June 1993, the seventeenth annual Women in Film luncheon took place at the Beverly Hilton Hotel in Beverly Hills, attended by some of the most powerful women in Hollywood. Michelle Pfeiffer took to the podium to accept a Crystal Award, where, dressed in a gray blazer and striped shirt, she made clear that she didn't buy into this feminist celebration, just one month after *Indecent Proposal* had topped the box office. As she looked back on 1992, which had been named Year of the Woman due to the record number of five female senators elected to the US Senate, she had some rather choice words.

"So . . . this is the year of the woman. Well, yes, it's actually been a very good year for women. Demi Moore was sold to Robert Redford for $1 million, Uma Thurman went for $40,000 to Mr. De Niro, and just three years ago, Richard Gere bought Julia Roberts for . . . what was it . . . $3,000? I'd say that was real progress," she said of *Indecent Proposal, Mad Dog and Glory*, and *Pretty Woman*, all of which featured women whose bodies were sold for sex. Her words were met with enthusiastic applause, but it was also noticed that Sherry Lansing, the producer of *Fatal Attraction* and *Indecent Proposal*, was seated close by, next to the latter film's star, Demi Moore.[1] Her character, Diana, makes a moral choice to sell herself to a millionaire for a night as a means of saving her architect husband's dream home.

"Now is not a pleasant time to be a woman in mainstream movies," agreed the *Independent* in May 1993. The reporter, John Lyttle, also used the example of Sarah Jessica Parker in *Honeymoon in Vegas*, whose fiancé, Nicolas Cage, offers her as a prize in a card game, where she is won by James Caan.[2]

The Threat Is inside the House   167

Just as the cinema of the fifties offered two contrasting female roles, the good wife or the bad girl, in the nineties, the wife was held up as a bastion of self-sacrifice, while the unmarried woman was not just a prize to be bought, but if she was in her thirties, she was susceptible to mental deterioration.

Pfeiffer had made her own extraordinary impact at the box office in 1992, as Catwoman in Tim Burton's *Batman Returns*. With her shiny red lips and black PVC dominatrix outfit, the feline villainess was a ferocious foe to Michael Keaton's brooding superhero, kicking him in the face with her sharp-heeled boots. It was another exhilarating moment after *Thelma & Louise* and a symbol of the repressed spinster fighting back.

Her alter ego, Selina Kyle, is the ultimate representative of the downtrodden working woman and childless cat lady, with the pressures of her life turning her into an anxious, frizzy-haired mess. At work, she is berated by her evil boss, Max Shreck (Christopher Walken). When she tries to put forward suggestions on a business deal, she is rebuffed and told to stick to making coffee. Selina Kyle returns home to her cloyingly pink apartment, with only her cat for company, and she listens to a series of depressing voicemail messages from her mother and a guy who breaks it off with her because she's too intimidating.

Realizing she's left a file at work, she heads back to the office to collect it but ends up overhearing Shreck's evil plot to take over Gotham City. By the time he's thrown her out of the window of the high-rise, she's had it with men. She survives the fall after being licked back to life by a coterie of cats and wanders home in a straggle-haired daze.

"Honey, I'm home," she calls as she enters her apartment, greeted only by her cat. "Oh, I forgot, I live alone."

Driven to madness by her voicemails, she sets about stitching her costume together from an old vinyl raincoat. As she tries it on, she tells her cat, "I don't know about you, Miss Kitty, but I feel so much yummier." The new Selina as Catwoman is empowered, ready to seek her revenge on men who oppress women and a society that holds them back.

"It's the so-called normal guys who always let you down. Sickos never scare me. At least they're committed," she explains of her reason for teaming up with the other villain in the movie, Penguin.

168   *Single & Psycho*

1992 was also the year of the domestic thriller, where a seemingly too-good-to-be-true stranger comes into a yuppie's life, initially disguising nefarious intentions and then slowly revealing a threat to domesticity. These women (and a couple of men) brought fear into the heart of the home in what has been dubbed as the "blank from hell" movie. In September 1992, Reggie Nadelson of the *Independent* described them as "the woman in jeopardy" film, or "the jep movie," the mother being *Fatal Attraction* and its offspring *Single White Female.*

"'Kill the bitch' the audience would shriek merrily; Jep Movies often elicit the kind of audience participation usually reserved for female mud-wrestling," she wrote.[3] Rather than sympathetically cheering for the success of Selina as archvillainess Catwoman, we were now expected to cheer for the single woman's death.

In January 1992, Disney's Hollywood Pictures promoted *The Hand That Rocks the Cradle* as the new *Fatal Attraction*, telling the story of a vengeful and infertile widow who poses as a nanny to infiltrate and destroy the nuclear family. The genre continued with *Single White Female,* this time with the depressed singleton trying to steal the life of her more beautiful, successful roommate. Any insights into the mental health of its female villains were only painted in broad brushstrokes, but the message was clear, that unwed women were increasingly deranged and would use their feminine trappings—which, in the case of *Single White Female*, was a stiletto—to kill.

There had been a dip in the horror genre by the beginning of the nineties because audiences had lost their appetite for slasher movies as the genre became oversaturated with franchises and spin-offs. With the fall of the Berlin Wall effectively ending the Cold War in November 1989, there was a new sense of stability in the West, but rather than communism and the nuclear threat, the paranoia was now focused on the status of security in the home. The AIDS crisis had proved that the most basic value of sexual intimacy could be deadly, and like the film noirs of the forties, domestic thrillers offered a direct connection between sex and murder.

Sleeping with the Enemy, The Hand That Rocks the Cradle, Single White Female, and the rest of the "blank from hell" offshoots satisfied the horror gap, with their glossy production values, luxurious aspirational homes, and beautiful actors who find that the person they

The Threat Is inside the House   169

thought was helpful to their life wants to destroy it. *Sleeping with the Enemy*, credited with starting the subgenre, had been one of the most successful films of 1991, and 1992 kicked off with a surprise banger when *The Hand That Rocks the Cradle* was released in January.

For a low-budget thriller with no major stars, it performed better at the box office than expected, knocking Steven Spielberg's *Hook* off the number one spot and grossing $140 million worldwide. It also provoked a strong response by latching on to a hot-button topic of what happens when the children of working mothers are placed in the care of nannies. It was the fear that Susan Faludi had alluded to in *Backlash*, where politicians sought to undercut the achievements of feminism by making women feel guilty and fearful of their choices. It also hit cinemas around the same time that a young nanny, Ann Franklin, from Westchester, New York, was charged with killing the three-month-old she was caring for.

Rebecca De Mornay is Peyton Flanders, a seemingly wholesome and flawless nanny who arrives at the picturesque Seattle home of Claire Bartel (Annabella Sciorra), her husband, Michael (Matt McCoy), and their two children—a little girl, Emma, and a baby boy, Joey—to offer her services. But Peyton has no intention of being the trusted helper. She wants to exact revenge on Claire, whose complaint of sexual harassment against Peyton's gynecologist husband encouraged a wave of women coming forward and leads to him killing himself. Peyton had also been heavily pregnant at the time, and after the stress caused her to go into early labor, she lost the baby. She was sterilized during the operation to save her life, and now in immense grief, she wants to take from Claire what she believes she took from her. Peyton gains the trust of their five-year-old daughter, Emma (Madeline Zima), and when everyone else has gone to bed, she sneaks into the nursery to breastfeed baby Joey, who then rejects Claire's milk.

Rather than blaming her husband for assaulting his pregnant patients when they are vulnerable, she aims her misplaced anger at the women. It was a depressing analogy to the way women who accuse men of sexual harassment are so often treated. In an interview with the *New York Times*, the director, Curtis Hanson, told the press at the time that he had been attracted to the script because it was a different, female, battleground than other thrillers as it explored

170 *Single & Psycho*

some of the fears and neuroses of women: "The house. The baby. The breast-feeding. The scene in the gynecologist's office."[4]

The movie is loaded with metaphors for fertility and the growth of family. Claire is a botanist who is building her own greenhouse, and she wants childcare assistance at home to give her more time to cultivate it. The Bartel family is connected to green and yellow, the colors of nature; Claire wears green, they have green paint in their home, and the children are often dressed in yellow. Peyton, on the other hand, who is childless and infertile, is connected to blue and gray, implying that no life can be sustained here. As she gains more power in the home, blue seeps into the new decor for the nursery and the new clothing worn by Joey, as if she's slowly killing off Claire's influence.

Rebecca De Mornay plays Peyton Flanders with icy control—the blond *Stepford Wife* villain with piercing blue eyes, who keeps the rage buttoned up under cardigans and blouses. The *Washington Post*'s Rita Kempley describes her as "the most unsympathetic villain-ess since the Alien," but as misplaced as her vengeance is, her reasons are more explainable than the villains of other "from hell" films.[5]

De Mornay was initially offered the role of "the good wife," but the antagonist was much more interesting to her. "The script was hypnotic," she said. "I kept thinking about it. I was disturbed by it, haunted by it. I kept thinking about the Peyton part. She was so chillingly deranged, a brilliant manipulator, one of the most three-dimensional villains I'd ever read."[6]

The film opens with a commentary on yuppie paranoia and prejudice. When Claire and Michael spot Solomon (Ernie Hudson) in the garden of their house, they immediately feel afraid of this Black man until they realize he is an intellectually impaired handyman who has been sent to help them. Peyton, on the other hand, with her WASPish looks, is never questioned when she turns up at their house without an appointment and instead is given immediate trusted access to the family.

Solomon is suspicious of her conniving nature, but with a mental disability, he is easily overwhelmed by her. The only other character who sees through her is Marlene, a brazen, red-haired career woman played with relish by Julianne Moore, who delivers her lines with biting sarcasm. Marlene is an ambitious Realtor who is free-spirited and undecided if she wants children yet. She wears short skirts and tailored jackets, chain smokes, takes no bullshit, and while she was an old flame of Michael's, it's obvious he was too boring for her. It would have been interesting to explore Marlene's relationship with Claire and how they'd become best friends despite the shared history.

She delivers some of the insightful lines of the film ("Never let an attractive woman occupy a power position in your home"), and her death, under shards of glass when the roof of the greenhouse collapses, is utterly symbolic—smashing the glass ceiling proves fatal. Peyton's death is also a knowing reference. She falls from the attic window and lands on the white picket fence, that classic symbol of the American suburban home.

Rita Kempley argued that the film targeted "a particularly vulnerable audience in expectant, new or busy mothers" and wryly described it as "Glenn Close with baby lust," "Fetal Attraction," and an "anti-feminist parable."[7] It crosses over into a subgenre of pregnancy horrors, including *Rosemary's Baby*, and its screenwriter, Amanda Silver, was pregnant with her son when she was editing her script to shape Peyton into a more realistic, complex character, "someone not as overtly crazy as I had her."

Silver was in her twenties when she wrote the script as part of her master's thesis at film school, inspired by the idea of a gender-reversed *Othello*. It may have been her debut work, but she had a writing pedigree as the granddaughter of Sidney Buchman, the screenwriter of such classics as *Mr. Smith Goes to Washington* and *Here Comes Mr. Jordan*, who was blacklisted in the late forties. Her husband, producer Rick Jaffa, helped find her an agent, and her script was quickly snapped up by Hollywood Pictures, a branch of Disney.

It may have been a commentary on Nineties domestic life, but it was a very Hollywood view in its exploitation of the fears around whether women could have it all, and at the time of its release, it was criticized for the sexist implication that women should do all the child-rearing themselves. "There are a lot of women in this country who are trying to work and have children at the same time. This film, I think, speaks to a lot of women's fears," Silver told the *New York Times* in January 1992.[8]

What it reinforced was this idea of a childless woman, or one going through the grief of not being able to have a family of her own,

172   *Single & Psycho*

being so deranged that she is willing to steal someone else's. Having experienced the grief myself, from the years of unexplained infertility with a volatile, unreliable partner and then a devastating miscarriage, I found humor in these depictions. I would joke that I was one step away from grabbing an ax and locking myself in the attic. At the time of my pregnancy, and just before my miscarriage, I'd been watching horror movies as research—*What Ever Happened to Baby Jane?*, *Rosemary's Baby*, *The Exorcist.* As Rosemary experiences her own horror pregnancy, and I was unexpectedly pregnant and scared about doing this all on my own, it struck me how out of control women feel during the whole process. My body didn't seem as if it were mine anymore; a parasite was feeding off it and sapping my energy so that I was bone-achingly exhausted every evening. I was also all too aware that once an embryo has burrowed into the womb, the only way it's coming out is through a great deal of pain, emotionally and physically.

Don't get me wrong—I was also very content to be in this state of early pregnancy, as unbelievable and overwhelming as it felt, but my heart breaks for women who have been forced to carry a child they don't want. After the shock of my miscarriage, and as I sank into despair, I scrambled for a reason why it happened. I believe now that it was a chromosome issue, but one of the more illogical thoughts was because I'd watched *The Exorcist* just a few days before and that I'd been cursed for it. So maybe Peyton's misplaced revenge on Claire comes from irrational, extreme grief rather than cold-blooded psychopathy. This anguish around infertility, miscarriage, and stillbirth wasn't openly discussed when the *Hand That Rocks the Cradle* was released, and so Peyton's pain isn't fully understood. Instead, as fun as the movie is to watch, she becomes a damaging stereotype. She's a barren witch who will try to steal the fertile woman's children. When it was shown in cinemas, Peyton elicited the same response as Alex in *Fatal Attraction*—whoops and cheers when Claire finally whacks her in the face.

"I simply had no idea how many buttons I was pushing when I wrote this, especially among women," Silver added in her interview with the *New York Times*. "I knew I was on to something, but I never felt I would get the screams and applause. People yell at the screen. Either people love this film or it really angers them.

The Threat Is inside the House   173

Frankly, I tell my pregnant friends not to see it until they have their babies."[9]

It delivered the same message as *Fatal Attraction* and *Basic Instinct*, that, according to Ella Taylor in *LA Weekly* in January 1992, "hell is other women. Especially women without families." She added, "*The Hand that Rocks the Cradle* preys nastily on every insecurity known to modern woman," and while it was less showy than *Fatal Attraction*, it was "very nearly as poisonous in the hatchet job it executed on single women. And it's far more poisonous in its divide-and-rule take on female friendship."[10]

When Susan Faludi was asked her opinion of the film, her major takeaway was the misdirection of Peyton's rage on the first female victim to speak out against her husband's sexual assaults:

> There's something sort of classic about women ripping each other down over a crime that was committed by a man. Women are either maniacs or morons—that's what is so frustrating about Hollywood's depiction of women. They're either compliant, beautiful wives, and therefore the good woman; or you've got a seething monster, a witch, who inserts herself in the family manse and tries to destroy the family. It seems like we only have one film a year where women are actually allowed to be buddies and go to the mat for each other. This year, it was "Thelma and Louise."[11]

Geena Davis may have become a feminist icon after playing the gun-toting Thelma, but after being elevated to the top tier in Hollywood, she refused to play these bitch roles. She had received such a warm response from women who had felt empowered by the movie that she didn't want to regress. In her September 1992 interview with *Vanity Fair*, she criticized the "whole rash of movies now where the whole goal is to incite the audience to scream, 'Kill the bitch!' I don't want to be a part of that. I'm careful. Even the parts I take, I want to be really aware of not demeaning women by what I do."[12]

The Hand That Rocks the Cradle's huge success was encouraging for upcoming domestic thrillers that followed the same tropes. As the *Los Angeles Times* wrote, "It should come as no surprise that the latest development fad seems to be movies about

174 *Single & Psycho*

terrifying women with hidden agendas, murder and mayhem on their minds."[13]

There was a report in the *Los Angeles Times* that Hollywood Pictures planned for De Mornay to play, in a film called *Outer Office*, an evil secretary who gathers information about her boss's life to use against him and in *The Crack in the Mirror*, as both the good and bad sisters. Neither came to fruition.[14]

"It does seem to be one of those mysterious trends that, at the moment, has overtaken studio development," said Ricardo Mestres, president of Hollywood Pictures, in April 1992. "It's not a new genre, but there is a real meat-and-potatoes business for this kind of movie."[15]

The next film in the subgenre was not about a single woman but a single man—a menacing police officer who infiltrates a domestic setting when he becomes obsessed with the wife. Released on June 26, 1992, *Unlawful Entry* was director Jonathan Kaplan's first big-budget thriller, and given that its production overlapped with the release of *Cradle*, and its box office domination, some of the latter's clichés inevitably made their way in. Kaplan acknowledged in press interviews that he was encouraged to include some "genre movie stupid moments" in the last reel, such as the cat jumping out of the closet and the villain coming back to life after he's supposedly been killed. He said, "You sit there and you argue with the studio and they tell you . . . 'Go see *Hand that Rocks the Cradle*' . . . and sure enough, every one of these moments where you're saying 'don't do that,' the audience loves it."[16]

Kurt Russell and Madeleine Stowe are Michael and Karen Carr, a yuppie couple living in a stylish home in suburban LA, where he works as a nightclub architect, and she's a primary teacher. One night, an intruder breaks into their home and holds a knife to Karen's throat. Feeling violated by this home invasion, they are comforted by the responding LAPD officer Pete Davis (Ray Liotta). At first he appears to be a blessing as he efficiently arranges home security for them, but he develops a dangerous fixation on Karen. Michael begins to realize how mentally unstable and dangerous Pete is, but when Karen refuses to accept this, it drives a wedge through their marriage.

While the villain, the police officer from hell, is male, there are a couple of "single women" tropes included for good measure. Pete

The Threat Is inside the House 175

has a friend with benefits, the slutty B-girl if this was a forties film noir, whom he kicks out of his police car when he's done with her, and Karen's best friend and fellow primary teacher, Penny, is single and guileless and just a little bit desperate, much like Carly's friend in *Sliver*. She's much plainer than the strikingly beautiful Karen, and she also takes a shine to Pete, whom she believes is a safe bet given that he's a handsome and charming police officer on the surface. This does not end well for Penny, and her demise is one of the obvious scares of the film.

Ray Liotta, who died in 2022, was all too aware of the by-the-numbers horror of the film and that it blatantly capitalized on the success of previous movies that had a similar story. "It's a delicate balance," he said at the time of the film's release. "There must have been 150 writers on this. It's hard to get a good ending without being corny. *Cape Fear, Hand that Rocks the Cradle, Fatal Attraction*. All of a sudden everyone's boiling rabbits."[17]

In May 1992, *Poison Ivy* hit cinemas as Drew Barrymore's first starring role after she had come out of rehab following her addiction problems as a young teen. It was the first of a few bad girl roles she took on before successfully transitioning to romantic comedies. In this gothic thriller, she plays a girl from the wrong side of the tracks who is invited into the wealthy but dysfunctional home of a new school friend, Sylvie (Sara Gilbert).

We don't know this girl's real name, but Sylvie dubs her "Ivy" because of a tattoo she has on her leg. Ivy is established as the trashy Lolita, with her bleached blond hair, the short skirts and cowboy boots, and the tattoos, and Sylvie is completely transfixed by her. So is her sickly mother (Cheryl Ladd) and her alcoholic television producer father (Tom Skerritt), who can't help but ogle this teenage girl. Controversial at the time, the sexual relationships are very inappropriate given that Ivy is only fifteen, but she's placed as the seducer who uses her charms to break up the family. There's sex, murder, lesbianism, and alcoholism, and this all helped it become a cult classic, even if it struggled at the box office.

New Line Cinema had approached Katt Shea, known for her work with Roger Corman, to create and direct a teenage *Fatal Attraction*. What was created was a shocking and polarizing movie that was described as "laughingly bad" and "brilliant and powerfully

176   *Single & Psycho*

disturbing." *Poison Ivy* caused a stir when it was shown at the Sundance Film Festival, and at a festival for women directors in Seattle, Shea came under attack for depicting violence against women and sex with a minor. As a woman, she faced much harsher criticism than she would have if a man had created the same vision, and in an interview with the *New York Times*, she defended her position. "I've been called a male-basher and a female-basher," she said. "At a screening, one woman said to me, 'How could you, as a woman, write a character like Ivy?' And at that point, I was really into saying, 'You can't censor art to be the way you want it depicted. Because pretty soon no one can be bad.'"[18]

Despite this controversy, the movie would inspire similarly inappropriate Lolita-esque thrillers, including *The Crush* (1993), with Alicia Silverstone as a teenage girl who develops a deadly infatuation for her much older neighbor (Cary Elwes), and three straight-to-video *Poison Ivy* sequels.

If there was one film that made the same cultural impact as *Fatal Attraction*, even entering the lexicon as an expression to describe an obsessed woman, it was *Single White Female*. Released in August 1992, it was the sleeper hit of the summer. Rather than the nanny from hell, it tells the story of the roommate from hell, feeding into the fears of independent young women living and working in big cities.

While *The Hand That Rocks the Cradle* featured a triangle of female archetypes and tapped into the paranoia around childcare, *Single White Female* pitted two types of single women against one another: the confident, beautiful, urbane woman who begins to suspect her life is being stolen from her and the devious wolf in sheep's clothing, a frenemy who initially appears to be trustworthy.

Screenwriter Don Roos adapted the 1990 novel by John Lutz, *SWF Seeks Same*, and with German auteur Barbet Schroeder at the helm, it had an arthouse sensibility in its use of a gothic apartment block to elicit anxiety and symbolize mental instability. Standing in for this location was the Beaux-Arts Ansonia apartment building on the Upper West Side, and with its long corridor shots, the creepy basement where terror can be unleashed, and the creaking wrought-iron elevator, it harks back to the way Roman Polanski shot the Dakota building in *Rosemary's Baby*.

The Threat Is inside the House   177

Schroeder, fresh from the huge success of *Reversal of Fortune* (1990), offered Bridget Fonda the choice of either female lead, the career woman or the unstable roommate. She chose the less flashy part, letting Jennifer Jason Leigh take the spotlight as a vulnerable woman who mentally deteriorates as she tries to get close to, and then emulate, her friend.[19]

For Bridget, the granddaughter of Henry Fonda, daughter of Peter, and niece of Jane, it was her first lead role, having costarred as a beauty queen in *Shag* (1989) and as British party girl Mandy Rice-Davies in *Scandal* (1989), and she created a memorable impression, particularly with that carrot-hued fringed crop. She plays Allie Jones, a trendy young software designer living in a cavernous Upper West Side apartment with her boyfriend, Sam—that is, until she discovers he's been cheating on her with his ex-wife, and she kicks him out. She's lonely living on her own, and she knows she'll struggle with the rent, and so she auditions a series of unsuitable roommates in a comical montage. Then Hedy (Jennifer Jason Leigh) arrives just at the right time, in the midst of Allie breaking down in tears at seeing a photo on the fridge of her and Sam in happier times. Hedy appears shy and unassuming; she works in a bookshop, and she immediately makes herself useful—she's a sympathetic shoulder to cry on, and she's also a substitute boyfriend who can fix a leaking pipe. With her insecurities and habit of putting herself down, at first she's no threat to Allie, but she reveals an aggressive side in the way she talks about the opposite sex. "Men are pigs, I don't care how nice they seem," she spits.

Slowly, Hedy begins to infiltrate Allie's life, copying her clothes and the distinctive haircut, which was so incredibly nineties that it sparked a real-life trend. As the *Los Angeles Times* noted, not since Bridget's aunt, Jane Fonda in *Klute*, had an actress "caused such a hairstyle sensation." According to the film's hairdresser, Candace Neal, the idea for this hairstyle came from costume designer Milena Canonero because she was "so aware of what's going on in the streets, as well as in fashion. She came to me with this idea for a sexy, easy haircut that would fit Bridget's character of a sexy, but very career-oriented, busy contemporary female."[20]

This hairstyle is so distinctive, so unique, that when Allie sees Hedy rocking it, the alarm bells start ringing. We can also see what

178 *Single & Psycho*

sort of a single woman Hedy is through her moaning masturbation session, which Allie can't look away from, and from her misery-filled consumption of Häagen-Dazs straight from the tub—a clear sign of unhinged behavior (see Alex Forrest). Hedy is also placed as a deviant when she dresses up as Allie to make a late-night sojourn to an underground sex club, complete with Enigma soundtrack and submissives and dominatrices in cages.

The title of the film reflected the trend of placing personal ads, yet the problematic specification of "white" as a sought-after quality was glossed over at the time (although the "seeks same" of the novel's title was corrected). But one person who took umbrage to it was Whoopi Goldberg, who, as a form of protest, insisted on doing an audition for the film. There had been a joke going around that an agent suggested to Rob Reiner, when he was struggling to cast *The Princess Bride*, that he should consider Goldberg for the blond titular character. When she heard it, she didn't find it funny. "They thought it was the stupidest thing they'd ever heard," she says of this casting joke. "It hurt so bad." She had the last laugh when she won an Oscar for *Ghost* and then starred in the blockbuster *Sister Act*.[21]

Fonda's live-in boyfriend at the time, fellow hot young actor Eric Stoltz, had previously dated Jennifer Jason Leigh, and this added a real-life frisson to the film, allowing for interviewers to try to suggest a female rivalry on set. While Bridget described this situation as "gold" to the *New York Times*, she must have been fatigued by the number of questions around it. "Eric went out with other actresses I know I'm going to work with, too," she said to another reporter. "What am I going to do? Only work with men?"[22]

Single White Female grossed over $48 million at the box office, and just as *The Hand That Rocks the Cradle* had sparked commentary about childless women, it further reinforced the dangers of letting a woman without a boyfriend or a husband into your life. Fahizah Alim in the *Sacramento Bee* wrote, "Mental instability. That's the overriding image perpetrated by many movies, TV and media about single women today. Single women aren't depicted as just desperate and lonely. They're certifiable."[23] She went on to say, "Wasn't it Sen. Orrin Hatch, R-Utah, who suggested to the world that Anita Hill was suffering from psychological problems? . . . Since the massive success of 'Fatal Attraction' . . . Hollywood has found a new villain: the

The Threat Is inside the House   179

predatory single woman. . . . Today, society seems no longer content with simply portraying single women as unfulfilled, unhappy, immoral, home-wreckers or destitute. . . . Today's single woman is a psychopath."[24]

The "from hell" subgenre phenomenon was inevitably going to reach oversaturation, as predicted by *Variety* on *Single White Female*'s release, which concluded it was "a concept that hasn't failed yet but inevitably will."[25] Unfortunately for 1993's *The Temp*, and for Lara Flynn Boyle as the dangerously ambitious single woman, it proved to be the one that did.

The Temp (directed by Tom Holland) was described by its producer, David Permut, as "'Working Girl' gone bad," and it was a thriller that very much tried to cash in on previous successes. Finally released in January 1993 after a scramble to create a new ending, it was a huge failure, partly due to its unevenness in tone, which even the screenwriter, Kevin Falls, described as a "mess." One of the main issues was that it didn't connect with women in the same way as its precursors. There was no heroine like Annabella Sciorra or Bridget Fonda who was forced to battle the crazy usurper; instead, Lara Flynn Boyle's temp was viewed completely through a male lens.

Falls, who had conceived the screenplay in 1989, was thrilled to finally have a script that made it to production. He initially envisioned it as more of a black comedy, but during its development, producers attempted to transform it into a yuppie paranoia thriller about the secretary from hell.

Lara Flynn Boyle had shot to fame as good girl Donna in the TV series *Twin Peaks*, and she was keen to break into movies. When she heard about the role, she jumped at the chance—turning up at the audition in a short skirt, push-up bra, and "enormous confidence." In a press interview in a West Hollywood hotel, she spoke of her admiration for *Fatal Attraction*: "I loved that movie because I remember how uncomfortable men were when they watched it. But I also loved Glenn Close in the movie. She just knocked my socks off. I was so scared of her that I was afraid to open my closet door when I got home. That's the kind of impact I hope I have with *The Temp*. If I can approach that type of performance, I'll be happy."[26]

She added, "I'm so tired of seeing women get smacked around in movies. I wanted to do the smacking for once. I'm tired of seeing

180 *Single & Psycho*

women as the victims just so the men can come off as macho. . . . Of course, I'm not condoning everything these women like my character do. Like, for instance, murder."[27]

Employing the ultimate symbol of domestic harmony, the action takes place at a Portland cookie-manufacturing company, Mrs. Appleby's, where its logo is that of a granny homemaker in apron and rocking chair, and a furor arises when a top-secret recipe is leaked. Arriving at the company is Kris Bolin (Flynn Boyle), who is hired as a temp for executive Peter Derns (Timothy Hutton) when his permanent assistant, Lance, goes off on paternity leave.

Kris is incredibly helpful, and she also provides some eye candy for the office, with her short skirts and low-cut blouses, and Peter, who is recently separated, joins his colleagues in leering at her. When Lance returns from leave, he is quickly dispatched via a gruesome shredder accident, which allows for Kris to be able to continue in her role. Peter begins to wonder if this almost too perfect assistant is really the temp from hell, particularly when his colleagues are dropping off one by one and her idea for including a touch of molasses to the cookie recipe, delivered with the utmost gravitas, is lapped up by the boss, Charlene (Faye Dunaway).

Kris has a photo of her supposed husband and child on her desk, but this turns out to be a ruse. She's single and deeply ambitious, and she sets out to use her sexuality to work her way up the ladder. It's never quite clear what Kris's motivation is, apart from a ruthless desire for promotion, or what the message of the film is—beware of an overly ambitious woman in the office? Maybe those characteristics were universally equated to being a conniving witch. In one confusing scene, Peter spies on Kris through the window of her bedroom, where she is masturbating, which is a clear code for deviant behavior in women (see *Presumed Innocent* and *Single White Female*).

Faye Dunaway, reprising her Oscar-winning role in *Network* as a highly strung, demanding boss, hams it up further, and there are signposts that suggest she is the real killer, right until the very last scene. This confusion was a result of a last-minute change to the ending following a negative reaction to the test screening. The final scene was originally to show Peter in a struggle to the death with Kris on a conveyor belt inside the bakery as they both tussle in cookie dough. When her hand is gruesomely cut off by the bladed chopper,

The Threat Is inside the House   181

she is then sent hurtling toward a huge flaming oven. It sounds like a homage to Hansel and Gretel, with the single career woman now the witch who is about to be baked like a cookie.

With test audiences repulsed by the ridiculousness of this final moment, Paramount insisted on a new ending, and a committee of writers was tasked with brainstorming new climaxes, some with Lara Flynn Boyle still as the villain, others with Faye Dunaway now the killer, and this uncertainty led to an ambiguous final cut.[28]

The *San Francisco Chronicle* movie critic was struck by the audience reaction to *The Temp* during one screening as it fell apart completely in the final showdown. He said the audience "groaned, hissed, laughed and yelled things at the screen when the end came. And walking out I heard several references to 'wasting two hours of my life.'"[29]

"The misogyny is pretty much a given here," Betsy Sherman wrote in the *Boston Globe*. "It's the norm in movies and television to portray women in the workplace, and especially executives, as predatory, manipulative and sexually threatening. Kris wants to be respected for her mind but uses her body as a weapon: She wears her skirts way-high and her blouses way-low, and it's not only Peter's eyes that wander all over her body, it's our eyes via the camera."[30]

After the failure of both *The Temp* and *Sliver* (released in September 1993), combined with the disaster that was Madonna's *Body of Evidence* (from April 1993), the trend for the domestic and erotic thriller fizzled out by 1994. Instead, it was replaced by a more cynical wave of neo-noir, which included *The Last Seduction* (1994). If Meredith in *Disclosure* is a bitch, then Bridget Gregory (Linda Fiorentino) is on a whole other level. With a switch in gender roles, it's Bridget who is the user and abuser of men; she dominates in the workplace, and she is utterly devoid of emotional attachments.

In *Sleeping with the Enemy*, Julia Roberts hides from her abusive husband by taking on an assumed identity in a small town, and in *The Last Seduction*, Bridget is in the same boat, although she has also arrived with stolen loot from her husband's pharmaceutical drug deal. Julia Roberts bakes pies; Bridget stubs a cigarette out in one, and while both have handsome local men falling for them, Bridget frames hers for rape and murder.

Having met her fall guy at a local bar, she uses him for sex and, in one famous scene, pins him up against a fence like a praying mantis.

182 *Single & Psycho*

Bridget knows how to tap into male weakness by going for their ego. A particularly successful technique is to ask them to show her their penis, which then places them in a vulnerable position.

We don't know her back story, and somehow it doesn't matter. She is just a cold, ruthless ice queen without any trauma or anxiety that helped to make her that way. There's something admirable about her humor, her put-downs, and her complete dominance over men. Her appeal to women is a form of wish fulfillment in that she is doing all the things that we would never be bold enough to do in real life. She allows for a fantasy where we can be as dismissive and cutting to the man who tries it on in the bar or to use them as a "designated fuck" rather than the other way round. With Bridget as the pinnacle of a dangerous career woman, there wasn't any place left for this trope to go. Instead, the chaotic single woman shifted into comedy as she became more sympathetic and much more disaster-prone.

CHAPTER 14

The Rise of the Singleton

In May 1994, Britain's *Daily Mirror* hailed the return of romance as cinema audiences were now snubbing erotic thrillers in favor of rom-coms that offered happy endings rather than jump scares. It was the huge success of Richard Curtis's *Four Weddings and a Funeral* that same month that was said to have sparked it. As the quintessential English rom-com, with its country house weddings bursting with meringue dresses and top hats, a cast of very sweary Brits, and that final declaration of love between Hugh Grant and Andie MacDowell in the pouring rain, it launched a new type of rom-com, and with it, a desire for more positive depictions of love.

"That's what people want now. They've had enough of the aggressive *Basic Instinct* approach," the article said. "In fact, it's grown-up romance—it's real, it's funny, it's touching."[1]

That same year, *Forrest Gump*, about a simple man who is an accidental contributor to the major historical moments of the mid-twentieth century and finds the meaning of life in a box of chocolates, won the Academy Award for Best Picture, beating the more violent postmodernist feast *Pulp Fiction*.

The romantic comedy had experienced a resurgence in the nineties with the huge success of *Pretty Woman* (1990). Its director, Garry Marshall, followed it with *Frankie and Johnny* (1991), which was designed to be a more tender, far less glamorous depiction of love between a short-order cook and a waitress in a New York greasy spoon. The porcelain beauty Michelle Pfeiffer played the supposedly dowdy waitress, with Al Pacino as the ex-con who decides that they are destined to be together. Pfeiffer's Frankie is scarred from a

184 *Single & Psycho*

previous abusive relationship, and she struggles to let anyone in. An amusing thread is that they both lie about their age; he tells her he's forty-two when he's forty-five; she says she is thirty-two when she later confesses she will be thirty-six soon, and in a twist, it's Johnny who is the one desperate to settle down. Still, his pursuit of her is quite uncomfortable to watch; he's too obsessive, too keen, and just too much into declarations of love after only knowing her for a short time. If it was the female character doing this, then alarm bells would absolutely be ringing.

The chaste romance in *Sleepless in Seattle*, which was the sleeper hit of summer 1993, had also shown that less was now more when it came to sex on screen as the closest Meg Ryan and Tom Hanks get to physical contact is holding hands. It had been inspired by 1957's weepy *An Affair to Remember* and was reflective of an apparent wish to turn the clock back to the fifties. Given this call for a return to traditional values, movies were harking back to the more conservative decade, as illustrated by the remake of *Father of the Bride* in 1991 (and its sequel in 1995). Similarly, bridal magazines were said to be experiencing a surge in sales as people planned out their dream wedding.

Bernie Herlihy, deputy editor of *Wedding and Home*, provided a quote to *Daily Mirror* as she explained that weddings were an escape from the anxiety-ridden nineties, with its AIDS crisis, the recession, and increasing divorce statistics. "Only yesterday we women were busy power-dressing our way to the boardroom and admiring Glenn Close's tactics in *Fatal Attraction*. Now we're going back to basics in a big way," she said. "We want to lose ourselves in the reassuring world of romance, to escape from a world which no longer looks exciting and dynamic as it did in the heady, hedonistic Eighties, but harsh and shallow. . . . Promiscuity and casual sex are a lethal gamble with our lives. A return to the old, romantic traditions of true love and a bond for life, is attractive."[2]

Conservative commentators treated the fifties as a utopia when men were in charge, women knew their place, and suburbia was a safe bubble to raise the perfect children. Newt Gingrich, Speaker of the House, posed the rhetorical question, "Why do we have all these problems we didn't have in 1955?" on an appearance on NBC's *Meet the Press* in May 1995. He blamed the Democrats for undervaluing the family by consistently favoring "alternative life styles,"

The Rise of the Singleton   185

which he likely defined as one-parent families and nonheterosexual couplings.

The fifties may have been idealized in the nineties as a golden, wholesome time, but it was also the era of segregated bathrooms and of Senator Joseph McCarthy's House Un-American Activities Committee stirring up a zealous desire to judge another's behavior. There was a record number of teenage girls giving birth (whose babies were often put up for adoption) and a huge rise in the use of tranquilizers for the generation of miserable housewives who would form the basis of Betty Friedan's study.[3]

Gerald Celente, director of the Trends Research Institute, offered a more cynical approach. He said, "Nostalgia is a distorted view of history. People look at the '50s as a simpler, better time, and it really wasn't. Remember, the people of the '60s rebelled because of the repression of the '50s."[4]

With this nostalgic desire to see gentle romance on screen, the way single life was portrayed in popular culture also shifted. The unwed woman was still fretting about her future, but she was doing this within the confines of comedy rather than terrorizing families in domestic thrillers.

In the nineties, sitcoms were increasingly depicting new forms of single life, but Candice Bergen's unmarried Murphy Brown caused political ripples when she gave birth to a boy at the end of the season four finale. The hard-bitten journalist was considered a feminine anomaly for her total focus on her career and her rejection of family life. When she became pregnant in her forties and chose to have a baby on her own, it led to a controversy that bled off-screen and onto the front page of the May 22, 1992, edition of the *New York Times.*

The hoo-ha was sparked by Vice President Dan Quayle when he gave a speech on family values as part of President George H. W. Bush's campaign for reelection. He criticized the show for sending a message that it was OK to be a single mother (which it is) and that by choosing to have a child alone she was "mocking the importance of fathers" and "calling it 'just another lifestyle choice.'" The pushback against Quayle was fierce, and as an early example of the culture wars that would dominate politics in the 2010s and 2020s, critics from the left said it was hypocritical to condemn both abortion and single motherhood at the same time.

186 *Single & Psycho*

As the *New York Times* reported, there were mixed messages coming from the Bush White House as they struggled to respond to the furor. Initially a spokesman criticized the "glorification of the life of an unwed mother" on the morning after Quayle's speech, but he swiftly shifted position to praise *Murphy Brown* for its "pro-life values." The creator of the show, Diane English, bit back: "If the Vice President thinks it's disgraceful for an unmarried woman to bear a child, and if he believes that a woman cannot adequately raise a child without a father, then he'd better make sure abortion remains safe and legal."[5]

If neither of those options is viable, then what choice is left for a single woman—abstinence? Or for women to be pushed into giving up their babies for adoption? The Magdalene Laundries of Ireland caused deep, lasting scars for the unwed women who were kept confined there while their babies were forcibly taken away. I've despaired at the antiabortion comments that offer adoption as the simple alternative. To force a woman to go through body-altering pregnancy, the pain of childbirth (which can do lasting physical damage), and then expect her to hand over this child seems inordinately cruel and dismisses her emotional and physical needs so that she's not much more than a baby factory.

In the meantime, Quayle became a joke, and the *Murphy Brown* creators got their own back when they used him as a punch line for the opening episode of season five, airing in September 1992. It showed Murphy watching his real speech on television and then addressing her audience as reality blurred with fiction. She concluded that "whether by choice or by circumstance, families come in all shapes and sizes, and ultimately what really defines a family is commitment, caring, and love."

Following her success with *Single White Female*, Bridget Fonda played Matt Dillon's girlfriend in Cameron Crowe's 1992 romantic comedy *Singles*, a zeitgeist-heavy movie that captured the Seattle grunge scene at its height. Alongside 1994's *Reality Bites*, it reflected a move toward films that represented Generation X's frustrations and cynicism around relationships. They were named as the slacker generation, too complacent to get married, and their lives were also depicted in the sitcoms, TV series, and movies about lonely singles in the big city.

The Rise of the Singleton   187

In August 1993, a new sitcom, *Living Single*, was launched on the Fox network. Starring Queen Latifah, it told the story of six Black friends living in a Brooklyn brownstone as they navigate love and their careers. Yvette Lee Bowser wanted to create a show that depicted young Black people in a positive way and reflected the life of her and her friends. There was a will-they-won't-they plot involving Kyle (Terrence C. Carson) and Maxine (Erika Alexander), a lawyer who later discovers her maternal side even though she hasn't met the right man yet. In a later season, she takes control of her destiny by going to a sperm bank and, in a twist of sitcom fate, unwittingly picking Kyle's sample.

Black women deserved positive representation in pop culture, and the film adaptation of Terry McMillan's 1992 novel *Waiting to Exhale*, directed by Forest Whitaker, was similarly embraced by audiences in December 1995. Centering on four female friends living in Phoenix, it was groundbreaking in how it told the stories of Black women, mothers, and divorcées. It offered a refreshing depiction of Black people, removed from the trend for ghetto-set films like *Boyz n the Hood* (1991) and *Juice* (1992). These affluent characters possessed enviable homes and wardrobes, and their private lives were relatable across different strata.

Robin (Lela Rochon) is successful in business, but she fails at love, even though she's desperate for a long-lasting relationship. In one resonant scene, she sleeps with a comically ungainly man she's not that into because she feels it's just what she needs to do as he appears good on paper. Another boyfriend is a cocaine addict, but he convinces her to stay with him on the heady promise that she can meet his mother. And there's the man she is so hooked on that she keeps coming back for more, even though she knows he's bad for her.

The moment when a woman destroys her ex's belongings in a fit of rage has been done many times before and after, but I don't think I have ever been moved by it in such a way as I was when watching Angela Bassett's Bernadine do so. Her anger permeates her grief as she bundles together her ex's expensive suits and shirts, shoves them in his car, and sets it all alight. Even more hurtful is that her husband, whom she accuses of being an Uncle Tom, has left her for a white woman.

"Would it be better if she were Black?" her husband asks.

188   *Single & Psycho*

"No—it would be better if you were Black!" she fires back.

As she attacks the "white bitch" who wronged her, it addresses for Black female audiences what Albert Yanney described in his British Film Institute review in 2016, the "abiding paranoia of the alluring white she-devil."[6] We can later see this trope play out in the Beyoncé and Idris Elba–starring *Obsessed* (2009), with Ali Larter as the single white professional driving a wedge between their family.

With a gross of more than $70 million, the success of *Waiting to Exhale* showed there was an audience for films focused on Black women, and this was further illustrated with the cult success of *Set It Off*. But it would be a rarely repeated experience until Tyler Perry in the 2000s. He carved out a niche in directing and producing Black ensemble films that focused on the intersectional issues facing Black women, beginning with 2005's *Diary of a Mad Black Woman*, about a woman who is kicked out of her home after eighteen years of marriage.

Following Fox's success with *Living Single*, NBC created its own version, *Friends*, and it piloted a year later, but this time with a cast of white actors playing single twentysomethings in Manhattan. Both sitcoms were filmed at Warner Brothers' studios, but from its launch in September 1994, *Friends* quickly outperformed its rival, and by the time the last episode of *Living Single* had aired in 1998, *Friends* was a worldwide phenomenon, and its stars were household names.

Just as the Spice Girls sparked a new topic of conversation in 1996—which one are you: Sporty, Baby, or Scary?—with *Friends*, everyone had an opinion about the character they thought was the funniest and whose dating disasters they most related to. Chandler (Matthew Perry) was arguably the funniest, while Jennifer Aniston's Rachel was considered the "hottest" and a favorite pinup for lads' mags. In the first season, the character who was positioned as more of the "straight man" for the others to bounce off was Courteney Cox's Monica Geller. Out of the six cast members, Cox was the most established in her career, having costarred with Jim Carrey in 1994's *Ace Ventura: Pet Detective*, and while Monica was the glue that held the group together, she rarely topped the favorite list.

The pilot episode of *Friends* reflects the double anxiety facing women. Rachel is a runaway bride who doesn't want to commit to

The Rise of the Singleton   189

the wrong man, and Monica is dating in the hope of finding the "one." She has a crush on Paul the Wine Guy, whom she met at the restaurant where she works as a chef. In advance of their date, she tells the gang in their local café, Central Perk, that she has no plans to sleep with him, but that promise goes out the window when, over dinner, he confides that he hasn't been able to have sex since his wife left him two years ago. After offering her the glimmer of hope of a future relationship by mentioning a "fifth date," she lets him stay over at her apartment. She is positively giddy with excitement the next morning, with the loved-up grin of someone who thinks she has a new boyfriend. During her shift at the restaurant the next day, one of her colleagues confesses that she, too, slept with Paul the Wine Guy to help him get over his divorce trauma, and Monica then realizes she has naively fallen for his line.

Friends creator Marta Kauffman later revealed that an NBC executive called Monica a "slut" for having first-date sex and that she "deserved what she got." After filming the pilot, the network gave the studio audience a questionnaire to ask whether they still had sympathy for Monica, and it was a strong yes. But to even ask this reveals the attitudes of the time—that it was the woman who was judged for being promiscuous rather than the man who had deceived her.[7]

Throughout the early seasons of *Friends*, until she gets together with Chandler, Monica frequently frets about her unsuccessful quest to find a serious boyfriend. The black humor around a single woman's anxiety was laid out in 1990's *When Harry Met Sally*, written by Nora Ephron. Meeting for the first time on a long-distance drive from college in Chicago to their new professional life in New York, Harry warns Sally that living as a single woman in a big city, she is liable to die alone, and "nobody notices for two weeks until the smell drifts out into the hallway." It's Harry who lays the seed of doubt in Sally's mind when she's still in her early twenties, and by the time she approaches thirty, she cries that time is running out. Single women were now telling themselves that unless they met a significant other, they would be fated to die lonely deaths.

When British journalist Helen Fielding created Bridget Jones, she not only helped to bring the word *singleton* into the mainstream, but her fictional character also became a spokesperson for single women in their thirties who were worried about being saddled with Miss

190 *Single & Psycho*

Havisham or bunny boiler comparisons and feared their bodies being eaten by their Alsatian. The concept wasn't new—Cathy Guisewite's comic strip *Cathy*, which ran from 1976 to 2010, was an early Bridget Jones prototype who diets and is bored of her job and boyfriend. But Bridget Jones's neuroticism around being single revealed the vulnerability many women felt at a time when women in their thirties were figuring out how to balance their careers with their biological clock.

What began as a column in Britain's *Independent* and *Daily Telegraph* became so popular that Fielding created a novelization based on the structure of Jane Austen's *Pride and Prejudice*. The BBC had recently aired its hugely popular 1995 adaptation, and Colin Firth's emergence from a lake as Mr. Darcy, his undershirt clinging to his body, had become the watercooler moment of the year for British viewers.

In her diary, Bridget records her trials and tribulations over the course of a year as she obsessively notes down her weight, her calorie intake, and how much she drinks, smokes, and dials 1471. In the United Kingdom, this was a service that revealed the last phone number that had called the landline, and if you were waiting for a call in the early 2000s, you would be compelled to check. Just as Dorothy Parker's single woman in the 1920s wills her telephone to ring, seventy years later, Bridget anxiously waits for her boss, and the object of her obsession, Daniel Cleaver, to call her.

Now that she's in her thirties, Bridget is constantly being made to feel bad about her single status. Her mother's friend Una is particularly annoying—"You career girls! I don't know! Can't put it off forever, you know. Tick-tock-tick-tock." Then there are the "smug marrieds," whose dinner parties make her feel like a freak when they ask her why she's not married yet. All her friends are the definition of a Sloane ranger, the nickname for a certain type of posh, tweedy Londoner in the eighties and nineties who lived in Chelsea. "You really ought to hurry up and get sprogged up, you know, old girl. Time's running out," they tell her. "Office is full of them, single girls over thirty. Fine physical specimens. Can't get a chap."

Bridget not only frets about her weight but also about becoming haggard as she ages, as if she expects Baby Jane Hudson to be looking back at her in the mirror. She scrutinizes her reflection for sagging skin and wrinkles and finds solace in the famous women who are fabulous

The Rise of the Singleton 191

in their forties, including, at the time, Jane Seymour, Joanna Lumley, and Susan Sarandon. The problem she finds is that the men her age suffer from what has become Leonardo DiCaprio syndrome—they don't find women their own age attractive and instead want to date early twentysomethings. She's constantly given the message that single women become more desperate with every passing year, and she shakes with anger at the thought of women being given a use-by date. When Mark Darcy asks her if she's read any good books recently, she has a brainwave. *Backlash* by Susan Faludi she tells him, in a knowing reference to the feminist criticisms of how single women are treated by mass media.[8]

Bridget has been taught that there's "nothing so unattractive to a man as strident feminism," but she is schooled by her friend Sharon, or Shazzer. As the voice of reason for both Bridget and Fielding's readers, she rants that there's a whole new generation of single women who have their own money and are having plenty of fun without having to "wash anyone else's socks." Bridget joins in the self-congratulation— "Hurrah for the singletons!"

In her book on *Bridget Jones's Diary*, Imelda Whelehan considers singleton more positive than *spinster* as it is a rebellion, a kind of subculture where women own their status, like the new woman and the bachelor girls of a century before. But singleness for women was also considered a social death. In 1983, Mary Strauss-Noll delivered an exercise on sex bias at Pennsylvania State University's Women's Studies Colloquium. She compared the connotations of the words *bachelor* and *spinster*. She found that while they may be related in their definition of an unmarried person, they were wildly different in their perceptions. A bachelor is positive, while a spinster is negative, and, she pointed out, there's no such thing as an "eligible spinster."[9]

Bridget Jones's Diary proved to be a celebration of the singleton when millions of women lapped it up on its release in 1996. It sold fifteen million copies worldwide and was named as the 1998 British Book of the Year at the British Book Awards. Fielding dedicated her much-anticipated, but more controversial, follow-up novel, *Bridget Jones: The Edge of Reason*, in 1999, to "the other Bridgets." At the same time, it was inevitable that a film adaptation was on the horizon.

Four Weddings creator Richard Curtis brought his brand of magic to help adapt Fielding's novel to the screen, but he wasn't the

192   *Single & Psycho*

director—rather, it was a woman, Sharon Maguire (and inspiration for the character Shazzer), who was at the helm. It was a smash success on its release in 2001, taking $281 million in the global box office and becoming one of the most successful female-directed films up to that point.

Despite the skepticism of an American playing a beloved British character, Renée Zellweger captured all of Bridget's bumbling neuroses and further deified the single woman who fights against the misery of her failing love life. In one of the first scenes in the movie, when Bridget overhears Mark Darcy (Colin Firth) calling her a spinster with a drink problem, she's suddenly hit with the realization that unless something in her life changed soon, her major relationship would be with a bottle of wine, "and I'd finally die fat and alone and be found three weeks later half-eaten by wild dogs. Or I was about to turn into Glenn Close in *Fatal Attraction*." Then we see her in her pajamas smoking on the sofa, dialing 1471, glugging down a glass of red wine, and letting the tears flow as she sings along to "All by Myself."

In both the book and the movie, Bridget thinks the reason nothing works out for her is because she's too fat, although it's obvious she isn't. Over twenty years on from its release, Generation Z writers took great delight in finding all the flaws in the movie. There was the apparent fat phobia, but the point wasn't that she was fat; it was that she *thought* she was, and it doesn't matter what anyone else tells you—it's how you feel about yourself. Fielding is skewering the society that makes Bridget, and other single women in their thirties, feel so neurotic around their bodies that they become obsessive. All these messages in newspapers and lads' magazines of what the perfect body looked like, of being simultaneously thin but with large boobs, would have a lasting impact on how I viewed myself and some of the punishments I did to my body. There were the brain waves that I should eat rice for breakfast and knock back wheatgrass shots to cleanse my body of all the pints of cheap lager consumed in the pub. But above all, there was the relentless quest to keep track of calories, as underpinned by the latest fad diet hailed in the media, and the criticism of celebrity bodies who fell short of the ideal. So I'm not sure if Bridget was the cause; rather, she was a reflection of how damaging the message was at the time.

The Rise of the Singleton   193

In an April 2021 article in *Bustle*, a young reporter, Diyora Shadijanova, watched *Bridget Jones* for the first time and recorded her thoughts. She can't understand why Darcy is Bridget's "the one" after calling Bridget a "verbally incontinent spinster who smokes like a chimney, drinks like a fish, and dresses like her mother."[10]

In the aftermath of the Me Too movement, Hugh Grant's Daniel Cleaver is jarring to this new generation, which is shocked at the casual way he pursues Bridget, his subordinate, in a predatory fashion and that she actually enjoys it. As Shadijanova writes, "Fuckboys of today aren't as physically aggressive in their pursuits. The most they'll do is ghost you on WhatsApp, after love bombing you for weeks. I feel like (hopefully!) Bridget would have had a lot to contribute to the Me Too conversations."[11]

Watching a film two decades after it was made, particularly when taking into account the enormous technological changes that have happened since Bridget waited by her landline phone, is always going to be jarring. But the reporter is balanced in her conclusion that "a lot of the messaging around relationships and body image is unhealthy, and parts of the storyline are incredibly ignorant, but it also manages to retain huge amounts of humour. It's almost a celebration of not being able to meet the unrealistic standards of society." And that is exactly what Fielding, and the movie adaptation, was going for.

On the other hand, a serious-minded article in the *New York Times* to mark twenty-five years of the novel's American release landed like Bridget going down a fireman's pole—badly. Elisabeth Egan wrote that Bridget's "nuttiness and self-loathing read like a relic from another time" and wondered whether it's "even remotely amusing in today's post-Roe, #MeToo, politically polarized world." She concludes that "Bridget deserved better. We all did." The writer clearly doesn't relate to Bridget, and that's fine, but it doesn't mean it's invalid for those who do.

She may have decried it as antifeminist, but she misses the point. Some of Bridget's notions sound dated in hindsight, but this was how women thought and spoke in the nineties. Times have changed, and it's a positive that girls and women expect to be treated differently—but it's interesting to wonder, to paraphrase Carrie Bradshaw, are they in a better or worse position than Bridget? She didn't have social media to make her feel even worse about her life. There were

194 *Single & Psycho*

no influencers on Instagram showcasing their perfect bodies and enviable lifestyles, no trolls sending mean comments, and she didn't have Tinder as a never-ending dating scroll.

While Elgin argues Bridget made "humor out of the premise that being neurotic is cute," it's more that it's a sort of embarrassment of humor—we laugh as Bridget digs herself into a hole and struggles to climb back out of it again. It's the type of humor that has served nineties sitcoms pretty well—I'm thinking of Ross in *Friends*, when he is welded into his leather pants or goes to the tanning salon and gets the instructions wrong while in the spray-tan booth. Bridget isn't trying to use her dizziness to be cute; she just happens to be accident-prone, puts her foot in it, and stumbles when trying to give a speech. All these things make her human and relatable to every other woman who feels as awkward and messy as she does.

It's also worth remembering Bridget is ultimately in control. She succeeds in finding a job in television, and she secures a big interview despite a slippery start. She rejects Daniel Cleaver when she realizes that what he is offering isn't enough for her, and it is she who chooses Mark Darcy, not the other way around.

Bridget may be lonely, but she is fearless, and her inner monologue is funny because it resonates with so many people: the awkward mingling at parties when you don't know someone, drinking too much wine with friends, obsessing over when someone is going to call, and feeling fat and unattractive, even when you're not. This was my experience of my twenties as the single friend, the one who was failing to find a date and whose neuroticism was probably very pitiful. And if we can't look back on films that were made decades before without condemning them for being problematic, then there wouldn't be any films left to watch that were older than ten years.

Having said that, there were also skeptics of Bridget at the time of the book's release in the States, including Alex Kuczynski, who in 1998 condemned Bridget as such "a sorry spectacle, wallowing in her man-crazed helplessness, that her foolishness cannot be excused."[12]

The cover of the American edition may have announced, sisterly, that "through it all, Bridget will have you helpless with laughter and shouting, 'Bridget Jones is me!'" but for Alex, Bridget's childish obsessions, her hankering after men, was sick-inducing, as if she had

The Rise of the Singleton   195

been programmed by the glut of women's magazines that fed her this information in the first place.

Bridget's life was also delivering the same tropes of the domestic thrillers of the eighties and nineties, of the lonely single woman who gorges on ice cream straight from the tub to help anesthetize the pain. In the words of Marcelle Clements, author of the 1999 study *The Improvised Woman: Single Women Reinventing Single Life*, "It's as if as women become more successful and powerful, they need to be punished for defying the old laws. They have to be with their nose in the Haagen-Dazs; they have to be made to look ridiculous and pitiful."[13]

For her article in the *New York Times* in 1998, Alex Kuczynski interviewed Candace Bushnell, whose weekly *New York Observer* column Sex and the City had recently been turned into a groundbreaking HBO series and who dismissed Bridget Jones as outdated by about ten years. "I think it's the kind of thing that would have been written here in the 80s," she said. "Now, in Manhattan, if you're over 35 and you're not married, frankly it's not a big deal. People say you're lucky and don't bother. But in England if you're 30 and you're not married, it's totally weird. It says more about the state of feminism in England."[14]

Candace Bushnell was working as a freelance writer for the *New York Observer* when she was offered the job of columnist in 1994. She suggested it explore the single life in Manhattan, with all its ups and downs. She was in her thirties and unattached, and she and her friends who were in the same boat often felt like outliers.[15] She struggled with the expense of maintaining a certain lifestyle in the city, going to book parties to grab free drinks and snacks, and mixing with celebrities and the wealthy Upper East Side denizens who invited her to the Hamptons. She was living the real life of the fictional Carrie Bradshaw.[16]

Bushnell's Sex and the City column became notorious. Like a nineties version of Taylor Swift, men approached her to tell her that they were afraid to date her in case she wrote about them. She typically blurred fact with fiction, with her supposed "friend" Carrie Bradshaw acting as her alter ego and who could safely describe her dating life in graphic detail without Bushnell's parents realizing it was her. She also created archetypes like "psycho moms," "international crazy girls," "modelizers," and "toxic bachelors."[17]

196   *Single & Psycho*

In Darren Star's television adaptation of the column, the pink tutu–wearing Carrie Bradshaw (Sarah Jessica Parker) would narrate the lives of her and her friends, who enjoy, in varying degrees, being single. When it made its debut on HBO in June 1998, *Sex and the City* was considered a breath of fresh air in the way it took ownership of some of the tropes single women in their thirties were saddled with, both by skewering and embracing them. As an updated version of Helen Gurley Brown's *Sex and the Single Girl*, credited with giving women permission to stay single for an extended length, it was unapologetic in its promotion of a particular lifestyle, of splurging on cocktails and luxury shoes and purses.

Carrie is a columnist who specializes in sex and relationships and has a fondness for puns as she offers her insight into the New York dating scene. Hung up on a rich businessman whom she nicknames Mr. Big, she has moments when she is a complete mess, even if she acts cool and put together. She drinks too much and stumbles out of bars, she gets stoned with a comic bookstore owner who lives with his parents, and stays up all night when she has a magazine shoot the next day—incidents that could be out of the pages of my own, less glamorous, diary. She is also uncertain as to whether she wants marriage and kids. In season four, when she discovers that boyfriend Aidan (John Corbett) has hidden an engagement ring in his bag, she throws up. Similarly, Carrie irritatingly breaks into hives when trying on wedding dresses and ponders whether women are only programmed to want marriage and babies.

As Jennifer Keishin Armstrong writes in her 2018 book, *Sex and the City and Us: How Four Single Women Changed the Way We Think, Live, and Love*, "Where Bridget was sweet and well-adjusted underneath her snark and borderline alcoholism, Carrie suffered mood swings and self-sabotaging behavior. In short, they sat at opposite ends of the single-woman character spectrum: Bridget an updated version of the single woman who knows her place, and thus is quite likable; Carrie an unsympathetic character, a true antiheroine at a time when unlikable lead female characters were rare."[18]

Her friends are all different in their approaches. Charlotte (Kristin Davis) is a traditional WASP who longs for the fairy tale of marriage and kids, Miranda (Cynthia Nixon) is the ambitious lawyer who is also softhearted and vulnerable, and Samantha (Kim Cattrall) is

The Rise of the Singleton   197

the fortysomething public relations expert who prefers sex without commitment. What was groundbreaking was that these confident women in their thirties and forties could talk freely and positively about former taboos such as masturbation and vibrators, oral sex and female ejaculation—in fact, absolutely anything was up for discussion over their brunch chats. Demand for Brazilian waxes swept the world after Carrie got one on a trip to Los Angeles. The cosmopolitan became the cocktail of choice for gaggles of friends hitting stylish bars, and along with the cupcake, the Manolo Blahnik was an access point into this oh-so-glamorous world.

Sex and the City would be a representation of the third wave of feminism, which had punctuated the nineties. While the previous generation of feminists had pushed for progressive views of marriage and equality in the workplace, now women were choosing their own pleasure and placing it before the traditional societal expectations of what the pattern of life should be. It was the same message that Madonna had pushed in her controversial 1992 book *Sex* and had been lambasted for.

The pilot episode dealt with women in their midthirties who were being overlooked by the toxic bachelor who wants to date younger women. The opening used the example of an English journalist who had a two-week relationship that seemed like it was going somewhere until he suddenly gave her the cold shoulder. Through a window weeping with drops of rain, we see her desperation as she tries to find out what happened. She talks to Carrie, who explains that men in New York don't want to commit. Carrie runs into her ex, says she's just seeing a couple of guys, nothing special, and propositions him for no-strings-attached sex. After he goes down on her, she doesn't let him have his turn and instead casually tells him, "I'll give you a call. Maybe we can do it again some time."[19]

As much as she is giving off cool vibes here, Carrie also has moments of being unhinged. In season one's "The Freak Show," as they enjoy dinner after attending a book launch, Miranda tells Carrie that if a man is over thirty and single, then there's something wrong with him: "It's Darwinian. They're being weeded out from propagating the species."

"What about us?" Carrie asks.

"We're just choosy," Miranda replies.

198　*Single & Psycho*

Carrie meets Ben at a Central Park fountain, and he's attractive and nice, but she can't help but wonder what's wrong with him. When he leaves her alone in his apartment while he goes to play soccer, she rummages through his fridge, his bedroom drawers, his books and pockets until he comes home early to find her trying to crack into a locked box. She's the one who's now the freak, "the frightening woman whose fear ate her sanity."

When Miranda, the lawyer, applies for her first mortgage as a single woman, she shares Bridget Jones's worry about dying alone in her apartment. She is informed by an elderly neighbor that the previous owner was a single woman who died in the apartment, and "rumor has it, the cat ate half her face." On her own one night, Miranda chokes on her Chinese takeaway, further emphasizing her panic.[20]

Rolling Stone named Kim Cattrall its "hot woman of a certain age" in 1999, and her fearless character, Samantha, was a refreshing representation of a single woman in her forties, who lives her life without regret. She shows what it's like to be unashamedly sexual, to be great at her job, and not to have any desire for marriage and children.

In the pilot, Samantha hails Linda Fiorentino's character in *The Last Seduction* as being a strong bitch who fucks a guy against a fence. Samantha is allowed to have the same consequence-free desire for commitment-free sex as a femme fatale, who would typically be punished for her transgression. Samantha, in the third season, moves to the Meatpacking District, where Alex Forrest had also lived; however, Samantha carries no burden of anxiety. She may be in her forties, but she has never had any desire to have a child, and she barely wants a relationship; rather, she loves her life as a wealthy PR executive with men falling at her feet.

As Cattrall said, "Women who have been 'sexually free' or 'promiscuous' have been punished through the ages. Whether it's *Looking for Mr. Goodbar* or Mata Hari or Sappho, whatever the scenario has been about a woman being sexual and being up front about her sexuality, each time she was punished, killed, or abused for it—until recently."[21]

In season one, the friends travel to Connecticut to attend a baby shower for a nemesis of Samantha's, and she arrives with her flat stomach exposed and a bottle of Scotch in hand to greet the mother-to-be.

The Rise of the Singleton   199

"I don't want to be one of those forty-year-old moms," Charlotte says as the four friends debrief in a dive bar back in Manhattan. Then she looks at Samantha. "No offense."

"Well, I don't want to be one of them either. There are no frozen eggs in my freezer," Samantha replies and holds her own "I'm not having a baby" shower party to celebrate.

The thread that ran through all six seasons, the two movies, and the spin-off series, *And Just Like That . . .*, was the importance of friendship because even if marriage was secured, happiness was not guaranteed. In "A Woman's Right to Shoes," Carrie is forced to remove her Manolos at the door, only to later discover that they've been stolen. Carrie is angered at the amount she's spent on gifts for friends for their weddings and babies, and so she creates a gift registry with one item, Manolos, for her celebration of her own "sologamy."[22] The shoe was a metaphor for women's independence—she may be unsuccessful in love, but she can have a killer wardrobe. It was also a Cinderella reference that Carrie was quite happy buying her own glass slipper, which wouldn't fall off at midnight.

In season two's episode "They Shoot Single People, Don't They?" Carrie is invited to be photographed for the cover of *New York* magazine, which is pitched to her as a feature entitled "Single and Fabulous." However, after having stayed out all night, she arrives to the shoot hungover, makeup free, and chain-smoking. When she sees the cover on the newsstand, with a photo of her smoking and looking rough, the headline is now "Single and Fabulous?"

This was echoed in a real *Time* magazine cover story for the August 28, 2000, edition, with the headline "Who Needs a Husband?" The four stars graced its cover, their heads tilted with a half-smiling expression on their faces, as if they were more powerful than coquettish. But it was more of a question than a statement as the subheading read, "More women are saying no to marriage and embracing the single life. Are they happy?"

The article celebrated the new status of the spinster, when previously "your best hope was to be seen as an eccentric Auntie Mame; your worst fear was to grow old like Miss Havisham, locked in her cavernous mansion, bitter after being ditched at the altar."

While it acknowledged the positives of women choosing a strong group of friends for company, rather than relying on finding a man,

200 *Single & Psycho*

Time also posed the question, "Do the burgeoning ranks of single women mean an outbreak of *Sex and the City* promiscuity? And what about children? When a woman makes the empowering decision to rear a child on her own, what are the consequences, for mother and child?"

In a joint *Time* and CNN poll, 61 percent of single women ages 18–49 answered yes when asked whether they would consider having a baby on their own. There were now options in choosing an "alternative lifestyle," and by not following the conventional path of heterosexual marriage, it didn't necessarily mean doom and gloom. With the advent of the new millennium, it seemed that the old tropes, the Alex Forrests and the Miss Havishams and the Bridget Joneses with her tubs of ice cream as a substitute for a man, were a thing of the past. Or were they?

CHAPTER 15

Playboy Bunnies, Slut-Shaming, and the Aughts' Double Standards

There's a crucial moment in 2001's *Vanilla Sky* when Cameron Diaz's Julie Gianni is speeding along the road at daybreak, with a terrified Tom Cruise in the passenger seat.

"You make a promise with your body, just as if you've spoken it," she cries, and as she puts her foot down on the accelerator, he begs her to stop. She is in love with him, yet he treats her as a "fuck buddy," and now she's just found out that he's been with another woman—a "moth" in a big coat who hasn't even slept with him. It's enough to drive her crazy.

Cruise is David Aames, the handsome but spoiled owner of a publishing company, which he inherited from his father. He's been having a seemingly no-strings-attached affair with Julie, a sexy, self-assured actress who is always taking calls on her cell phone. Even though she pretends to be the cool girl, willing to drop by as a sexual distraction when he's sick, she has a focused intensity in her eyes, and when he says he'll call her later, she shouts after him, "When?" As the psychotic single woman and destroyer, her confident aura disguises a desperate need to be loved.

One evening, when David hosts his birthday party in his luxury apartment, his best friend, Brian, brings along achingly beautiful and free-spirited Sofia Serrano (Penélope Cruz), who is all dark hair and bee-stung lips, and her bulky puffer coat only serves to enhance her charms. Julie gatecrashes the party by appearing in David's bedroom, her naked body wrapped in a duvet, in contrast to Sofia's huge coat that needs its own room.

"I'm mad at you, Dick. We made love four times the other night," she says, hungrily kissing him, not wanting to let him go, even when

202 *Single & Psycho*

he stops reciprocating. "When will you call me? Don't say soon. I hate it when you say soon."

Back at the party, David finds Sofia and confesses to her he has a problem, a stalker, that he needs help with. "Red dress, strappy shoes? She's really staring at you," says Sofia. "And she seems to be crying. Less happy. I think she's the saddest girl to ever hold a martini."

Hours later, the celebrations have ended, and a sad Julie has desperately wrapped herself around a waiter who is still holding a tray of martinis, while David and Sofia chat and spark off each other as he walks her home to her apartment. David feels the possibility of a real connection for the first time. When he leaves her place at daybreak, he's buzzing at having experienced what might be love, and this time he's in no hurry to sleep with her. However, Julie has stalked him there, and he makes the fateful mistake of getting into her car to talk.

She's still drunk and emotional, and after accusing him of treating her disrespectfully, she cries out over and over that she loves him as she slams her hands on the steering wheel: "You fucked me four times the other night, David. You've been inside me. I've swallowed your cum. That means something!"

She charges through a red light, putting her foot on the accelerator as he pleads for her to stop. But it's too late—the car swerves off a bridge and crashes into a wall, leaving David with life-changing injuries. He will try to recreate his love for Sofia through a *Jules et Jim* poster, Bob Dylan cover art, and the vanilla sky of a Monet painting, but it's all been destroyed by the actions of an obsessive woman. Even after Julie has apparently been killed in a car crash, she makes a return in David's bed, where this time he smothers her with a pillow.

If it sounds much like the actions of Alex Forrest, the *Californian* advised, "Don't let the trailer fool you—this is NOT a hip, new age variation of 'Fatal Attraction.' There is nothing 'vanilla' about the plot."[1] Instead, the movie is a trick of the mind, in which David scrambles to recreate the reality that he should have had, before Julie stole it from him.

In the original Spanish version, *Abre Los Ojos* (1997), Diaz's character was supposed to be older and less attractive than Penelope Cruz's (who played the same role in both versions). To make it less implausible that Cruise would reject the willowy blond Diaz, so often billed as every man's dream, director Cameron Crowe made her much more unhinged as she flashes her Joker smile, laughs wildly, and then lets the mask slip. She's the single woman who appears to adore her life of cocktails and work calls, yet it covers a desperation that can break into psychotic behavior at any moment.

Twenty years after *Fatal Attraction*, and in a world of *Sex and the City* and *Bridget Jones*, it appeared on the surface that there was a greater appreciation of single life. By the midnineties, the straight single woman was more visible than ever, as the first generation to benefit from second-wave feminism had now grown up. Betty Friedan had focused on marriage and workplace equality, but single women and, in particular, lesbians had largely been forgotten. What the flourish of feminism in the early to midnineties switched to was abortion rights and sexual violence, and with its spokespeople the powerful riot grrrl bands like Bikini Kill, it made single women much more visible. Thanks to Bridget Jones, there was a shift from *spinster* to *singleton*, and she was celebrated as long as she was doing it in the acceptable way—being feminine, soft, and sexual.

Television's *Ally McBeal*, debuting in 1997, was often hailed as the spirit of the third wave. Calista Flockhart plays Ally, a talented lawyer at Boston firm Cage and Fish, who finds herself working with her ex-boyfriend, whom she still has feelings for and who is now married to another lawyer. Ally's life plan, of starting a family at twenty-eight, isn't going smoothly. We see her inner world with comedic hallucinations around motherhood, including the famous dancing baby soundtracked with "Hooked on a Feeling," which brings to life the idea of the ticking clock. "How did I get to be such a mess so soon in my life?" she typically asks herself, and she uses the lessons of her personal life in her court summations, which she delivers wearing her characteristic short skirts and business jackets. Her loneliness is further emphasized by her thoughtful solo walks, often at the end of episodes, as she contemplates which way her life is going.

As the most popular female character on television at the time, she was the stereotype of a woman whose success has hindered her private life, but if Ally could be seen as an American Bridget, there was one difference; Ally is great at a job, whereas Bridget manages to jinx all areas of her life, including her career. Both, however, believe that the root to their happiness is finding a long-term relationship. On the cover of the June 29, 1998, edition of *Time* magazine, Ally

204 *Single & Psycho*

McBeal's head appeared as a cutout on a black background, alongside the suspended heads of feminists Susan B. Anthony, Betty Friedan, and Gloria Steinem, with the question "Is Feminism Dead?" The accompanying article opined how nineties feminism had descended into silliness, visible through a popular culture that is "insistent on offering images of grown single women as frazzled, self-absorbed girls." It questioned whether Ally McBeal was really progress, or if it marked the death knell for feminism: "Maybe if she lost her job and wound up a single mom, we could begin a movement again."[2]

"She's not a hard, strident feminist out of the '60s and '70s," said the creator of *Ally McBeal*, David E. Kelley. "She's all for women's rights, but she doesn't want to lead the charge at her own emotional expense."[3]

Time described Ally McBeal and Bridget Jones as the products of "Camille Paglia syndrome," where their feminism was linked to their sexuality. In her 1990 book, *Sexual Personae*, Paglia believed that women held power over men, who were weakened by their desire for the female body. Following the same argument as the sexologists from the twenties, she told women that they shouldn't expect men to be able to control themselves with sex, so it was up to them to own their power. Further, former Princeton student Katie Roiphe's controversial book *The Morning After*, published in 1993, argued that heightened date rape awareness on college campuses was creating an unnecessary culture of sexual fear. She insisted that feminism had created a hysteria where *harassment* was a blanket term for feeling uncomfortable, and with date rape an accusation for any regrettable encounter, this victimhood was undermining real victims.

Another ambitious single woman who found that her sexuality was used against her, and who was thrust into an international scandal, was Monica Lewinsky, a young White House intern. When news of her affair with President Bill Clinton broke, she was subjected to the double standards of the late nineties and became, in her words, the "patient zero" of being shamed on the internet.

She was only twenty-two years old, and there was a clear power imbalance between a young intern and the commander-in-chief, but the criticism was targeted mainly at her, as she was labeled a "slut," a "home-wrecker," and a *Fatal Attraction* type. When the full report of the affair was released by Kenneth Starr, it provided salacious insight

Playboy Bunnies, Slut-Shaming, and the Aughts' Double Standards   205

into what, and who, went down in the Oval Office. In a piece in the *Washington Post*, Megan Rosenfeld and Michael Colton wrote that it provided "a keyhole view of a young woman's hopes, dreams and sexuality," with readers of the report imagining her "as the star of either 'Fatal Attraction' or 'Seduced and Abandoned'—or 'Dumb and Dumber.'"

Maureen Dowd in the *New York Times* wrote an op-ed following Monica's appearance before the grand jury, where she was forced to give evidence of her affair. She was painted as both frivolous and obsessive, with her attention-seeking need to give gifts of ties to the president. When the news was filled with reports of Clinton trying to repair his relationship with his wife, Hillary, and daughter, Chelsea, "that woman stamped her feet. Like the Glenn Close character in 'Fatal Attraction,' Monica Lewinsky issued a chilling ultimatum to the man who jilted her: I will not be ignored."[4]

While it was Clinton's team who had spread the rumors she was a stalker living in a fantasy world, Dowd conceded that while "she is not a stalker, since Mr. Clinton encouraged her interest for quite some time, she is certainly aggressive. Otherwise, as a mere intern, she could not have barged through all the protective layers around the president . . . Monica has at least one special talent: she is relentless. It was the quality that got her noticed by Bill Clinton, and it is the quality that will prevent him from ever escaping her."[5]

Some of the second-wave feminists came to President Clinton's defense. Gloria Steinem, in an op-ed piece for the *New York Times*, insisted the relationship was consensual, and therefore he couldn't be accused of sexual harassment.[6] *Backlash* author Susan Faludi also made excuses for the president when she said, "If anything, it sounds like she put the moves on him."[7]

If feminists were quick to defend him it was because, as a Democrat, he was pro-choice and had made positive changes to women's rights, such as signing into law the Family and Medical Leave Act, making childcare a priority, and appointing Ruth Bader Ginsburg to the Supreme Court. It not only set up Monica to be slut-shamed and depicted as a stalker, but it was also a dramatic reverse from the victories made, that men should not use their power in the workplace to take advantage of women for sex.

206 *Single & Psycho*

It also marked a shift into a postfeminist Camille Paglia and *Sex and the City* landscape. By the millennium, the gains of the women's movement had been twisted and co-opted to demonstrate that the job of feminism had been done. A generation of women had grown up with the idea that they could work and earn their own money in a world that had moved beyond misogyny. They had achieved equality and independence; they were more visible than ever in film, television, and literature; and they were driving culture and consumerism as they moved on from the "old maid" and "spinster" stereotypes.

In 2001, the *Economist* coined the term "the Bridget Jones Economy" to celebrate this new demographic that was being courted by advertisers: "More than any other social group, they have time, money and a passion for spending on whatever is fashionable, frivolous and fun."[8]

The article noted that in the US 2000 census, one-person households outnumbered married families with children for the first time. While it also included divorced, widowed, and elderly singles, the biggest rise in the nineties was young people living alone. The explanation given for this shift was the increasing number of women in higher education who were studying law and medicine. As they enjoyed the salary and the challenging work, they delayed having marriage and children.[9]

On November 5, 2000, Britain's *Observer* newspaper, in a special "Singles" issue, dubbed the 2000s as the "Singles Century," with the prediction that by 2010, half the UK population would be unmarried. For the first time in history, being single was "a proactive lifestyle choice, like the car you drive, the food you eat, or the books you read."

As the single stigma was supposedly fading, they claimed that "even the late-90s stereotypes already seem out of date. Single woman doesn't ring 1471 (à la Bridget Jones) as soon as she gets in through the door. She isn't hung up on her first love (à la Ally McBeal). And single man doesn't go through his little black book the minute he's been dumped (à la High Fidelity)."[10]

Women celebrated being a Carrie or a Miranda, and even a voracious Samantha, with their independence and freedom, the shoe fetishes and boozy brunches that came along with it. As *USA Weekend* said at the time, *Sex and the City* told viewers that "being single is no longer a disease." The show was also a huge success in Japan, as young

Playboy Bunnies, Slut-Shaming, and the Aughts' Double Standards   207

single women, who had previously been nicknamed the "parasite single" for still living with their parents or "Christmas cake" because it goes stale after December 25, began to claim more power in their relationships. It also appealed for its fashion—Japanese women were style conscious and expressed themselves in unique ways, as seen with the Harajuku street style, which flourished at the turn of the twentieth century.

Yet despite the supposed liberation, there was a new challenge to contend with—postmodern sexism. Misogyny was covert, disguised within the double standards of the times. It was Janet Jackson being canceled after accidentally, and very briefly, flashing her breast during the 2004 Super Bowl half-time show, while her co-performer, Justin Timberlake, was allowed to thrive.

As Anthea Taylor in *Single Women in Popular Culture* wrote, "Postfeminism, rather than a simple backlash, signals how feminism is being reworked and renegotiated in media culture, often in politically troublesome ways. It led to a panic around single women and their marriage prospects. Women aren't considered viable unless they are partnered."[11]

There were new terms popping up to describe single women, which helped create this idea that they were frivolous and immature. There were *freemales* and *TWITS* (teenage women in their thirties); the SYF, or single young female, independent and driven by consumerism; and for women in their forties who were living like Samantha Jones, they were predatory *cougars*. There were other phrases such as *quirkyalones*, which was coined by author Sasha Cagen in 2004 to describe "a person who enjoys being single (but not opposed to being in a relationship) and generally prefers to be alone rather than being on a date for the sake of being a couple."[12]

Vanilla Sky demonstrated that there were different ways to be single. You could be a martini-swilling, stiletto-wearing Julie who masks her desperation, but it was better to be Sofia, the unjaded girl, who holds back as she knows she is the prize. At the same time, there were mixed messages that in this postfeminist world of the aughts, women were expected to be empowered by being sexual.

In the early 2000s, Cameron Diaz, the woman who had launched her career by spinning through a revolving door in a tight red dress in *The Mask* (1994), had a reputation as a sexy goofball. Despite her

208 *Single & Psycho*

obvious model looks, she was taken seriously because of her decision to play against type in films like *Vanilla Sky*, for which she was nominated for a Golden Globe, *There's Something about Mary* (1998), *Being John Malkovich* (1999), and as the voice of an ogre in *Shrek* (2001).

Her singleness was typically celebrated, and male journalists salivated over her being a "guy's girl" who, in the words of an *Esquire* journalist, is the type of girl "men can drink and golf and wrestle and fish and cuss and spit and fart and shower with. These would also be girls who can do all those things and never not be easy on the eyes while doing them."[13] She was the type who was so accurately described in Gillian Flynn's *Gone Girl* as "the cool girl."

As well as being game for uglifying herself in movies, she also played up to being the sweet, fun-loving Natalie in the hit movie *Charlie's Angels* (2000), which reflected a new era of strong, kick-ass women who were as adept at karate as they were dressing up as yodeling Heidis. In its 2003 sequel, the Angels team up with burlesque troupe the Pussycat Dolls for one action sequence where they tease by performing in skimpy clothing before chasing the bad guy down an alleyway. This was the dichotomy of the aughts era, as empowerment was so entwined with being sexy. There had been a massive shift from nineties androgyny, of the Generation X slackers in plaid and punk singers like Courtney Love, Shirley Manson, and Alanis Morissette, the women I was raised on, to something much pinker, girlier, and raunchier.

Betty Friedan in 1997 celebrated the closing down of the Playboy nightclubs as a result of the women's movement—"it no longer seemed sexy, evidently, for women to pretend they were 'bunnies,'" she wrote. But she spoke too soon.[14] Just two years after Betty Friedan's reflections, it was clear that a new drive for femininity was being pressed on girls and women. Precocious teen singers Britney Spears and Christina Aguilera were in the charts, wearing their jeans low-slung (riding on their hips) and flashing belly-button rings, and Playboy's bunny ears were perkier and more marketable than ever.

As an outdated relic, the last Playboy Club had closed in 1986, but with a sense of postmodern irony, it was ripe for a return. The bunny logo was featured on pencil cases and mobile phone covers and on a gold pendant worn by Carrie Bradshaw. Bridget Jones arrives at a

Playboy Bunnies, Slut-Shaming, and the Aughts' Double Standards 209

garden party in bunny ears and corset, and in *Legally Blonde* (2001), Reese Witherspoon's Elle Woods makes an overdressed (or underdressed) entrance at a Harvard party in the hopes she can win back the man who dumped her.

In an interview with Italian journalist Oriana Fallaci in 1967, *Playboy*'s founder, Hugh Hefner, revealed why he chose the bunny as the symbol of the Playmate. The soft and playful animal, he believed, was the perfect representation of the sexually compliant, desirable woman who is always pleasing, never difficult: "She is never sophisticated, a girl you cannot really have. She is a young, healthy, simple girl—the girl next door . . . we are not interested in the mysterious, difficult woman, the femme fatale, who wears elegant underwear, with lace, and she is sad, and somehow mentally filthy. The Playboy girl has no lace, no underwear, she is naked, well-washed with soap and water, and she is happy."[15]

Feminists in the seventies had protested against Miss World and *Playboy* to show that women were more complicated than the naked and scrubbed Playboy bunny, that their existence wasn't merely for being looked at and caressed. But culture spoke otherwise in the aughts. Instead of burning their bras, women were told that a pushup bra enhanced their powers.

It was what Ariel Levy described as "raunch culture" in her 2004 book *Female Chauvinist Pigs*, where the aesthetics of the sex industry had become mainstream by being marketed to young women as "empowering." Playboy Bunny T-shirts, thongs, pole-dancing classes, Brazilian waxes were all essential tools for desirability. Overnight, it seemed that having a mound of pubic hair was considered unattractive and unfeminine. "We'd earned the right to look at Playboy; we were empowered enough to get Brazilian bikini waxes. Women had come so far, I learned, we no longer needed to worry about objectification or misogyny," wrote Levy.[16]

In 1997, an opportunistic entrepreneur from LA called Joe Francis founded his own videotape company, Girls Gone Wild, by convincing college-age girls (and some underage girls) that they would find freedom in flashing for the camera or by making out with their friends and even performing sex acts. By the 2000s, it had become an empire, with an increasingly explicit catalog raking in millions, with trucker caps and bikinis for sale, celebrity endorsements from Ashton

210   *Single & Psycho*

Kutcher and Paris Hilton, and a growing number of young women waking up the next morning with a hangover and huge regrets that their drunken moment would be readily available for all to see.

Throughout the aughts, there were mixed messages for women around whether to celebrate being single or if they were wasting their years working hard and playing hard rather than trying to secure a family. While Carrie Bradshaw may have been a role model whose life many young women wished to emulate, it was made clear that the goal was for heterosexual coupling, and there was a raft of dating manuals that could be used as a guide.

Reality television included shows where single women competed for the attention of one man, including *The Bachelor, Joe Millionaire, Average Joe*, and Australia's *The Age of Love*, in which twentysomething "kittens" were pitted against fortysomething "cougars" to win over tennis ace Mark Philippoussis. The contestants on these shows, whose looks generally followed the beauty queen standard, were expected to strip off to bikinis, to be flirty and flattering to the man, and to prove that they were honest and deserving of the ultimate prize—marriage. The best way to survive elimination was to show restraint by not drinking too much or having sex too early. If they exhibited any *Fatal Attraction* behaviors, they would be punished with a swift removal from the house.

Despite the celebration of singleness, marriage was still the end goal for women, and with an increase in the numbers of unmarried women, relationship guides thrived in the 1990s and 2000s as a tool to help women navigate their escape from a spinster fate. Some of these guides had messages about learning to love yourself first, but by far the most popular were the ones that instructed women to do the opposite of what feminists had taught. *The Rules: Time-Tested Secrets for Capturing the Heart of Mr. Right* became a cultural phenomenon when it was published in 1995 and provoked much discussion for being either outrageously regressive or incredibly insightful. Authors Ellen Fein and Sherrie Schneider marketed their guide to the modern, educated single woman who couldn't work out why she was mangling her love life.

To secure that ring on the finger, as promised on the cover of the book, women were advised to follow the strict rules, which included never approaching or initiating a conversation, avoiding eye contact, or acting like you wanted sex too much. Women were never to phone the man first or even call back, and they were advised to withhold their real personality for as long as possible. The message was not to be too emasculating, which was code for "too feminist."

"In a relationship, the man must take charge," the authors schooled. "He must propose. We're not making this up—biologically, he's the aggressor." This was clearly where Alex Forrest had gone wrong. Traces of *The Rules* could be seen in the rom-coms coming out of Hollywood in the 2000s. Typically they dealt with the modern travails of the career girl (often working in media, perhaps on a snappy women's magazine) who leads an ultra-glamorous life, but all that's missing is the love of a good man.

How to Lose a Guy in 10 Days (2003) took the idea of following a dating manual like *The Rules* and flipping it to demonstrate all the crazy things a woman should not do if she wanted to maintain a relationship. Kate Hudson plays Andy Anderson, a blonder version of Carrie Bradshaw who works as the how-to girl at a women's magazine, but has ambitions to be a "serious" journalist. Beautiful, confident, cool, and with the ability to turn on any man, she's the opposite of her best friend and colleague, Michelle (Kathryn Hahn), who is a Bridget Jones mess, down to thinking she's too fat. We first meet her in her chintzy apartment, sobbing to Andy after another breakup despite it being "the best week of my life." As far as she's concerned, things were going great, but then he started "getting really busy, and I didn't know where he was. I kept calling him, calling him, but he was never home."

"You kept calling him?" Andy cringes.

"I didn't leave him a message. He didn't know it was me. My number's blocked."

As Andy tells her, "Michelle, if the most beautiful woman in the world acted the way you did any normal guy would still go running in the other direction."

Michelle insists that no man would ever run away from Andy, and so it becomes a basis for a new how-to article on how to drive a guy away, using the classic mistakes women like Michelle make—calling too much, being clingy, accusing him of thinking she's too fat, crying during sex. When Andy meets advertising executive Ben (Matthew McConaughey) at a bar, she selects him as her hapless victim, but

212 *Single & Psycho*

what she doesn't realize is that he's been assigned a bet himself, to make a woman fall in love with him in ten days. No matter what Andy throws at him, the stakes of his bet—to win the account of a diamond company—are too high.

In reality, Andy munches burgers with bacon without worrying about the calories, loves basketball, and is down with hanging with the guys in the restaurant kitchen so that she doesn't miss a second of the game. She'd be any man's fantasy, but for the sake of her article, she must hide her true personality by pretending she'd prefer Celine Dion over sports, filling his bathroom cabinet with her tampons, and giving his penis a cutesy name. Ben can't fathom why she switched from the "good Andy," who is amazing, fun, cool, sexy, into "evil Andy," who, his colleague cracks, is probably bipolar.

Her pinnacle of unhinged behavior is displayed at Ben's weekly poker night with the guys. Frustrated at being unable to break Ben, Andy ramps it up by invading this male space, knocking beer over the poker table, ripping the pizza from their mouths and replacing it with healthy snacks, and crying over Ben's neglect of their "love fern."

"Is she on something?" his friend Thayer asks. "God, I hope so," says Ben, doing a crazy symbol with his hands. By the end of the movie, after Andy and Ben have been "outed" for their ulterior motives, Ben discovers Andy's true "good" nature, and they are able to have the happy ending.

In 2004, *Sex and the City* came to its conclusion after six celebrated and revolutionary seasons. In the final episodes, Carrie feels she's ready to settle down with Russian artist Aleksandr Petrovsky (Mikhail Baryshnikov), but knowing that she's approaching forty and is therefore at a crucial point for her fertility, he reveals he's had a vasectomy. As she confides her dilemma to Charlotte over a black-and-white cookie, her friend schools her, "We're thirty-eight! These are the years."

"Yes, I know. I've heard. I'm running out of time. I don't even have time to eat this cookie. . . . It's so good I forgot to have children."

By the end of the final episode of the series in 2004, each woman was now in a committed relationship, and Carrie had secured the love of the elusive Mr. Big. Even though Carrie, in a voiceover, insists that the greatest love is the one "you have with yourself," it reinforced the message that a happy ending was to be found in coupledom. In 2008, Beyoncé hailed the single woman in her hit "Single Ladies (Put a Ring on It)." However, it wasn't so much a celebration of being uncoupled but rather a clapback to men that they better propose, or she'll dance with another.

The anxiety around singledom versus marriage was further nourished by alarmist advice from experts. In 2002, Sylvia Ann Hewlett's book *Creating a Life: Professional Women and the Quest for Children* was a warning to women that their egg quality would begin to decline at twenty-seven. The claim that women had been lied to when they were told they could wait until forty or later to have babies helped to turn her book into a bestseller.

Time featured the themes of Hewlett's book in an article, "Making Time for a Baby," in the April 15, 2002, edition: "Listen to a successful woman discuss her failure to bear a child, and the grief comes in layers of bitterness and regret. This was supposed to be the easy part, right? Not like getting into Harvard. Not like making partner. The baby was to be Mother Nature's gift."[17]

The figures revealed were startling—at twenty, the risk of miscarriage was about 9 percent; it doubled again by the time a woman reached her early forties, and at forty-two, 90 percent of a woman's eggs were abnormal. Hewlett described it as an "epidemic of childlessness," and she said her message was being cruel to be kind, by giving women a wakeup call in the face of false optimism as to the reality of whether they can achieve it all.

That word, *abnormal*, to describe her aging eggs further emphasized what was wrong with women in their forties who had left it too late. In the 1970s, one in ten American women didn't have children. By 2010, it was almost one in five.

In the age of the internet, and with a huge market in celebrity gossip magazines, famous women in the aughts faced tougher scrutiny than ever. Tabloids beat down on them for their weight, their skin, their fashion choices, their love lives—whether they were tragically single, with too many relationships under their belts, or were lovelorn after a divorce. This was the ailment placed on Jennifer Aniston. Her stereotyping in the media epitomized the "creeping nonchoices" described by Hewlett because, as a single thirtysomething, she, of course, would be tormented by the ticking clock.

214 *Single & Psycho*

When Aniston was profiled in *Vanity Fair* in May 2001, she was painted as the woman who had found the golden goose—a career and love in the shape of Prince Charming, husband Brad Pitt (whom she married in 2000). A happily-ever-after with children was all but guaranteed. As she chatted to reporter Leslie Bennetts, the actress was pragmatic as she insisted she was still figuring life out herself. Raised by divorced parents, she said she "didn't have a fantasy of what marriage would be like." She also exclaimed that she didn't "feel like a role model—god, no, I'm a mess!" She backtracked at this candor: "I mean, I'm not a mess, but we're all just trying to figure it out, to do the best we can."

She struggled with feelings of not being good enough—of being told to lose weight by her agent to make her castable and then criticized for losing too much weight as she became sleeker and glossier with each season on *Friends*. As one of the most popular figures on television, she wasn't in any hurry to have a baby, although, she confided, Brad was keen on having seven children: "He loves the idea of having a huge family. But you just never know. Whatever will be, will be." By 2004, with her ten-year run on *Friends* coming to a close, she and Pitt would have more time to start planning.

By the time of her second *Vanity Fair* interview in 2005, she was divorced from Brad and was now a much sadder Jen. Leslie Bennetts returned to interview her, and as she opened the door to her Malibu bungalow, she burst into tears. The reporter detailed the aftermath of her breakup with Brad Pitt, when endless cover stories in tabloids and gossip magazines splashed with the tragedy of her love life and her fertility.

America's sweetheart had been replaced in Brad's affections by Angelina Jolie, a woman who was not only considered sexier and more mysterious but also more maternal. Following the announcement of their separation, there was wild gossip that he and Jolie's relationship had heated up after costarring in the action movie *Mr. and Mrs. Smith* (2005), and they were captured in paparazzi photos together with Brad acting as father to her adopted son.

Aniston, on the other hand, who was thirty-six and had, according to Bennetts, "expected to spend the past year being pregnant, the pain of watching this spectacle unfold was compounded by vicious rumors about herself."[18] There were sensational stories that the reason the marriage ended was because she refused to have Pitt's baby as she was too hung up on her career.

"A man divorcing would never be accused of choosing career over children," she said. "That really pissed me off. I've never in my life said I didn't want to have children. I did and I do and I will! The women that inspire me are the ones who have careers and children; why would I want to limit myself? I've always wanted to have children, and I would never give up that experience for a career. I want to have it all."

Across the covers of tabloids, her life became a soap opera. Headlines blared that she was "devastated," "furious," or seeking "revenge." Jen's love life was a focus of media gossip for the next decade following her relationships with actors Vince Vaughn and Justin Theroux and with much speculation about whether she was ever going to have that elusive child. She cleared it up in an interview with *Allure* in 2022. "It was really hard," she said. "I was going through IVF, drinking Chinese teas, you name it. I was throwing everything at it. I would've given anything if someone had said to me, 'Freeze your eggs. Do yourself a favor.' You just don't think it."

Like Aniston, when I was in my early thirties, it never occurred to me to freeze my eggs. It wasn't promoted as an option in the same way as it is now, and I was unaware that egg quality diminishes. I just knew that the age of forty was supposedly the cut-off point for all sorts of things—marriage, children, hope. I even made half-hearted pacts with male friends that if we were still single by the time we were forty, we'd have a child together. One even jokingly typed it into the calendar on his phone to remind him in seven years as we sat in the pub firing around banter about the future. After the miscarriage, I thought about my options as a forty-one-year-old. I posted on a women's Facebook group because I had this desperate desire desire to express my pain, and a suggestion was put out there—Why not single motherhood? Why not do IVF on your own with a sperm donor? There were options available, but they cost money, and I also wondered if I could cope on my own and if it was fair to a child not to know their father. Maybe I could ask one of those male friends who, like me, were still single but didn't have the pressure of time weighing down on them. All these choices had to be weighed up, and at my age, and with the statistics telling me that my egg quality was diminishing

216 *Single & Psycho*

every month, if it was truly what I wanted, I had to act quickly. But what if I wasn't meant to be a mother after all, and I could embrace being child-free? I could try to accept the situation because I loved my independence, I was happy in my own company, and maybe I was only thinking I wanted children because of the messaging that had fixed itself in my brain. I had been an avid reader of the celebrity gossip magazines that placed "Sad Jen" on the front cover, making assumptions and judgments about her choices, and no doubt they had made an impression on me too.

The movies that Jennifer Aniston specialized in also reflected some of the dilemmas she, and I, and other women in their thirties and forties faced. *The Break-Up* (2006), costarring Vince Vaughn, detailed the aftermath of a crumbling long-term relationship. In *The Switch* (2010), her single character chooses donor sperm, only to find that her best friend switches it for his own when drunk, and in *He's Just Not That into You* (2009), her character, Beth, can't understand why her long-term boyfriend (Ben Affleck) won't marry her.

Back in 2010, after I rented the DVD, my roommate came home to find me curled up on the sofa with her cat on my knee completely absorbed by what was on the television screen. When she asked me what movie I was watching, she burst out laughing when I told her *He's Just Not That into You*. I think she found it particularly funny given she knew that I was stressing over someone I'd been chatting to on Match.com who was continually flaking out on me and I hadn't heard from in five days. I was quite the pitiful sight.

He's Just Not That into You was adapted from a 2004 self-help book that was not only penned by a *Sex and the City* writer but was based on a popular line from the series. The character of Berger, who Carrie dates in season six, utters the famous phrase in the episode "Pick-a-Little, Talk-a-Little" in response to Miranda, who is fretting that her date turned down her invitation to come up to her apartment. When Berger gives her the hard truth, she feels great relief that she can now move on. The expression caught on among viewers, and given its popularity, writer Liz Tuccillo felt it was the beginnings of a self-help guide. When script consultant Greg Behrendt came on board, they shaped it into a funny, more sympathetic version of *The Rules*. Their book was published months after the airing of the final episode of *Sex and the City* and became a *New York Times* bestseller,

Playboy Bunnies, Slut-Shaming, and the Aughts' Double Standards   217

with its success boosted when Oprah Winfrey said it "should be on every woman's night table."

The film rights were snapped up by Drew Barrymore's production company, Flower Films, and it was developed into a Baltimore-set rom-com with an all-star cast, including Aniston, Barrymore, Scarlett Johansson, Jennifer Connelly, and with Ginnifer Goodwin as the thread that connects the different characters. Her character, Gigi, does all the wrong things, much like Michelle in *How to Lose a Guy in 10 Days*, and with the help of barman Alex (Justin Long), who tries to rein in her craziness, must decode the messages from men to help her find a fulfilling relationship.

Goodwin had played a similarly desperate young woman in *Mona Lisa Smile* (2003), a *Dead Poets Society* for girls, with Julia Roberts as the inspiring bohemian teacher of female students at Wellesley College in the fifties, who are all just filling time before their inevitable marriage. Goodwin plays the supposedly "chubby one" who is mocked ruthlessly by Kirsten Dunst's icy bitch for having limited prospects with men.

In this more contemporary dating drama, Goodwin's Gigi comes across as crazy rather than bubbly, and after her date with a real estate agent, Conor (Kevin Connolly), with her eyes wide in hopeful expectation that he could be the one, she's mystified to find he's not called her up to ask her out again. There's a montage of Gigi waiting anxiously by her landline, keeping an eye on her cell phone in yoga class and in the shower, and she then picks over every exact detail of the date with her colleagues, looking for any clues as to how the date really went. Once she has established that Conor isn't into her, she turns her attention to Alex, who has been trying to help her out with solid advice. In a particularly cringy scene, she misreads the signals when he invites her to a party in his apartment by hanging around even after all the other guests have gone and then leaping on top of him on the sofa. Despite the book's aim being to convince women that they weren't the "exception" to the rules, the film adaptation gives in on this final message by allowing Gigi to be rewarded for her crazy behavior by being the exception for Alex.

The *New York Times*, in its review, described it as "a grotesque representation of female desire" that followed the current trend of creating patronizing content for women:

218   *Single & Psycho*

The good Dr. Freud once asked, what do women want? To judge by the recent crop of what are often sneeringly referred to as chick flicks, today's woman wants designer threads, extravagant weddings and a generous helping of public humiliation served up with laughs, most at her expense. Where have you gone, Thelma and Louise? Oh, right: those gun-toting runaway heroines played by Geena Davis and Susan Sarandon, who wore old blue jeans and confidently put the moves on the men in their lives in Ridley Scott's 1991 outlaw female fantasy, drove off the cliff at their big finish. You have been missed, ladies.[19]

I'd gone from cheering on *Thelma & Louise* as a teenage girl to now, at the age of thirty, lying on the sofa with a cat on my lap that made me sneeze if I stroked her too much, all too aware that I was as pathetic as Gigi in my expectations and misreading of signals.

Another single character in the movie, Anna, played by Scarlett Johansson, is a yoga instructor and up-and-coming singer who has an affair with Bradley Cooper's married Ben. It was the type of temptress role that the actress specialized in. Considered confident and direct, and protective over her private life, Johansson was sexualized from the moment she broke out at the age of eighteen with *Girl with a Pearl Earring* and *Lost in Translation* (both 2003). She was number one on *FHM*'s list of the "100 Sexiest Women," and in 2006, *Esquire* named her the Sexiest Woman Alive.

In polls, she was frequently praised for her lips and her breasts, but when asked about this by reporters, she rolled her eyes at being reduced to her body parts: "I'm sure my mom will be proud. You work hard making independent films for fourteen years and you get voted best breasts. . . . What about my brain? What about my heart? What about my kidneys and my gallbladder?"[20]

For the article accompanying her win in *Esquire*, the male reporter documented his meeting with Scarlett. He had hoped to scroll through the internet with her, finding and commenting on all the sites devoted to her, and she flatly said no. She knew where her boundaries lay, and instead they did the interview over a game of pool in a billiards hall in lower Manhattan. "Just don't write anything pervy," she advised.[21]

Her body parts made an appearance in the first line of the *Time* review of Woody Allen's *Match Point* in January 2006, where she was

Playboy Bunnies, Slut-Shaming, and the Aughts' Double Standards   219

described as "curvaceously configured, and she has those remarkably proportioned lips." In *Match Point*, Scarlett plays Nola Rice, an American actress in London who is dating wealthy, privileged Tom (Matthew Goode). Through him she meets Chris (Jonathan Rhys Meyers), a former tennis pro who has ingratiated himself into this family and married Tom's sister Chloe (Emily Mortimer), purely for the prestige and money that comes with it. He's as calculating as Tom Ripley and as ambitious as George in *A Place in the Sun*. As George is infatuated with Angela, Chris is immediately attracted to Nola. One rainy afternoon, when Tom's snobby mother questions Nola's profession as an actress, she leaves in a fury, and she and Chris then have passionate outdoor sex despite the rainstorm. They embark on a torrid affair at the same time as Chloe is desperately trying to have a baby. When Nola discovers she's accidentally fallen pregnant with Chris, she pushes him to take responsibility. Nola's youth is reflected in her lack of understanding of the privileged world she's in, her desire to be adventurous, and then her naivety that a man like Chris, who has come from nothing and grifted his way into wealth, will do the right thing.

As desirable as Nola is, she's in the same position as Alice in *A Place in the Sun* as she tries to cajole the father into taking responsibility for his unborn child. In her pregnant anxiety, Nola turns shrewish and unstable as she begs Chris to divorce Chloe, and she causes a scene on the street when she realizes he has no intention of doing so. Chris knows that this will jeopardize his marriage, and he would rather kill her than risk losing his position.

Scarlett had been brought in at the last minute to replace Kate Winslet, and even though she was only nineteen at the time, she confidently plays Nola as an outsider who is inevitably punished for her coquettish charms. The actress didn't consider Nola a femme fatale; rather, she calls her a "survivor—trying to make it any way she can."[22]

The first decade of this new millennium was marked by its conflicting morality. On one hand, it encouraged raunch culture and on the other puritanically condemned "sluts," and while the cosmopolitan-swilling singleton had at times been celebrated, women in the same boat as Bridget Jones were also being blamed for the ills of society. After the September 11, 2001, attacks on the World Trade Center, and the devastating wars in Afghanistan and Iraq that followed, there

220   *Single & Psycho*

was a greater push in the United States for family values, which tied in with the sweeping patriotism of the era.

Overeducated women who weren't having children were further scapegoated following the global economic crash in 2007, which triggered a deep recession. In a September 2008 speech at the Conservative Party Conference, British politician David Willetts blamed Bridget Jones for not only causing the downfall of the modern family but of British society as a whole. His argument was that there were now more women going to university than men, and with their increased success, they were depriving men of "being the breadwinner," particularly with rising unemployment.[23]

Kira Cochrane, writing in the *Guardian,* saw the irony in his comments, given that "there has hardly been a character in popular literature more devoted to finding a man than Bridget Jones."[24] There were others who gave credit to Bridget for encouraging women toward marriage, lest they have the same fate as her.

In an article in the *Daily Mail,* Kate Mulvey spoke of how a child's birthday party had triggered her feelings of despair at being childless and almost forty. She wrote that she was one of a "growing number of women—the proportion of women under 50 without children has doubled over the past two decades—who have simply forgotten to have a baby." She blamed her predicament on seventies feminism as, being a Generation Xer, she was the "fallout generation from the sexual revolution, the real-life Bridget Joneses who spend their evenings getting drunk instead of reading bedtime stories."[25]

Leaving it too late to have children was considered the biggest threat for single women. Lori Gottlieb's *Marry Him: The Case for Settling for Mr. Good Enough* (2010) urged women to settle in order to find happiness. She described how every woman, no question, "feels panic, occasionally coupled with desperation, if she hits 30 and finds herself unmarried."[26]

A June 2008 *Daily Mail* article entitled "Rise of the Freemale: The Women Who'd Rather Be Single than Share Their Time and Money" highlighted the latest figures from the Office of National Statistics, which revealed that 8 percent of British women between twenty-five and forty-four lived alone—double the number from twenty years before. Kylie Minogue and Cameron Diaz were mentioned as examples of this breed of women who were choosing independence over a

Playboy Bunnies, Slut-Shaming, and the Aughts' Double Standards   221

long-term relationship, and with its illustration of Kylie in her famous gold hot pants, she was quoted as saying she would never have a conventional family life. Despite her fabulousness, the insinuation was that women who chose that lifestyle were selfish.[27]

Kylie was also at odds with the depiction of Susan Boyle on *Britain's Got Talent*, which further emphasized old-fashioned notions of the spinster as a frumpy middle-aged woman living alone with her cat. When she first walked onto the audition stage in 2009, she was met with condescension and the assumption that she would be one of the joke acts. She was the unacceptable form of single woman as she was considered dowdy and aging—the opposite of the dynamic Carrie Bradshaw or the cute Bridget. Yet she defied all those scathing comments with her pitch-perfect and powerful voice, and in that one audition, she supposedly beat the stereotypes of a sad woman who had never been kissed.

The narrative in self-help books was that single women, no matter their professional success, were deeply miserable and living with regrets. With the subprime mortgage crisis triggering a global recession and deep economic anxiety, and with a rising alt-right movement on the back of Barack Obama becoming the first Black president of the United States when he was inaugurated in January 2009, now was the time for a return to the domestic thriller, where the single woman was once again the threat.

CHAPTER 16

Alcoholic, Divorced, and Highly Anxious

The American Film Institute in June 2003 unveiled its list of one hundred heroes and villains in Hollywood cinema from the last hundred years. Coming in at number seven on the villains list was Alex Forrest. The top three may have been Hannibal Lecter, Norman Bates, and Darth Vader, but the psycho single woman was considered more villainous than the shark in *Jaws* and the killer cyborg in *The Terminator*.

In the romantic comedies and television shows and dating manuals of the 2000s, the message had been ingrained in women that they must not, at any cost, act like the *Fatal Attraction* bunny boiler. Now firmly part of popular culture, she was the frightening witch whose presence was felt when any single woman demanded too much or implored, "I will not be ignored." It was clear that in the pursuit of love and marriage, women should do everything to avoid being compared to her.

The aughts had only seen a few films in the same vein as *Fatal Attraction*, such as 2002's *Swimfan*, which exploited the popularity of teen movies to shift the tropes to high school. A sequel to *Single White Female*—with its subtitle, "The Psycho," clearly reveling in its intentions—went straight to video on its release in 2005. Adrian Lyne in 2002 created a reverse *Fatal Attraction*, *Unfaithful*, with Diane Lane as the cheating wife and Richard Gere as the betrayed husband who lashes out at the handsome French man who seduced her. Lyne even gives a little nod to the bunny when the couple's son is dressed as a rabbit for a school play.

If the slew of *Fatal Attraction*–style thrillers in the nineties had boomed on the back of a recession and a backlash against feminism,

Alcoholic, Divorced, and Highly Anxious 223

the exact same conditions would lead to a new set of domestic thrillers inspired by the 2007 financial crash and its aftereffects. The foreclosures on homes and the skyrocketing unemployment rates created a mass feeling of anxiety around the stability of home life.

If you took the premise of *Fatal Attraction* and imagined what would happen if the wife was the one who had the affair with the temptress, then you would land on the 2009 erotic thriller *Chloe*, directed by Atom Egoyan and adapted from the 2003 French film *Nathalie*. . . . Its director, Anne Fontaine, had been disappointed that her movie didn't have the lesbian flavor she had intended, because its two stars, Fanny Ardant and Emmanuelle Béart, weren't comfortable doing sex scenes together.

In the remake, Julianne Moore plays Catherine, a Toronto gynecologist who suspects her music professor husband (Liam Neeson) is having an affair with one of his college students. Catherine feels the distance in their marriage, and she finds it painful to see her husband flirt with younger women. At a restaurant one evening, she meets a call girl, Chloe (Amanda Seyfried), in the ladies' room and is transfixed by, almost afraid of, the younger woman's beauty. She hires Chloe as a means of testing her husband's infidelity, and as Chloe reports back in graphic detail about what happened between them, Claire is turned on. She and Chloe spend a night together, but afterward, realizing there are consequences to her affair with a woman, Claire tells Chloe there can't be any other encounters. The younger woman refuses to take no for an answer because it's Claire she has been obsessed with all along. As she's ushered out of Claire's office, her eyes red from the emotion, she looks directly into the camera as if she's challenging the audience, "Just you wait and see what I'll do."

In obsessive, Alex Forrest moves, she calls Claire incessantly at work, turns up unannounced, and then shifts her attention to Claire's teenage son. She insists they have sex on Claire's bed, and as she rides him, she focuses on the clothes in Claire's wardrobe, particularly the spiked heels, to make herself orgasm. When it came to the ending, it was as if the director acknowledged its debt to *Fatal Attraction*. As Chloe becomes fanatically violent, there is only one way out for her.[1] Elizabeth Weitzman, writing in the *New York Daily News*, gave it one star and described it as tacky and predictable: "Still, if you've been

224 *Single & Psycho*

waiting desperately for a lesbian 'Fatal Attraction' that manages to be simultaneously slick and tawdry, your wish has finally been granted."

Another twist on the love triangle was 2009's *Obsessed*, where Beyoncé and Idris Elba are Black professionals under threat from a predatory female. The interracial dynamic of a psychotic white woman (Ali Larter) trying to destroy the lives of a happily married Black suburban couple could have made powerful commentary, but this was never fully explored. The *New York Times* in its review was critical of Idris Elba's apparent similarity in appearance to O. J. Simpson and Ali Larter to Nicole Brown Simpson, which lent the film "a distasteful taint of exploitation." This was likely unintentional, given the film's hesitance to dig deeper into much beyond the surface of its simplistic narrative.

Derek Charles (Elba), his wife, Sharon (Beyoncé), and toddler son, Kyle, are first seen arriving at their new home, a gorgeous villa in a leafy suburb of Los Angeles, and with the earthy interiors and the Norah Jones soundtrack, it's clear this is true domestic bliss. Derek, an asset manager, meets the new office temp, Lisa (Ali Larter), in the elevator of one of those sterile glass and steel offices that contrasts with the warmth of his home. She's a tall and thin blond in sharp tailoring who tries to attract his attention by flashing her thigh and giving him the come-hither with her icy blue eyes. When Sharon visits him in the office with Kyle, she doesn't trust Lisa for a second—after all, this was how Sharon met Derek in the first place.

The office is a hotbed of sexism—"Whose legs are those? . . . Always nice to have a pretty girl around the office," says the company boss in a meeting with Derek, and Ben (Jerry O'Connell), the office letch, informs Derek that women now view the workplace as their hunting ground, and Lisa has Derek in her crosshairs. The outdated language and sexual harassment clearly hadn't moved on from 1993's *The Temp*, although Lisa is more in line with what audiences expected to see from Lara Flynn Boyle's character.

Despite Lisa's best efforts, Derek isn't up for workplace flirtations, and he also refuses to join in with the sexist banter because he really is devoted to his family. Derek's no Michael Douglas—he doesn't need to wrestle with his guilt because he refuses to cheat on his wife. Instead, he bats the predatory single woman away at every step of her seduction attempt. When she joins him for a drink at a bar, just before the office Christmas party is about to begin, she insists on ordering two dirty martinis, making sure they're "filthy." Lisa grinds up against Derek on the dance floor, but despite being woozy from alcohol, he refuses to even give her a peck on the cheek under the mistletoe, and when she corners him in a bathroom cubicle, he fights her off. The next day, he realizes the full extent of her craziness when she climbs into his car and strips down to her underwear.

There was limited chemistry between Ali Larter and Idris Elba or any backstory that would offer an explanation as to why she was so unstable. Her obsession comes out of nowhere because we know nothing about her except for her skills in manipulation and that she appears to believe there's something happening between her and Derek. The behavior intensifies when she gatecrashes a work retreat, spiking Derek's drink and sleeping over in his hotel room. Was this a sexual assault? We're not shown what she actually does to him, but later he returns to the room to find her having overdosed on sleeping pills. From there, it descends further into *Fatal Attraction* by numbers (without the illicit sex or dead animals) as Lisa kidnaps Kyle and then returns him unharmed, which provokes Beyoncé's Sharon to the breaking point.

Sharon has been a bland character up to the point where she finds out about the supposed "affair," and now enraged, she kicks Derek out of the home. This is the Beyoncé of her hit single "Irreplaceable," who sends her man packing as she acknowledges that she can find another him tomorrow. Sharon is also a foreshadow of the vengeful wife of her cultural touchstone album, 2016's *Lemonade.* The album was considered a response to husband Jay-Z's infidelity, and in the track "Sorry," she is unapologetic and empowering as she raises her finger and tells her husband he better grow up, because she's ready to say goodbye. She also takes aim at the mistress, who she labels as a "Becky." It was a line that could have been aimed at Lisa, and it left in its wake internet-breaking speculation as to who this Becky, a derogatory term for a white woman, was.

Sharon eventually softens and allows Derek to move back in, but after Lisa comes into the house and takes their son from his bedroom, this is the final straw. She goes further than Beth Gallagher when she shouts at Lisa down the phone, "You think you're crazy? I'll show you crazy. Just try me, bitch!"

226 *Single & Psycho*

What the trailer promised, and what audiences came out to see, was a catfight between Beyoncé and this skinny white woman. Anne Archer and Glenn Close may have kept the fight to the bathroom, but here no room is off limits as they kick and punch at each other throughout the house until there's a final showdown in the attic.

Derek phones Sharon midfight, and she tells him she's going to have to call him back. He is no use in this fight—it's between two lionesses who are battling for dominance. Lisa, barefoot and in a white shirt that makes her appear as if she's escaped from the hospital, is no match for Sharon, who deftly avoids her swings and punches until Lisa steps on a loose floorboard. She plummets through the ceiling of the attic, shattering the glass coffee table in her fall and then bringing the chandelier down on top of her. The literal homewrecker has been destroyed. This scene was also an allegory of how women are so often pitted against one another—the curves of Beyoncé versus the skinny blond, the stability of home versus the marriage-wrecking force of a single seductress. Despite its poor reviews, with the criticism that it was just another "crazed-bitch-stalker movie," *Obsessed* took in $28 million on its opening weekend in the States, partly thanks to the appeal of Beyoncé kicking butt.

Beyoncé would be criticized a decade later for her similar swaggering reaction to a rival woman who is trying to steal her man in her reinterpretation of Dolly Parton's "Jolene." On her 2024 album, *Cowboy Carter*, Beyoncé adapted the iconic song (which had dozens of previous cover versions) to give a bolder pushback to the predatory single woman. The album was critically acclaimed, but it was this version of "Jolene" that led to a negative reaction, particularly on social media.

She had, critics said, erased the vulnerability of the 1973 original as Parton appeals to the flame-haired minx through flattery, whereas Beyoncé was too confrontational in her response. In Parton's version, she doesn't place the blame on the man as she believes it's the bewitching beauty of Jolene that would lead him to stray, so she begs for her compassion to leave him alone.

In an article in the *Conversation*, Dr. Kadian Pow, a lecturer at Birmingham City University, offered her interpretation that Beyoncé was reworking the track in African American women's language (AAWL). Parton, on the other hand, is negotiating on "conventions of the white southern womanhood and the gentility expected" of these strict gender roles. Parton had recorded it in the seventies, when Southern women were still expected to follow conservative values. While Parton is using charm, Beyoncé taps into her identity as a Black woman, the unapologetic force of her album *Lemonade*, who protects her family and chastises Jolene for being desperate. She also uses the support of her husband, voiced by Willie Jones, to stand as a family unit.

As Kadian Pow says, "The threat of infidelity is the same, but how the two women negotiate it is a reflection of their age, race and experiences of womanhood. Why would we expect the song to be the same when these two women are far from?"[2]

Similarly, Nadira Goffe wrote in *Slate*, "Black women don't have time to beg—or, rather, historically, begging has gotten us nowhere. Instead, we have learned that we must defend what we've worked so hard to create—even, potentially, our own delusions about our relationships."[3]

Like her character in *Obsessed*, Beyoncé in "Jolene" is the scorned woman fighting back, who is empowered in her demand to be treated with respect. It was an assertive defense of her marriage, a form of boundary-setting feminism in the same way "Single Ladies" told the man he better put a ring on it, or he would lose her.

In an article in the *Paris Review*, Amy Gentry described *Obsessed* as the first and "whitest" of a subgenre of Black-fronted thrillers released by Sony's Screen Gems division. After its success with *Obsessed*, and then the 2014 all-Black remake of *About Last Night*, the low-budget studio released a series of hot-button domestic thrillers with a Black cast, including *No Good Deed* (2014), *The Perfect Guy* (2015), and *When the Bough Breaks* (2016), where professional middle-class characters are stalked and threatened in their homes.[4]

The *Hollywood Reporter* described *When the Bough Breaks* as a "lazily written and generically directed Fatal Attraction knockoff."[5] What it does tap into is the controversial topic of surrogacy and how motherhood is determined. Regina Hall is Laura, a professional chef in her forties who lives in New Orleans with her husband, John (Morris Chestnut), and their cat, Miss Havisham. Unable to carry a child to full term, they sign up to a surrogacy service, and Laura feels an immediate connection to a young woman, Anna (Jaz Sinclair),

228   *Single & Psycho*

who agrees to carry their last embryo. Anna has an abusive boy-friend, and to protect her and their embryo, the couple agrees to let her move into their home. But inevitably Anna becomes obsessed with John, and she wishes to destroy Laura so that she can keep John and his baby for herself. Here there are two sides of the problematic woman on display. Laura is too career-focused and unable to carry a child because she left it too late, and Anna is a single, unstable seduc-tress who wants to steal what isn't hers.

While the effects of the 2007–8 economic crash were only given a passing mention in *Obsessed*, the blight of the foreclosure crisis, where millions of Americans lost their homes as they failed to keep up their mortgage payments, was the driving force of the home invasion movie *Mother's Day* (2010). It was a welcome return for Rebecca De Mornay as the psychotic family matriarch who, it turns out, is much like her *The Hand That Rocks the Cradle* character in that she can't be trusted around newborn babies. When her violent bank-robbing sons plan to hide out at their family home, they are dismayed to dis-cover that the house was repossessed and is now owned by a yuppie couple who happen to be hosting a gathering with their friends. The three criminals invade the home, threaten the occupants, and then call in "Mother" to take control. There is no father in this situation; De Mornay is a single mother (who hasn't given birth) whose icy blue eyes are once again put to chilling effect as she reveals her ruthless-ness and the control she wields over her children.

    In this new wave of domestic thrillers, it wasn't just single women who were the problem—unhappily married and divorced women were just as transgressive. Being unable to find a mate is judged as inexplicable in popular culture, but divorce is also consid-ered a failure. In the miserable anxiety of being in a dysfunctional marriage, perhaps because having children hasn't gone to plan, the divorced or separated woman attempts to find solace from her sim-mering resentment in a bottle of wine or to plot something much more nefarious.

    In 2012, *Gone Girl*, the third novel of former *Entertainment Weekly* writer Gillian Flynn, swept to number two on the *New York Times* bestseller list, where it spent ninety-one weeks in the chart. It was a true literature phenomenon, one of those cultural touchstone books that is used as a descriptor—there was "the Gone Girl twist" and the "Gone Girl effect" to apply to the raft of domestic thriller novels and films that followed its lead.

Flynn sparked discussions around the concept of the "unlikable female character," the way women shrink in marriage, and "the cool girl" who must bend like a willow to fit with how men want them to be. And even when they act in a palatable way, they are dismissed for getting older or being crazy. As the character of Nick says, "Women are fucking crazy. No qualifier: Not some women, not many women. Women are crazy."

The story was inspired by the Scott Peterson case in 2002, where a California man, considered handsome and successful, was charged with the murder of his wife, Laci Peterson, and unborn child. The media frenzy was further heightened when his mistress revealed herself at a news conference.

Flynn also used the 2007 housing crash as a metaphor for the slow death of a marriage and the poison that follows. Nick Dunne and his wife, Amy, are forced to move from their comfortable existence in New York's Brooklyn Heights back to his hometown in Missouri after they lose their magazine writer jobs in the recession. They move into one of the McMansions that make up a ghost-town housing development, where all atmosphere has been obliterated due to most of the homes being abandoned by foreclosure.

Amy's psychologist parents made a fortune by using their only daughter's childhood as inspiration for their wildly successful *Amazing Amy* series of novels. While it gives her trust fund privilege, she feels stifled by the fictional Amy, whose great choices are almost a corrector for the bad ones Amy makes. After her parents lose their money in the recession and need her trust fund for themselves, she has no choice but to return to Nick's hometown.

Here, Nick teaches at a local college, where he has an affair with one of his students while neglecting his now listless and bored wife. He spends much of his time at the bar he owns with his sister, and he begins to hate Amy for being far removed from the cool version he thought he had married. When he comes home one day to find the house ransacked and his wife missing, a huge search is launched for her, but Nick doesn't play the part of distraught husband well, and suspicion turns to him.

230 *Single & Psycho*

There are two unreliable narrators in this first half of the novel as the story is alternately told from Nick's point of view and then from Amy's, through extracts from her diary as she hints at his creeping abusiveness. Amy's diary is, in fact, a construct, and in the second section, we switch to her real voice as she reveals she faked her death to escape this life that was forced on her. She wants to make Nick suffer for his infidelity, and so she goes to psychopathic extremes in her pursuit of her punishment.

Her elaborate plan also involves creating a construct of an anxious thirtysomething singleton who was grateful to settle down. In the entries before she meets Nick, she writes that her friends are baffled by her singleness because she's smart and pretty with a cool job and a lovely, wealthy family: "I know that they secretly think there's something wrong with me, something hidden away that makes me unsatisfiable, unsatisfying."

In reality, there are three Amys—the diary Amy, the version she pretended to be when she met Nick, and then the real her, who is cold, detached, and psychopathic. As she reveals herself in the second half of the novel, she describes the woman she pretended to be—a construct known as the "cool girl."

The "cool girl" speech resonated completely with women as it was so true; it was the girl from the dating manuals who never nags or complains, who mustn't exhibit cloyingly desperate behavior for fear of driving him away. The "cool girl" was Cameron Diaz in *Esquire* and *GQ* features, Kate Hudson in *How to Lose a Guy in 10 Days*, and Jennifer Lawrence at red carpet events. They were hot, they loved sex, and they drank beer and chowed down on burgers, all the while maintaining that perfect figure. "Men actually think this girl exists," muses Amy. "Maybe they're fooled because so many women are willing to pretend to be this girl."

Nick is also pretending to be a better, more charming version of himself, but in reality, he's misogynistic in his hatred for women, the way he mumbles "stupid bitch" under his breath. In her diaries, she claims that Nick, after a night out, would describe the "lost causes" in the bar—the kind of desperately overdressed and made-up woman close to forty, whom he sneered at: "Now I am his Lost Cause, and he's trapped with me, and maybe that's why he's so angry."

Alcoholic, Divorced, and Highly Anxious   231

The psychopathic Amy, the real Amy, is a calculating genius when it comes to fakery. As well as faking her own death, she also fakes her own pregnancy by stealing the urine of her pregnant neighbor. After her rich ex-boyfriend imprisons her in his high-security property, she murders him to offer a plausible means of returning home. She is reunited with Nick and seeks for them to have a happy marriage so that he will suffer. At the end of the novel, Amy has trapped Nick with a real pregnancy. He has his own revenge, creating a manuscript that he has entitled *Psycho Bitch*, although he knows it will never be published.

Given the book's success, it would be inevitable Hollywood would call, and David Fincher worked with Flynn as she adapted her own novel into a screenplay. Fincher's previous works include *Panic Room* (2002), with Jodie Foster as a divorcée who numbs herself with alcohol, and after moving into a New York townhouse with the money from the settlement, she and her daughter are vulnerable to home invasion. "I was looking for something I'd never seen before," said Fincher. "The book talked about narcissism in a really interesting way—the way we concoct not only an ideal version of ourselves in hopes of seducing a mate, but in hopes of seducing someone who is probably doing the same thing."[6]

What is further set up, with the help of Emily Ratajkowski as the student Nick is having an affair with, is the *Fatal Attraction* triangle. Fincher asked Affleck to suggest someone men desire and women dislike, and they landed on Ratajkowski, known for the polarizing Instagram posts that make her both desired and envied.

When examining *Gone Girl* through the lens of *Fatal Attraction* and *Presumed Innocent*, Amy is the cheated-on wife who now takes her vengeance on her husband rather than the mistress. It's the wife, not the other woman, who is portrayed as if she needs a mental health diagnosis. There's something disturbed going on in Amy's mind, and it's reflected in the schizophrenic way she pretends to be other people—the sad single, the "cool girl," the dutiful wife, the inspiring daughter. Now that she's had enough of her sexist husband, who spends more time at his bar than at home and cheats on her with a younger woman, she claims her power against the stereotypes. But in the movie, she is reduced to a further series of tropes.

The scenes in New York, which flash back to the "meet cute" between Amy and Nick, are straight out of an Adrian Lyne movie.

232 *Single & Psycho*

They walk through the city at night, past warehouses that are similar to the ones Michael Douglas and Glenn Close stroll past and where a baker's bag of confectioners' sugar creates a blizzard of sweet snow. And they have lustful, loud sex in a library, ignoring all the other people around. Amy's desire to possess every man leads to her framing them for rape and murder. Just as Alex screams, "I will not be ignored," Amy will not lose. Amy is also Catherine Trammell in *Basic Instinct*—her icy blond perfection breaking into sexual aggression in the bedroom as she seduces Desi and then slits his throat with a letter opener, allowing the blood to cascade over her. She's every woman in a domestic thriller who fakes a pregnancy so that a man will stay with her.

Both the film and the novel led to accusations of misogyny against Flynn for her creation of a female character who lies about rape and domestic abuse and tries to frame her husband for murder. The *Washington Post* headlined a piece "Is 'Gone Girl's Amy a Misogynist? A Misandrist? Or Both?"

As Eliana Dockterman wrote in *Time*, the movie "forces the audience to debate and pick apart its gender dynamics. There's no question that Amy is a monster when she slashes Desi's throat during sex or when she fakes her death to trap Nick. But she does these things to rebel against the boxes others have tried to put her in—'Amazing Amy' by her parents, 'Cool Girl' Amy by Nick, beautiful and doting Amy by Desi."[7]

As Flynn told the *Guardian*, "The one thing that really frustrates me is this idea that women are innately good, innately nurturing. In literature, they can be dismissably bad—trampy, vampy, bitchy types—but there's still a big pushback against the idea that women can be just pragmatically evil, bad and selfish."

At the same time, she rejected the idea of Amy as the psycho bitch as she was far more complicated than that: "I don't write psycho bitches. The psycho bitch is just crazy—she has no motive, and so she's a dismissible person because of her psycho-bitchiness."[8]

Gone Girl was a massive success on its release in fall 2014, earning just over $369 million worldwide and an Oscar nomination for Rosamund Pike. It also sparked a wave of female domestic thrillers that followed "the Gone Girl effect." In the mid-2010s, if you put a "Girl" in the title of a novel or a film, you were likely to have a hit.

Or maybe it was more to do with an appetite for reading and seeing complicated, messy, destructive women who owned their craziness. Paula Hawkins's *The Girl on the Train* was the fastest-selling adult novel in history when it was published in 2015, and Universal hoped to achieve the same success as *Gone Girl* for its 2016 adaptation, directed by Tate Taylor and starring Emily Blunt.

Paula Hawkins, in an interview with the *Hollywood Reporter*, insisted that the protagonists were widely different. "Amy Dunne is a psychopath, an incredibly controlling and manipulative, smart, cunning woman—and Rachel's just a mess who can't do anything right," she said. "Amy is deliberately unreliable, while Rachel is accidentally unreliable because she got so pissed drunk."[9]

As a domestic thriller, *Girl on the Train* tapped into the dark side of suburbia, where the threat is inside the house. There were similarities in its use of multiple narrators and the twisty storyline that is centered on a missing middle-class woman who may have been killed by her lover. There is also a complicated female protagonist, divorcée Rachel Watson, who has descended into alcoholism because of her failure to have a child during her marriage. It explores how a woman's status is designated by her fertility and mothering skills and that if she fails at marriage, if she fails at having children or being a good mother, then she is dismissed by society. The three narrators, Rachel, Megan, and Anna, are all defined in different ways by motherhood or their lack of.

Rachel may have lost her job after being caught drinking at work, but she continues to commute to and from the city on the train, observing an attractive young couple in one of the houses by the railway track. It's in the same block of houses that Rachel once lived with her husband, Tom, but she's been replaced by blond and beautiful Anna, who is also now the mother of Tom's child. It's particularly painful, given the unexplained fertility issues Rachel had, and now that she finds comfort in drinking, she knows that people can see the damage all over her, not just in her puffy face but in the way she holds herself.

She misses her husband, her life that she once had, and she blames the other woman, Anna, who has now moved into her home, sleeps in her bed, is tending her garden, and has even had the child Rachel longed for. "Fucking bitch," thinks Rachel in drunk, foggy anger.

234   *Single & Psycho*

"She's a cuckoo, laying her egg in my nest. She has taken everything from me."

Rachel becomes the madwoman, calling her ex's phone incessantly, leaving messages, turning up uninvited, and even breaking into their home and taking their newborn baby into the garden. She plays over how her marriage went wrong, the realization that having a child wasn't as easy as it was supposed to be, and the isolation she felt as her friends were having children and celebrating first birthdays. Tormented by grief and loneliness, she dulled the pain with alcohol, which became more frequent and more necessary.

Megan, the woman she watches, is plagued by her own dark past, and she finds solace with other men to escape raw, visceral mother's guilt. One day, Rachel reads in the papers that Megan has gone missing, and she is haunted by a flashback from when she was blackout drunk, that she may know something about what happened to Megan.

Rachel feels the weight of people's opinions of her, that the other passengers on the train and the detectives investigating Megan's disappearance see her as delusional, unhinged, a "barren, divorced, soon-to-be-homeless alcoholic" who is unwilling to move on and accept that her ex has a new family.

Anna enjoyed being a mistress; she never felt guilty for it or bad for Rachel, even after finding out she had turned to drink. She finds being the other woman a "huge turn-on" because it means that she must be irresistible. When she suspects that maybe Tom is seeing Rachel again, she becomes the jealous woman she hates—guessing his laptop password, drinking alone, spying on him.

Megan is also painted as a stalker. She simmers with anger as she waits for text messages and calls from her mystery lover. In words that echo Alex Forrest, she thinks, "If he thinks I will just disappear, go quietly, he's mistaken. If he doesn't pick up soon, I'm going to stop calling his mobile and call him at home. I'm not just going to be ignored."

By showing these three sides of womanhood—the infertile divorcée who turns to alcohol, the unapologetic mistress who wins the prize, and the grieving mother who becomes an obsessive lover—Hawkins, like Gillian Flynn, reveals the way society treats women who don't have it all. It is also about gaslighting, in which all three women are manipulated by one man so that they are unable to trust what's real.

At different points in my life, I've felt like all three women, at times obsessive in my quest not to be single, gaslit by my partner, infertile and grieving. I connected with Rachel's words, that she liked her job but didn't have a glittering career, and that she was all too aware "women are still only really valued for two things—their looks and their role as mothers." If she's not beautiful and she can't have kids, she asks, then does that make her worthless?

At my lowest ebb with Gavin, I felt like a shell of the person I was. I couldn't sleep because I was expecting him to burst in at 3 a.m. to wake me up and rant at me, and I was miserable in my job as a government press officer. My boss there was an intimidating bully, and given that I was also being bullied at home, I wasn't equipped to deal with her and instead retreated into my own insecurities. I came into work one day shaking from Gavin having spat in my face in anger that morning, but I couldn't tell them that I wasn't myself, that I was scared and self-conscious and timid because of everything else that was happening around me. The only solace, like Rachel, was to drink wine in the evenings. I paid for some personal training sessions to try to improve my health, but I was so tired in the mornings from the sleepless nights, and I felt so puffy and haggard and bloated, that I didn't enjoy the forced hour spent with an overly confident trainer in his twenties who I was convinced was judging me.

After leaving Gavin, I'd had a good year, recovering under lockdown and experiencing a reawakening. But after the miscarriage, I sank into my grief. Two months on from the loss, I went on vacation to Greece with my parents. They'd rented a villa on one of the islands to celebrate their fiftieth wedding anniversary, and it had been hard work doing all the required COVID-19 tests and getting the results back in time to catch the flight.

Even under the balmy heat of a Greek summer, the tranquility of the turquoise sea that I just wanted to plunge into, the hum of cicadas and motorboats in the harbor, I was so depressed. My stomach was twisted and knotted, and the anxiety gripped every part of my body. I just wanted to drink to drown the pain—so at 4 p.m. every day, I went down to a bar by the sea to sit with a cocktail and read a book. It was a beautiful spot overlooking the harbor, where I could

236 *Single & Psycho*

gaze at the spiky sea urchins clinging to the rocks below the surface and watch the moored yachts, imagining what type of people were on board. As much as I enjoyed the company of my parents, these were times when I just wanted to be on my own to draw closer to oblivion with every sip of my cocktail. We've never been a family who could speak in depth about our emotions, and besides, I didn't think they'd understand. They'd perfected compromise and companionship, and in my forty-plus years as their daughter, I'd never seen them argue. I couldn't see a future like that, particularly when grieving my fertile years and having been all but ghosted by Paul.

It was coming up to forty days since I'd had my first bleed after the miscarriage, and this lack of a period was also stressing me out. It wasn't that I thought I was pregnant again; it was more that I was worried my ovaries were giving up on me. What's more, I hadn't heard from Paul since he'd sent me photos of his latest Star Wars toys the week before. To be fair, I hadn't told him I was going to Greece, only because his messages had become fewer and fewer, as if he was trying to do the slow fade while still convincing himself he was the good guy. All I'd been receiving from him were links to TikTok videos and pictures of his assembled Lego. And this was a thirty-nine-year-old man. My desperation and hurt was palpable. I was aware that over the past five years, I'd become one of these women in *Gone Girl* and *Girl on the Train*, and I needed to stop. But I struggled, like Rachel, to let go of the anger and resentment and the desire to keep picking at the wounds. I couldn't face up to the fact that Paul didn't want me because I didn't know what my value was as a fortysomething single woman who had been unable to have a child or forge a decent, lasting relationship.

I enjoyed these domestic thrillers because they offered me an outlet for my own pain, and the gaslighted "Girl" and "Woman" phenomenon continued with A. J. Finn's 2018 novel *The Woman in the Window*, which again featured a confused narrator who is dismissed by all those around her because of her abnormal situation.

Anna Fox is a middle-aged psychologist who lives alone in her New York brownstone and is terrified of leaving her house after a tragic accident that resulted in her separation from her husband and daughter. She drowns her pain by knocking back anxiety medication with red wine as she watches Hitchcock movies and spies on her new neighbors, a married couple and their son.

One evening, she is convinced that she has witnessed a ghastly crime—the husband from across the street stabbing to death his wife. Anna calls the police, but after the husband insists that his wife is very much alive and well, and because Anna is a heavy drinker on medication, the detectives doubt her sanity.

She is, like Rachel in *Girl on the Train*, being gaslighted as her weaknesses are used against her. This was an important factor in these mysteries—that the characters aren't taken seriously. Because they are without a man to speak for them, because they are close to middle-aged and distasteful due to drinking too much, they are dismissed. One could even draw a parallel to historical witch hunts. It's easy to condemn a woman when she doesn't fit into society's idea of acceptable womanhood.

The film adaptation starred Amy Adams as Anna Fox and Gary Oldman and Julianne Moore as her neighbors and was directed by Joe Wright. But after receiving poor test audience scores, 20th Century Studios sold it off to Netflix, and it was lambasted in reviews for its overly self-conscious homage to Hitchcock.

The phenomenon of the Girl and Woman domestic thrillers was satirized by the 2022 Netflix series *The Woman in the House across the Street from the Girl in the Window*, which starred Kristen Bell as a woman who, according to the blurb, "mixes wine, pills, casseroles and an overactive imagination."

While these characters owe a debt to *Fatal Attraction* in their depiction of unstable women who struggle with love and fertility, they are now more clearly understood to have mental disorders, at a time when society is talking more freely about, and taking seriously, emotional health. This shift in the way women were taking control of their complicated narratives and owning their life in disarray would be a marker for a whole new genre of female-led television series.

CHAPTER 17

Fleabag, Fourth-Wave Feminism, and the Destructive Single Woman

In the opening moments of Taylor Swift's 2015 music video for "Blank Space," we see her resting on a four-poster bed in a black nightgown and eye mask, clutching a kitten to her chest. The setting is a luxury mansion, and Taylor is a femme fatale who lures men into her world before her crazy behavior inevitably drives them away. Erupting in jealousy when she suspects him of texting someone else, she drops his phone in her pool, rips up his clothes, cries mascara tears, and stabs a heart-shaped sponge cake with a knife. It was this character, a nightmare dressed up as the dream woman, that she felt the press was trying to turn her into.

"Blank Space" was written from the point of view of, she said, "a girl who's crazy but seductive but glamorous but nuts but manipulative? That was the character I felt the media had written for me, and for a long time I felt hurt by it. I took it personally. But as time went by, I realized it was kind of hilarious."[1]

From her early days as a teen country star, songwriting was a means for her to express her heartbreak, and in the age of social media, it became a game for cyber-sleuth fans to work out exactly which famous ex she was referring to in her lyrics. Swift never directly named names, but she dropped clues into the liner notes of her albums and, as a naive teen, offered tantalizing burns to talk-show hosts like Ellen DeGeneres, where she revealed Joe Jonas had dumped her over the phone. "While some women are content to just leave an angry voice-mail message or throw the guy's clothes in the street, Swift lets the whole world know he's been a heel," wrote *Vanity Fair*'s Nancy Jo Sales in a 2013 profile.[2]

Fleabag, Fourth-Wave Feminism, and the Destructive Single Woman   239

One paramour, John Mayer, didn't take kindly to the song she wrote about him, the bluesy ballad "Dear John," which painted him as an exploiter of a nineteen-year-old girl's heart. He told *Rolling Stone* that it was a "really lousy thing for her to do."[3] Others, like Jake Gyllenhaal, whose presence was felt throughout her fourth album, *Red,* have had to endure being teased and trolled mercilessly by her fans.

Despite being the highest-earning musician in the United States in 2014, Taylor was often dismissed as a frivolous pop star who used her songs as a tool for revenge. Celebrity magazines and tabloids focused on her love life by curating photo spreads with all her previous boyfriends and speculating on the next targets on her list.

"For a female to write about her feelings," she said, "and then be portrayed as some clingy, insane, desperate girlfriend in need of making you marry her and have kids with her, I think that's taking something that potentially should be celebrated—a woman writing about her feelings in a confessional way—that's taking it and turning it and twisting it into something that is frankly a little sexist," she told *Vanity Fair* in 2013.[4] She noted that men like John Mayer were labeled "playboys," whereas women doing the same things were "sluts" or "clingy."

In 2011, she spoke to the *New Yorker* about her fascination with the Kennedy clan, and as well as being seen with Ethel Kennedy at the Sundance festival in January 2012, she had also started dating Ethel's grandson Conor Kennedy. Having been taken under the Kennedy wing, she even bought a house near theirs on Rhode Island, which, it was speculated, was designed to place her close to Conor. The move led to comparisons with Alex Forrest. *TMZ* host Harvey Levin described her as a "nutcase" for buying a home so close to her boyfriend's family, and the story was accompanied by a clip from *Fatal Attraction.*

"I like you, I will apparently buy up the real-estate market just to freak you out so you leave me. Like that makes sense, like that's something you should do," she said sarcastically to Nancy Jo Sales.[5] Despite her protests, the Glenn Close comparisons were a common feature in profiles of Taylor. Jon Caramanica in the *New York Times* said she was "her own TMZ, 'Fatal Attraction' by way of Hannah Montana."[6] The

240 *Single & Psycho*

irony was that while she was being painted as the stalker, she needed to have her own security, because there was a file of people "who want to take me home and chain me to a pipe in their basement."[7]

Despite the satire of "Blank Space," Taylor would continue to be mocked for her love life, and it intensified over the summer of 2016 as she embarked on a very public relationship with Tom Hiddleston, not long after breaking up with Scottish DJ Calvin Harris. There was a backlash against the public displays of affection, as if she was faking it for attention. As she would sing in "I Did Something Bad" on her revenge-laden 2017 album *Reputation*, society has a habit of accusing women of being witches and psychos.

Bridie Jabour wrote in the *Guardian*, "When stories are published calling Taylor 'insane' and a 'control freak,' and when entire Tumblr threads are devoted to how 'annoying' she is, we're sending a message to young girls and women: You are not allowed to be seen enjoying your success or your sexuality—and you are certainly not to appear to think you deserve either."[8]

I'd been listening to Taylor Swift since 2010, when I discovered that her music—heartbreaking songs about love and shitty guys—resonated with me and my quest to find a partner. I threw myself into online dating and singles meet-up events, but I typically focused my attention on the wrong, unavailable ones. I'm a decade older than Taylor, but as a thirty-year-old, I was still living the postadolescent existence of first dates and short-lived, doomed relationships (including with a Merchant Navy cadet who was going to be away at sea for four months), clubbing all night, and then spending the next day unable to do much more than veg out and eat pizza. Now that I look back on it, it was a glorious time as I was constantly indulging in the exquisite pain of confused heartbreak. But I wish I had been less wrapped up in my mission. I was far from being a career woman, just working as a communications officer and dreaming that I could give it all up to be a writer. So, in my case, it wasn't as if I was neglecting relationships for a high-flying job; I was just an avoidant with a tendency to be attracted to the wrong people, no doubt because their very unavailability was a twisted way of protecting myself.

Nine years later, I was on a stagnant salary that hadn't shifted much from my early thirties and dealing with the dawning realization, after googling the signs, that I was in an abusive relationship. It

Fleabag, Fourth-Wave Feminism, and the Destructive Single Woman   241

was all there. Gavin had spat at me, he'd pushed me against walls and screamed in my face, and then cried and apologized until I forgave him. I also wondered about the financial abuse—he didn't control my money, but he withheld his. He refused to contribute to the bills unless, he said, I was a "better" girlfriend who was more obliging to his needs. I knew I needed to escape, but I was too weak to do anything about it because I was going to be forty soon, and that was a cliff dive into being an unwanted hag.

Summer 2019, I'd given up the government job to do PR for a gallery in Edinburgh. I thought that if I quit the job I hated, then everything would be better, but the problems followed me to this new one. My stomach was perpetually knotted like a pretzel, I could feel anxious flutters in my heart to match the constant twitch in my eye, and I hated having to be in an office every day because I struggled to focus when my mind was fizzing with what was happening at home. Besides, I was hungover a lot of the time because, despite our issues, Gavin and I still went to the pub frequently.

The place where I worked was near a river, surrounded by woodland, and it felt far removed from the city center, despite it only being a fifteen-minute walk away. I can remember that summer, the smell of damp vegetation, the leaves and mud underfoot as I spent my lunchtime ambling by the river listening to Taylor Swift, and her words about relationships soothed me. I walked so much, maybe two hours a day, and she allowed me to forget the pain for a moment, to help ease that sick, helpless feeling that was constantly there. She sang of being an outsider and a nerd, the pain of heartbreak, the casual cruelty of an ex, and she had flitted between bad relationships, just like me. But if she was criticized for being unable to keep a man, for being flighty and sluttish and clingy, then I wondered, did that not mean I was exactly the same?

Taylor also has a delicious tendency to be petty and to hold on to resentments as she exacts revenge through her lyrics on those who wronged her. She was the "Mad Woman" on 2020's *Folklore* album, who goes crazier every time she's called crazy, and who is prodded and poked until she explodes in anger. By the time of her 2024 album, *The Tortured Poets Department,* on the track "Who's Afraid of Little Old Me?" she was now a spitting, levitating banshee who had been poisoned by all the jokes and sneers at her expense.

242   *Single & Psycho*

After I finally left Gavin, I was relieved that I was now free, but at the same time, I also experienced an overwhelming feeling of bitterness. I was angry at myself for having let it go on for so long, and I also questioned what it was about me that had attracted this situation. I knew I was a pushover, I was too soft and not assertive enough, I could be bumbling and awkward, and all my past grievances came back with a bite. I raged at all those from my past who I felt had put me down, and so I deleted them from Facebook—the girls from school I hid from in the toilets, the supposed friends I believed didn't have my back.

I'm all too aware that I share a sense of victimhood with Taylor, a persecution complex where I want to blame others in response to my own self-sabotage. I was angry at the injustice, but I didn't know where to target my rage. Perhaps this is what happened to Hedy in *Single White Female* or Peyton in *The Hand That Rocks the Cradle*. They didn't have an outlet for their grievances, and so they took it out on new victims rather than on the actual, root cause of their despair. This rage would have a palpable presence in the 2010s as an updated feminist movement, one centered on social media, sparked a fresh representation of women. It was the underlying theme of *Gone Girl* and *Girl on a Train*, and this new generation, who wore their feminism like a badge of anger, was owning their bad lifestyle choices and fully embracing their destructiveness and despair.

Taylor hadn't started out as a feminist; she first emerged as a teen country star in 2007, when the "F" word was practically taboo. Other famous women struggled with their response when they were asked if they aligned themselves with the movement; Lady Gaga, who had embraced her status as a gay icon and played with the conventions of sexuality, stated, "I'm not a feminist. I hail men, I love men, I celebrate American male culture—beer, bars and muscle cars."

In 2012, Nigerian author Chimamanda Ngozi Adichie's TEDx talk "We Should All Be Feminists" went viral. When Beyoncé sampled her words in her 2013 track "***Flawless," she made it clear what line she stood on. "Because I am a female, I am expected to aspire to marriage," Adichie says. "I am expected to make my choices always keeping in mind that marriage is the most important. Marriage can be .. . a source of joy and love and mutual support. But why do we teach girls to aspire to marriage and we don't teach boys the same?"

Fleabag, Fourth-Wave Feminism, and the Destructive Single Woman   243

The message of "***Flawless," of the strength in loving and appreciating every part of your body, and her use of the words by Adichie made a huge impact as she reversed the negative stereotypes of feminism. This was further emphasized at the 2014 MTV Video Music Awards, when Beyoncé performed "***Flawless" with the word *FEMINIST* illuminated behind her.

Adichie was asked her thoughts on her words being used in a pop song, and while she described Beyoncé as "lovely" and praised her for spreading the message to a global audience, she also insisted "her type of feminism is not mine" because she "gives quite a lot of space to the necessity of men. I think men are lovely, but I don't think that women should relate everything they do to men: did he hurt me, do I forgive him, did he put a ring on my finger? We women are so conditioned to relate everything to men."[9]

As the 2010s rolled on, feminism was becoming more visible thanks to thought-provoking but humorous books by journalist Caitlin Moran and comedian Tina Fey and with television shows like *Girls,* which explored the tumultuous lives of single twentysomethings through a feminist lens. Following the shock election of Donald Trump in November 2016 and the October 2017 allegations against Harvey Weinstein, this new feminism peaked with the Me Too and Time's Up movements.

Hollywood actresses Ashley Judd, Rose McGowan, Gwyneth Paltrow, and Salma Hayek first spoke out against their experiences of sexual harassment in the business that had long treated the casting couch as a joke. The movement spread to other, less lucrative, industries, making clear that all women had the right to feel safe in their work environment. It became a call to arms to stand up to sexual harassment and abuse and to push for pay equality.

All the negative stereotypes of feminism, of the "feminazis" and man-haters, were reversed as feminism was now co-opted by pop culture into a cool, trendy movement with high-fashion T-shirts such as Dior's "We Should All Be Feminists." The celebrities who had previously denied being a feminist were ready to declare their support, perhaps because it would be more suspicious if they didn't announce these credentials.

Time named 2014 as the Year of Pop Feminism, as it was to modern pop stars what "sex was to 1964 rockers: it's nothing new, but

244 *Single & Psycho*

it's suddenly become electrifying." There were discussions on social media and in opinion pieces on how to do feminism: Could you watch porn? Could you be sexy? How did this relate to dating? On the flip side, women were also grappling with a rise in misogynistic abuse on social media, not just from men but also from other women.

Taylor Swift, as a teen country singer, had initially thought feminism was about hating men rather than "just saying that you hope women and men will have equal rights and equal opportunities." She had listened to and learned from her close friend Lena Dunham, whom she connected with over Twitter to profess her love for Dunham's show, *Girls*, which Dunham wrote and coproduced. Debuting on HBO in 2012, it detailed the lives of four twentysomething single women living in the hipster enclave of Brooklyn, who learned about relationships from growing up with *Sex and the City*. Still figuring out their careers in their postcollege years, they struggle for money and navigate the modern rules of sex and dating. *Girls*, arriving on the scene to coincide with this burgeoning fourth wave of feminism, introduced a new female stereotype, the comically destructive single woman. They were morally questionable, narcissistic, and they threw away the dating rule books, and this new wave first became apparent with Judd Apatow's *Bridesmaids* (2011).

On *Girls*, Lena Dunham plays Hannah, a budding writer who so often makes narcissistic declarations like being the "voice of a generation" and struggles with her vague "situationship" with Adam (Adam Driver). Dunham wasn't shy to strip off, and she was quick to acknowledge that "I have a body that is outside of the Hollywood norm, and it's not the kind of body I ever thought would be seen naked on television."[10] Hannah is open in her discomfort; she begs for attention and affection and has a habit, like Dunham, of rubbing people the wrong way.

Just as Taylor played with her public image in "Blank Space" and Lena Dunham skewered herself as a self-centered millennial, female writers were owning the stereotypes and amping up the crazy, needy, and reckless. Their soundtrack was Swedish pop singer Robyn, whose hit singles "Dancing on My Own" and "Hang with Me" were the anthems of the postadolescent condition. They were the tracks that I was listening to in my early thirties, and I felt just like the characters depicted in the lyrics: the outsider trying to connect with something

Fleabag, Fourth-Wave Feminism, and the Destructive Single Woman   245

real while still indulging in a hedonistic, untethered lifestyle for want of anything else to do and feel.

Robyn's electronic-infused pop dealt with teenage issues for an adult audience, expressing the type of heightened emotions that people, as I could testify all too well, still felt in their thirties and forties, when they were supposed to be beyond this. They were, as the *Guardian* described, "songs that make you want to dance through tears," and her lyrics drew an image of a woman spinning around on the dance floor, heels crunching on broken glass, as she watches the man she is obsessed with kiss another woman. As Robyn told *Pop Justice* in April 2010, "I think those teenage lyrics and that mood is, to me, also this thing that I sometimes feel no matter how old I get. I'm always going to feel like this person on the outside looking in. And I think it's an important subject and it's one that I'm always going to be interested in because it's the driving force behind what a lot of people do. 'Nobody understands me, I've got to tell them how I feel'—that emotion is amazing to me."[11]

In July 2016, a new female-created comedy-drama series aired on BBC3 and immediately gained a loyal audience and critical acclaim. The titular character, Fleabag, is a millennial antihero who is perpetually skint and seeks comfort in fleeting, meaningless sex. She embodies the fearful image of the single woman, blowing cigarette smoke from her red lips before she breaks the fourth wall to reveal her real trauma and loss. "Fleabag's a control freak who wants to convince you everything's OK. It's a kind of tortured complexity that we've all felt," *Fleabag* creator, Phoebe Waller-Bridge, said. "It would be described as 'mysterious' and 'sexy' for a male character, but can be labeled as 'difficult' or 'needy' from women."[12]

Waller-Bridge first conceived of the show in response to a challenge to do a ten-minute skit during a friend's standup storytelling night. She then adapted it into a one-woman play at the Edinburgh International Festival, and it was nominated for an Olivier award and then commissioned for the BBC.

As she was writing the play, feminism was emerging in the United Kingdom with discussions around the pornification of mainstream culture and with progressive actors like Ryan Gosling wearing T-shirts that said "This is what a feminist looks like." Women were proudly stating they were giving up shaving and waxing as a protest

246 *Single & Psycho*

against the tyranny of exacting beauty standards, and online magazines like *Vagenda, Feminist Times,* and *gal-dem* were a reaction to "post-feminism" and the continued push for sexualization through a male lens.

One of the most insightful lines for Waller-Bridge was when Fleabag insists she's not obsessed with sex, but she can't stop thinking about it. As she lists everything she likes—the power, the validation, the touch—the one thing she doesn't love is the feeling of it or the actual act itself: "Actually, loads of women after the end of the play were like, 'Yeah! Me too! I don't like the feeling of it.' I was like, Oh, no. That's so sad that so many women feel like that. Again, that contradiction in her about sex."[13]

As with the stage show, over the six episodes of season one, Fleabag (which was Waller-Bridges's own family nickname) appears to be an urban single woman in London who jokes about her sex life in an unapologetic, confident way, but the black humor is a coping mechanism—she wants people to think she's fine, but inside the cracks are getting deeper. She reveals she is struggling with the tragic death of her best friend, Boo, her guinea-pig themed café is failing, she's split from her boyfriend, and her overachieving sister and stepmother are pains in her life.

In the flashbacks with her deceased friend, we see the warmth and connection they shared. They both enjoyed a drink and they railed against a society that was indifferent to their status as single women. In the present, Fleabag uses sex to forget as she compulsively brings it into every situation, such as masturbating to a speech by Barack Obama. She is now owning that deviant behavior that would have had her condemned as a psychopath if this were in the nineties.

She shares the same traits as the more egotistical Hannah in *Girls* in drinking too much, having random sex with strangers, and falling out with her family. They are also both wildly inappropriate in meetings—Fleabag flashes her bra during an appointment with her bank manager because, she claims, she thought she was wearing a T-shirt underneath. Hannah sabotages a job interview by making a date rape joke that does not go down well.

Fleabag exhibited what *Buzzfeed* writer Emmeline Clein referred to as dissociative feminism, of numbing yourself, embracing self-indulgent behavior, and turning it into a joke. She doesn't wallow;

Fleabag, Fourth-Wave Feminism, and the Destructive Single Woman   247

rather, she separates herself from the pain in the same way women sometimes disassociate from their bodies during sex, going through the motions of the act as they think they should rather than fully being present to enjoy it.

After the second season was released in 2019, there was a trend on TikTok for posters to show their "Fleabag era" of going to sleep in mascara and relishing their prettiness after crying. As Sophie Peyser wrote in *Lithium* magazine, "When the Fleabag woman is hurt—by society, by men, whomever—she responds by sinking deeper into that pain. Fleabag—and the real-life women on TikTok who identify with her suffering—medicates through sex, alcohol, and inflicting pain on others."[14]

She concluded that this tendency for self-destruction was damaging to the feminist movement as Fleabag directed her anger toward herself rather than at the patriarchy—although, as women, have we not always inflicted pain on ourselves? It's a form of self-flagellation to be so critical of our appearance, to compare ourselves to others, feeling envy at the perfect body in magazines and on Instagram.

At the end of season two, Fleabag bonds with the "hot priest" whose celibacy means there will never be a physical relationship between them. He teaches her that it's a human connection, rather than meaningless sex, that can help her soothe her pain.

Lena Dunham had been heavily criticized for employing a fashionable feminism in *Girls* that was exclusionary to those who were nonwhite and nongender-conforming. While there had long been a lack of representation of people of color, screenwriters including Mindy Kaling, Michaela Coel, and Issa Rae filled the void by creating their own works to redefine how a modern woman of color was depicted on the screen. By taking control of the narrative, they shifted typical one-dimensional supporting characters to create complicated stories that explored sexuality, trauma, relationships, and the type of awkward behavior that had mostly, up until that point, been reserved for white women.

Airing the same year as *Fleabag* was *Insecure,* a comedy-drama created by Issa Rae to depict the lives of twenty- and thirtysomething Los Angelenos based on her friends, and in particular, the experiences of a young Black woman who is removed from the angry, assertive stereotypes and instead is unsure, awkward, and trying to

248   *Single & Psycho*

find her place in the world. In the pilot episode, Issa introduces herself to a classroom of disinterested youths with whom she's trying to connect through her nonprofit organization to reach children in the projects. She describes herself as a twenty-nine-year-old, college-educated Black woman who has been with her boyfriend for five years and is then bombarded with questions as to why she's not married.

"I'm just not right now," she replies with a defensive smile.

"My dad said ain't nobody checking for bitter-ass Black women anymore."

"Tell your dad Black women aren't bitter. They're just tired of being expected to settle for less."

At work, she feels she's treated like the token Black person with all the answers, and she's also having doubts about her relationship with Lawrence, who spends his days on the sofa as he struggles to find work. Instead, she fantasizes about an ex, Daniel, who has reappeared in her life. She doesn't want to waste her time lounging with Lawrence while missing out on her future.

Her best friend, Molly, is a corporate lawyer who appears to have her life in order yet struggles with dating. She wants to find the one but often comes on too strong too soon. Rather than sending a text, she chooses to call a guy she's been on three dates with, and this forwardness scares him into rejecting her: "Sorry, I'm not looking for a relationship right now."

Molly jokes she cries tears of singleness, frustrated about the dating scene as a Black woman. She tells her coworker that Black guys love Asians and Latinos and white women, but it's the Black women they don't date.

"It's not happening for me," Molly cries to Issa over the phone in the bathroom at work, but she's constantly told that she needs to lower her standards. She's desperate to get into The League, an elite dating site, and even though she's been seeing good guy Jered, she ditches him in favor of the high flyers solely because he's not college-educated. But then, whenever she tries to pin them down to commit, they run scared.

Rae believed there was an obvious gap in on-screen representations of the women she could identify with, that of "a regular, insecure Black girl . . . I don't feel fierce, flawless all the time, and that's OK."[15] The overriding stereotype in popular culture had been the

Fleabag, Fourth-Wave Feminism, and the Destructive Single Woman   249

"angry Black woman" or the supportive secondary character. There was limited space for the one burdened with insecurities, who struggled with societal injustices, and who was held back by damaging stereotypes.

In the 2019 novel *Queenie* by Candice Carty-Williams, the titular character also contends with the expectations placed on her as a Black woman. She is fetishized by the white men she dates, who see her just as tits and ass to be abused—and with the prevalent stereotype of the assertive Black woman, and the constraints within her own British Caribbean community, she feels she's not allowed to be vulnerable. She wants to use her junior position at a newspaper to support the Black Lives Matter movement, as she's increasingly stirred up by the incidents of injustice that she reads about, but she is consistently told by her white editor that it's too much for audiences.

Queenie is always being told she's too much, that she's too angry and too sexual, and she feels like she's cracking up under the pressure and stress. She discovers, at the beginning of the novel, that she had a miscarriage despite being on contraception, and her live-in boyfriend breaks up with her before she gets the chance to tell him. Dealing with the aftermath of having grown up in an abusive household, she uses casual encounters as a coping mechanism while dealing with the racism and fetishization of Black women on dating apps. After being pursued by a tweed-wearing work colleague, Ted, who pressures her into having sex with him in the work toilets, he ghosts her and then puts in a complaint that she's the one stalking him. Queenie's been taught to hold all her emotions in, as it's just what's expected of her cultural background, but faced with all this racist and sexist oppression, of being wrongly accused of being the aggressor, what she needs to do is embrace the anger.

In 2020, Michaela Coel's *I May Destroy You* was the series to watch on the BBC during the pandemic. Following the success of her Channel 4 sitcom *Chewing Gum,* Coel had been given creative freedom to deliver a new series in the way she envisioned it. In *Chewing Gum,* she had played an awkward twenty-four-year-old raised in a strict Christian Ghanian household in a London council estate and, with the empowerment of Beyoncé ringing in her ears, is on an accident-prone mission to lose her virginity.

250   *Single & Psycho*

For her follow-up, *I May Destroy You*, Coel drew on the aftermath of her own sexual assault in 2016 to play a hip young London writer, Arabella, whose confidence is shattered when she is drugged and assaulted by a stranger. Her rape forces her to come to terms with her vulnerability as a woman, whereas previously all her focus had been on being "Black and poor." The supporting characters must also grapple with their identities, with Kwame (Paapa Essiedu) as a Black gay man who indulges in casual Grindr encounters and is then shaken up by a sexual assault, and Terry (Weruche Opia) as an actress who has a terrible audition for a feminist brand after being asked if it's "her real hair."

Arabella is on deadline to complete her much-anticipated follow-up to her viral *Chronicles of a Fed-Up Millennial*, but rather than buckling down for an all-nighter, she procrastinates and is persuaded to go out with friends. She blacks out after her drink is spiked, and she's left with only the haziest memories of what happened—a cracked phone screen, a cut on her head, and a flashback to a man assaulting her. It takes her a while to piece it all together, and as she realizes she's not crazy and didn't imagine it, the assault rocks her foundations. Later, as she connects with another author, Zain (Karan Gill), the first man she sleeps with after her assault, she discovers he removed the condom without her knowing, and it's like she's been violated all over again. At a literary event where they have both been invited to speak, she chooses to out him as a rapist who gaslit her, and when her speech spreads on social media, she becomes an Instagram sensation—the avenging angel standing up for women.

But the double assaults have left her a shell of who she was, and as resentments simmer under the surface, she returns to Ostia, a beachside city near Rome, where she had spent time writing her novel on the publishing company's dime. It had been a drug-fueled trip, and the sex with the Italian drug dealer Biagio (Marouane Zotti) was blissful. But this time, ungrounded and grasping for that connection with him, she arrives at his door uninvited and lets herself in. He's shocked to find her in his home, and when she runs down to get pizza, she comes back to find he's locked the door behind her. It's as if he's now scared of her as the mentally unstable, abused woman who has turned up uninvited, and rather than talking with her, he effectively ghosts her by locking her out. She erupts in anger, kicking and

Fleabag, Fourth-Wave Feminism, and the Destructive Single Woman   251

beating on the door again and again. To get rid of this madwoman, he opens the door, and when he shows her that he has a gun, she flees into the night.

Arabella's life, and career, further nosedives until one evening she recognizes her attacker, a white man, who has returned to the scene of the crime. She chooses to bite back and play him at his game by becoming the avenging angel, and in a series of scenes that are part fantasy, part reality, she plays with different narratives in her mind. In a moment that would be similarly replicated later in 2020 in *Promising Young Woman*, she pretends to be unconscious in the nightclub toilet, and as he tries to rape her once more, she opens her eyes and, in all soberness, confronts him. This bold depiction of vengeful femininity, of furiously reacting to the injustice inflicted on her, was one that very few women of color had been allowed to express. Not since the days of Cleopatra Jones and Coffy had Black women been given their chance to be as fucked up and raging as Alex Forrest or other supposedly psychotic women whose trauma manifests into anger. By being given a chance to tell her story in the way she wanted to, Coel tapped into a subject that she explored subversively. While it felt like an original celebration of being Black and British, it also had a wide appeal as the themes connected with women of all backgrounds. There's a very frank moment when Arabella and Biagio have sex while she's on her period, and rather than being repulsed, he is fascinated by the blood clot on the sheets. This was a bold acknowledgment for all women that they shouldn't feel ashamed of their bodily functions and in fact should rejoice in being open about it.

One of the reasons shows like *Insecure* also touched a nerve was their reflection of the modern confusion of dating via app. In *Insecure,* Molly talks Issa through the different dating apps: "Ok Cupid. It's free, so it's like bottom-of-the-barrel dudes. Tinder used to be cool, but now it's basically a fuck app. Hinge at least pulls up your network of friends . . . basically most of these dudes are not looking for a relationship. They're just trying to fuck."

The rise of internet dating was supposed to make it even easier to find a date, but instead it caused more anxiety among people who struggled to match. With the dominance of apps and Instagram DMs, single women steered their love lives with new dating expressions

252   *Single & Psycho*

such as *gaslighting, ghosting,* and *breadcrumbing*—words that Alex Forrest would no doubt sympathize with.

Donna Freitas used surveys of students in 2006 as a basis for her 2013 book *The End of Sex: How Hookup Culture Is Leaving a Generation Unhappy, Sexually Unfulfilled, and Confused.* There was a sense that this hookup culture, as propagated by *Sex and the City,* was damaging to women, but if fleeting connections and one-night stands were worrisome in the first decade of the Millennium, then it would reach a whole new level with this proliferation of dating apps. Their introduction in the 2010s was the equivalent to the pill in the 1960s—it was a sexual revolution that allowed for easier, consequence-free transactions. But when it came to searching for a meaningful, long-term relationship, it often proved to be a bitter experience.

When Tinder was launched in September 2012, its format of swiping images of potential dates was revolutionary. It was the fast food of online dating, where people could accept or reject purely based on an image. Other companies adapted to Tinder's proliferation by developing their own apps with swipe function, and Hinge and Bumble followed, all placing photographs as the main attraction. Previously, the descriptions had been as important as the photographs, but now what you wrote didn't really matter—it was how you looked, and the front-facing camera on the phone made it so much easier to post your own selfie. There were the duck pouts, the bathroom selfies, the lying on your bed and taking the picture from high above, and then there was the (mostly unsolicited) dick pic.

In a 2015 feature in *Vanity Fair,* Nancy Jo Sales was on a mission to observe how the app was being used. She came across a table of professionals in a sports bar in Manhattan's financial district, letting off steam from their high-powered jobs on Wall Street by scrolling through Twitter and comparing matches. They might have declared, "Tinder sucks," but that didn't stop them from swiping.

The guys who were using it admitted there was competition to sleep with the hottest girls, whom they referred to as "Tinderellas." As one said, "I sort of play that I could be a boyfriend kind of guy . . . but then they start wanting me to care more . . . and I just don't."[16]

All that choice was devaluing relationships. Because it was so easy to find a new match, people wanted to hedge their bets and embrace

Fleabag, Fourth-Wave Feminism, and the Destructive Single Woman   253

hookups and short-term dating rather than commit too quickly. There was a degree of pressure on women not to come off as overly keen, for fear of being accused of bunny boiler behavior. They had to act the "cool girl," whether they were drip-fed promises of commitment or ghosted after a few dates. In an example of gender inequality, often it was men who had the power to decide whether something was serious or not or whether, in the words of J. Cole in his 2011 single "Work Out," he's only here for the night.

Online dating also proved to be more of a challenge to people of color, a frustration expressed by Molly in *Insecure* and by Queenie. Ok Cupid research revealed that Black women received fewer replies from men and that "every race—including other blacks—singles them out for the cold shoulder."

Coupled with the Me Too movement, issues of consent and bad dating practices were endlessly debated and depicted in a wide variety of content. In the 2022 Netflix documentary *The Tinder Swindler*, the women who bravely told their story about a compulsive and dangerous con artist were trolled online. Criticized for their own apparent desperation, they became the target of ridicule and were placed under far greater scrutiny than the deceptive criminal who conned them out of huge sums of money.

Kristen Roupenian's short story "Cat Person," which was published in the *New Yorker* in 2017, went viral for its description of a sad and disappointing sexual encounter. It was hailed as a defining touch point of the Me Too movement for exploring the gray areas of consent and its depiction of a woman who puts her own discomfort to the side to manage her date's feelings.

The 2023 movie adaptation opens with a voice-over as if from a vintage movie trailer as the heroine, Margot (Emilia Jones), a twenty-year-old student, stands behind the cinema concession stand, where she works: "You will cringe as the demented doctor experiments with a girl's trusting innocence." Here she meets Robert (Nicholas Braun), an awkward and much older customer whom she swaps numbers with.

We see a full moon and the caption of Margaret Atwood's famous quote, "Men are afraid that women will laugh at them. Women are afraid that men will kill them." It's a heavy-handed way of explaining the aim of this movie, which gives the seven-thousand-word story

254 *Single & Psycho*

a horror makeover. The idea of turning it into a thriller must have been encouraged by the success of *Promising Young Woman* in 2020, which also explores issues around consent and sex dynamics, but the bizarrely over-the-top conclusion burns down much of the subtlety of the story.

It plays up to the scariness of dating by posing those universal questions: Do we really know who we are messaging and flirting with over text and who we've arranged to go for drinks with? We see Margot's growing fear and paranoia around her own safety as she walks across empty parking lots at night, ramping up Britney Spears's "Gimme More" to give her faux confidence.

Margot is advised by her best friend, Taylor, never to double text, yet after she sends a racy selfie and doesn't get a response, she continues to message until Robert asks her out on a date. It's hard to know what she sees in him. She feels afraid of being alone with him, and not only does he destroy the ant colony in her college lab and inadvertently (and symbolically) kills the queen ant, but he also bulldozes her into seeing *The Empire Strikes Back* on their first date and turns out to be a terrible kisser. He tells her he has cats, perhaps as a way to make him sound gentle, but at his house, she realizes there's no sign that they even exist. Did he lie about being a cat person? In the movie, it turns out he's been keeping them in the basement, the appropriate place for a creature so aligned with femininity.

Margot hopes that if they have sex, she might feel more attracted to him, but now that she's on his bed and he's taking off her clothes, it doesn't feel right. In the unsettling sex scene, the device of a doppelgänger is used as she explains why it's easier just to go along with it, in the way that women often disassociate. This doppelgänger isn't the bad side of her, like Nina's in *Black Swan*, as discussed in the next chapter. It's the rational, straight-talking side of Margot who encourages her to say no, but it's so hard to listen to these sensible voices when you are right in the thick of it.

As soon as the sex is over, she is hit by a wave of repulsion at all those porno moves he puts her through, and she is adamant that she doesn't want to see him again. There is one very effective scene that is framed like a horror movie. Sitting in darkness, with their faces lit by the phone, Margot and Taylor are hunched together as they watch Robert's drunken messages ping one after the other, and as they

Fleabag, Fourth-Wave Feminism, and the Destructive Single Woman   255

become more unhinged, it culminates in him calling her a "whore." This was a moment that hit home for me, having been subject to a torrent of text abuse by Gavin whenever I ran away from the flat to escape his rages—the "whore" and "slut," "disgusting," "smelly," all fired at me one after the other until they eventually made way for pity and apologies. It's one of the most common tactics for abusers—they wear you down with insults, undermining your confidence until you start to believe it.

This was where the short story ended, but in the movie, Margot ups her own paranoid behavior by breaking into Robert's garage and attempting to plant a tracking device on his car, and when he catches her, it turns into a full-blown home invasion thriller.

Here, there was no clear answer to the modern dating conundrums or to the question of who was really the unstable one. After being ghosted, it's inevitable to ask what went wrong and to blame yourself, and this frustration drives Robert to stalkerish behavior. Margot, on the other hand, is right to feel scared; she is ingrained with the knowledge that she is vulnerable when walking alone at night, and she is perfectly within her rights not to reply to him ever again. Dating can be like walking on a tightrope—trying to act interested without coming across as needy, trying to handle rejections and bad dates without being disheartened, and the real fears around whether the person you've met online is who they say they are.

For women like Taylor Swift and the messy millennials in popular culture, playing up to the stereotypes of the chaotic single woman was a means of taking control. With dating apps encouraging even more uncertainty in relationships, and with the bunny boiler legacy of Alex Forrest still lingering like smoke trails, sometimes it's good to own the crazy before someone else can accuse you of it.

CHAPTER 18

"I'll Show You Crazy"

In December 2019, the first trailer for *Promising Young Woman* was unveiled, and it offered a tantalizing snapshot into a neon-lit candy-colored world of revenge. We first see Carey Mulligan slumped on the maroon leather booth of a nightclub as a group of men discuss the state that this lone, drunk woman is in: "They put themselves in danger. . . . You'd think they'd learn by that age, right?"

She's taken home by a supposedly good guy (Adam Brody), plied with more drinks, and placed on his bed when she's clearly too drunk to consent. And then, like Arabella in *I May Destroy You*, she comes around, sits up, and looks soberly at the camera: "I said, what are you doing?" Next, we see her adding another count to a notebook in which she records, it's presumed, the men she's targeted.

For people who saw this original trailer, there was an assumption that Mulligan's Cassie would do more than just scold these men, that she had a psychopathic desire to physically hurt them. The selected clips from the movie show her smearing lipstick across her face like a madwoman, and to the strains of Britney's "Toxic," she is dressed as a campy nurse with Harley Quinn hair in one of those sexy Halloween costumes. As she addresses the man who is restrained on a bed, she insinuates that she's about to perform amateur surgery on her victim. This vengeful Me Too queen was targeting the type of privileged white man who could use his influence to get away with rape on campus.

The film's release date was delayed until the end of 2020 due to the coronavirus pandemic, and when it finally came out, it was hailed as a feminist masterpiece, a fizzing critique of the Me Too movement and Hollywood's voice of conscience to Harvey Weinstein's downfall. Yet it turned out that Cassie wasn't quite the psycho as promised in that trailer. In actuality, the film was a rainbow-striped black comedy that delivered a gut-punch twist.

Writer and director Emerald Fennell was hit with the concept for the film at a dinner party in her flat in London, when one of her guests mentioned a creepy encounter on the tube. The men were shocked, but the women could all relate, and they chipped in with their own horror stories. Emerald thought of the paranoia women so often feel about their drinks being spiked on a night out and the men who think a drunk woman would be easier to persuade to come home with them.[1]

"What if I went to a nightclub and pretended to be really, really drunk, and somebody took me home, and then just as they were removing my pants, I revealed I wasn't drunk?" she thought. An image formed in her mind of a woman sitting up in bed, suddenly sober, and asking, "What are you doing?" She later described this very scenario to a producer: "I said, 'And then she sits up, and she's not drunk!' And he went, 'Holy [expletive], she's a psycho!'"[2]

She was particularly scornful of the type of guy who is convinced they are on the right side and support feminism, yet they would also be willing to take advantage if the opportunity presented itself. In words that could apply to Dan from *Fatal Attraction*, Emerald said, "Everybody thinks of themselves as a good person—so what happens when someone comes along and shows you that you're not?"

Thirty-year-old Cassie is a medical school dropout who still lives with her parents, and her girlishly pink bedroom indicates she hasn't made the full transition to adulthood. She works in a cupcake café by day, and at night, she prowls nightclubs, pretending she's drunk so she can root out those supposed good guys.

She may be single, but she's the opposite of Diane Keaton in *Looking for Mr. Goodbar*. She's not looking for a man for excitement and thrills; rather, she has a desire for revenge. She pretends she's close to blackout drunk to make herself vulnerable and then waits to be picked up, so she can give him a surprise he's not expecting.

She isn't just seeking revenge on men who take advantage of drunk women; she's also on a vengeance campaign to get justice for

258 *Single & Psycho*

her friend Nina, who committed suicide after she was gang-raped at a college party and was then slut-shamed for it through the circulation of a video of the attack.

The colorful candy-sweet costume and production design, with Cassie's nails painted different pastel shades, was what Emerald Fennell described as "poison popcorn." Cassie dresses in an unthreatening manner to disarm, and tonally, the movie flirts with being a rom-com, with the inclusion of a scene where Cassie and her new boyfriend dance to Paris Hilton's "Stars Are Blind" in a drugstore aisle.

During an early screening of *Promising Young Woman*, Carey Mulligan observed members of the audience becoming animated during the tragic twist. "No one was sitting comfortably," she said. "It provokes a reaction that is unlike anything I have seen in a long time."[3]

It also was polarizing among critics. Similar to the criticism of Glenn Close, Mulligan took exception to the *Variety* reviewer who implied that she wasn't pretty enough for the role, as if Margot Robbie would be a more tempting prospect to fool the predatory men. *Slate* lambasted it for not addressing Cassie's white privilege and for costar Laverne Cox being relegated to "the Magical Black Cupcake Boss with no apparent backstory or life goals other than to support the fragile Cassie," although I'd say it's definite progress to have a trans woman playing a character whose identity is unquestionably a woman.

The movie succeeded in turning the psycho single woman trope on its head and reevaluating the raunch culture of the 2000s, as punctuated with its Paris Hilton and Britney Spears soundtrack. In the nightclub scenes, Cassie is the threat, and this time it's the man brought up on *Girls Gone Wild* who should be afraid. The easy pickup who is too drunk to say no to flashing her breasts or performing sex acts won't be so easy this time, and she could, in fact, cause harm.

The point that Emerald made with the devastating twist that saw the tables turned on Cassie was that the neat empowerment of Hollywood revenge movies was not the reality for women who are assaulted. They don't get the chance to execute the perfect revenge. She said, "That's not how it works when women are angry and upset and traumatized."[4]

Emerald Fennell was head writer on the second season of the BBC series *Killing Eve*, taking over from Phoebe Waller-Bridge, whose first season aired on BBC3 and BBC America in 2018. Based on Luke Jennings's novels, it starred Jodie Comer as deadly assassin Villanelle, who is obsessed with Eve (Sandra Oh), the British intelligence officer tasked with investigating and capturing her. Villanelle has an exquisitely frivolous taste in fashion and a childlike demeanor that belies her psychopathy. *Promising Young Woman* shares a similar dark undercurrent beneath a glittering, colorful surface, and just as Cassie uses costume to disarm, Villanelle's couture gives her cover to appear less threatening as she plots violent murders.

The fixation between Eve and Villanelle is played out as a skewering of all those movie clichés of obsessive love in the domestic thrillers of the nineties. Villanelle steals Eve's suitcase and insists her lover tries on Eve's clothes and even single white females her identity, using her name as an alias as she travels across Europe to assassinate her targets.

Adding a twist to the way bathrooms are often the setting for a woman's violent death, Villanelle breaks into Eve's apartment and stifles her screams by turning the tap on her head. And in one of the more shocking moments, she hunts her prey in a nightclub and, under the heavy strobe lights, stabs him to death. Not only does this scene allude to, and subvert, the danger women often feel on a night out, but it is also reminiscent of a nightclub scene in an erotic thriller—although this time there's no Michael Douglas in a green V-neck sweater, and rather than sex with Sharon Stone, it ends with death.

Eve is in her forties; she's going through a midlife crisis and is burdened with worries that her career and her marriage have reached a plateau. Villanelle awakens something in her, a sense of excitement and danger, and Eve admires her rule-breaking, her lack of inhibitions, and her love of a luxury lifestyle. She wants to hunt her down and arrest her, but she also wants to be with her, and this depiction of an obsessive relationship outside of heterosexual norms was incredibly unique in popular culture.

As Eliana Dockterman wrote in *Time*, "Writers typically portray female obsession as one-sided. Crazed women stalk the wives of the men they can't have (*Fatal Attraction*, *Obsessed*) or try to subsume another's life (*Single White Female*, *Ingrid Goes West*). Eve and Villanelle's mutual fascination is rare."[5]

260   *Single & Psycho*

Eve is also attracted to Villanelle because her mind frequently goes to dark places. Eve, in one scene, asks her husband how he might murder her. "Flatter you to death?" he offers. When he asks her the same, she comes up with an elaborately gruesome plan: "I'd paralyze you with saxotoxin and suffocate you in your sleep. Chop you into the smallest bits I could manage. Boil you down. Put you in a blender. Take you to work in a flask and flush you down a restaurant toilet."

The dark side of femininity was bubbling to the surface throughout the 2010s on the back of the new wave of feminism. Rather than obsessions centered on love, female writers created complicated characters as a means of being part of a more open discussion on mental health, anxiety, and the untapped rage at the violence and fear women experience in everyday life.

After being breadcrumbed and ghosted by Paul in the weeks following the miscarriage, I now fantasized about taking revenge on him. I imagined what I could do—perhaps sending him something awful in the post, maybe mass deliveries of pizza or an anonymous email of complaint to his work. It was an obvious step too far; petty vengeance is never really a solution and instead is more damaging to the perpetrator, but at least it was cathartic to imagine it. When we'd been dating, Paul would always, without fail, comment on women he fancied, from the "hot" Brazilian at the gym to the actresses in every movie we watched, and even during something seemingly harmless like *The Great British Bake Off*. It really bothered me and made me feel like I wasn't good enough, to the point where I was trying to think of movies to watch that wouldn't have an attractive actress in it.

He took a particular shine to one of the contestants on the latest series of the baking show, and it wasn't just a casual mention; it was all the time, without fail. It culminated in him sending her an Instagram message saying, effectively, he wanted her in his stocking at Christmas, and then when she replied, he sent me the screenshot. I was devastated. I felt disrespected and betrayed, and I didn't respond to his messages until he apologized a few days later. I was quick to forgive him, but it continued to be a sore point, and when I'd told one of my friends, she took an immediate dislike to him and thought he was a loser.

This particular *Bake-Off* contestant was on Cameo, where she would send a personalized video message for a reasonable double-digit fee. I imagined paying her to create a video to send to Paul where, after I explained that he had ghosted the woman who had miscarried his child, she could tell him what an asshole he was. Playing it out in my head was incredibly satisfying, but I knew that doing it in real life wouldn't exactly help me heal. Thoughts of revenge are better left as a fantasy rather than spilling into reality. But my imaginings were an outlet for my anger, in the same way that it was manifested in popular culture at the time. I'd watched *Promising Young Woman* and *I May Destroy You*, and I'd found a catharsis in Elisabeth Moss's depiction of escaping an abusive relationship in *The Invisible Man*. That someone who painted himself as the good guy—who spoke up for women's rights and claimed to be a feminist in his deep concern for women's safety—could not only objectify women on a daily basis but also be so callous was infuriating.

Phoebe Waller-Bridge told *Vogue* in May 2018, "It feels like, recently, a lot of female anger has been unleashed. Articulated anger. Which is exciting for me because I've always found female rage very appealing."

Rage was brewing when Donald Trump was elected as president in 2016, even after being caught on tape boasting of "grabbing them by the pussy." It was also there when women shared their stories of sexual assault and for the media coverage of cases where white male college students used their privilege to escape prison sentences after raping intoxicated young women. The female characters created by Waller-Bridge and Fennell deal with their rage either by disassociating or by expressing it through violence. Rather than suppressing their bad side, they fully allow it to run riot.

Black Swan (2010) was one of the first of a new wave of movies that provided a deeper insight into women's mental health. Darren Aronofsky was inspired by Michael Powell and Emeric Pressburger's ballet classic, *The Red Shoes*, to create a twisted fairytale about a ballet dancer, Nina (Natalie Portman), who is consumed by her own obsession for perfection.

She punishes her body by vomiting up her food, cracking her bleeding toes, and pulling at the broken toenails, and this single-mindedness will culminate in psychosis and a mental breakdown. She may find freedom in expression, but when she unleashes her dark side, she becomes a destructive force.

262 *Single & Psycho*

Nina, with her little girl voice, lives in a form of stunted growth as her mother, Erica (Barbara Hershey), still treats her like a child. They both coo "pretty" over a pink grapefruit, and her girlish peachy-pink and frilly bedroom (much like Cassie's in *Promising Young Woman* and Selina Kyle's in *Batman Returns*, as if the confines of overt, girlish femininity will erupt like a volcano of molten sugar) is filled with stuffed animals to watch over her. She is given little privacy as her mother sometimes sleeps in a chair by her bed—not great when Nina wants to experiment with touching herself. Erica gave up her ballet career for her daughter and now lives vicariously through her. At the same time, she's overprotective and tries to block Nina's first performance when she thinks it's too much for her and forces her to have a slice of cake even though Nina is so conscious of what she eats.

The artistic director of the ballet company, Thomas (Vincent Cassel), wants to put on a visceral, real performance of *Swan Lake*, and to start afresh, he retires his prima ballerina, Beth, in favor of a younger dancer. The others bitch about Beth, insinuating she's a hag close to menopause. It's perfect casting to have Winona Ryder play Beth as she was edged out of Hollywood by a new generation of stars like Natalie Portman. Nina secretly enters Beth's dressing room, sitting in her chair to admire her reflection as she tries on her lipstick, and imagines that she can step into her place. After being ousted by the company, Beth is hit by a car, and Thomas believes she walked into traffic on purpose, because everything she does "comes from within, from some dark impulse." As Beth lies on pink sheets in her hospital bed, surrounded by flowers and with a mangled leg that will no longer be able to dance, Nina sees her own future, when she might be made redundant too.

While Nina embodies the innocent White Swan, "the virginal girl, pure and sweet," Thomas wants her to explore her darker side to prove she can play the Black Swan, the "lustful twin" who "tricks and seduces" the prince. Thomas is the alpha male who claims dominance over the dancers and appears to expect sexual favors in return for championing their career. He encourages Nina to masturbate as a way of awakening her sexual repression, and in his office, he kisses her aggressively. She bites him in response to this assault, and it's the first reveal that she has a power inside her.

"I'll Show You Crazy"   263

When a new girl, Lily (Mila Kunis), rocks up at the studio, she is completely unapologetic for being late or for smoking indoors, and she's confident in the way she moves and acts. Lily looks like Nina; they're mistaken for sisters, and after inviting Nina out for drinks, she encourages her to take MDMA, even though they are due on the stage the next day. Back in Nina's bedroom, Lily appears to give Nina her first orgasm, but then Nina sees her own face between her legs, as if she is being tormented by her doppelgänger.

Rather than her sexual awakening being a positive transition to adulthood, it's a destructive force, as it so often is for mentally fragile female characters like Nina. As her anxiety intensifies, she picks at her skin until it bleeds; imagines feathers are sprouting from textured skin; and in the fracture of mirrors, her evil doppelgänger is taunting her as she fully inhabits the Black Swan. Convinced that Lily has been trying to steal her role, she lashes out at her and stabs her in the abdomen with a piece of a shattered mirror. It's a hallucination; in reality, she's the one who is injured, and as the White Swan dives into oblivion, Nina's expression is one of ecstasy, like Norma Desmond finally ready for her close-up. By embracing her ambition and sexuality, Nina has to destroy herself.

The *New York Times* described *Black Swan* as a "witchy brew of madness and cunning" as it linked Nina's descent into obsession and madness to a bewitching.[6] It's the eternal struggle of womanhood—the desire to be good and the repressed "bad" side, which, when set free, will inevitably lead to her death. This twinning is a classic gothic horror trope, straight from the pages of Robert Louis Stevenson's *Strange Case of Dr. Jekyll and Mr. Hyde*. In Brian De Palma's *Sisters*, the deviant twin must die for the good girl to survive, and Taylor Swift also played with this concept in her music video for "Anti-Hero." Here, the bad Taylor provokes negative thoughts about her body while also encouraging her to stay up late and drink too much.

Black Swan is a film about an obsession that takes over a woman's mind until she can no longer tell what's real, in the same way that Alex Forrest becomes deluded in her pursuit of Dan. It's also about a mother's suppression of her daughter, the cost of seeking perfection, and the bliss of giving in completely to madness. It took home Oscars for Best Picture, Best Director, and Best Actress for Natalie Portman,

264   *Single & Psycho*

and its huge success encouraged a line of new movies that portrayed complicated single women whose obsessions feed their dark side.

In *Red Sparrow* (2018), for example, Jennifer Lawrence is an ambitious ballerina in Russia who violently beats members of her company whom she believes sabotaged her career. After a nasty leg break, she is no longer able to dance and instead is recruited by her uncle to work as a spy for Putin. She uses her cunning and aggression, when needed, to survive.

With the launch of Instagram in 2011, and its colossal impact on mainstream life, there was a subgenre of social media thrillers that acted as a commentary on the damage it can do to self-esteem. Rather than hankering after a relationship and a family, the obsessive single woman of the social media era is after fame and money.

Ingrid Goes West (2017) paints the toxicity of social media and the narcissism and envy it creates. Aubrey Plaza is Ingrid, just released from a psychiatric facility for stalker behavior. Now that she has her phone back, she goes to Los Angeles, where she is fixated on a social media star, Taylor (Elizabeth Olsen), who uses Instagram to monetize her perfect life, complete with husband, beautiful home, and wellness lifestyle. Ingrid orchestrates a meeting by pretending to rescue Taylor's dog, and the two strike up a friendship, despite the suspicions of Taylor's husband and brother, who mooches off his sister.

It's a modern, satirical update on *Single White Female*, and *Influencer* (2022) is a thriller that follows a similar theme. Emily Tennant plays Madison, whose Instagram fame allows her to travel in Thailand, as long as she keeps her followers updated with dreamy photos from her trip. She was supposed to be traveling with a boyfriend, but after an argument with him, she goes alone. At the resort bar, she is hassled by a sleazy guest, and coming to her rescue is CW (Cassandra Naud), an American traveler whose easygoing persona belies something darker. When Madison's room is robbed and passport stolen, we wonder what CW has to do with it, and soon we discover her ruthless intent when she takes Madison on a trip to a remote island and leaves her there. With Madison now disappeared, CW takes over the villa she rented, and we also meet Jessica (Sara Canning), another influencer, and Madison's boyfriend, Ryan, who both become suspicious of her. The question is: Whose life is fake? CW appears to hate influencers and their lifestyle, but she steals their

"I'll Show You Crazy"   265

identity and their lives, with the understanding that their world is so shallow that her sociopathy can slip under the radar.[7]

Sometimes these women are just psychotic—they haven't been wronged by men; they just like to kill, or they're driven by greed. In *I Care a Lot* (2020), Rosamund Pike excels as the Amy Dunne–esque Marla Grayson, who uses the legal system to place vulnerable elderly people under her conservatorship so she can seize their assets. Marla is a psychopath who doesn't experience fear or empathy and will go to extremes in her manipulation as she works the system for her own personal gain.

Cinema has always thrived on its depiction of violent acts perpetrated by men, but for women to display such brutality is a rarity. If not for a political cause, such as the women using violence to campaign for suffrage, it could be triggered by the loss of a child or as a response to male aggression, where female purity was compromised. The rape-revenge exploitation movie of the seventies suggested that once she had been violated, she had nothing else to lose. With rape being considered worse than death, it tied into notions that a woman's true value is her virtuosity and virginity, and if those are taken from her, then she has lost everything. *I Spit on Your Grave* (1978) features an excruciating twenty-five-minute-long rape scene, and given the female nudity, it was designed to both tantalize and horrify a male audience. Now, in the era of Me Too, women were angered by the double standards as they refused to be treated as objects.

The Me Too movement also highlighted how few female directors were being given the chance to tell female-centric stories. Traditionally, female characters tended to be drawn from a masculine point of view. Catherine Tramell, for example, was very much the male fantasy of an ice-cold but sexually voracious bad girl, and Alex Forrest a desperate single woman in her thirties—and these characters only became more nuanced due to the talents of the actresses who played them. As more women than ever were given a chance to helm movies, they created complex female characters who expressed their anger at the world through violence.

In Ana Lily Amirpour's *Mona Lisa and the Blood Moon* (2021), a young woman with telekinetic powers escapes from a mental institution and into a lurid New Orleans with its neon fast-food restaurants and strip clubs. The patient, Mona Lisa (Jeon Jong-seo), is an outsider,

266 *Single & Psycho*

having escaped from North Korea as a child, and she awakens from a catatonic state with the arrival of a blood moon. It opens like a classic horror movie as she seizes control of the hospital wardens' bodies, making them stab themselves and bash their heads against a television screen. When she meets a tough-talking stripper, Bonnie Belle (Kate Hudson), at a burger bar, the single mother invites her into her life as she finds a way to exploit the girl's powers by extracting cash from unwilling strip club patrons.

Mona Lisa feasts on junk food throughout the movie, and as she munches down on a burger, Bonnie Belle tells her she had a sense something weird was going to happen that night because "when it's a full moon, I feel it in my ovaries." Similarly, Mona Lisa's powers are linked to the pain of menstruation. "I bleed violently every month and feel pain," said Amirpour. "Every month inside my body, there's a violent war that some people can't understand. Women push humans out. We know violence even deeper, internally."[8]

It harks back to the telekinetic ability of *Carrie* (1976), whose powers are unleashed when her period arrives in the communal high school showers. Shocked at the sight of blood when she had been told nothing about her body by her religious zealot mother, she is teased mercilessly by the other girls. Now that she has entered womanhood, she is able to harness that rage to exact revenge on those who have wronged her.

There's horror in the female body; pregnancy, periods, and aging bodies trigger fear and repulsion in men because they break the fantasy. For female protagonists, the lunar cycle of their period allows them to tap into their psyche, a place that is so unknowable to men and makes them all the more terrifying.

Sometimes it's also unknowable to women. I wasn't taught at my all-girls school about ovulation or lunar cycles, and I hadn't even seen a vagina, including my own, until confronted by the images in my first boyfriend's porn mag collection. In my late twenties, I began to experience a grinding pain in my lower back, made worse if I stood still for too long, and despite trips to the doctor and a consultancy with a chiropractor, it was only a decade later that I worked out that it was most painful during ovulation. I realized I'd probably been suffering from endometriosis without any knowledge of it. Women are forced to put up with the afflictions of painful periods and irregular

"I'll Show You Crazy"   267

bleeding, and there's limited research into why this is, so seeking an explanation for it becomes an arduous, often futile, task.

Women are also continually warned that safety from predatory men can't be guaranteed, and instead, they should stay home at night. We've been taught to walk with keys between our fingers so we can use them to jab at our attackers, but the long-held message has been that good girls respect a self-imposed curfew. It's the bad girls who are out and asking for danger. Amirpour's directorial debut, *A Girl Walks Home Alone at Night* (2014), tapped into her Iranian heritage to tell the story of a woman in a chador who is a blood-sucking vampire. By switching the power dynamics, it becomes an analogy about the fears women feel when walking at night. Instead of being afraid, she is a vigilante figure as she defends the women who work the streets and attacks and then feeds off the pimps.

Amirpour said, "We inherit this fear that all women carry from the beginning: 'how do you exist in this big bad world?' Wherever we are, there's always some degree of danger. If I psychoanalyze my films, I can see me giving myself that fearlessness."[9]

Modern horror movies are tied to concerns around male violence against women and the fears and anger around real cases where women have been picked out and targeted by men on the streets. There's a fantasy element there, that a woman is given more powers than she would normally possess and can take revenge on those who wrong her. Or maybe we just want to imagine the possibilities of going a little crazy sometimes. There is something empowering about Bridget in *The Last Seduction*, despite her odiousness, or Mona Lisa, who can take control of others' bodies, and there's a wish fulfillment in being able to turn the tables on predatory men by becoming the danger that they should fear.

The British singer Self Esteem, real name Rebecca Taylor, has earned comparisons to Fleabag and built up a millennial fan base who feels kinship with her lyrics that explore her insecurities and anxiety around her appearance and single status. In one of her tracks, "I'm Fine," written for the cinema version of the Broadway and West End play *Prima Facie*, she describes how she and her friends bark like dogs if they feel threatened when being approached by a group of men. This is because "there is nothing that terrifies a man more than a woman that appears completely deranged."[10]

268 *Single & Psycho*

Just as there was a backlash against feminism when *Fatal Attraction* came out in 1987, in the 2020s, women's autonomy and reproductive rights were increasingly under threat. Horror movie cycles can be considered a response to contemporary fears, such as the zombie and alien invasion movies of the fifties as an allegory of the atomic age. The German-born writer Curt Siodmak was inspired by his experience as a Jew in Nazi Germany to create 1941's *The Wolf Man*, about a man who has a horrific fate placed on him. He later said, "When the war ended, the bottom fell out of the horror film business. When they began testing the atom bomb, it all started again. . . . In times of peace of mind, there's no place for horror films; times of fear—like now—bring out the need for violence in people."[11] He spoke those words in the eighties, but they could equally apply in the 2020s.

The horror movies of the late sixties and early seventies, such as *Night of the Living Dead* (1968), were a response to the Vietnam War, while the hagsploitation subgenre reflected concerns around the rising feminist movement. The hags in *What Ever Happened to Baby Jane?*, *Strait-Jacket*, and *Die! Die! My Darling* (also known as *Fanatic*) acted as a subliminal warning to younger women that if they chose to be so independent, they might end up as an ax-wielding Joan Crawford. Every time she looks in the mirror, she sees her aging reflection, grotesque in her efforts to remain young, and her resentment bubbles like a cauldron until it inevitably boils over.

By the 2020s, there was a new wave of hags, and this trend was driven by increasing intergenerational misunderstanding. In the sixties, the hippies who protested war and championed peace and love were at odds with those who had lived through World War II. Now it was boomers versus Gen Z, and they blamed one another for the ills of society.

The new generation of horror movies like Ti West's *X* (2022) and Zach Cregger's *Barbarian* (2022) features a female (at times sympathetic) villain whose elderly, sagging body is grotesque and frightful. In *X*, Mia Goth plays both an adult film star and an old woman whose insatiable, and unfulfilled, desire for sex leads to violence.

The 2022 prequel to *X*, *Pearl*, was developed by Ti West and Mia Goth to explore the backstory behind the murderous old woman of the first. Set in 1918, Pearl is obsessed with the idea of stardom and the movies as a means of escaping her domineering mother and catatonic father. Like her elderly incarnation in *X*, she possesses an insatiable sexual appetite, and looking like the farm girl Dorothy in her dungarees, she simulates sex with a scarecrow that is strung up on a cross in a corn field. When there's a chance to audition for a touring dance revue, she is convinced she'll be given a ticket out of this town, but when it doesn't come to plan and her audition piece fails, her rage takes over. The tension is ramped up when we realize the full scale of her instability, and it's only a matter of time before she reveals her murderous fury.

The unpredictable, violent hag was also central to the plot of *Barbarian* (2022). Tess (Georgina Campbell) has booked an Airbnb in Detroit so she can attend a job interview, but when she arrives late at night at the house in a rundown area, she is shocked to find that a man, Keith, is already staying there and that it appears to have been double-booked. Tess is concerned for her safety, and while she reluctantly accepts Keith's offer to share the property for the night, she tries to safeguard herself as much as possible by at first refusing to accept a drink from him.

This initial setup, given that Keith is played by Bill Skarsgård, most known as Pennywise in *It* (2017), makes us wonder whether he's the threat to this young single woman who's in such a vulnerable position. Throughout the narrative, there's a connecting thread of dangerous sexual behavior in men, yet the real terror lies in the basement of the house.

We know that in a horror movie, characters should stay away from the basement, the symbolic womb of the house. It's where Norman Bates hides his dead mother in *Psycho*, after all. When Tess explores this basement, she enters into a world of barren spinsterhood—a place where dreams of nursing babies can only be achieved vicariously. In this way, the movie can be read as a warning to women about the horrors of growing old, the grotesqueness of an aging woman's body, and, in true "hag horror" style, the regret of lost youth and the mourning of children.

2024's *The Substance* was striking in its nod to the "hag horror" genre. All the key elements are there; a once huge star, Demi Moore, who, like the character she plays, was cast out from the starring roles as she aged. She frets over her appearance in the mirror, and she struggles to deal with being increasingly invisible in a world that connects youth with beauty. She thought that creating a beautiful doppelganger to act out her fantasies would be the answer, but instead it triggers a rapid mental deterioration. When she smears lipstick over her face, like Tallulah Bankhead in *Fanatic* and Diane Ladd in *Wild at Heart*, it's her rebellion and defiance against the trappings of femininity.

There's nothing more fearful for a woman than being over forty, single, and childless. Once past menopause, she becomes invisible as her supposedly sagging body is an affront—something to be kept hidden. Youth is so entwined with beauty, and relevance is only found in someone who possesses the approved looks, that the feeling of being ignored becomes evident once you slip into that downward spiral of middle age.

CHAPTER 19

Tradwives and Childless Cat Ladies

When *M3GAN* hit cinemas in 2022, its zeitgeisty marketing campaign launched it as one of the most talked-about films of the year. There was one scene in particular that went viral on TikTok—the dance sequence performed by a murderous AI doll, its delectable creepiness enhanced by the Victorian governess costume. As some commentators delighted in pointing out, she's literally *slaying* while slaying people.

The premise of the movie is simple. Allison Williams is Gemma, a robotics engineer who is forced to care for her niece, Cady, after her sister and brother-in-law are killed in an accident. Gemma has zero experience of children; all the toys she owns are collectibles that are not allowed to be touched, and, she says, "I don't even take care of my own plants." At a loss over how she should help a grieving Cady, Gemma decides to bond with her over a prototype toy she has been working on—a life-size AI doll, which is programmed to adapt and learn how to educate and protect the child it has been gifted to.

The next part is not quite so conventional as it descends into a mash of *Mary Poppins* and Chucky when M3GAN becomes the deadliest of best friends to Cady. As the doll embeds itself within the family, a glitch in her programming turns off the safeguarding systems as she fights to be the dominant carer. From there, the craziness is ramped up with inventive killings of school bullies to viral dances as a means of distracting her victims from her murderous intent.

The thread that runs through this movie is that technology can have a negative effect on children and that it's dangerous for parents to rely on tablets and apps to entertain their kids. It was an updated

272   *Single & Psycho*

warning for the AI age that shared its message with *The Hand That Rocks the Cradle*—that a good mother shouldn't outsource childcare. Here, the single woman also realizes that her life, which had been so focused on progressing her career, would be much richer with the presence of a child. With global concerns around falling birth rates, including in the United Kingdom and the United States, the new message in the 2020s was that by their thirties, women should be having children as a duty. These concerns were led by right-wing figureheads who leaned toward eugenics in their not-so-subtle argument that it was white women who bore the responsibility to preserve Western civilization.

Fatal Attraction and the domestic thrillers that followed were made at a time of anxiety over the AIDS crisis and of the moral panic around the choice to delay marriage and children and its effect on the sanctity of the family. The modern nineties woman was more open to casual relationships than the generations before, and rather than being submissive, she was acting in the same uncommitted way as men. For some factions, this was scary. This fear of sexually aggressive women was expressed through the homicidal maniacs and vamps of films like *Basic Instinct* and *Fatal Attraction*. Alex's angry response to Dan, that she refuses to be used by him and will make him take responsibility, was the language of feminism. She was also aware that she needed to play the cool girl to initially win him over. It was the notion later defined by Gillian Flynn but one that women had known for decades—she mustn't let him think she is too emotional, too invested. Alex just gives up playing the game because she is so filled with rage at the unfair treatment.

Adrian Lyne, *Fatal Attraction*'s director, said on the film's release in 1987, "You hear feminists talk, and the last ten, twenty, years you hear women talking about fucking men rather than being fucked, to be crass about it. It's kind of unattractive, however liberated and emancipated it is. It kind of fights the whole wife role, the whole childbearing role. Sure, you got your career and your success, but you are not fulfilled as a woman."

Because men were worried that their dominant position was in jeopardy, and with a recession in 1992 that led to a surge in unemployment, there was a growing resentment around shifting gender roles. As Michael Douglas's character in *Disclosure* passionately argues to his wife, it's men who are suffering. They were the ones who had to fight in the wars, they were being ousted from their jobs, and as their mental health suffered, there were higher rates of male suicide. Thirty years later, this same message was now being exploited by divisive provocateurs Andrew Tate and Jordan Peterson and the vice president, J. D. Vance.

The new wave of feminism in the 2010s, with its mass social media movements Time's Up and Me Too, was inevitably going to be followed by a backlash. A new strain of toxic masculinity thrived on TikTok with figures like Tate appealing to young men who believed they were being unfairly maligned by feminism. According to a 2020 survey by the British antiracist campaign group Hope Not Hate, almost half of the young men surveyed, whose ages were between sixteen and twenty-four, agreed that feminism has "gone too far and makes it harder for men to succeed."[1]

Tapping into this push for procreation and family values, conservative women and misogynistic alpha males called for a return to a traditional template, where the woman would once again be submissive to her man. The "tradwife" gained traction on social media from 2018, as predominantly Christian and conservative millennial and Gen Z influencer housewives like Hannah Neeleman, known by her social media handle "Ballerina Farm," extolled the benefits of staying at home to raise their family and to practice traditional domestic chores. Neeleman's Instagram was filled with videos of churning butter and milking cows, making apple sauce on the Aga while cradling her baby, and wearing linen smocks in muddy fields. As a piece on *Today* pointed out, the tradwife lifestyle sometimes crossed into the alt-right movement on social media by using hashtags like #FeminismSucks, #ConservativeWomen, and #TwoGenders and by promoting images of happy housewives doing the laundry, cooking, and always looking like a vintage pinup.[2]

In Greta Gerwig's 2019 adaptation of *Little Women*, Emma Watson plays the older March sister, Meg, whose ambition to be a wife and mother is in opposition to Jo, who considers marriage the end of freedom. She tells Jo, "Just because my dreams are different than yours doesn't mean they're unimportant." Emma Watson considered the many different ways to be a feminist, and for Meg, "her way of being a feminist is making the choice—because that's really,

274 Single & Psycho

for me anyway, what feminism is about. Her choice is that she wants to be a full-time mother and wife."[3]

The key word here is *choice*. If someone wishes to be a home-maker and stay-at-home mother, then that's her prerogative, but not every woman has that option or privilege or want.

Fully committing to being a tradwife comes with the expectation that a woman must sacrifice her own desires and suppress her creativity and ambition, all in the name of a performative fifties domestic bliss. And surely, that would once again lead to the "problem with no name," as identified by Betty Friedan. When a July 2024 profile in the *Times* on Ballerina Farm went viral, it burst the bubble on her Instagram-perfect life as a former ballerina raising eight children on a farm in Utah. Instead, her husband was depicted as an oppressive force, discouraging her from getting epidurals during childbirth, refusing the help of a nanny, and controlling the finances.[4]

The tradwife subculture was placed in the spotlight following the guest graduation speech of football star Harrison Butker of the Kansas City Chiefs at the Catholic Benedictine College in May 2024. As he addressed the women in the audience directly, he warned them about the "diabolical lies" that they could find happiness in their careers: "I would venture to guess that the majority of you are most excited about your marriage and the children you will bring into this world." What a thing to tell a room full of young graduates who have worked hard to achieve degrees in their chosen fields. But with the tradwife movement, a woman's value lies in her baby-making abilities.

The television adaptation of Margaret Atwood's *The Handmaid's Tale* offered a grim insight into a future where women are subjugated and categorized by their fertility, and protesters around the world donned the red smock and white bonnet of the handmaids as they took a stand for a woman's right to autonomy over her own body.

But by the 2020s, and with this retreat to "traditional" values soaked in religious virtuosity, the dystopian future felt increasingly possible. When Trump appointed right-wing justices to the Supreme Court, it pushed through the reversal of *Roe v. Wade* in 2022, ending American women's constitutional right to abortion. As states now set their own laws, strict abortion laws were introduced in more conservative states like Texas, and in Alabama in 2024, restrictions were placed on IVF when it was deemed that a five-day blastocyst, a

Tradwives and Childless Cat Ladies   275

clump of up to one hundred cells, had human rights. In the nineties, much of the blame was placed on feminists who had encouraged, in the words of Newt Gingrich, "alternative lifestyles," and they were depicted as man-hating hags. Just as the women who were living outside the bounds of what was considered "normal" in the seventeenth and eighteenth centuries were hanged and burned, the witches in eighties and nineties movies were demonized and destroyed.

Now, in the 2020s, with this panic around declining birth rates, the blame was laid at the feet of feminism. Over the summer of 2024, as the world was gripped by the drama of the presidential election campaign, there were two types of women at play—the trad wife and the childless cat lady, as coined by J. D. Vance in 2021 to criticize Kamala Harris for failing to birth children. His provocative statements were tied to his belief that women without children have little value and were part of a long tradition of using "cat lady" as an insult to scare women into complying. Over the past few years, single women have been increasingly blamed for society's failings, including, of all things, the decline of Tupperware parties.

The headline of an article in the *Daily Mail* in April 2023 announced, "How the Rise of Women Triggered the DOWNFALL of Tupperware: Even the Queen Liked Their Little Plastic Pots, but the Firm Is Teetering on the Brink of Collapse because Dutiful Housewives No Longer Exist."[5] The article was more balanced than the headline would suggest, but the gist was that the Tupperware company, first founded in the years after World War II and famous for helping housewives become saleswomen with their Tupperware parties, selling the convenient plastic storage tubs from their homes, was now struggling for business. The dip in sales and the ultimate closure of the brand were down to a postpandemic slump and an increase in manufacturing costs, but the media laid the blame at the feet of working women who were rejecting a domesticated life.

With a new backlash against feminism that threatened contraceptive health, and with greater awareness of mental health issues, the domestic thriller made a comeback with a host of television adaptations of classic nineties movies. There was Netflix's *Obsession*, which was based on *Damage* (1992); Paramount's eight-part drama *Fatal Attraction*; and Apple TV's eight-part series based on 1990's *Presumed Innocent*, with Jake Gyllenhaal in the Harrison Ford role

276 *Single & Psycho*

and Ruth Negga as his wife, Barbara. Domestic thrillers had once been a midbudget cinema staple, but now they were expanded for television. In the nineties, a thriller wasn't complete without an erotic scene, but after the Millennium, this had all but been eradicated in favor of sanitized, family-friendly content. Sex thrived on cable channels like HBO, and so it was up to streaming platforms to create more grownup content as an alternative to the domination of superhero movies.

The major difference between the originals and their modern adaptations is the greater focus on mental health, which offers a deeper analysis of the previously maligned female characters to explain why they act in such a self-destructive way. While audiences in 1987 literally cried out for Alex Forrest to be murdered, modern viewers are more sympathetic to her. In the early nineties, conservatives sought to preserve the traditional homogenous family unit, while in the 2020s, the definition of a family is much more inclusive and diverse.

The trashy domestic thriller is a fantastic piece of escapism, an outlet for all the uncertainty we feel in our lives. These new adaptations hit screens in the midst of a cost-of-living crisis, with rising inflation and the knock-on effects from the war in Ukraine and the COVID-19 pandemic. And they were also tweaked to provide a voice for all the rage of the post–Me Too era.

It was inevitable, and vital, that *Fatal Attraction* be given a feminist makeover for its television incarnation, and with a female writer, Alexandra Cunningham, and director, Silver Tree, they opted to give Alex a backstory. This time, Dan is punished with a prison sentence, but Alex still loses her life, and rather than being killed during her invasion of the Gallagher home, her murder is more deliberate. She may have the excuse of a troubled childhood, but somehow she seems more poisonous, less sympathetic. We also see the little girl, Ellen, now as a young adult coming to terms with the reason her father was sent to prison, while he protests that he is innocent of murdering Alex. Through this adult Ellen, the series suggests that the obsessive instability of Alex can be passed down the generations. Rachel Cooke in the *Guardian* described it as "dealing with mad women is a bit like playing Whac-a-Mole. Uh-oh. No sooner have you dealt with one than up pops another, eyes rolling like marbles in a saucer."[6]

Tradwives and Childless Cat Ladies   277

In 2024, a new female stalker became a focus of ridicule and revulsion on the back of the viral Netflix series *Baby Reindeer*. Written and starring Richard Gadd, a Scottish comedian, and, like *Fleabag*, based on his one-man show at the Edinburgh Festival Fringe, it was billed as the true story of what happened when he was stalked by a woman for three years. Gadd plays struggling standup comedian Donny Dunn, a fictionalized version of himself, and his stalker, Martha (Jessica Gunning), was supposedly a fictionalized version of his real tormentor. When she walks into the London bar where he works and claims to be too poor to afford a cup of tea, he feels sorry for her and offers it for free. This one act of kindness leads to a terrifying ordeal, where she bombards him with forty-one thousand emails littered with typos and hours and hours of voicemails.

Donny Dunn is a damaged man as he is struggling to come to terms with his rape by a male producer who groomed him with drugs and promises of helping him break into the big time. It's this vulnerability that leads to his susceptibility in allowing Martha, who is also damaged and mentally ill, into his life. As Gadd said of his real-life abuse, "It destroys you from the inside out, those secrets and that kind of disempowerment and that rumination and obsessive anger and wrath and self-hate."[7]

His story is harrowing, but it proved to be cathartic to him in using dark humor to share it with the world. Gadd said in an interview with the *Times* that he blamed himself for it, that he had encouraged her or had been flattered by the attention, and besides, when he went to the police, he wasn't taken seriously. He believed that his story was so shocking because it reversed the normal rules of harassment, of a female victim and a male aggressor, particularly given that he knew he was stronger than his stalker.[8]

"I would always take umbrage to the bunny-boiler-style stories where somebody's really normal, usually quite good looking, and then it's chipped away and they're sociopathic or psychotic," he said. "Real stalking is a mental illness—it isn't as contained or insidious or malicious as it has been portrayed on film and TV before. I saw a lot of humanity in her."[9]

But as *Fatal Attraction* proved, to have a woman as the villain made it all the more deliciously thrilling, as audiences enjoyed yelling for her to be taken down. Given that it was billed as a true story, online sleuths were quick to track down the alleged "real" Martha, and after she was outed and set up to be a hate figure, she was interviewed by Piers Morgan, where questions were raised about the ethics of Netflix in allowing her to be so easily traced. Ultimately, more time was devoted to discovering the identity of the female stalker than the powerful man who sexually abused Gadd because, since medieval times, it's a woman who is ripe for blame, and it's a woman who must be burned.

The series, and the obsession surrounding her identity, further served to illustrate that an unmarried woman, particularly when she is considered frumpy and middle-aged, could only be the villain we love to hate.

Conclusion

As you have seen in the pages of this book, throughout history and in popular culture, the single woman has so often been dismissed and derided as an old maid, an evil witch, or a selfish career woman. Even with the push of the tradwife and the childless cat lady trope, it's become more acceptable than ever to choose not to have children. By retaining her independence, a child-free woman's contribution to society is often greater because she has the time to excel in her field.

It was unmarried women in the nineteenth century, after all, who made world-changing contributions, even when they were decried for going against the accepted true path. Jane Austen and Louisa May Alcott wrote great novels, Florence Nightingale transformed professional nursing, Christabel Pankhurst led the call for suffrage in the early twentieth century. But at the same time, single women who were rejecting the expected path were labeled as deviant, as lesbians, or as pitiful, unattractive, and bitter old maids and spinsters. It was the women without a man to speak for them who had been burned at the stake.

Whenever women made solid ground in progress, in being given the right to choose whether they wanted to work and when, and if they wanted to get married and have children, there was a pushback, and Hollywood was often there to capture the mood and reinforce the message. The femme fatale of film noir was a reaction to the suspicions men felt when they returned home after the end of World War II, and in the following decade, there would be a drive to convince women that their only source of happiness was found in domestic work. By the sixties, a political and social shake-up led to the sexual revolution and a burgeoning feminist movement, but in the seventies,

280 *Single & Psycho*

as women's liberation made important gains, movies like *The Beguiled* and *Play Misty for Me* questioned whether women could really handle free love. By the eighties, there was a fully formed backlash against feminism, now blamed for a plague of miserable single women. With the end of the Cold War and with popular culture now reflecting a more conservative bent, the domestic thriller boom tapped into yuppie paranoia and the fear that the threat was closer to home. There were a few bright sparks—*Thelma & Louise* had given women the chance to have their own punch-the-air moments, but it was condemned for encouraging women to be violent man-haters. There was Cher, who compared men to dessert and told her mother it was she who was a "rich man." But above all, the message drilled into the single woman was that she must be compliant and accepting for fear of being accused of being a bunny boiler. At the same time, forty was the crucial cutoff point for being able to secure marriage and children as, beyond that, any sense of dignity and purpose would wilt away.

By the 2000s, the singleton was a sympathetic, relatable hot mess like Bridget Jones or Carrie in *Sex and the City*, while at the same time dating manuals and the pornification of culture ensured women were kept on the right path. There were standards to be met, and if they deviated, if they forgot to wax, if they were too sexual, or they weren't sexual enough, then they were likely to end up alone. In the 2010s, supported by a new wave of feminism, single women owned their chaotic lives. They wallowed and indulged in their misery, or they fought back as the vengeful angel against the injustice in the world. In the face of another conservative backlash in the 2020s, there was a drive to instruct women that their duty to have children was all the more vital, given the supposedly catastrophic drop in birth rates. Horror movies reflected the anxieties of the time, of a loss of body autonomy, of the everyday dangers facing women, and of aging bodies no longer able to birth children.

Women had once been labeled hysterics for expressing their emotions because being feminine was to be passive and accepting. But by suppressing their anger, this buttoned-up rage exploded into psychopathy. She became the madwoman in the attic, the bunny boiler, and the single white female. Just as we have finally accepted that men should be vulnerable for the sake of their mental health, women are finally embracing their imperfections. They are "brat," the word of

2024, after Charlie XCX's album, to celebrate someone who is defiant, rebellious, and chaotic. The term *spinster* was removed from official usage on the marriage register when the Civil Partnership Act was introduced in the United Kingdom in 2005. Yet being single or childless can still feel isolating and ostracizing. There's this awareness of not quite fitting in or having much in common with the friends who drop off one by one to focus on being parents. They rent cottages together with their families or go for bracing day trips together, whereas the single friend is often excluded. This was one of the things I longed for as I struggled with my fertility. I wanted to go on vacation with my friends who had children, imagining the blissful woodland cottages or beachside villas we could rent, or to be able to chip in to their child-rearing stories with my own experiences. I was also envious of the friends who knew they definitely didn't want children. They were resolute that there were too many people in the world as it was, and for environmental and personal reasons, they didn't feel the need to procreate.

If Alex Forrest were alive in the 2020s, maybe she wouldn't be so worried about her status as a childless thirty-six-year-old. More women than ever are choosing to have children later in life, as evidenced by data from the UK's Office for National Statistics in 2022, which revealed that half of all thirty-year-old women in Britain were child-free.

Maybe Alex would also be comforted by the fact that being single isn't a barrier to starting a family. There are many different options for both straight and same-sex-coupled women to have a child without a man, such as using a sperm donor, an egg donor, or both. The Alex Forrest stigma, of being thirty-six and approaching barren status, is outdated, and even after forty, it doesn't mean that you are going to turn into a full-blown psychopath due to the relentless torment of a ticking clock.

Australian pop singer Natalie Imbruglia, for example, was single when she had a child at the age of forty-four through IVF. Mindy Kaling spoke about her choice to have children with a sperm donor. Women are much more open in their discussions around issues that affect their midlife fertility, such as perimenopause and declining egg quality, with egg freezing a valid, and popular, way to remove any pressure around time limits.

282   *Single & Psycho*

After I'd fallen pregnant with Paul and I'd been devastated at the miscarriage at eleven weeks, the pain of that empty womb shook me. All I wanted was to replicate the feeling of a life growing inside me, but I didn't have a partner. The last time I saw him was when we went to the cinema to see *Cruella*, and after his own cruel slow-fade, he'd finally ghosted me. I tried to reach out, pathetically sent him a message to see if he wanted to meet up, but after a week, there was still no response, and he'd left my message on two gray ticks. I stalked his social media, and with the exacting forensic detective work of an unhinged woman, I discovered through a wine-sharing app that he'd been drinking bottles of Argentinian and Spanish wine. I knew that he tended to drink craft beer when on his own, so I pieced it all together to come up with the only possible answer—he must have been drinking it with someone else, and this could only be another woman. I didn't know for certain, obviously, but it seemed pretty clear-cut, and I was devastated. I felt like a fool, accepting his breadcrumbs for the last six weeks, and I sank into a destructive depression as I coped with the rejection. Yet at least it gave me closure.

I needed to take control of my own destiny, and so I began to read about solo parenting. It dawned on me that I didn't need to have a partner; I could go to an IVF clinic and do it myself. My parents even drove me to the clinic on the outskirts of Glasgow for my appointment to examine my egg follicle count, which, I was told, was good for my age. Afterward, we ate our sandwiches by a bench on the grounds of the center, soundtracked by the roar of traffic from the adjacent motorway. I joked that all those people driving past would be wondering why we were having a picnic outside a fertility clinic.

I continued dabbling with the dating apps. I enjoyed going on dates with new people, and as long as I didn't pressurize myself into thinking that I needed to find the one, then it was a way of boosting my confidence and proving that I may be forty-one, but I was still attractive. I told myself I was just looking for company and casual relationships because I had another mission to follow—one that would no doubt freak out all those single men in their forties whom I was chatting with. As much as I wanted to forge ahead with IVF via sperm donor, I wondered if I was truly in a good place mentally to go through the process. I'd had a rough few years, and I didn't want to use the IVF as a sticking plaster to try to fix the pain.

Conclusion   283

There are three types of women—single, childless, and aging—who are either mocked or considered a threat, particularly if they check all three boxes.[1] By the age of forty, I was ticking all three, but for that year during the pandemic, now that I had left Gavin, I felt free.

On a summer's day in 2020, as Scotland's lockdown restrictions eased, I met a dear friend in Princes' Street Gardens, where we sat on a sunny patch of grass with Edinburgh Castle looming above us. We hadn't seen each other since March, and so we drank mini bottles of prosecco as we caught up on all that had been happening and ruminated about our futures. What she had realized in lockdown was that her relationship wasn't satisfying enough. She needed excitement, something more, but at the same time, she didn't want to throw away a good thing, considering she was approaching her midthirties. I told her how scared I'd been of breaking it off with Gavin, particularly because I didn't know how volatile he'd be, but that I only wished I'd done it sooner.

I told her that even though I had cried myself to sleep for a few years over the tragedy of not being able to have a child due to my relationship with Gavin, now, at forty, I was feeling OK about it. I'd pushed the idea of a baby out of my mind. Maybe it was the freezing of time under the pandemic, as if the world had been cast under a sleeping spell, but I wasn't anxious anymore, and I wasn't going to live by silly biological timelines. Besides, I didn't think I could get pregnant easily. I tried with Gavin, it hadn't happened, and I assumed it was both our fertilities that was the issue. But thank goodness it didn't happen, because having a child in an abusive relationship would have been a terrible thing.

I was now convinced I could carve out an exciting life as a single, childless woman. I was imagining a future of world travel, and with this complete freedom, I could work really hard to achieve the writing career I desired. I tried to frame my experiences with Gavin as a positive. I knew what it was like to be heartbroken, to be fearful, and I could fully understand the reasons someone stays in an abusive relationship, and this would all help to shape my storytelling. Perhaps it could form the basis of a novel one day. I wanted to fully explore who I was supposed to be, and maybe my identity was meant to be as a single woman. And maybe that was fine. I'm allergic to cats, so being a cat lady was not going to be in my destiny unless I got one

284 *Single & Psycho*

of those hypoallergenic ones, but I could be an explorer, writing as I travel. I still had Korea and Japan to experience, I wanted to ride the California Zephyr Amtrak from Chicago to the West Coast, and a writing retreat in Bali was on my wish list.

Sitting on the grass with my friend, all we were waiting for was life to return to normal, for international borders to open up, for the contagion to come to an end. It was about trying to live in the present, without any plan for even the next few months. At this point, Gavin was still in my flat while I lived with my parents. I didn't know when he would leave, but I was safe, and I was breathing again. I was in my situationship with Paul, unable to see each other very much due to restrictions, but I liked him and was excited to see where it would go.

A year on from this moment in the park, basking in sunshine and drinking prosecco, I would be pregnant, and shortly after that, I would miscarry. After being ghosted by Paul, I went on Tinder dates, all the while thinking that I shouldn't become seriously involved with someone because they would inevitably be repelled by my plans for single motherhood. But then I met a man I really liked. Long-distance at first, we met up in Edinburgh a month after our first message, and I felt an overwhelming sense of excitement in the lead-up to it.

I'm sure my friends felt like I hadn't learned my lesson from my impulsivity of throwing myself into a new relationship, but it felt right, and what's more, he didn't drink, which had once been a red flag for me but was now quite welcome. Instead of boozy pub meet-ups, our dates involved hill-walking in the Yorkshire Dales and trips to the Lake District. When I told him my plans, he was very accepting of it, and we decided to do it together. There was another painful miscarriage and an unsuccessful round of IVF, which made it all feel so hopeless.

After that expensive, failed IVF, I'd booked a trip to the writer's retreat in Greece, and here I met two women who were my age, also single, also child-free, and they helped me realize I could be happy with whatever the outcome because you can make your life as you want it to be. I had so much I wanted to see and do, and I knew that having a child would be a big sacrifice to the freedom I enjoyed. But I decided I needed to try everything I could because I didn't want to look back in ten years and wonder what if. So we did another round of IVF, and this time, it worked.

I'd been conditioned to think that being in a relationship was the key to happiness, that the promise of a committed relationship would ground me and force me out of the postadolescent haze of my early thirties. I'd been sold the message through movies and popular culture that normal women were the ones who were in relationships and ticking off the checkboxes on the accepted timeline. The abnormal ones were like Alex Forrest, grasping and desperate, and as they edged closer to forty, they would unleash their terror on unsuspecting men. The single woman without a child was a predatory figure; she wanted to steal another woman's husband or children for herself, like Carolyn in *Presumed Innocent* or Peyton in *The Hand That Rocks the Cradle*, or she was so selfish in her chasing of her career or her indulging in shopping and swilling cocktails that she would miss her chance and become a tragic lost cause. There was nothing worse, after all, than a woman brushing forty who was still trying to act like she was young. Cohabitation, marriage, and children were the supposed guarantee to not being cut adrift in the rocky, treacherous oceans of perpetual singledom.

I'd discovered by living with Gavin that a long-term relationship could be the loneliest, most helpless position to be in. Someone asked me during that time, "What does happiness mean?" And I said, "Safety," because my elusive happiness was linked to an imagined place where I wasn't scared in my own home. When I think back to my joyful days in my early thirties, living in my own rented apartment, where I delighted in getting up early and writing before work, inviting friends around for drinks, or doing baking experiments and dancing around the room with no one to judge me, it was about the happiest I'd ever been.

Given my feline allergies, I'll give the last word to Taylor Swift. Named as *Time*'s 2023 Person of the Year, she appeared on the cover as a poised, strong Wonder Woman in a black leotard, with a cat draped around her shoulders. In this one image, she was answering all those mocking comments about her dating life and owning her own unmarried status as a self-confessed cat lady who dotes on her felines. It was defiant and strong and a statement of intent against all those who try to pigeonhole her and other women who are on their own path.

Acknowledgments

This book is the most personal I've ever written, and while I initially paused at sharing some of the stories, the more I researched and rewatched the movies I had loved when I was younger, the more I saw a real connection as I evaluated some of the experiences in my life over the past few years.

I'd dived into the world of psychotic women previously, but I felt much more of a connection to the women of *Single & Psycho*, and I could absolutely see something of myself in that 2010s creation of the chaotic, messy women, the ones who haven't managed to get it together just yet.

Thanks as always to my agent, Isabel Atherton at Creative Authors, and to Caroline Montgomery at Rupert Crew for their support of this project. Thank you also to Natalie O'Neal at the University Press of Kentucky—your enthusiasm and guidance are very much appreciated.

Notes

Introduction

1. Helen Fielding, *Bridget Jones's Guide to Life* (New York: Penguin, 2001).
2. Anne Taylor Fleming, "Sperm in a Jar," *New York Times*, June 10, 1994.
3. Susan Faludi, *Backlash: The Undeclared War against Women* (New York: Vintage, 1993).
4. Jake Horton, "Who Could Be Most Affected by US Abortion Changes?," BBC .co.uk, May 3, 2022.
5. Joshua Zitser, "Matt Gaetz Says Women Who 'Look Like a Thumb' Don't Need to Worry about Getting Pregnant, Video Rant Shows," *Business Insider*, July 24, 2022.
6. Jane Caputi and Lauri Sagle, "Femme Noire: Dangerous Women of Color in Popular Film and Television," *Race, Gender & Class Journal* 11, no. 2 (2004): 90–111.

1. "I'm Not Going to Be Ignored"

1. Carrie Rickey, "A Femme Fatale Pulls Down a Lawyer," *Philadelphia Inquirer*, September 18, 1987.
2. Michael Wilmington, "The Mad Love in a Fatal Attraction," *Los Angeles Times*, September 18, 1987.
3. Rickey, "A Femme Fatale."
4. Connie Benesch and Deborah Caulfield, "What's the Attraction Here?," *Los Angeles Times*, October 15, 1987.
5. Jamie Portman, "Close Worked Hard to Achieve 'Blow-Your-Mind' Performance," *Windsor Star*, October 22, 1987.
6. Portman, "Close Worked Hard."
7. Bruce Fretts, "Fatal Attraction Oral History: Rejected Stars and a Foul Rabbit," *New York Times*, September 14, 2017.
8. James Dearden, "Fatal Attraction Writer: Why My Stage Version Has a Different Ending," *Guardian*, March 9, 2014.
9. Benesch and Caulfield, "What's the Attraction."
10. Rebecca Humphries, *Why Did You Stay?: The Instant* Sunday Times *Bestseller: A Memoir about Self-Worth* (London: Sphere, 2022).
11. Laura Kavesh and Cheryl Lanvin, "One Tantrum Doesn't Make You a Bunny Boiler," *Gazette*, May 7, 1989.

290   *Notes to Pages 22–40*

12. "Close Encounters," *Liverpool Echo*, March 9, 1989.

13. "Names 'n' Faces," *Miami Herald*, December 5, 1990.

14. Helen Fielding, "The Bridget Jones Effect: How Life Has Changed for Single Women," *Guardian*, December 20, 2013.

15. Helen Fielding, *Bridget Jones's Guide to Life* (London: Picador, 2001).

16. Paisley Gilmour, "'I'm a "Bunny Boiler" Girlfriend'—What It's Like to Be a Serial Love Addict," *Cosmopolitan*, January 9, 2019.

17. Bruce Fretts, "'Fatal Attraction' Oral History: Rejected Stars and a Foul Rabbit," *New York Times*, September 14, 2017.

2. The Madwoman in the Attic

1. Elaine Showalter, "Victorian Women and Insanity," *Victorian Studies* 23, no.1 (Winter 1980): 157.

2. Patsy Stoneman, *Charlotte Brontë* (Tavistock, England: Northcote House Publishers, 2013).

3. Clement King Shorter, *Charlotte Brontë and Her Circle* (London: Hodder and Stoughton, 1896).

4. Showalter, "Victorian Women and Insanity."

5. Palko Karasz, "Charles Dickens Tried to Banish His Wife to an Asylum, Letters Show," *New York Times*, February 23, 2019.

6. Edward H. Clarke, *Sex in Education, or a Fair Chance for Girls* (Boston: James R. Osgood, 1875).

7. Amy Froide, "Spinster, Old Maid or Self-Partnered—Why Words for Single Women Have Changed through Time," *Conversation*, December 2, 2019.

8. Philippa Gregory, *Normal Women* (Glasgow, Scotland: William Collins, 2023).

9. Froide, "Spinster, Old Maid or Self-Partnered."

10. Alison Weir, *The Six Wives of Henry VIII* (London: Vintage, 2011).

11. Gregory, *Normal Women*.

12. Gwendolyn B. Needham, "New Light on Maids 'Leading Apes in Hell,'" *Journal of American Folklore* 75, no. 296 (April–June 1962): 106.

13. Weir, *The Six Wives*.

14. Katherine Howe, *The Penguin Book of Witches* (New York: Penguin, 2014).

15. Howe, *Penguin Book of Witches*.

16. Philippa Levine, "So Few Prizes and So Many Blanks: Marriage and Feminism in Later Nineteenth Century England," *Journal of British Studies* 28, no. 2 (April 1989): 150.

17. Lee Virginia Chambers-Schiller, *Liberty, a Better Husband: Single Women in America—The Generation of 1780–1840* (London: Yale University Press, 1984).

18. Betty Friedan, *The Feminine Mystique: The Classic That Sparked a Feminist Revolution* (London: Thread, 2021).

19. Rebecca Traister, *All the Single Ladies* (New York: Simon and Schuster, 2016).

20. Louisa May Alcott, *The Complete Works of Louisa May Alcott: Novels, Short Stories, Plays and Poems* (Prague, Czechia: e-artnow, 2015).

Notes to Pages 43–68   291

3. Bachelor Girls

1. "Etiquette of the Bachelor Girl," *Philadelphia Inquirer*, August 30, 1903.

2. Ella Hepworth Dixon, "Why Women Are Ceasing to Marry," *Humanitarian* 14 (1899): 391–96.

3. Emma Liggins, "The Life of a Bachelor Girl in the Big City: Selling the Single Lifestyle to Readers of *Woman* and the Young Woman in the 1890s," *Victorian Periodicals Review* 40, no. 3 (Fall 2007): 216.

4. Sheila Jeffreys, *The Spinster and Her Enemies: Feminism and Sexuality, 1880–1930* (North Melbourne, Australia: Spinifex Press, 2003).

5. Jeffreys, *The Spinster and Her Enemies.*

6. Jeffreys, *The Spinster and Her Enemies.*

7. Jeffreys, *The Spinster and Her Enemies.*

8. Jeffreys, *The Spinster and Her Enemies.*

9. Nichi Hodgson, *The Curious History of Dating* (London: Robinson, 2017).

10. Molly Haskell, *From Reverence to Rape: The Treatment of Women in the Movies* (Chicago: University of Chicago Press, 1987).

4. The Good Wife and the Bad Girl

1. Oscar Shepard, "Spotlight Parade," *Bangor Daily News*, June 2, 1941.

2. Susan Hartmann, *The Homefront and Beyond: American Women in the 1940s* (New York: Twayne Publishers, 1983).

3. Dan C. Fowler, "The Problem of Unwed Mothers," *Look*, July 29, 1949.

4. Leontine Young, *Out of Wedlock: A Study of the Problems of the Unmarried Mother and Her Child* (1954; Westport: Bloomsbury Academic, 2008).

5. Robert Coughlan, "Modern Marriage," *Life*, December 24, 1956.

6. Lynn Peril, *Pink Think: Becoming a Woman in Many Uneasy Lessons* (New York: W. W. Norton, 2002).

7. Clifford Rose Adams and Vance Oakley Packard, *How to Pick a Mate: The Guide to a Happy Marriage* (New York: E. P. Dutton & Company, 1946).

8. Peril, *Pink Think.*

9. Betty Friedan, *The Feminine Mystique: The Classic That Sparked a Feminist Revolution* (London: Thread, 2021).

10. Friedan, *The Feminine Mystique.*

11. Paulina Bren, *The Barbizon: The Hotel That Set Women Free* (London: Two Roads, 2021).

12. Rona Jaffe, *The Best of Everything* (London: Penguin Modern Classics, 2011).

13. Lloyd Shearer, "Why Actresses Try Suicide," *Parade*, November 6, 1960.

14. Charles Casillo, *Marilyn Monroe: The Private Life of a Public Icon* (New York: St. Martin's Press, 2018).

15. Casillo, *Marilyn Monroe.*

16. Donald Zec, "The Problem of Being Marilyn Monroe," *Daily Mirror*, February 13, 1961.

17. Clare Booth Luce, "What Really Killed Marilyn," *Life*, August 7, 1964.

18. Sarah Churchwell, *The Many Lives of Marilyn Monroe* (London: Granta Books, 2005).

292   *Notes to Pages 69–97*

5. 5 a.m. Breakfasts on Fifth Avenue and a Countercultural Shake-Up

1. Mary Quant, *Mary Quant: My Autobiography* (London: Headline, 2012).
2. Helen Gurley Brown, *Sex and the Single Girl: The Unmarried Woman's Guide to Men* (New York: Open Road Media, 2012).
3. Betty Friedan, *The Feminine Mystique: The Classic That Sparked a Feminist Revolution* (London: Thread, 2021).
4. Friedan, *The Feminine Mystique*.
5. Friedan, *The Feminine Mystique*.
6. Ariel Levy, *Female Chauvinist Pigs: Woman and the Rise of Raunch Culture* (New York: Simon & Schuster, 2006).
7. Friedan, *The Feminine Mystique*.

6. The 1970s

1. Charles Higham, "Suddenly, Don Siegel's High Campus," *New York Times*, July 25, 1971.
2. Kevin Thomas, "Dust on Her Star Buildup," *Los Angeles Times*, May 10, 1971.
3. Wesley Morris and Jenna Wortham, "History's Crucial Role in the Films 'All Eyez on Me' and 'The Beguiled,'" *New York Times*, June 29, 2017.
4. Vincent Canby, "Clint Eastwood Is Star of Siegel's The Beguiled," *New York Times*, April 1, 1971.
5. "Gloria Steinem's Cheerful Captivity," *Washington Times*, September 14, 2000.
6. Marcia Cohen, *The Sisterhood: The Inside Story of the Women's Movement and the Leaders Who Made It Happen* (Sante Fe, NM: Sunstone Press, 2009).
7. Ariel Levy, *Female Chauvinist Pigs: Woman and the Rise of Raunch Culture* (New York: Simon & Schuster, 2006).
8. Peter Biskind, *Easy Riders, Raging Bulls* (London: Bloomsbury, 2016).

7. Is It Really Free Love?

1. Paula J. Caplan, "Sex and the Myth of Women's Masochism," *Psychology Today*, August 14, 2012.
2. Lacey Fosburgh, *Closing Time: The True Story of the "Goodbar" Murder* (1977; New York: Open Road Media, 2016).
3. Richard Thompson and Tim Hunter, "Clint Eastwood Interview," *Film Comment*, January/February 1978.
4. Judy Fayard, "Who Can Stand 32,580 Seconds of Clint Eastwood? Just about Everybody," *Life*, July 23, 1971.
5. Yohana Desta, "The Triumph and Tragedy of Sondra Locke," *Vanity Fair*, December 14, 2018.
6. Roger Greenspun, "Play Misty for Me Review," *New York Times*, November 4, 1971.
7. Adam Knee, "The Dialectic of Female Power and Male Hysteria in *Play Misty for Me*," in *Screening the Male: Exploring Masculinities in the Hollywood Cinema*, ed. Steven Cohan and Ina Rae Hark (New York: Routledge, 2012), 97.

Notes to Pages 98–123 293

8. From Feminism to Fighting for the Nuclear Family

1. Susan Faludi, *Backlash: The Undeclared War against Women* (London: Vintage, 1993).
2. Gloria Anzaldúa, *Interviews/Entrevistas* (New York: Routledge, 2020).
3. Jenni Murray, "What Did Margaret Thatcher Do for Women?" *Guardian*, April 9, 2013.
4. Bettijane Levine, "As the Ankle Turns," *Los Angeles Times*, June 18, 1982.
5. Joe Eszterhas, *Hollywood Animal* (2004; Reading, England: Cornerstone Digital, 2008).
6. Eszterhas, *Hollywood Animal*.
7. Eszterhas, *Hollywood Animal*.
8. Eszterhas, *Hollywood Animal*.
9. Diane Haithman, "Glenn Close Has Had Enough of Being Square Jawed and Sturdy," *Evening Sun*, October 17, 1985.
10. Eszterhas, *Hollywood Animal*.
11. Rita Kempley, "Jagged Edge: Cut and Run," *Washington Post*, October 4, 1985.
12. Kempley, "Jagged Edge."
13. Stephen Schiff, "What Dynasty Says about America," *Vanity Fair*, December 1984.
14. L. J. Waite, "US Women at Work," *Population Bulletin* 36, no. 2 (May 1981): 1.
15. Jane See White and Scott Kraft, "Older Women Fear Time a Biological Thief," Associated Press, November 27, 1980.
16. Bayard Webster, "Study Shows Female Fertility Drops Sharply after Age of 30," *New York Times*, February 18, 1982.
17. Faludi, *Backlash*.
18. Ginny Dougary, "One Step Forward, Two Steps Back—Susan Faludi," *Times*, March 14, 1992.
19. Faludi, *Backlash*.
20. Molly McKaughan, *The Biological Clock: Reconciling Careers and Motherhood in the 1980s* (New York: Doubleday, 1987).
21. Lynn Darling, "Still Tough after All These Years," *Newsday*, February 1987.

9. Burnout, Biological Clocks, and Boiling Rabbits

1. Beverly Beyette, "The Mrs. Myth," *Los Angeles Times*, January 30, 1998.
2. Mr Manchester's Showbiz Diary, "Men and Me, by Cher," *Manchester Evening News*, April 9, 1988.
3. James S. Kunen, "The Dark Side of Love," *People*, October 26, 1987.
4. Bruce Fretts, "*Fatal Attraction* Oral History: Rejected Stars and a Foul Rabbit," *New York Times*, September 14, 2017.
5. Susan Faludi, *Backlash: The Undeclared War against Women* (New York: Vintage, 1993).
6. "Taste of My Life with Miranda Richardson," BBC Television, January 8, 2010.
7. Fretts, "*Fatal Attraction* Oral History."
8. Kunen, "The Dark Side of Love."
9. Michael Wilmington, "The Mad Love in a Fatal Attraction," *Los Angeles Times*, September 18, 1987.

294 *Notes to Pages 123–140*

10. Nancy Webber and Lowell Alexander, "*Fatal Attraction*—The Mad Woman's Case," *Los Angeles Times*, October 4, 1987.

11. Connie Benesch and Deborah Caulfield, "What's the Attraction Here?" *Los Angeles Times*, October 15, 1987.

12. Jamie Portman, "Close Worked Hard to Achieve 'Blow-Your-Mind' Performance," *Windsor Star*, October 22, 1987.

13. Wilmington, "The Mad Love in a Fatal Attraction."

14. Benesch and Caulfield, "What's the Attraction."

15. Kunen, "The Dark Side of Love."

16. Peter Larson, "Film 87," *Belleville News-Democrat*, January 17, 1988.

10. Baby Booms and Working Girls

1. Tom Scanlon, "Ford Plays 'a Woman's Part,'" *Times Tribune*, December 18, 1988.

2. Chris Gardner, "Working Girl Turns 30," *Hollywood Reporter*, December 3, 2018.

3. Gardner, "Working Girl."

4. P.D.Z., "Movies: Ripe Fear," *Newsweek*, August 4, 1975.

5. Gardner, "Working Girl."

6. Gardner, "Working Girl."

7. Jesse Kornbluth, "Melanie's Place in the Sun," *Vanity Fair*, April 1989.

8. Nikki Finke, "Griffith Grows into an Actress, Not a Star," *Los Angeles Times*, December 21, 1988.

9. Myra Forsberg, "That's Melanie Griffith Everywhere," *New York Times*, April 17, 1988.

10. John Runyan, "A Working Woman in Corporate Manhattan," *Seattle Gay News*, December 23, 1988.

11. Sheila Benson, "Latest Film Women: Smart But Cuddly," *Los Angeles Times*, January 8, 1989.

12. Susan Schindehette, "A Baby for Don and Melanie," *People*, February 27, 1989.

13. Schindehette, "A Baby for Don and Melanie."

14. "Sigourney Plays Role for Laughs," *Spokesman-Review*, December 25, 1988.

15. "Sigourney Plays Role."

16. Lewis Beale, "New Challenges Threaten Gains of Feminism," *Los Angeles Daily News*, February 24, 1989.

17. Beale, "New Challenges."

18. Caryn James, "Film," *New York Times*, November 20, 1988.

19. Gabrielle Bruney, "The True Story of Cheryl Araujo's Sexual Assault, as Revisited in Netflix's *Trial by Media*," *Esquire*, May 18, 2020.

20. Sonia Taitz, "Jodie Foster, Tough Hero," *New York Times*, October 16, 1988.

21. Charles Champlin, "Private Diane Keaton Well-Hidden," *Los Angeles Times*, October 4, 1989.

22. Jay Boyar, "Actress Diane Keaton Comes Back to Comedy," *Orlando Sentinel*, November 20, 1987.

23. James, "Film."

24. Susan Faludi, *Backlash: The Undeclared War against Women* (New York: Vintage, 1993).

Notes to Pages 140–163 295

11. Bitches from Hell

1. "Aids Goes to Hollywood: Movies and Morals," *Sunday Times*, March 25, 1990.
2. "Aids Goes to Hollywood."
3. "Aids Goes to Hollywood."
4. John Lyttle, "Film: To Love, Honour and Dismay," *Independent*, May 7, 1993.
5. Lynn Hirschberg, "The Misfit," *Vanity Fair*, April 1991.
6. Kevin Sessums, "Geena's Sheen," *Vanity Fair*, September 1992.
7. Geena Davis, *Dying of Politeness: A Memoir* (Glasgow, Scotland: William Collins, 2022).
8. Davis, *Dying of Politeness*.
9. Davis, *Dying of Politeness*.
10. Davis, *Dying of Politeness*.
11. Richard Johnson, "Wash. Post Casts Stones at JFK Flick," *New York Daily News*, May 29, 1991.
12. Davis, *Dying of Politeness*.
13. Davis, *Dying of Politeness*.
14. Sessums, "Geena's Sheen."
15. Sessums, "Geena's Sheen."
16. Susan Faludi, *Backlash: The Undeclared War against Women* (New York: Vintage, 1993).
17. Felicity Barringer, "One Year Later, Anita Hill Interprets Thomas Hearings," *New York Times*, October 17, 1992.
18. Wilson Morales, "Celebrating 'Set It Off' 15 Years Later," Blackfilm.com, November 10, 2011.
19. Stephen Holden, "Just Trying to Get Even While They Get Rich," *New York Times*, November 6, 1996.

12. Sex and Fear

1. Margarette Driscoll, "All for Love? Violence by Women," *Times*, June 7, 1992.
2. Camilla Paglia, "Deadlier than a Male—Amy Fisher," *Sunday Times*, February 14, 1993.
3. Kevin Sessums, "Stone Goddess," *Vanity Fair*, April 1993.
4. Kevin O'Sullivan, "Free Spirit under Fire, Michael Douglas," *Sunday Times*, April 26, 1992.
5. Joe Eszterhas, *Hollywood Animal* (Reading, England: Cornerstone Digital, 2008).
6. Sharon Stone, *The Beauty of Living Twice: Sharon Stone* (London: Allen & Unwin, 2021).
7. Stone, *The Beauty of Living Twice*.
8. Liz Smith, "People Talk," *Philadelphia Inquirer*, August 31, 1990.
9. Eszterhas, *Hollywood Animal*.
10. Eszterhas, *Hollywood Animal*.
11. Stone, *The Beauty of Living Twice*.
12. Sessums, "Stone Goddess."
13. Sessums, "Stone Goddess."
14. Eszterhas, *Hollywood Animal*.
15. Eszterhas, *Hollywood Animal*.

296   *Notes to Pages 164–181*

16. W. Speers, "A Woman Scorned Vents Fury over Sharon Stone," *Philadelphia Inquirer*, April 6, 1993.

17. Stone, *The Beauty of Living Twice*.

18. Carol Sarler, "Women Behaving Badly," *Sunday Times*, February 21, 1993.

19. Owen Gleiberman, "Sleeping with the Enemy," *Entertainment Weekly*, February 8, 1991.

13. The Threat Is inside the House

1. "Pfeiffer Spices Up Award Show," *Los Angeles Times*, June 14, 1993.

2. John Lyttle, "Film: To Love, Honour and Dismay," *Independent*, May 7, 1993.

3. Reggie Nadelson, "Men Are Nervous, Women Are Terrified," *Independent*, September 3, 1992.

4. Bernard Weinraub, "Say Hello to the Nanny from Hell," *New York Times*, January 5, 1992.

5. Rita Kempley, "The Hand That Rocks the Cradle," *Washington Post*, January 10, 1992.

6. Weinraub, "Say Hello to the Nanny."

7. Kempley, "The Hand That Rocks."

8. Weinraub, "Say Hello to the Nanny."

9. Weinraub, "Say Hello to the Nanny."

10. Ella Taylor, "Hollywood's Latest Catfight," *LA Weekly*, January 30, 1992.

11. Weinraub, "Say Hello to the Nanny."

12. Kevin Sessums, "Geena's Sheen," *Vanity Fair*, September 1992.

13. Andy Marx, "Trend Alert: Looks Like the 'Cradle' Rocked Hollywood," *Los Angeles Times*, April 12, 1992.

14. Marx, "Trend Alert."

15. Marx, "Trend Alert."

16. James Ryan, "A Thriller Filmed in the Shadow of the King Case," *Record*, June 21, 1992.

17. Ryan, "A Thriller Filmed."

18. Laurie Halpern Benenson, "How 'Poison Ivy' Got Its Sting," *New York Times*, May 3, 1992.

19. Frank Sanello, "Bridget Carries Burden Beautifully," *Edmonton Journal*, August 17, 1992.

20. Barbara Foley, "The Single Hottest Cut," *Los Angeles Times*, September 2, 1992.

21. Jess Cagle, "Entertainers of the Year: Whoopi Goldberg," *Entertainment Weekly*, December 25, 1992.

22. Sanello, "Bridget Carries Burden."

23. Fahizah Alim, "The Outcasts," *Sacramento Bee*, August 16, 1992.

24. Alim, "The Outcasts."

25. Todd McCarthy, "Single White Female," *Variety*, August 10, 1992.

26. Barry Koltnow, "*Fatal Attraction* Inspires Boyle in *The Temp*," *Pittsburgh Post-Gazette*, February 13, 1993.

27. Ryan Murphy, "They're Hell on Heels," *Daily News*, February 18, 1993.

28. Robert W. Welkos, "'The Temp': Why Things Didn't Work Out," *Los Angeles Times*, March 1, 1993.

Notes to Pages 183–205 297

29. Welkos, "'The Temp': Why Things Didn't Work Out."

30. Betsy Sherman, "*The Temp* Doesn't Come Through," *Boston Globe*, February 13, 1993.

14. The Rise of the Singleton

1. Charlotte Lamb, "Romance Reigns—Return of Weepie, as Audiences Snub Sex," *Daily Mirror*, May 14, 1994.

2. Lamb, "Romance Reigns."

3. Frank Rich, "Gingrich Family Values," *New York Times*, May 14, 1995.

4. Lisa Anderson, "'90s America Trying So Hard to Recreate Its Fantasy of the '50s from TV to Fashion, Nation Embracing Ideas It Perceives as Representing a Simpler Time, Trend Watchers Say," *Chicago Tribune*, March 2, 1995.

5. Michael Wines, "Views on Single Motherhood Are Multiple at White House," *New York Times*, March 1, 1992.

6. Albert Yanney, "In Praise of Whitney Houston and the Cast of *Waiting to Exhale*," BFI.com, December 8, 2016.

7. Samantha Highfill, "*Friends* Co-Creator Reveals the Monica Story NBC Tried to Cut," *Entertainment Weekly*, September 11, 2019.

8. Helen Fielding, *Bridget Jones Omnibus: The Singleton Years* (London: Picador, 2013).

9. M. Strauss-Noll, "An Illustration of Sex Bias in English," *Women's Studies Quarterly* 12, no. 3 (Spring 1984): 36.

10. Diyora Shadijanova, "15 Thoughts I Had Watching *Bridget Jones's Diary* in 2021," *Bustle*, April 13, 2021.

11. Shadijanova, "15 Thoughts."

12. Alex Kuczynski, "Dear Diary: Get Real," *New York Times*, June 14, 1998.

13. Kuczynski, "Dear Diary."

14. Kuczynski, "Dear Diary."

15. Jennifer Keishin Armstrong, Sex and the City *and Us: How Four Single Women Changed the Way We Think, Live, and Love* (London: Simon & Schuster, 2018).

16. Keishin Armstrong, Sex and the City *and Us.*

17. Keishin Armstrong, Sex and the City *and Us.*

18. Keishin Armstrong, Sex and the City *and Us.*

19. Ariel Levy, *Female Chauvinist Pigs: Woman and the Rise of Raunch Culture* (New York: Simon & Schuster, 2006).

20. Anthea Taylor, *Single Women in Popular Culture: The Limits of Postfeminism* (Basingstoke, England: Palgrave Macmillan, 2011).

21. Keishin Armstrong, Sex and the City *and Us.*

22. Keishin Armstrong, Sex and the City *and Us.*

15. Playboy Bunnies, Slut-Shaming, and the Aughts' Double Standards

1. Jack Garner, "Nothing 'Vanilla' about Cruise-Cruz Thriller," *Californian*, December 13, 2001.

2. Gina Bellafante, "Feminism: It's All about Me!" *Time Magazine*, June 29, 1998.

3. Bellafante, "Feminism."

298   *Notes to Pages 205–232*

4. Maureen Dowd, "Liberties; Monica Gets Her Man," *New York Times*, August 23, 1998.

5. Dowd, "Liberties."

6. Gloria Steinem, "Feminist and the Clinton Question," *New York Times*, March 22, 1998.

7. Marjorie Williams, "How Bill Clinton Neutered the Feminist Movement," *Independent*, April 3, 1998.

8. "The Bridget Jones Economy," *Economist*, December 20, 2001.

9. "The Bridget Jones Economy."

10. "The Singles Issue," *Observer*, November 5, 2000.

11. Anthea Taylor, *Single Women in Popular Culture: The Limits of Postfeminism* (Basingstoke, England: Palgrave Macmillan, 2011).

12. Sasha Cagen, *Quirkyalone: A Manifesto for Uncompromising Romantics* (San Francisco: Harper San Francisco, 2004).

13. Bill Zehme, "Cameron Diaz Loves You," *Esquire*, April 1, 2002.

14. Betty Friedan, *The Feminine Mystique: The Classic That Sparked a Feminist Revolution* (London: Thread, 2021).

15. Oriana Fallaci, *The Egotists: Sixteen Surprising Interviews* (Chicago: H. Regnery, 1968).

16. Ariel Levy, *Female Chauvinist Pigs: Woman and the Rise of Raunch Culture* (New York: Simon & Schuster, 2006).

17. Nancy Gibb, "Making Time for a Baby," *Time*, April 15, 2002.

18. Leslie Bennetts, "The Unsinkable Jennifer Aniston," *Vanity Fair*, September 2005.

19. Manohla Dargis, "Film Review: *He's Just Not That into You*," *New York Times*, February 13, 2009.

20. A. J. Jacobs, "Scarlett Johansson Is the Sexiest Woman Alive," *Esquire*, November 1, 2001.

21. Jacobs, "Scarlett Johansson."

22. Richard Schickel, "Movies: Scarlett Johansson: *Match Point*," *Time*, January 8, 2006.

23. Taylor, *Single Women in Popular Culture*.

24. Kira Cochrane, "Did Bridget Jones Destroy Family Life?" *Guardian*, September 30, 2008.

25. Kate Mulvey, "Duped Out of Motherhood," *Daily Mail*, February 24, 2006.

26. Lori Gottlieb, *Marry Him: The Case for Settling for Mr. Good Enough* (New York: Penguin, 2010).

27. Gwyneth Rees and Lucy Ballinger, "Rise of the Freemale: The Women Who'd Rather Be Single than Share Their Time and Money," *Mail Online*, June 1, 2008.

16. Alcoholic, Divorced, and Highly Anxious

1. Elizabeth Weitzman, "Call-Girl Calamity Is Atom Bomb," *New York Daily News*, March 26, 2010.

2. Kadian Pow, "Beyoncé and Dolly Parton's Versions of Jolene Represent Two Sides of Southern Femininity," *Conversation*, April 22, 2024.

3. Nadira Goffe, "Why Everyone Is Arguing about Beyoncé's Cover of 'Jolene,'" *Slate*, April 2, 2024.

4. Amy Gentry, "White-Lady Tears," *Paris Review*, January 26, 2017.

Notes to Pages 232–266 299

5. Sheri Linden, "'When the Bough Breaks': Film Review," *Hollywood Reporter,* September 9, 2016.

6 "David Fincher Interview: 'I Was Looking for Something I'd Never Seen Before,'" *Time Out,* September 22, 2014.

7. Eliana Dockterman, "Is *Gone Girl* Feminist or Misogynist?" *Time,* October 6, 2014.

8. Oliver Burkeman, "Gillian Flynn on her Bestseller *Gone Girl* and Accusations of Misogyny," *Guardian,* May 1, 2013.

9. Tatiana Siegel, "'Girl on the Train' Author Shoots Down 'Gone Girl' Comparisons," *Hollywood Reporter,* September 28, 2016.

17. *Fleabag,* Fourth-Wave Feminism, and the Destructive Single Woman

1. Chuck Klosterman, "Taylor Swift on 'Bad Blood', Kanye West, and How People Interpret Her Lyrics," *GQ,* October 2015.

2. Nancy Jo Sales, "Taylor Swift's Telltale Heart," *Vanity Fair,* March 15, 2013.

3. Sales, "Taylor Swift's Telltale Heart."

4. Sales, "Taylor Swift's Telltale Heart."

5. Sales, "Taylor Swift's Telltale Heart."

6. Jon Caramanica, "Taylor Swift Is Angry, Darn It," *New York Times,* October 20, 2010.

7. Jonathan Van Meter, "Taylor Swift: The Single Life," *Vogue,* January 2012.

8. Bridie Jabour, "Taylor Swift's 'Downfall': What the Online Celebrations Really Say," *Guardian,* July 18, 2016.

9. Jackson McHenry, "Chimamanda Ngozi Adichie Doesn't Think Beyonce's Feminism Is Flawless," *Vulture,* October 7, 2016.

10. Dave Itzkoff, "Cable's New Pack of Girls, Trying on the Woman Thing," *New York Times,* March 2, 2012.

11. P. J. Gold, "Robyn Talks 'Body Talk,'" *Pop Justice,* April 12, 2010.

12. Emma Bullimore, "Seven Reasons Why Feminist Comedy *Fleabag* Will Be Your Latest TV Addiction," *Stylist,* July 19, 2016.

13. E. Alex Jung, "Phoebe Waller-Bridge on her Amazon Show *Fleabag,* Sex Jokes, and Ryan Gosling Feminism," *Vulture,* September 20, 2016.

14. Sophia Peyser, "The 'Fleabag' Era of Dissociative Feminism Must End," *Lithium Magazine,* January 19, 2022.

15. "Upending the 'Angry Black Woman' Myth with Issa Rae and Ziwe," *Archetypes with Meghan,* October 25, 2022.

16. Nancy Jo Sales, "Tinder and the Dawn of the 'Dating Apocalypse,'" *Vanity Fair,* August 6, 2015.

18. "I'll Show You Crazy"

1. Carina Chocano, "Emerald Fennell's Dark, Jaded, Funny, Furious Fables of Female Revenge," *New York Times Magazine,* December 17, 2020.

2. Chocano, "Emerald Fennell's Dark."

3. Susannah Butler, "The Film That's Dividing Feminists," *Evening Standard,* April 15, 2021.

4. Chocano, "Emerald Fennell's Dark."

300 *Notes to Pages 267–283*

5. Eliana Dockterman, "*Killing Eve* Isn't Your Average Mystery Series. Here's How It Breaks the Mold," *Time*, April 5, 2018.

6. Manohla Dargis, "On Point, on Top, in Pain," *New York Times*, December 2, 2010.

7. Brian Tallerico, "Influencer," *Roger Ebert*, May 26, 2023.

8. Miriam Balanescu, "Female Rage: The Brutal New Icons of Film and TV," *BBC Culture*, October 12, 2022.

9. Balanescu, "Female Rage."

10. Julia Llewellyn Smith, "Self Esteem: 'This Is the Body I Can Have without Killing Myself,'" *Times*, July 15, 2023.

11. Tom Weaver, *Return of the B Science Fiction and Horror Heroes* (Jefferson, NC: McFarland Classics, 2000).

19. Tradwives and Childless Cat Ladies

1. Sabrina Barr, "Half of Generation Z Men 'Think Feminism Has Gone Too Far and Makes It Harder for Men to Succeed,'" *Independent*, August 4, 2020.

2. Elise Solé, "Cooking, Cleaning and Controversy: The 'Tradwife' Movement Embraces a 1950s Housewife Ideal," *Today*, March 7, 2023.

3. Paris Lees, "Emma Watson on Transcending Child Stardom," *British Vogue*, December 2019.

4. Megan Agnew, "Meet the Queen of the 'Trad Wives' (and her Eight Children)," *Times*, July 20, 2024.

5. Lindsay Nicholson, "How the Rise of Women Triggered the Downfall of Tupperware," *Daily Mail*, April 13, 2023.

6. Rachel Cooke, "Lock Up Your Bunnies: Fatal Attraction Is Back, and Still Stuck in the 80s," *Observer*, April 16, 2023.

7. Julie Miller, "Baby Reindeer: Meet the Scottish Comedian Who Turned His Stalker Experience into a Netflix Show," *Vanity Fair*, April 11, 2024.

8. Susannah Butter, "Richard Gadd: How I Turned My Stalking Nightmare into a Netflix Drama," *Times*, April 11, 2024.

9. Miller, "Baby Reindeer."

Conclusion

1. Emma John, "How a New Wave of Literature Is Reclaiming Spinsterhood," *New Statesman*, March 16, 2022.

Index

About Last Night (2014), 227
Abre Los Ojos (1997), 202
Abzug, Bella, 82
Accidental Tourist, The (1988), 130, 132
Ace Ventura (1994), 188
Adams, Amy, 237
Adichie, Chimamanda Ngozi, 242–43
Adjani, Isabelle, 92
Affair to Remember, An (1957), 184
Affleck, Ben, 216, 231
Age of Love, The (reality show), 210
Aguilera, Christina, 208
AIDS crisis, 7, 113, 140, 160, 168, 184, 272
Alcott, Louisa May, 37, 40, 279
Alien queen (character), 45, 96–97, 170
Alien (1979), 95–97, 170
Aliens (1986), 11, 95–97, 112, 148
Alien 3 (1992), 148
"All by Myself" (song), 192
Allen, Woody, 59, 82, 135, 218
Allman, Gregg, 110
Ally McBeal (TV show), 203–4, 206
American Tragedy, An (Dreiser), 58
Amirpour, Ana Lily, 265–67
Anderson, Judith, 47
And Just Like That. . . (TV show), 199
Aniston, Jennifer, 109, 188, 213–17
Annie Hall (1977), 82, 135
Anthony, Susan B., 37, 204
Apatow, Judd, 244
Araujo, Cheryl, 133–34
Archer, Anne, 115, 226
Ardant, Fanny, 223
Atkins, Susan, 77, 81
Atwood, Margaret, 253, 274
Austen, Jane, 40, 190, 279
Average Joe (TV show), 210

Baby Boom (1987), 134–36
Baby Reindeer (TV show), 277–78
bachelor girls, 43–44, 49, 191
Bachelor, The (TV show), 210
Backlash (Faludi), 7–8, 109, 136, 150, 169, 191, 205
"Bad Girl" (song), 86, 145
Baldwin, Billy, 162
Ballerina Farm, 273–74
Balls of Steel Australia (TV show), 24
Bankhead, Tallulah, 47, 105, 270
Bara, Theda, 47
Barbarian (2022), 268–69
Barbizon Hotel, 61–62
Bardot, Brigitte, 64
Barrymore, Drew, 175, 217
Basic Instinct (1992), 10–11, 101, 155, 157–62, 164, 173, 183, 232, 272
Basinger, Kim, 104, 115, 130, 158, 164
Bassett, Angela, 187
Bates, Kathy, 143
Bates, Norman (character), 10, 92, 222, 269
Batman Returns (1992), 167, 262
BBC (British Broadcasting Corporation), 12, 21, 87, 98, 119, 190, 245, 249, 258–59
Beals, Jennifer, 102
Béart, Emmanuelle, 223
Beatty, Warren, 70, 100–101
Bedelia, Bonnie, 141, 143
Beguiled, The (1971), 77–82, 84, 88, 90, 92, 280
Beguiled, The (2017), 79
Being John Malkovich (1999), 208
Bell, Kristen, 237
Berenger, Tom, 111
Bergen, Candice, 126, 185
Bergman, Ingrid, 18

302 Index

Best of Everything, The (Jaffe), 62–64, 73, 90, 126, 131
Best of Everything, The (1959), 62–63, 73, 90, 131
Best Years of Our Lives, The (1946), 55
Bewitched (TV show), 76
Beyoncé (Beyoncé Knowles), 188, 213, 224–27, 242–43, 249
Biehn, Michael, 95
Big Chill, The (1983), 102–3, 105
Bikini Kill, 203
Binoche, Juliette, 164
Black Lives Matter movement, 249
Black Swan (2010), 254, 261–64
Blanchett, Cate, 82
"Blank Space" (song), 18, 238, 240, 244
blaxploitation genre, 80–81, 251
Blond Ambition World Tour, 144
Bloomer, Amelia, 37
Blue Lagoon, The (1980), 82
Body Double (1984), 99–100, 128–29
Body Heat (1981), 99
Body of Evidence (1993), 181
Boleyn, Anne, 32, 163
Boothe Luce, Clare, 68
Born Yesterday (1950), 130
Bow, Clara, 47
Bowser, Yvette Lee, 187
Boyer, Charles, 18, 55
Boyle, Lara Flynn, 179–81, 224
Boyle, Susan, 221
Boyz n the Hood (1991), 187
Bracco, Lorraine, 111–12, 141
Bradshaw, Carrie (character), 37, 62, 193, 195–99, 206, 208, 210–12, 216, 221, 280
Brando, Marlon, 70
breadcrumbing, 114, 252, 260
Breakfast at Tiffany's (1961), 71–72
Break-Up, The (2006), 216
Bridesmaids (2011), 244
Bridges, Jeff, 102
Bridget Jones's Diary (Fielding), 4, 7, 23, 63, 189–96, 198, 200, 203–4, 206, 208–9, 211, 219–20, 280
Bridget Jones's Diary (2001), 7, 191–96, 198, 200, 203–4, 206, 208–9, 211, 219–20, 280

Bridget Jones's Guide to Life (Fielding), 4, 23
Bridget Jones: The Edge of Reason (Fielding), 191
British Broadcasting Corporation (BBC), 12, 21, 87, 98, 119, 190, 245, 249, 258–59
Brittain, Vera, 46
Brontë, Anne, 27, 38
Brontë, Charlotte, 27–28, 38, 40
Brontë, Emily, 27, 38
Brook, Kelly, 24
Brooks, Louise, 129
Brooks, Richard, 85
"Brown Eyed Girl" (song), 165
Brownmiller, Susan, 100
bunny boiler, 1, 10, 14, 16–18, 22–25, 51, 165, 190, 222, 253, 255, 277, 280
Burton, Tim, 167
Bush, George H. W, 185–86
Bushnell, Candace, 73, 195–96
Business as Usual (1987), 126
Butker, Harrison, 274
Buttafuoco, Joey, 157
Buttafuoco, Mary Jo, 156–57

Caan, James, 143, 166
Cameron, James, 95–96, 100
Canonero, Milena, 177
Cape Fear (1991), 150–51, 175
Capote, Truman, 71
Capra, Frank, 50
Career Girl Murders, 73
Carrie (1976), 266
Carty-Williams, Candice, 249
Catherine of Aragon, 32
Cat People, The (1942), 36, 48
"Cat Person" (Roupenian), 253–55
Cat Person (2023), 253–55
Cattrall, Kim, 196, 198
Catwoman (character), 167–68
Charlie's Angels (2001), 208
Charlie's Angels: Full Throttle (2003), 208
Cher (Cherilyn Sarkisian), 110, 280
Chewing Gum (TV show), 249
Chisholm, Shirley, 82

Index 303

Chloe (2009), 223
Civil Rights Act of 1964, 75
Clarke, Edward H., 30
Cleopatra Jones (1973), 251
Clift, Montgomery, 10, 56
Clinton, Bill, 204–5
Clockwork Orange, A (1971), 99
Close, Glenn, 1, 13–17, 22, 102–4, 115, 122–24, 163, 171, 180, 184, 192, 205, 226, 232, 239, 258
Closing Time (Fosburgh), 86
Coel, Michaela, 12, 247, 249–51
Coffy (1973), 80, 251
Colbert, Claudette, 80
Collins, Joan, 104–5
Columbia Pictures, 62
Comer, Jodie, 259
Connelly, Jennifer, 217
Connor, Sarah (character), 95–96, 112
Coppola, Sofia, 79–80
Cosmopolitan (magazine), 24, 72, 75
COVID-19 pandemic, 118, 138, 235, 276
Cox, Courteney, 188
Cox, Laverne, 258
Crawford, Joan, 9, 29, 48, 55, 63, 105, 159, 268
Cruella (2021), 122, 282
Cruise, Tom, 110, 140, 201–2
Crush, The (1993), 176
Cruz, Penélope, 201–2
cult of Single Blessedness, 37
Curtis, Richard, 183, 191–92

Damage (1992), 164
Dance with a Stranger (1985), 115
"Dancing on My Own" (song), 244
Dangerous Liaisons (1988), 22
Danson, Ted, 136
Davis, Bette, 9, 29, 49–50, 105, 131, 159
Davis, Geena, 130, 132, 146–50, 158, 173, 218
de Acosta, Mercedes, 47
Dead Poets Society (1989), 217
Dearden, James, 16, 114
"Dear John" (song), 239
DeGeneres, Ellen, 238
de Havilland, Olivia, 55–56

de Lempicka, Tamara, 47
Demme, Jonathan, 129
De Mornay, Rebecca, 36, 169–70, 174, 228
De Niro, Robert, 150, 166
De Palma, Brian, 84, 99, 100, 128, 263
Desmond, Norma, 263
"Diamonds Are a Girl's Best Friend" (song), 66
Diaz, Cameron, 24, 201–3, 207–8, 220, 230
Dickens, Catherine, 28–30
Dickens, Charles, 26, 28–30
Dickinson, Emily, 37
Didion, Joan, 61
Die! Die! My Darling! (1965). See *Fanatic*
Die Hard (1988), 98
Die Hard 2 (1990), 98–99
DiMaggio, Joe, 67
Disclosure (1994), 152–54, 181, 272–73
Diversion (1979), 16, 114
Don't Bother to Knock (1952), 66
Double Indemnity (1944), 54, 158
Douglas, Illeana, 151
Douglas, Kirk, 54
Douglas, Michael, 1, 15, 22, 115–16, 124, 152–53, 158, 160, 224, 232, 259, 272
Dressed to Kill (1980), 99–100, 128
Driver, Adam, 244
Dunaway, Faye,180–81
Dunham, Lena, 11, 244, 247
Dunne, Amy (character), 5, 229–33, 265
Dunst, Kirsten, 79, 217
Dworkin, Andrea, 83, 100
Dylan, Bob, 18, 202
Dynasty (TV show), 104–5

Eastwood, Clint, 77–78, 80–81, 87–90, 92
Edinburgh Festival Fringe, 277
Edinburgh International Festival, 245
Eisenstadt v. Baird, 83
Elba, Idris, 188, 224–25
Ephron, Nora, 109, 189
Equal Pay Act of 1963, 75
Equal Rights Amendment, 82–83, 97, 106, 132

304   Index

Eszterhas, Joe, 101–4, 158, 160, 162–63
Evans, Robert, 101, 160, 163
Exorcist, The (Blatty), 151, 172
Exorcist, The (1973), 172
"Express Yourself" (song), 145

Fallaci, Oriana, 209
Falling Down (1993), 153
Faludi, Susan, 7–8, 52, 106, 109, 136, 149–50, 169, 173, 191, 205
Fanatic (1965), 76, 268, 270
Fatal Attraction (1987), 1–3, 7, 10, 13–17, 21–25, 32, 47, 88, 92, 99, 113–19, 122–25, 132, 139–40, 142, 144, 156–58, 163–65, 167–68, 172–73, 175–76, 178, 180, 184, 192, 202–5, 210, 222–25, 227, 231, 237, 239, 257, 259, 268, 272, 275–77
Father of the Bride (1991), 139, 160, 184
Feminine Mystique, The (Friedan), 37, 61, 74–75, 83, 106–7, 185, 274
femme fatale trope, 2, 11, 47, 54–55, 99–100, 105, 157–58, 161–62, 181–82, 198, 209, 219, 238, 280
Fennell, Emerald, 257–58, 261
Fey, Tina, 243
Fielding, Helen, 4, 23, 189, 191–93
film noir, genre, 2, 52–55, 99, 158, 175, 181–82, 280
Final Analysis (1992), 164
Fincher, David, 145, 231
Fiorentino, Linda, 181, 198
Firth, Colin, 190, 192
Fisher, Amy, 15, 156–57
F.I.S.T (1978), 101
flapper movement, 46–47
Flashdance (1983), 101–2, 114
"***Flawless" (song), 242–43
Fleabag (TV show), 11, 245–47, 267, 277
Flynn, Gillian, 5, 208, 228–32, 234, 272
Fonda, Bridget, 10, 177–79, 186
Fonda, Jane, 102, 177
Forrest Gump (1994), 183
Forrest, Alex (character), 1–2, 4, 7, 9–10, 12, 14–18, 22–25, 36, 45, 64, 68, 88, 90, 113, 115–19, 122–23, 140, 162–63, 172, 178, 198, 200, 202, 211,

222–23, 232, 234, 239, 251–52, 255, 263, 265, 272, 276, 281, 285
Fosburgh, Lacey, 86–87
Foster, Jodie, 132, 134, 231
Four Weddings and a Funeral (1994), 183, 191
Foxy Brown (1974), 81
Frankie and Johnny (1991), 183–84
Freud, Sigmund, 30, 46, 218
Friedan, Betty, 37, 61, 74–75, 82–83, 106–7, 131–32, 185, 203–4, 208, 274
Friends (TV show), 108, 188–89, 194, 214
"from hell" genre, 10–11, 125, 165, 168–82

Gadd, Richard, 277–78
Garbo, Greta, 47–48
Gardner, Ava, 54, 64
Garner, Erroll, 88, 91
Gaslight (1944), 18
gaslighting, 18, 21, 59, 234, 252
Gay and Lesbian Alliance against Defamation (GLAAD), 160
Gentlemen Prefer Blondes (1953), 66
Gere, Richard, 86, 94–95, 164, 166, 222
Gerwig, Greta, 273
ghosting, 114, 122, 236, 252–53, 255, 260–61, 282, 284
Gibson, Charles Dana, 43
Gibson girl, 43
Gilda (1946), 158
"Gimme More" (song), 254
Gingrich, Newt, 184, 275
Ginsburg, Ruth Bader, 205
Girl on the Train, The (Hawkins), 10–11, 233–37
Girl on the Train, The (2016), 10–11, 233–37
Girls Gone Wild franchise, 209
Girls (TV show), 11, 244, 246–47
Girl Walks Home Alone at Night, A (2014), 267
GLAAD (Gay and Lesbian Alliance against Defamation), 160
Goldberg, Whoopi, 178
Gone Girl (Flynn), 5, 11, 208, 228–33, 236, 242

Index   305

Gone Girl (2014), 231–33, 236, 242
Good Mother, The (1988), 135–36
Goodwin, Ginnifer, 217
Goth, Mia, 268
Grant, Hugh, 183, 193
Great British Bake Off, The (TV show), 260
Great Expectations (Dickens), 29; and Miss Havisham (character), 23, 29, 190, 199–200, 227
Greer, Germaine, 8
Grier, Pam, 80–81
Griffith, Melanie, 100, 125–32
Guisewite, Cathy, 190
Gunning, Jessica, 277
Gurley Brown, Helen, 72–73, 196
Guttenberg, Steve, 136
Gyllenhaal, Jake, 239, 275

hag horror. *See* hagsploitation
hagsploitation, film genre, 9, 76, 143, 268
Hall, Regina, 227
Hamer, Fannie Lou, 82
Hand That Rocks the Cradle, The (1992), 2, 11, 36, 157, 168, 172–73, 176, 178, 228, 242, 272
Handmaid's Tale, The (Atwood), 274
Handmaid's Tale, The (TV show), 274
"Hang with Me" (song), 244
Hanks, Tom, 109, 184
Hanson, Curtis, 169–70
Harris, LaDonna, 82
Hartman, Elizabeth, 79
Haskell, Molly, 48
Hawkins, Paula, 233–34
Hayward, Susan, 57
Hayworth, Rita, 64, 99, 146, 158
HBO, 195–96, 244, 276
Hedren, Tippi, 127
Hefner, Hugh, 209
Heiress, The (1949), 56
Hemingway, Mariel, 82
Henreid, Paul, 49–50
Henry VIII, 32
Hepburn, Audrey, 71–72
Hepburn, Katharine, 48

Hepworth Dixon, Ella, 43
Herrmann, Bernard, 10
Hershey, Barbara, 262
He's Just Not That into You (2009), 64, 216
Hill, Anita, 151–52, 154, 178
Hillis, Marjorie, 48, 61
Hilton, Paris, 6–7, 210, 258
Hippocrates, 30
His Girl Friday (1940), 131
Hitchcock, Alfred, 10, 47, 99, 164, 237
Hite, Shere, 100
Holden, William, 51–52
Holliday, Judy, 130–31
Hollywood Pictures, 168, 171, 174
Honeymoon in Vegas (1992), 166
Hopkins, Matthew, as Witchfinder General, 34
House Un-American Activities Committee, 185
How to Lose a Guy in 10 Days (2003), 90, 211–12, 217, 230
How to Marry a Millionaire (1953), 66
Hudson, Kate, 211, 230, 266
Hunter, Holly, 147
Hurley, Elizabeth, 117
Hush . . . Hush, Sweet Charlotte (1964), 76
hysteria, as diagnosis, 30–31

I Care a Lot (2020), 265
"I Did Something Bad" (song), 240
I Dream of Jeannie (TV show), 76
I Love Lucy (TV show), 139
I May Destroy You (TV show), 12, 249–51, 256, 261
"I'm Fine" (song), 267
Imitation of Life (1934), 80
Indecent Proposal (1993), 166
Influencer (2022), 264–65
Ingrid Goes West (2017), 264
Insecure (TV show), 11, 247–48, 251, 253
in vitro fertilization (IVF), 39, 137, 215, 274–75, 281–82, 284
"Irreplaceable" (song), 225
I Spit on Your Grave (1978), 265
It's a Wonderful Life (1946), 50

306 Index

IVF. *See* in vitro fertilization
I Wanted Wings (1941), 51–54, 56, 90, 117

Jaffe, Rona, 62, 126
Jaffe, Stanley R., 113, 115
Jagged Edge (1985), 102–4, 163
James I, 34
Jane Eyre (Brontë), 27–28, 50
Jay-Z, 225
Jennifer's Body (2009), 11
Jennings, Luke, 259
Jeon, Jong-seo, 265
Joe Millionaire (TV show), 210
Johansson, Scarlett, 59, 217–19
Johnson, Dakota, 131
Johnson, Don, 128–30
"Jolene" (1973 song), 226–27
"Jolene" (2024 song), 226–27
Jolie, Angelina, 214
Jones, Bridget (character), 4, 7, 23, 63, 189–95, 198, 200, 203–4, 206, 211, 219–20, 280
Jones, Samantha (character), 196, 198–99, 206–7

Kaling, Mindy, 247, 281
Keaton, Diane, 85, 134–35, 145, 257
Kelly, Grace, 61–62
Kempley, Rita, 104, 170–71
Kennedy, John F., 66–67
Kennedy, Robert, 66
Kent State shooting, 101
Khouri, Callie, 146–47
Kidder, Margot, 84
Kidman, Nicole, 79, 141
Killers, The (1946), 54
Killing Eve (TV show), 258–60
Kitty Foyle (Morley), 48–49
Kitty Foyle (1940), 48–49, 55, 62
Krenwinkel, Patricia, 77, 81
Kunis, Mila, 263
Kutcher, Ashton, 209–10

Lady Gaga (Stefani Joanne Angelina Germanotta), 242
Lady in the Dark (1944), 55
"Lady of Shalott, The" (Tennyson), 41

Lake, Veronica, 51–53, 99
Lancaster, Burt, 54, 78
Landis, Carole, 65
Lange, Jessica, 115, 150
Lansing, Sherry, 113–15, 166
Larter, Ali, 188, 224–25
Last Seduction, The (1994), 181–82, 198, 267
Latifah, Queen, 154–55, 187
Lawrence, Jennifer, 230, 264
Lecky, Nicôle, 12
Legally Blonde (2001), 23, 209
Leigh, Janet, 10
Leigh, Jennifer Jason, 10, 177–78
Lemmon, Jack, 67
Lemonade (album), 225
Lewinsky, Monica, 27, 204–5
Lewis, Juliette, 150
Lichtenstein, Roy, 108
Lilith (1964), 70–71
Liotta, Ray, 174–75
Little Women (Alcott), 40
Little Women (2019), 40, 273
Living Single (TV show), 187–88
Locke, Sondra, 89–90
Looking for Mr. Goodbar (Rossner), 85
Looking for Mr. Goodbar (1977), 85–87, 116, 133, 145, 151, 198, 257
Love, Courtney, 208
Loy, Myrna, 55
Lyne, Adrian, 16, 25, 104, 113–15, 123, 222, 231, 272

Macbeth (Shakespeare), 33
MacDowell, Andie, 183
Madame Butterfly (Puccini), 88, 123
Madonna, 86, 144–46, 181, 197
Maguire, Sharon, 192
Malice (1993), 141
Manolo Blahnik shoes, 62, 197, 199
Manson, Charles, 78, 81; and Tate-LaBianca murders, 77, 81
Manson, Shirley, 208
Mary Tyler Moore Show (TV show), 83
Match Point (2005), 59, 218–19
McConaughey, Matthew, 211
McGillis, Kelly, 132, 159

Index   307

McGowan, Rose, 243
McKinnon, Kate, 13
M3GAN (2022), 271–72
Mercer, Mae, 80
Me Too movement, 243, 253, 256, 265, 273, 276
Meyers, Jonathan Rhys, 219
Meyers, Nancy, 134
Midnight Cowboy (1969), 99
Miller, Arthur, 65, 67
Mills, Donna, 91, 109
Minogue, Kylie, 220–21
Miss America protest, 1968, 75
Mona Lisa and the Blood Moon (2021), 265–67
Mona Lisa Smile (2003), 217
Monroe, Marilyn, 2, 65–69, 130
Mood (TV show), 12
Moon over Miami (1941), 65
Moonstruck (1987), 110
Moore, Constance, 51
Moore, Demi, 10, 102, 129, 152–53, 166, 269
Moore, Julianne, 170, 223, 237
Moran, Caitlin, 243
Morning in America, 1984 advertising campaign, 97
Mortimer, Emily, 219
Mother's Day (2010), 228
Mrs. America (TV show), 82
Mulligan, Carey, 256, 258
Murphy Brown (TV show), 126, 185–86
My Stepmother Is an Alien (1988), 130

Nathalie. . . (2003), 223
National Organization for Women (NOW), 75
National Women's Political Caucus, 78, 82
Neeson, Liam, 111, 135–36, 223
neo-noir, film genre, 99, 111, 181
Netflix, 237, 253, 275, 277–78
New England Journal of Medicine, 8, 106
New Hollywood, 76, 84
new woman, 43–44, 191
Nichols, Mike, 129
Nightingale, Florence, 36, 279

Night of the Living Dead (1968), 268
Nimoy, Leonard, 135–36
9 1/2 Weeks (1986), 104
9 to 5 (1980), 126
No Good Deed (2014), 227
No Man of Her Own (1950), 58, 70
Now, Voyager (1942), 49–50
Nun's Story, The (1959), 72

Oates, Joyce Carol, 68
Obama, Barack, 221, 246
Obsession (TV show), 275
O'Donnell, Rosie, 109
Officer and a Gentleman, An (1982), 94–95, 117
Oh, Sandra, 259
Oldman, Gary, 237
Olivier Awards, 245
Olsen, Elizabeth, 264
One Million B.C. (1940), 65
online dating, 138, 216, 240, 252–53, 284
Ophelia (Millais), 41
Othello (Shakespeare), 171
Out of the Past (1947), 54

Pacino, Al, 183
Page, Geraldine, 77–79
Paglia, Camille, 157, 161, 204, 206
Paltrow, Gwyneth, 243
Panic Room (2002), 231
Pankhurst, Christabel, 45, 279
Paramount Pictures, 16, 101–2, 123, 181, 275
Parker, Dorothy, 17, 190
Parker, Sarah Jessica, 166, 196
Parton, Dolly, 126, 226–27
Pearl (2022), 268–69
Perfect Guy, The (2015), 227
Perry, Matthew, 188
Perry, Tyler, 188
Peterson, Laci and Scott, 229
Pfeiffer, Michelle, 29, 147, 158–59, 166–67, 183
Phantom Thread (2017), 81
Picasso, Pablo, 143
Pickford, Mary, 47
Pike, Rosamund, 232, 265

308 Index

Pitt, Brad, 149, 214–15
Place in the Sun, A (1951), 10, 58–60, 69, 219
Plath, Sylvia, 61
Platt, Oliver, 127
Playboy (magazine), 23–24, 75, 83, 93, 208–9
Playboy Club, 83, 208
Play Misty for Me (1971), 88, 90–92, 280
Plaza, Aubrey, 264
Poe, Edgar Allan, 16
Pogrebin, Letty Cottin, 83
Poison Ivy (1992), 175–76
Polanski, Roman, 81, 176
Portman, Natalie, 261–63
Possessed (1947), 55
Postman Always Rings Twice, The (1946), 55
Postman Always Rings Twice, The (1981), 99
Predator (1987), 96
Presumed Innocent (1990), 141–43, 152, 157, 180, 231, 275–76, 285
Presumed Innocent (TV show), 275–76
Pretty Baby (1978), 82
Pretty Woman (1990), 95, 139, 148, 164–66, 183
Pride and Prejudice (Austen), 190
Pride and Prejudice (TV show), 190
Prima Facie (Miller), 267
Princess Bride, The (1987), 178
Promising Young Woman (2020), 251, 254, 256–59, 261–62
Psycho (1960), 10, 16, 92, 222, 269
Pulp Fiction (1994), 129, 183

Quaid, Dennis, 111
Quant, Mary, 69
Quayle, Dan, 185–86
Queenie (Carty-Williams), 249, 253
Queer Nation, 160
Quinn, Roseann, 85

Rae, Issa, 11, 247–48, 251
Rains, Claude, 50
Ramis, Harold, 135
Ransohoff, Martin, 102–4, 163

Ratajkowski, Emily, 231
Reagan, Ronald, 96–97, 112, 132
Reality Bites (1994), 186
Rebecca (1940), 11, 47
Rebel without a Cause (1955), 69
Red (album), 239
Red Shoes, The (1948), 261
Red Sparrow (2018), 264
Reed, Donna, 50
Reiner, Rob, 143, 178
Reputation (album), 240
Richardson, Miranda, 115
Ripley, Ellen (character), 95–96, 112, 148
Robbie, Margot, 258
Roberts, Julia, 164–66, 181, 217
Robyn, 244–45
Roe v. Wade (1973), 9, 97, 274
Rogers, Ginger, 48, 49, 55
Rogers, Mimi, 111–12, 115
Rolling Stone (magazine), 198, 239
Roman Holiday (1953), 71
Ronstadt, Linda, 109
Rosemary's Baby (1968), 36, 76, 78, 81, 17–72, 176
Rosie the Riveter, 53
Rossetti, Dante Gabriel, 41
Roupenian, Kristen, 253
Ruckelshaus, Jill, 82
Rules, The (Fein and Schneider), 210, 211, 216
Russell, Kurt, 174
Russell, Rosalind, 131
Ryan, Meg, 109, 137, 184
Ryder, Winona, 262

Sabrina (1954), 72
Salem witch trials, 35
Sales, Nancy Jo, 238–39, 252
Salt, Jennifer, 84
Sarandon, Susan, 147–48, 191, 218
Saturday Night Live (TV show), 13–14, 22, 122
Sawyer, Diane, 109
Scacchi, Greta, 141
Schlafly, Phyllis, 82, 97
Schroeder, Barbet, 176–77
Schwarzenegger, Arnold, 113, 159

Sciorra, Annabella, 169, 179
Scorsese, Martin, 150
Scott, Ridley, 95, 111, 114, 147, 218
Screen Gems, 227
Seacole, Mary, 36
Seberg, Jean, 70
Self Esteem. *See* Taylor, Rebecca
Selleck, Tom, 136–37
Seneca Falls Convention, 37
Set It Off (1996), 154–55, 188
Seven Year Itch, The (1955), 66
Sex and the City (TV show), 1, 24, 43, 73, 159, 195–97, 200, 203, 206, 212, 216, 244, 252, 280
Sex and the Single Girl (Gurley Brown), 72–73,196
Seyfried, Amanda, 223
Shaw, Fiona, 137
Shea, Katt, 175–76
Shearer, Lloyd, 64–65
Shields, Brooke, 82
Short, Martin, 160
Siddal, Elizabeth (Lizzie), 41–42
Siegel, Don, 78, 90
Silence of the Lambs, The (1991), 160, 222
Silver, Amanda, 171–73
Silverstone, Alicia, 176
Simpson, Don, 100–102
"Single Ladies (Put a Ring on It)" (song), 213, 227
Singles (1992), 186
Single White Female (1992), 2, 10, 51, 165, 168, 176, 178–80, 186, 222, 242, 259, 264, 280
Single White Female 2 (2005), 222
Siodmak, Curt, 268
Sisters (1972), 84, 263
Skarsgård, Bill, 269
Skerritt, Tom, 175
Sleeping with the Enemy (1991), 164–65, 168–69, 181
Sleepless in Seattle (1993), 109, 184
Sliver (1993), 162–63, 175, 181
Smith, Jada Pinkett, 154
Snake Pit, The (1948), 56
Some Like It Hot (1959), 67

Someone to Watch Over Me (1987), 111–13, 115, 141
Something Wild (1986), 129
"Sorry" (song), 225
Spears, Britney, 208, 254, 256, 258
Spielberg, Steven, 84, 100, 169
Splendor in the Grass (1961), 69–70, 86
Stallone, Sylvester, 101
Stanton, Elizabeth Cady, 37
Stanwyck, Barbara, 48, 54, 58, 69
Star Wars franchise, 96, 138, 142, 236, 254
Steinem, Gloria, 8, 77, 82–83, 100, 204–5
Stewart, James, 50
Stoltz, Eric, 178
Stone, Sharon, 11, 158–63, 259
Story of Adele H, The (1975), 92–93
Stowe, Madeleine, 174
Strait-Jacket (1964), 268
Strange Case of Dr. Jekyll and Mr. Hyde (Stevenson), 263
Sundance Film Festival, 176, 239
Suspect (1987), 110
Sutherland, Donald, 152
SWF Seeks Same (Lutz), 176
Swift, Taylor, 2, 17–18, 195, 238–41, 244, 255, 263, 285
Swimfan (2002), 222
Switch, The (2010), 216

Taming of the Shrew, The (Shakespeare), 33
Tandy, Jessica, 55
Tate, Sharon, 81
Taylor, Elizabeth, 10, 58–59
Taylor, Rebecca, 267
"Telephone Call, A" (Parker), 17, 190
Temp, The (1993), 179–81, 224
Terminator, The (1984), 95–96, 222
Thatcher, Margaret, 97–98, 104
Thelma & Louise (1991), 95, 114, 146–51, 153–54, 156, 158, 167, 173, 218, 280
There's Something about Mary (1998), 208
Theroux, Justin, 215
This Is Paris (2020), 6
Thomas, Clarence, 151
Three Men and a Baby (1987), 136

310   Index

Three Men and a Little Lady (1990), 136–37
Thurman, Uma, 129, 164, 166
TikTok, 119, 138, 236, 247, 271, 273
Timberlake, Justin, 207
Time (magazine), 148, 199–200, 203–4, 213, 218–19, 232, 243–44, 259, 285
Tinder Swindler, The (2022), 253
Titanic (1997), 95
TMZ, 239
To Each His Own (1946), 56
Tortured Poets Department, The (album), 241
Total Recall (1990), 159
"Toxic" (song), 256
tradwife movement, 12, 273–74, 279
Tramell, Catherine (character), 158–62, 164, 232, 265
Truffaut, François, 92
Trump, Donald, 13, 104, 126, 243, 261, 274
Turner, Lana, 55
Turn of the Screw, The (James), 28
20th Century Studios, 237

Unfaithful (2002), 222
Universal Studios, 90, 101, 233
Unlawful Entry (1992), 174–75

Van Houten, Leslie, 77, 81
Vanilla Sky (2001), 201–2, 207–8
Vanity Fair (magazine), 105, 144–46, 149, 173, 214, 238–39, 252
Vaughn, Vince, 215–16
Vélez, Lupe, 64–65
Verhoeven, Paul, 158–59, 161
Vogue (magazine), 83, 261

Waiting to Exhale (1995), 187–88
Walken, Christopher, 145, 167
Waller-Bridge, Phoebe, 11, 245–46, 258–59, 261
Walt Disney Studios, 168, 171
Walter, Jessica, 90
Warner Brothers, 89, 188
Watson, Emma, 273
Weaver, Sigourney, 125, 127, 129, 131–32

Weinstein, Harvey, 243, 257
"We Should All Be Feminists" (TEDx talk), 242–43
West, Ti, 268
What Ever Happened to Aunt Alice? (1969), 79
What Ever Happened to Baby Jane? (1962), 9–10, 29, 76, 143, 172, 190
What's the Matter with Helen? (1971), 11
When Harry Met Sally (1989), 137, 189
When the Bough Breaks (2016), 227–28
"Who's Afraid of Little Old Me?" (song), 241
Wilkes, Annie (character), 45, 143–44
Williams, Allison, 271
Willis, Bruce, 98
Winfrey, Oprah, 217
Wing, Leslie, 102
Winger, Debra, 94, 115
Winkler, Irwin, 158
Winters, Shelley, 10–11, 58
witch trials, 33–36
Witherspoon, Reese, 209
Wolf Man, The (1941), 268
Wolstenholme-Elmy, Elizabeth Clarke, 44
Woman in the House across the Street from the Girl in the Window, The (2022), 237
Woman in the Window, The (Finn), 236–37
Woman in the Window, The (2021), 237
Woman's Vengeance, A (1948), 55
Women, The (1939), 131
women's liberation movement, 8, 75, 77, 84, 92, 113, 280
Wonder Woman, 53, 285
Wood, Natalie, 69
Working Girl (1988), 125–27, 129–34, 179
"Work Out" (song), 253
Wright, Joan, 35
Wylie, Max, 73

X (2022), 268–69
X-rated movies, 99–100

Zellweger, Renée, 192